11-2012

A MIRACLE OF GRACE

MERCER
UNIVERSITY PRESS

Endowed by
TOM WATSON BROWN
and
THE WATSON-BROWN FOUNDATION, INC.

A MIRACLE OF GRACE

An Autobiography

E. GLENN HINSON

MERCER UNIVERSITY PRESS
MACON, GEORGIA

MUP/ H856

First Edition

Books published by Mercer University Press are printed
on acid-free paper that meets the requirements of American
National Standard for Information Sciences—Permanence of
Paper for Printed Library Materials.

Mercer University Press is a member of Green Press
Initiative (greenpressinitiative.org), a nonprofit organization
working to help publishers and printers increase their use of
recycled paper and decrease their use of fiber derived from
endangered forests. This book is printed on recycled paper.

Library of Congress Cataloging-in-Publication Data

Hinson, E. Glenn.
  A miracle of grace : an autobiography / E. Glenn Hinson. -- 1st ed.
     p. cm.
  Includes bibliographical references and indexes.
  ISBN-13: 978-0-88146-394-1 (hardback : alk. paper)
  ISBN-10: 0-88146-394-9 (hardback)
  1. Hinson, E. Glenn. 2. Baptists--United States--Biography. 3. Christian college
teachers--Biography. 4. Southwestern Baptist Theological Seminary--History. I.
Title.
  BX6495.H525A3 2012
  286'.1092--dc23
  [B]
                        2012021587

CONTENTS

ACKNOWLEDGMENTS

Because an autobiography offers many opportunities to say thanks to people who figure prominently in my story, I will restrict my expression of appreciation here to some who have assisted me in the production of it.

At the head of my list is Dr Charles Deweese, recently retired Executive Director-Treasurer of the Baptist History and Heritage Society. Charles, once my student at Southern Seminary, pored over every page and made helpful suggestions of both general and specific nature. He then addressed to Marc Jolley an enthusiastic recommendation to publish the book. Dr Daniel Avery, assisting priest in Bruton Parish Church, Williamsburg, VA, and quality of life counselor to U.S. military personnel, read an early draft and offered valuable comments. I have weighed carefully and incorporated many of the observations and suggestions both of them made, but I will not hold either one accountable for the final product.

The list of persons who encouraged me to write a memoir or autobiography and then kept asking when I would finish it is too long to record here. I should mention, however, dozens of participants in the Academy for Spiritual Formation sponsored by The Upper Room of the United Methodist Church who pressed me to tell my full story on the basis of what they heard me relate in part. Friends who heard me speak in churches and who attended retreats I led also prompted me to do this. Academic colleagues and friends conscious of the buffeting I experienced during the Southern Baptist "holy war" gave their thumbs up to the undertaking too and inquired frequently about my progress. Would I have undertaken such a lengthy and heavy labor without such encouragement? Even if I would have, I gained an immeasurable boost from these friends.

On sheer production I must thank the late Dr Hugh Peterson, Administrative Dean at Southern Seminary when I entered in 1954. Whether as a requirement or not I can't remember, Dr Peterson introduced seminarians to his Eureka Filing System, a simple way of collecting materials for sermons, papers, or other church doings. From that time on, I filed everything of importance in my work as a student and later as a professor. My collection led eventually to seven four-drawer filing cabinets packed with two types of folders: (1) correspondence and (2) subjects. Not a day went by as I wrote chapters of my story that I did not silently thank God for Hugh Peterson's Eureka, which put at my fingertips the information I needed to document my story.

Regarding production, I also must express appreciation for the editor and staff of Mercer University Press. Transforming a 600-page manuscript into an attractive and readable book is no small undertaking, and the press takes some risk in publishing biographies. So I am grateful to Marc Jolley and others at MUP for their willingness to take a risk on my story and to expend the great energy they needed to bring it to fruition.

Finally, I thank my wife, Martha, my son, Christopher, and my daughter, Elizabeth for permitting me to tell this story, which involves them, too. Perhaps I should offer an apology to hundreds of others whom I speak about with candor. I do not mention any person to embarrass or diminish them. If they feel I have done so, I pray that they will accept my sincere apology in advance.

E. Glenn Hinson
Louisville, November 22, 2011

PREFACE

It takes a big ego to write an autobiography or memoir. Doing so is based on the assumption that your life story has in it something worth the attention of other people, something from which they can learn. It seems a little immodest of me to say so, but that is why I have written *A Miracle of Grace*. Like Augustine writing his *Confessions*, John Bunyan *Grace Abounding to the Chief of Sinners*, or Thomas Merton *The Seven Storey Mountain*, I am telling my story as honestly and transparently as I can, so that you can learn not so much about me, how good or bad I am, as about the way God enters into an ordinary human life. I look at my own life as "a miracle of grace," that is, a life that I could not have planned but one that was given to me. You will hear me use the word "grace" with a number of nuances. At bottom it means "gift." Like Henri Nouwen I think that life is grace, given to us more than earned or merited by us. In one sense I'm trying to express thanks to God for the gift of my life, and, conscious of its troubled beginning, I look back with mouth agape at the way it has turned out.

Autobiographies or memoirs usually have an apologetic aim—to explain why we did what we did. Anyone who has lived as long as I have, of course, has much to apologize for and to put in perspective. In my own case the apology has several different dimensions to it. One of those is simply to be as honest and straightforward as I can in confessing shortcomings and limitations, and you will see plenty of them as you read my story. I suspect that all of us feel deep within that we could have done better than we did. I flagellate myself again and again for taking on far more projects than I could effectively discharge with the result that much of my work seems trite and superficial. May God forgive me and accept what I have tried to do anyway.

A second is to explain a curious career path—from New Testament to Church history to Spirituality. In the Missouri Ozarks we labeled such a person "jack-of-all-trades and master-of-none." I don't think I'm making excuses when, in the story that follows, I point to a number of factors that help to explain why and how my vocational interest shifted and expanded since the time I met Thomas Merton in 1960, when I took my first students of Church history to the Abbey of Gethsemani to expose them to the Middle Ages. Concern for spirituality heightened as I tried to respond to the needs of ministers and students for something Protestant seminaries did not adequately supply. The urgent need to start a new seminary opened an opportunity to do with spirituality what I never dreamed I would do.

Another dimension of my apology is to put in perspective my relationship with Southern Baptists, particularly the Southern Baptist Theological Seminary, where I taught for more than thirty years. Biblical inerrantists let no opportunity pass to feature me as the major reason for the "Baptist reformation" or "conservative resurgence." Sometimes your critics compliment you more than your friends! Their attacks peaked in 1991 when the fundamentalist-dominated International Mission Board defunded the International Baptist Theological Seminary at Rüschlikon, Switzerland, because I was teaching there. Subsequently a trustee at Southern Seminary did his best to demonstrate that I violated the Seminary's doctrinal statement, *The Abstract of Principles*, and the Personnel Committee of the trustees sent me a "warning" based on his charges.

My response to attacks has permitted me to put in perspective my career-long involvement in the ecumenical movement revitalized and enlarged by Pope John XXIII (1958–63) and the Second Vatican Council (1962–65). In some ways a powerful ecumenical current has wafted me aloft to gaze upon some of the most momentous events in Christian history. When exiled by a part of my own church family, I found my larger Christian family throwing a lifeline toward me, pulling me in, and administering life-giving CPR. I am agog personally as I look back on the affirmation and certification I have experienced from my world Christian family. The extent to which denominational lines have broken down seems still open to debate, but I cannot find words adequate to express my awe at the love others have beamed my way. You will see later why I sometimes refer to myself as a Bapto-Quakero-Methodo-Presbytero-Lutherano-Episcopo-Catholic.

You will find in this book also some effort to apologize for the fact that I have tried to hold together a commitment both to the Church and to the Academy. In their best representatives, I believe both want to bear witness to the Truth in the way their respective spheres permit them to do with integrity. Training ministers weighted my scales a bit on the side of concerns of the Church. However, a look at my bibliography will show that I have expended a considerable amount of effort in engaging my peers in the Academy. Thankfully, too, on occasions when I found myself disenfranchised by Southern Baptists, I earned accolades from academic peers and institutions. Had both rejected me, I'm not sure where I would have headed.

Throughout my career story you will discern references to impairment of hearing, a physical disability that clearly created challenges for me as a scholar and teacher. It would be futile and unproductive to speculate as to how much it cost. I'm sure, for instance, that it kept me from developing a speaking knowledge of German, French, Italian, and other modern languages; yet, I may have become more proficient in reading those languages because I focused more on the written word. One clear lesson from all of this, however, is: you have to play the hand you are dealt in life. Dealing with deafness has sensitized, tenderized, and made me more conscientious of other persons, especially students, with handicaps. Moreover, I have been the recipient of an immense amount of grace from others as a handicapped person, beginning with my wife, children, colleagues, students, and friends. Even as my deafness has worsened, as you will see, many people everywhere made allowances and continued to rely on me as a person who had something to offer. In a word, I received grace abundantly.

I hope that you will read my story, to adapt a phrase from John Bunyan, as an account of the merciful kindness and working of God in my life.[1]

Louisville, Kentucky
August 30, 2010

---

[1] John Bunyan, *Grace Abounding to the Chief of Sinners* (London: Dent; New York: Dutton, 1666, 1928) 4.

1

A FRACTURED FAMILY

You may think it strange, but any personal account I give of my life must begin with my birth family breaking apart like Humpty Dumpty. My earliest memories are of my mother and father fighting, physically and verbally. My father was an alcoholic—sadly one who could never admit that he had a problem and thus never sought help. When he was sober, Lloyd Allen Hinson, or Al, as his cronies called him, was a gentle, thoughtful, intelligent person. But when he was drunk, demons took control and made him an angry, abusive, impulse driven madman who used his superior size and strength to manhandle his wife.

My mother, Docia Frances Crow Hinson, was no match physically. At five feet two she couldn't begin to get in any effective blows against a six-footer, try as she might, although the level of his inebriation helped her. Were it not for the terrible tragedy of shattered lives, it would have been comic to watch such ill-matched foes fight. It's not hard to understand, though, why my diminutive mother wanted both my older brother and me to be boxers. She needed bodyguards. Quite logically, she named him Gene after Gene Tunney, who took the heavyweight-boxing crown away from Jack Dempsey in 1929, the year my brother was born on December 2. His other name, Allen, came from our father.

Many of my early memories aren't very distinct, but my early vocabulary would have embarrassed sailors. I won't repeat some of the words my dad coined. One, however, particularly stayed with me because it helps me to understand where part of the family's crisis may have come from. "Wooden ear." My dad would yell that over and over as he slapped my mother all around the kitchen or the bedroom. "Wooden ear." I was too young at first to comprehend what it meant, but by age three or four I knew: my mother was losing her hearing, just like I did at about the same age.

Although "Mother," as she always insisted Gene and I call her, did not match up physically, save for her deafness, she was more than a match mentally. She had a high school diploma, whereas my dad completed only elementary school. She had taught for two years in the elementary school my dad had once gone to. As a matter of fact, that is how they met. Al Hinson was the pick of the big Silas Hinson clan of Lone Dell, Missouri, a charmer, a natural-born salesman, and he won her heart. They married in 1926, and moved to St. Louis, where they lived for a while with her parents, Albert and Dena Crow. Later they rented a bungalow on Potomac Street and then a larger house on Shenandoah Avenue nearer Hinson's Auto Sales, a new and used car dealership at the confluence of Jefferson and Gravois, which my dad had miraculously gotten started despite the depth of the Great Depression. Apt as he was as a salesman, however, he relied on my mother to keep the books.

Mother did not have a high level of tolerance. With her increasingly poor hearing she may have misunderstood much that my dad was trying to say. If he came home drunk, however, as happened more and more, she would roast him like a pig on the spit. "Been to Heine Mueller's again, huh? I told you never to go near that place again, you sot."

"I'll go there when I damn well please, bitch." Whack. And the fight was on.

Heine (short for Heinrich) Mueller's Tavern was just a couple of blocks from Hinson Auto Sales in a heavily German-populated section of South St. Louis. It was a favorite place to close a deal. Sometimes at night, when Dad got the worst of a fight with Mother, he would drag Gene and me with him down to Heine Mueller's, sit us up on one of the bar stools, and order us cokes. Never beer, though I remember one cute little four-year old whom some of the other drinkers would set up with beer to see him do his comic act. He also smoked a pipe for them.

The fights were fierce. One just after Christmas 1935, when I was four, sticks in my mind like a leech. The Hinson family had had a big Christmas that year. Toys littered the floor around the Christmas tree. One that I especially cherished was a little tool kit—hammer, saw, and screwdriver. Grandma Crow was already calling me "Mr. Fix-it." I handled family traumas by staying busy.

Mother had prepared a special dinner of chicken, dressing, mashed potatoes, gravy, and green beans—on top of putting in a full day at Hinson Auto Sales doing the books.

When Mother left the office, Dad had a customer. He promised that he'd be home soon, no later than six o'clock. Six o'clock came. Seven o'clock. Eight o'clock. No Dad. Finally, a little after nine he staggered in, stoned, barely able to totter up the two front steps into the house. Mother lit into him.

"Where have you been, Allen? You're drunk."

"I ain't drunk, Dosh. Just had a couple of three/two beers."

"The heck you aren't. You can't even stand. And you've let my supper ruin." Big tears dribbled down her cheeks.

"Shut up, bitch! I ain't gonna listen to such sniveling." Wham! This time Mother got in the first punch, and the fight was on. It went on for God knows how long. Fists flailed wildly.

There was a choking sound, a gasping for breath. Not knowing what to do, I went over and grabbed my dad's pants leg and yanked on it a few times. "Daddy! Daddy! Don't! You're killing Mother. Stop it! Stop it!" I screeched.

I don't think he knew quite what to do, but he let go and stumbled away to the bathroom. I could hear his pee hitting the water in the commode, water running to wash his hands and face, and some clunking around as he tried to get the door open again. Then he stumbled into the bedroom and fell across the bed. He slept in his rumpled suit and didn't move until morning.

Many people probably wouldn't expect a four year old to think much about what he'd seen, but I can remember a fear settling over me. "What's happening to my family?" I loved and respected both my mother and my father just as all children do, their faults notwithstanding. Here I'd just witnessed something awful, my father choking my mother. I didn't sleep well that night or quite a few other nights later as I picked up other evidences of the gradual submission of a soul to an addiction he seemed powerless to resist.

I had no idea then, and most people I knew didn't either, that alcoholism is a disease. "Drunks" were comic, people to be laughed at, not pitied. If they wanted to, they could control their drinking and straighten out their lives—especially someone like my Dad. He came from a devout Baptist home that didn't look kindly on drinking any kind of alcoholic beverages. "Hardshell Baptists," my mother called them. And I'm afraid, looking backward, that the black-and-white, judgmental approach only increased my Dad's inferiority complex and rebelliousness. Held back in earlier years, when he reached age twenty-one, he kicked off the traces and let drinking be the chief kicker.

Success, without the education to undergird it and carry it further, assured a steeper downhill slide into an ever-greater dependency. Like many another salesperson, Al Hinson depended on affability and sociability to make sales. All too often, sales were sealed around a table at Heine Mueller's Tavern or one of the endless numbers of beer joints in South St. Louis. Most people could probably stop drinking after one or two beers. Not Al Hinson. Once he started, he couldn't stop, sure that he could drink anybody else under the table and was convinced that, no matter how much he drank, he was never drunk. He never made contact with Alcoholics Anonymous.

The episodes occurred more and more often. I didn't know the reason for it, but our aunt and uncle, Fleta and Ossie Marsh, often took Gene and me to stay with them or to the farm they owned at Cuba, Missouri, so Mother and Dad could try to work out their problems. I remember the first time I went by myself. Aunt Fleta picked me up on Saturday afternoon so they could leave before dawn on Sunday morning. I got so homesick I thought of a jillion reasons the Marshes needed to run me home. At their house I had to mind my manners, something that didn't matter too much at our house. It was nice when we acted friendly sometimes. But at the Marshes I had to be quiet during the blessing, stir my iced tea without tinkling the ice, sit up straight at the table, eat what was on my plate, and say "Please" and "Thank you." When Aunt Fleta was home, I had to be quiet because she usually had migraines. The Marshes made me very nervous. But those excursions had a commendable purpose—to get Gene and me away from home for a while.

When we went to the farm, Aunt Fleta and Uncle Ossie got me up at 4 a.m. and sat me between them in their little 1930 Model A Ford Coupe for the eighty-mile ride down old US Highway 66. Usually they made one stop on the way—at the Diamonds, a round-the-clock restaurant about half way to Cuba. It gave everybody a chance to wake up.

Grandma and Grandpa Crow lived on the Marshes' farm, and when we got there, they put everybody, including me, to work. I didn't like the farm very much. To go to the toilet, you had to walk half way to the barn and, in winter, freeze your bottom off. The one thing I did like was fishing in Brush Creek that we forded on the way to the farm.

Fishing in Brush Creek at age four was where I experienced my first touch of grace. I stood holding my pole until the fish or little minnows had nibbled the whole worm off my hook. Uncle Ossie noticed. He sidled over, got between me and my line, and said, "Glenn, let's see what we've got here." He slipped a little perch onto my hook and dropped it into the water. You can't imagine the joy of my first catch or my first touch of grace.

Sometimes cars got stuck in the treacherous gravel at the ford. Although the water was usually shallow there, heavy rains caused the sand and gravel to shift. The wheels could sink quickly all the way to the axle. When that happened, there was nothing a driver could do but wait until someone brought a team of horses to pull the car out. I laughed the first time it happened as I rode with the Marshes. What tickled me was the way Uncle Ossie "cussed" when it happened. "Oh, fiddlesticks!" That didn't sound anything like my dad would have said.

The Hinson family had occasional outings of our own, usually to Lone Dell to the Hinson homestead which my great-grandfather had settled in 1856, moving there from Tennessee. The large Hinson clan liked to gather for jamborees on Saturday nights. None of them had formal training in music, but they could all play by ear and sing. If they picked around on a fiddle, banjo, guitar, or blew on a harmonica for a while, they could match the Grand Ole Opry. My dad usually sang. The challenge was in getting to Lone Dell.

The more he drank, the less comfortable Dad felt going home. Prospect Baptist Church stood at the corner of the Hinson homestead on land ceded by my great-grandfather. The Hinson family had attended faithfully throughout their lives—Grandpa Silas and Grandma Maggie, Bill, Floyd, Allen, Lasco, Elbert ("Eb"), and the only daughter, Zella. Bill, Dad's oldest brother, was a lay Baptist preacher. Under a mantle of bravado and cockiness Dad wore a hair shirt of guilt and resentment, and he sought to stiffen himself for these meetings with a couple of extra glasses of Griesedick or Budweiser. Most of the time he made quick stops along the forty-mile trip from South St. Louis to Lone Dell to reinforce the reinforcement. He seemed to know personally just about every bartender along the way.

One of these trips is especially memorable. It was already getting dark when we drove west on Gravois, US 30, out of the city toward Lone Dell. Dad's mood was nasty, and everybody tried not to irritate him further. He drove the new Dodge sedan very slowly, his reflexes badly impaired. When headlights approached from the opposite direction, he slowed to a snail's pace. At House Springs, about half way to Lone Dell, the lights started flickering and then went out completely—very dangerous on that curvy, hilly, two-lane highway. He let out a few "son-of-a-bitches" but managed to steer the car to a safe stopping place. In the dark he fumbled around in the glove compartment. "No fuses, God dammit!" He sat thinking a few minutes, his mind not clear. After several minutes he took a packet of Lucky Strikes out of his shirt pocket, took the inside wrapper out, separated the foil, took out the fuse from under the dash, and wrapped foil around it. The lights went on and we slowly crept back onto the road.

We hadn't gone very far before the lights went off again and he had to repeat the process. How many times I can't say because I eventually went to sleep in the back seat. I don't think we got to Grandpa Hinson's that night. I don't know whether we got back home either. All that my four-year old mind could make of it was that Dad wasn't himself again and that this was happening more and more often.

Mother was doing her best to cope. She had grown up in a solid and happy family. She idolized her father, Albert N. Crow, a gentle, loving, salt-of-the-earth person. He exhibited all of the qualities and habits her husband lacked. He felt secure in who he was and what he did, which was mostly farming. He neither smoked nor drank. He was loved and admired by all who knew him. It was not easy, therefore, for her to understand or help a husband who sought security in a bottle.

Her mother, Dena, was the daughter of German immigrants from Westphalia named Helling and Kluszmaier. They were devout Lutherans and had played a major role in the settlement of Franklin County, Missouri. My grandmother, though, joined the Baptist church when she married Albert Crow.

Mother wanted to be a model for the rest of her family like her dad and mother were. She was the oldest of the four Crow children, born 11 October 1901, and her dad's pet. After her, spaced four years apart, came Fleta, Raymond, and Alvie. For a time Raymond and Alvie lived with my mother and dad as they took the only jobs either of them ever held, as mechanics at Big Four Chevrolet just a block or two up Jefferson Street from Hinson Auto Sales. As it turned out, Mother had to turn to her sister and brothers for the familial example she expected to supply for them. All three of them had secure, happy marriages; she alone had made an unfortunate choice of spouse.

Mother sought help in religion. That was natural, for the Crow family took faith seriously. They were Baptists. My great-grandfather Ross Crow whittled off a corner of the Crow homestead at Reed's Defeat, a farm settlement about three miles from Sullivan, Missouri, for a community cemetery—Crow Cemetery—and built a chapel on it.

Mother, however, did not find the help she sought among Baptists, and instead joined a Spiritualist Church located on Potomac Street as it crosses the little triangle where Grand and Gravois avenues meet. Spiritualists emphasize communication with the spirits of the departed, which they believe remain in the vicinity of the earth for three years after death. Besides proximity to our house on Potomac Street, Mother's link with the Spiritualists came through Mummy and Daddy (pronounced Doddy) Eynon.

The Eynons were Welsh immigrants who suffered grievously with the death of their only son, Joe, not long after they arrived. Mother had known Mummy and Daddy from youth, for they lived near the Crow homestead at Reed's Defeat. She renewed acquaintance with them in St. Louis, where they attended the Spiritualist Church on Potomac Street. They deepened their friendship when we moved to a farm no more than a quarter of a mile from theirs in 1937 just before my sixth birthday. I'm shading the facts only slightly when I say that my earliest memories of "church" are of attending séances in the Eynon home shortly after we moved to Sullivan. Actually, I can remember attending a Christmas party at the Spiritualist Church on Potomac once before we moved to Shenandoah, but that did not involve a worship service. It was Santa Claus and presents for kids, and I was too timid even to go talk to Santa Claus.

My mother was trying to bear up at this point under a heavier load than anyone should have to carry. Her family, which she had hoped would be exemplary, was in complete disarray. Alcoholism scars not only the alcoholic and the spouse; it affects every member of a family. In the Hinson family it sliced deep into the very psyches of two children, marking them for life.

Violence seeped into my life from the beginning. Oh, how subtly it did so. When I was four or younger, I don't know the age for sure except that we moved from the house on Potomac Street when I was four, I committed an act of cruelty which has symbolized my potential for violence throughout my life. A bird built her nest in the guttering at the corner of our house and laid eggs in it. Shortly after the eggs hatched, one of the little birds clad in nothing more than pinfeathers fell out of the nest and was peeping and scrambling around helplessly on the ground when I discovered it. For a long, long time I played with the bird, petting and trying to comfort it. Then, suddenly, on impulse I cruelly wrung its neck.

I can't give his perspective on the story I'm relating because Gene was killed in the Coast Guard Air-Sea Rescue Unit at Norfolk, Virginia, in 1966 at thirty-six years of age. He had never quite gotten his life together. He left high school after two years, joined the Merchant Marine, and then, at age seventeen, joined the Coast Guard. Sadly, he, too, like our father, had become an alcoholic. He had married and had two children, Cheryl and Mark Glenn, but drinking had resulted in divorce not long before he died.

Some who knew him would probably characterize Gene as a "Dennis the Menace," but I thought he was mean. He picked on me. Admittedly, I was not a pleasant child or easy to get along with, but Gene, a truly gifted child, could think of a thousand ways to torment me and make me angry. And neither of us knew another way to express anger than the way we saw our parents do it—by fisticuffs and wrestling. Hitting, kicking, scratching, pulling hair, throwing toys or whatever else was handy.

From as early as I can remember Gene I remember fighting him. He was a year and a half older, so he won pretty handily most of the time. A lot of it was not lethal. My dad had sense enough not to leave his "Over/Under" rifle/shotgun loaded and ready to fire. Sometimes, though, we had weapons that could have done permanent damage. One of those was a little penknife someone gave me when I shined the chrome on the used car they had bought at Hinson Auto Sales. It was about the size of a large crayon—white with a little red button. Push the button and the blade would fly out. I loved it.

Gene and I were lolling around on the new sofa Mother had just had delivered when I pulled out my pride and joy, pressed the red button, and watched the blade flip neatly into place.

"Hey, Glenn. That's neat. Let me see it. I'll give it right back. I promise."

"Uh. Uh." I knew better than to trust Gene's promises. "You won't give it back."

"Yes, I will. Promise."

"No." And with that the fight was on. At first I tried to keep the knife away from him. Then I stabbed at him. By the time we were both completely worn out from wrestling small knife pricks dotted Mother's new sofa. Luckily, neither of us had a scratch. I can't remember whether either parent administered any discipline. My dad's favorite was the razor strap he used to whet his barber razor, and he did not hesitate to use it when in full control of his faculties.

Gene and I were out of control. We learned very quickly, like most children in codependent and dysfunctional families, how to take advantage of the tension between warring parents to do just about anything we wanted.

One thing we liked to do was to smoke cigarette butts dropped under the bleachers at the softball park just one block down Shenandoah from our house. When Mother and Dad were fighting, we would sneak box matches from the kitchen and creep out the back yard and down the alley to the park. There was a fence behind the bleachers, but they were open on the ends. So we simply walked in, scouted out larger cigarette butts, lit up, and puffed away. We liked to imagine that we were Raymond and Alvie, our uncles.

One day, Mother missed us and sent Dad to look for us. We weren't supposed to go out of the yard or smoke or, above all, use matches. Our four-year old next-door neighbor had gotten a box of matches, lit them, threw them up in the air, and watched them drop. Unfortunately one of them dropped into his shirtfront, caught his clothes on fire, and burned him from his chin to his toes. He had to have skin grafts from his mother for a year or more. Dad caught us in violation of all three. He came with a little switch. Gene, of course, could run fast enough to keep ahead several steps, so my short little legs caught the brunt of the punishment. It was a day to remember.

I have no idea how the business was doing—probably only passably in that deeply depressed period. Dad employed two nephews, Richard and Lloyd, sons of his older brother Bill Hinson, and several others. At some point he took in a partner named Davenport. On a trip to Indianapolis, Davenport and his wife were involved in a very serious car wreck. That set the stage for my first visit to a hospital as Dad hustled all of us into a car to race by night to Indianapolis to visit Mrs. Davenport, the only one injured seriously. Fortunately, he didn't make any stops along the way. Her husband, who was definitely "driving under the influence," escaped without a scratch. Her room reeked of ether and other antiseptic smells with which I was not familiar, but her husband reeked of beer smells with which I was quite familiar. Dad had chosen a partner with whom he felt comfortable because they had the same problem.

Alcoholism casts a wide net. To feel okay, alcoholics seek out people of the same stripe who can bolster them in their habits. If they don't find ready-made company, they will entangle others in the same snares.

During the Depression, just after the lifting of Prohibition, of course, they never had to look far to find drinking buddies. One of the axioms I heard repeated over and over with monotonous regularity in those bar visits was: "Never drink alone!" There was logic behind this. Drinking alone is the sign of alcoholism. So you must always find one other person or, better still, a group to drink with. If you do that, you are not an alcoholic. My four- and five-year-old mind remained unconvinced that Dad and his cronies at Heine Mueller's didn't need to look at the glazed eyes, slurred speech, stumbling steps, wife beatings, child abuse, and a slew of other signs before they closed the case. Besides, the beer smelled an awful lot like horse pee. But I dared not say anything.

However the business was going, the stress of it doubtless made drinking more likely. Not only so, in St. Louis Dad had a network of cronies who did not recognize the problem he had with drinking but actually egged him on. If Dad were to get out of this destructive habit and get his life back in order, he would have to get out of the environment that contributed so much to his downfall. That, at least, is what Mother concluded. With counsel and encouragement of family and friends she and Dad decided to turn the business over to Davenport and move to a farm about three miles from the old Crow home-place at Reed's Defeat and, as I mentioned earlier, just a quarter mile from the Eynons. The eighty-acre farm belonged to a family named Kleinert.

Geographical solutions seldom solve deep interior dilemmas, and, sad to say, they didn't work in Dad's case either. The move may have helped for a little while. Coming in the middle of the summer in 1937, it kept everybody busy. Mother and Dad had to sell the new Dodge they drove to buy milk cows, a team of mules, all kinds of farm implements, and whatever else they needed to get a farm going. They had to mow hay and store it in the barn for winter and plant what they could in the garden when the season was already too late to grow most vegetables. It was hard, but they set about it vigorously. Dad stayed sober for a month or two, but not long.

Dad had grown up on a farm. He knew how to farm. He liked many aspects of farm life. One was the cooperativeness among farmers in planting, harvesting, putting up hay, barn raising, and doing other tasks requiring joint effort. By nature a gregarious person, he liked to get together with neighbors as they threshed wheat or put up hay. Like other farmers, he hitched up old Beck and Kate and followed the only threshing machine in the county from farm to farm until it had harvested everybody's wheat. In something he intended for good and which should have brought healing, however, lurked his old nemesis.

Most farmers around the community did not drink heavily, but they did keep a little whiskey for medicinal purposes. One of our immediate neighbors, Mr. Beiers, a German immigrant, kept a vineyard and made wine. A few, going back to Prohibition, brewed their own beer and refrigerated it by tying a string around the neck of each bottle and letting it down into their cisterns to cool. Electricity had not yet reached the countryside around Sullivan in 1937. All the volunteer help Dad offered others began to pay off in invitations to share whiskey, wine, and homemade beer, and he proved powerless to resist once more. Within two years Mother gave up any effort to reclaim him.

One would have thought that these good folks would have understood that "wine is a mocker," that they would have seen enough examples of drunkenness to know that some people can't drink at all, that they would have resisted the urge to be hospitable in this way. To expect this level of awareness in 1937, however, is to forget that our perspective two generations on is conscious of things that these people could not have known. Some of these people were teetotalers and would never have offered Dad anything stronger than spring water. Some who drank did so in moderation and could not imagine drinking to excess. The Kemps, for instance, another family of German immigrants, drank beer as the normal mealtime drink. Some who made homebrew probably drank more than they should have, but they weren't alcoholics. Jim Landing, for instance, suffered from loneliness and needed companionship. Being hospitable with his brew was the easiest way to get it. But some others had the same problem Dad did. They were alcoholics.

One in particular stands out: Frank Sotebier. Frank's was a tragic story. I know only part of it, but enough to know what drew Dad to him and him to Dad. Just before we moved to that area, Frank had married a young woman with two daughters from a previous marriage. When Dad first met him in a bar in Sullivan, he learned that Frank's wife had tuberculosis and was dying. Frank was trying to wash away his grief, anger, and frustration. Fundamentalist preachers attributed her illness to sin, hers for remarrying and Frank's for marrying a divorced woman. Then, they declared that he had no reason to get angry because the fault was his, not God's. Frank wallowed in a pit of despair.

Frank Sotebier and Allen Hinson were sorrowfully suffering souls. Neither had a lot of education, but both were bright and sensitive. Their pain magnetized them and pulled them toward one another. When Frank and his family moved, Dad hauled their meager belongings. He was there when Frank's wife died in 1938. He helped them in whatever way he could. And he drank when Frank did.

Anyone who has lived with alcoholics will have memories both tragic and comic. I've seen comic routines very similar to the memory that is flashing in my mind at the moment. Dad and Frank had spent part of the day boozing up with Jim Landing. They only had to walk up a fairly steep hill from Jim's to get to our house, but Frank still had a couple of miles to go to get to his. Dad thoughtfully wanted to loan him our tamest mule, Kate. Getting a near helpless drunk aboard even a little mule, however, proved to be a colossal challenge for an almost equally helpless drunk. It took at least ten or fifteen minutes of huffing and puffing, grunting and groaning, cussing and swearing before Frank got on the first time looking at the mule's rear end. He had to slide off and go through another fifteen minutes of the same. I doubt whether Frank got home that night, but Dad did go down to the Sotebier's to retrieve Kate the next day.

Then there's the part in which we find no humor at all. Rebecca Sotebier's was the second funeral I had attended. The first was in St. Louis for a young man who had accidentally shot himself. None of the words spoken at Rebecca's funeral has stayed with me. What I remember is the terrible grief of my classmate in the first grade, Betty Lou Riske, watching the burial of her twenty-eight year old mother in the frozen, snow-covered earth. It tore my heart out. All through that first year of school I had felt deep pain for this blonde, curly headed beauty who seemed too distracted to answer the questions asked of us. Dad had told us about her mother's illness, but at this moment it took on a life it had not had before. I never again saw Betty Lou. She hadn't attended second grade classes at all that fall.

I don't know what Frank's theology was, but my dad's was contradictory. When he was sober, he professed atheism; when he was drunk, he was a fundamentalist. He dragged us all with him to Cave Spring Landmark Missionary Baptist Church a mile or so down the road from our farm. He used that beautiful baritone and good ear to belt out the hymns he had learned growing up in Prospect Baptist Church. I've spent a lot of time thinking about this contradiction and have come to this conclusion: When Dad was sober, he had the courage to reject a false God, the judgmental God which caused people like Frank Sotebier to wallow in despair. When he was drunk, he lapsed back into the dogmatic thinking of his youth.

This story of my fractured family has lots of side angles that will come out here and there, but the main part of the story is coming toward its end. Far from providing an exodus from his alcoholism, the move to the farm made the family's financial situation still more desperate with all the worry attendant on it, added a new set of drinking buddies to the ones he left behind, and made way for new episodes which led to divorce initiated by Mother in 1939.

Heine Mueller and a bunch of old drinking buddies came out to the farm to hunt. The Kleinert place and many other local farms had rabbits and quails in abundance, and Heine brought lots of good things to eat and toys for Gene and me. What I can't readily erase from my mind, though, was our behavior on one of those occasions. It was fall. The corn had been cut and shocked. Gene and I caught Heine down in the cornfield, picked up cornstalks, and started whacking him on the legs and buttocks. He yelped and begged us to stop, but we kept on. We both hit just as hard as we could. Play turned to cruel passion, and passion overwhelmed reason. Were we retaliating for some part we imagined that he might have had in Dad's fall, or did we, like Augustine stealing pears and throwing them to the pigs, do it just for the hell of it? Or did some evil possess us? Heine's canvas hunting pants and high top boots probably prevented too much damage, but Dad told us later that we had left welts all over Heine's backside. I don't believe Heine or the others ever came back after that. It was another of those deeds for which I must say, "God, forgive. I don't know what possessed me." Yet I think I do, too, for I saw the same misguided, or should I say insane passion in my father.

One painful episode that I can scarcely relate came not long before Dad left once and for all. He came home drunk more and more frequently the last year. On this occasion, murderous anger about something consumed him, most probably aimed at Mother. As he stumbled toward the house, a little dog which someone had let out of a car in front of our house, and which Gene and I had adopted, got in his way, as friendly little animals do. Dad tripped and almost fell down.

He swore. "I'll kill that goddamned dog. Get me my gun."

Gene dutifully trotted into the house and brought the "Over/Under" gun out with a box of shells for the 110 shotgun.

Dad ordered us to tie the little dog to the pasture fence. We didn't dare to question him. He jammed a shell into the chamber, put the barrel right into the dog's face, and pulled the trigger.

Emboldened by this macabre act, he then headed diagonally across the little field that ran alongside the roadway. "I'm going to go over and shoot those goddamned Eynons. They're the ones who have caused all this trouble."

"What trouble, Dad?" Gene asked.

"Between your mom and me."

Dad had long legs and, at age seven, I had trouble keeping up. Filled with fear about what might happen, I began to whimper. Mummy and Daddy Eynon were only about four feet eight inches tall—gentle souls who would offer little resistance. And they were Mother's best friends.

"Son-of-a-bitch," he swore. "What is it now?"

"My leg. My left leg hurts," I complained. I had learned in my brief life that, even at his worst, Dad would respond to my laments.

"Oh, shit! We'll go back."

"No. No. I can make it," I replied bravely, knowing that he would chicken out somewhere along the way anyway.

"No, goddamn it. I said we'd go back."

All three of us turned around and headed for the door at the side of the house. He couldn't walk. He had to crawl up the three steps into the living room.

I'm not sure how much Mother knew about some of these happenings. She missed a lot because of her deafness, although she was a very observant person. Dad's mushrooming anger aimed chiefly at her made her realize that she had no more than a snowball's hope in hell of rescuing him from himself and preventing great harm to herself and her children. She was proud, and she didn't want to admit failure in one of life's most important ventures. But she had to. And what probably freed her to do so was the unexpected death of her father in 1939.

Grandpa Crow died of a stroke, which if I am not mistaken, seems to have been brought on by his last heroic act. Aunt Fleta and Uncle Ossie were visiting their farm at Cuba one Sunday. A threatening storm developed quickly. Fearful that they might not get across Brush Creek if it rained heavily, they prepared to leave immediately. Grandpa Crow, knowing how treacherous the ford was, hitched up his team to the wagon and followed them to the creek. Taking no chances as it began pouring rain, he hooked their car to his wagon and pulled them across the creek. They went on their way and he headed back toward the house. Suddenly it started hailing. The horses, frightened by golf-ball size hail, lurched forward. Grandpa was thrown out of the wagon box between the horses as they reared in fright. He grabbed the tongue of the farm wagon and held on for dear life. Badly battered, he made it home, but during that harrowing experience or shortly after that had a stroke. He died at age sixty-three. His funeral was the last public event my mother and father attended together.

Grandpa Crow's death cut the last restraint to dissolving this unhappy marriage. So long as he lived, Mother felt she had to do the best she could to hold it together. She did not want her father to know she had failed. In the Great Beyond he would understand better than he might have in the Now. She could get assurances of that in séances at Mummy and Daddy Eynon's conducted by Mrs. Oerdrop, the minister of the Spiritualist Church on Potomac Street. More than anything, she needed and got his okay. And divorce would be better for her and Gene and me, and even for Dad. It took courage, but ten or eleven years of hell had prepared her. She did not flinch.

What about me? What had all of this done to my life? One thing that I was learning was to avoid conflict. Except in dealing with my brother, I steered around it. All of these things going on in my life were creating ambivalences and insecurities. My natural tendency was to hold back. If a teacher called for volunteers, I waited and let others go first. If someone handed out gifts, I let others go first. If Dad started cussing and beating Mother, I stood back. This *modus operandi* could have been due in part, I realize, to my being a second child. Second children, psychologists say, tend generally to be less assertive than first children. In my case, though, I think something else operated more powerfully—erosion of self-confidence in the ethos of alcoholic family life. My engine whirred at 5000 rpms, but my transmission stayed in neutral. It would take a heap of living and amazing grace to transform this into a life that mattered.

2

A LONG LONELINESS

A long loneliness followed Dad's departure. More accurately, I should say that I was lonely before, but now my loneliness was growing bigger and bigger. Loneliness is deeply painful. It is not something human beings choose for themselves. It's something that they would do almost anything to avoid. The pain of it seems at times unbearable.

It would have helped had Dad kept in touch, made at least occasional contact, a visit here and there. Or wrote and sent a care package or the alimony the divorce settlement called for. But he didn't. Between his abrupt departure with scarcely a goodbye, until I moved to St. Louis and enrolled in Washington University I saw him twice—at funerals for his father and his mother. He paid no alimony. He sent no money. The heavy woolen suit I wore to Grandfather Hinson's funeral in the summer of 1948 so embarrassed him that he did buy me a white cotton shirt and seersucker pants at the General Merchandise Store in Lone Dell.

He doesn't deserve all of the blame here. He and Mother parted with such bitterness that she didn't want him around. She gave Gene and me her side of the story, but she said nothing good about Dad or any of the Hinson family. She made it a point not to let us have contact with any of them. As a matter of fact, when Mother remarried a couple of years later, she persuaded Gene legally to take the surname of her spouse, John Helms. I kept the name Hinson. Whether I still clung to some tattered shred of love for Dad and his family, or harbored an ill-defined and perhaps indefinable feeling that the name I'd had up to that time was sacred, or was just holding back because I'd already learned not to leap without being able to see where I would land, or was plain scared, I can't say. There's probably truth in all of those factors. I respected John Helms, but I had very ambivalent feelings about taking *his* name. I took pride in my name and hoped someday I would add to its luster.

The separation came on the eve of the Second World War. Germany had already run roughshod over Poland and Czechoslovakia. Soon the

German army overran France and much of the rest of Europe. For a time it looked as if England alone would have to hold back the Nazi tide. I don't have very precise information about what happened, but, leaving his shattered family behind, Dad enlisted at age forty as a mechanic in what was then the Army Air Corps. Because he had been too young at the time, he had not served in World War I, but at this point the Air Corps was desperate to enlist anyone competent with engines, as Dad was. He spent some of the war in England—I don't know how long— and I've often wondered how he could have functioned effectively, but his alcoholism may not have been much worse than that of countless others living in such a terrifying situation.

War service should not exonerate him, but it perhaps shows that he was not in a situation in which he could do much about his former family's desperate plight, and laws had not yet been thought of that would do something about "deadbeat dads." At any rate, I never heard from him once.

My loneliness was magnified by a second separation, that of my brother Gene. This time it hurt much more deeply because, our battling notwithstanding, Gene and I were very close. Like any other "little brother," I both admired and envied Gene. He got to go places I didn't get to go and do things I didn't get to do. He got new clothes, and I got hand-me-downs if there was anything left to hand down. We were close enough in age, however, less than a year-and-a-half, that, by the time I was five, I could compete in many ways. And competition usually led to conflict. As I've recounted earlier, he and I fought fiercely without remission.

Dad's departure opened still more occasions for those fights, and Mother could not control us. She pleaded, she begged, she cajoled, she threatened. Her pleas went unheeded. In a period when she had to manage the task of both mother and father, we posed a real danger to ourselves and to one another. Incidents were numerous, but I will only cite a few.

One of our chief chores was to milk the five or six dairy cows Mother kept before we left for school in the morning. We had to get out very early, before daylight in winter, because we had a two-mile hike to Cave Spring Elementary School. Milking a cow by hand is not an easy chore for a six- or eight-year-old, and it can get boring. To liven it up, Gene began playfully to squirt milk from a cow's teat, initially at our white cat but then at me. He discovered that he could do this most effectively if he milked the cow in front of mine and kept his back to me.

"Hey, Glenn! Look at this!"

At first not expecting anything like that, I scrunched down under the cow's belly to see what he wanted. He squeezed with all his might. A thin stream of milk hit me right in one of my eyes, and milk dribbled down my face and onto my clothes. Not one to let such an offensive act pass unnoticed, I began to squirt milk all over his backside.

On a farm without running water or electricity you didn't go in and take a quick shower and put on clean bib overalls. We wore what we had on to school. If we sat near the pot-bellied stove, after a while we would reek of soured milk and usually a little cow manure we had stepped in.

On one of these early morning fights we got into an argument over whose cow gave the most and best milk. The argument led to shouting and shoving and then wrestling and hitting. Gene grabbed a half-filled bucket of milk and sloshed it all over me. By that time I was in tears, so angry I could hardly see. Passion pushed reason out of the way. I was determined I would pay him back. I picked up a six-inch scrap of wagon tire iron lying on the floor and hurled it at him. It landed right on the crown of his head. If the heavy hunting cap with earflaps we wore in the winter hadn't covered his head, it could have knocked him unconscious or even killed him. As it was, it left a huge knot.

I mentioned the difficulty of bathing. People accustomed to hot and cold running water, well-heated bathrooms, and plenty of clean clothes may have trouble visualizing the primitive way we did that. In winter Mother heated water in a teakettle and perhaps another large pan or two on the wood stove in the kitchen. We put a large tub used for washing clothes behind the stove in the corner of the living room. We would pour the hot water into about a half tub of cold until the water reached a comfortable temperature. To save water, which had to be drawn up by hand from the cistern in the back yard, Gene and I would usually take our bath at the same time, a custom bound to lead to trouble and in one case near tragedy.

I can't recall what triggered the wrestling while we were in the tub, but we didn't have much leeway either toward the walls where they joined one another to make a corner or toward the potbellied stove. The great danger, of course, lay in the direction of the stove because, to heat the room enough to make it comfortable for bathing, you wanted its metal sides hot. If you lost your balance, … In this particular melee it turned out to be Gene who found out what it's like to be branded with red-hot iron. I shoved him and he went spiraling into the side of the stove at its hottest point. I could hear the sizzle as it sautéed his right hip and smell flesh burning. He carried the ugly scar till the day he died.

Looking backwards over those early years, I'm amazed sometimes that either Gene or I survived. Once, I barely did. It was the winter of 1938–39 when I was seven and a second-grader. My nemesis this time was not Gene but pneumonia.

Mother never knew why I came down with pneumonia because neither Gene nor I ever told, but it happened like this: At the front of our property where it adjoined the gravel road (now Missouri 185) was a large pond made, I was told, by earthquake tremors. During winters like the icy one in 1938–39, it froze over with a thick coat of ice. Skaters from all around gathered to skim over its wonderful sleek surface. They built bonfires on the bank and often stayed late at night.

Our cows used that same pond for their drinking water. During winter, Gene and I had to cut square holes near the bank so the cows could drink. We would take a chopping axe, cut a floe, push it down with our foot and slide it under the ice. A cow could drink before it froze again.

One day in January, when Mother had gone over to the Eynons, we came up with a devilish trick on the skaters. In addition to cutting holes for the cows, we would cut holes in the center of the pond for the skaters to slip into. They would give us quite a show. The scheme didn't turn out quite as expected, but rather set me up for a bout with pneumonia. Gene cut a hole and slipped the floe neatly under the ice. Then he handed the axe to me. I hacked a two by two feet square in the four to six inch ice, put my right foot on the floe, and pushed. It is not easy to push a block of ice like that down into the water, and I had to exert myself. When the floe finally started slipping under, it carried my right foot with it. My left foot slipped off of the solid part of the ice and I plunged into the hole and kept going down, down.

I don't know how deep the pond was. It was deeper than the average human-made pond, I think. To me, who didn't know how to swim, it seemed like a hundred feet. My feet finally hit bottom, though, and I pushed upward as hard as my legs could push. Fortunately, I surfaced exactly on the hole. Gene grabbed me by my soaking wet denims, pulled me up onto the ice, teeth chattering, and chilled to the bone. We raced to the house. I yanked off every stitch, including my long johns, and huddled behind the stove to warm as Gene collected me some other clothes.

The next morning I awakened with a horrible headache, the first I had ever experienced. Mother went over to the Taylors, our nearest neighbors, and called a doctor. It took a while for him to get to our house, but it didn't take him but a minute's listening with his stethoscope to decide. I had double pneumonia, a very serious case. "Not much I can do," he said. Alexander Fleming had discovered Penicillin in 1928, but scientists didn't learn how to use the first of the antibiotics to cure things like pneumonia until 1940, a year or so after my battle. The doctor gave Mother some kind of heavy syrup to keep me from coughing too much. In the next day or so I slipped into a semi-conscious state. I remember hearing voices but could not make out what was happening. In the midst of it I dreamed, but the whole experience seemed like a dream. The only tangible memory I have is that Mother moved me out of the back bedroom, which had no heat, into her bedroom, which opened to the room where the pot-bellied stove stood.

One month to the day after I went to bed with pneumonia, I awakened and felt well. I wanted to get up and go outside to ride my tricycle in the sunshine, which bathed our house that day. Reluctantly, Mother bundled me up warmly and let me go. My legs were weak, but I was well. It was a miracle I had made it. Yet it left me an important legacy, a confidence that God's eye was on me and that I should learn how to relax and, as Thomas Kelly has phrased it, let life be willed through me.[1]

Somewhere along the way here, Mother decided she could not take care of two rambunctious, boisterous boys. For one thing, she could not afford it. I don't suppose many can imagine in the present prosperous era the poverty of people living in the Ozarks of Missouri or Arkansas in those years. The average per capita income in Arkansas in 1933 was $50.00 a year (equivalent to $815 in 2012), and it did not pass $200 until 1940.[2] Missouri's was just slightly higher. There was real poverty there, and we knew it firsthand.

Mother's main expense was $6 a month rent on the eighty-acre Kleinert farm we lived on. Next was probably clothing for Gene and me.

[1] Thomas R. Kelly, *A Testament of Devotion* (New York: Harper & Brothers, 1941) 61.

[2] E. Glenn Hinson, *A History of Baptists in Arkansas, 1818–1978* (Little Rock: Arkansas Baptist State Convention, 1979) 251.

We wore out overalls, shoes, socks, and coats more quickly than Mother could get money together to buy them. Once, when she bought each of us new bib overalls at a dollar a pair, we wore the seat of them out sliding down some unfinished oak boards we had leaned against one of the big sassafras trees in front of the house. And Mother didn't have time to mend clothes all the time. I remember the way she fixed our socks when we wore holes in the toes. Because darning took too much time, she just sewed diagonally across the toe and cut off the defective part, leaving the heel about where the arch should be. This interesting mending technique had the effect of pulling the rest of the sock down into the shoe and leaving the ankle completely exposed.

We raised most of our food in the garden; we had milk from the cows, but we could not keep meat because there was no electricity. We did have chickens and could sometimes butcher hogs in the winter. I trapped rabbits in a homemade rabbit trap.

That little trap left me with one of my most poignant memories and perhaps, etched a little deeper in my mind, a conviction that, by God's grace, things will work out somehow. For Thanksgiving 1939, Aunt Fleta and Uncle Ossie had invited us to have dinner with them at their farm. We knew it would be a super meal because the Marshes had a comfortable living, and Aunt Fleta was a superb cook. But we had no car. Even if we had had one, Mother could not have driven it the twenty-five or thirty miles to their farm at Cuba, even by back roads. So she and I were to have dinner alone.

The one question that took possession of my thought that morning was: "Will I have a rabbit in my trap so we can have meat for Thanksgiving dinner?" I caught rabbits with such regularity that it seemed likely. When I got to my trap this time, I could see that something had sprung the little trigger. Excited, I picked it up to carry it to the house. It felt heavy, heavier than I had ever felt it. "Oh, no. I've caught a 'possum," I said to myself. And one thing I can tell you is that 'possum meat isn't "good and sweet," as that song claims. My mother once tried to bake a 'possum in the oven—it's nothing but grease. But I needn't have worried. When I reached in, I found not *one* but *two* rabbits! You can't imagine the exhilaration, the thanksgiving of an eight-year-old heart on that bleak November day!

The times were tough, and Mother's only cash income came from cream. We separated it from milk with our De Laval separator, kept it cool, and put it down by the front gate to be picked up by truck and shipped to a dairy for processing. She earned $12 to $14 a month that way.

Had it not been for G.C. Busch and Sons, the Hinson family remnant would not have made it. G.C. Busch owned the General Merchandise store in Spring Bluff, Missouri, about five miles from the farm we lived on. The store handled everything farmers would need, from farm implements to clothing for the body and food for the table. When we needed feed for our cattle or food for our table or anything else, Busch's little truck always came. His sons, Von and Lowell, always told my mother the same thing: "It's alright if you can't pay now, Mrs. Hinson. Dad won't mind." I have no idea how many people in those depression years were not able to pay G.C. Busch back, but he wouldn't have minded so long as he could survive. When my mother could no longer pay the $6 a month rent on the farm we lived on, we moved to a farm owned by G.C. Busch rent-free. He reminds me of the "inasmuchers" of what I call Jesus' Parable of Kingdom Righteousness in Matthew 25:31–46. He was downright good. He did good without even thinking about it.

Mother did her best to keep us together. She forestalled the separation for a while by inviting Grandma Crow to live with us. Although they didn't get along too well, Grandma was in robust health and energetic enough to help with all the chores both inside and outside the house. She could have continued to live on the farm at Cuba with the Marshes after Grandpa's death, but it seemed best for her to move to Sullivan and help us in a time of desperate need. Although she did a lot of housework and gardening, she made a special point of keeping her eye on Gene and me. She stayed about a year. By that time, I think, we had nearly exhausted her patience with some of our shenanigans.

Sometimes Gene and I really tried to be helpful, but at eight and ten that was not easy. In one of our efforts to help, we put Grandma Crow and ourselves at some risk. Mother had kept saying that she wished somebody would clean the manure out of the barn. We didn't have the kind of equipment we needed to do that, but we did have a horse named Prince and a one-horse buggy. The buggy was made for riding, but we took the seat off and made a wagon bed to haul the manure. Our more serious challenge, however, was to put some harness together for Prince.

We had seen enough harness mended to know how it was supposed to be done. Unfortunately we lacked one essential for mending: rivets. Properly installed, rivets will smoothly fasten different pieces of leather together and avoid irritation. But we had no rivets. So we decided to use the universal farm fastener, bailing wire, which we had in abundance from the hay we fed the cows. However carefully you may install it, we soon learned, bailing wire does not make a smooth fastener of leather. We did our best to see that all sharp points headed away from the horse, but that proved difficult for boys our age with limited tools. We knew that we had rigged up a contraption that might evoke a lively reaction from Prince, but we thought he was gentle enough that we could take the risk.

After several days work we finally assembled a harness that looked like most of those we had seen. We piled manure high on the little buggy, excited that the day had at last come when we, though only eight and ten, were doing men's work. Next came the outfitting of Prince. He stood very still as we slipped the collar onto his neck and fastened it. But when we lifted our laboriously crafted harness onto his back, slipping the harness around the collar, we noticed that he was a little jumpy. He hadn't worked lately, we thought, so we could attribute his jumpiness to that. Gene led Prince out of the barn and backed him between the buggy shafts.

"Glenn, you stay down," he commanded, clambering over the wheels and onto the top of the manure pile. "I'll drive the buggy."

He clucked, "Gidayap!" Prince took a step and hesitated. A second step, and hesitated, then a third. It was obvious that something was making him jumpy. Getting slightly exasperated, Gene snapped the lines down toward Prince's rump.

Prince leaped and stopped. Gene snapped the lines again. This time, Prince took off like a rocket. He raced as fast as he could run through the open gate into a forty-acre pasture where we had intended to spread the manure. The buggy bounced up and down on the hard, bumpy ground, much of the time on two wheels as Prince made a wide arc and headed straight for a deep, wide gulley.

How Gene stayed aboard as long as he did I will never know. A pile of manure doesn't make a very secure seat. Gene evidently braced himself against the sideboards we had installed to hold the manure, and they held until the buggy hit the ditch. At that time the shafts broke and an exhausted horse slowed down little by little and stopped at the edge of a grove of trees growing around a huge sinkhole.

As all of this was taking place, Grandma Crow was busy in the garden hoeing and weeding. She didn't hear well, but she couldn't miss the wild melee taking place just a few hundred yards from her. When she saw Gene bouncing up and down and then finally disappearing out of sight into the gulley, she raced in his direction waving her arms wildly. In her path, however, stood a barbed wire fence with four or five strands designed to keep cows out of the garden. During the summer, Grandma Crow always wore a bonnet and long dresses. Because she sunburned easily, she pulled long stockings over her arms when she worked in the garden. Covered with far more than enough to get hung up on any fence, she thrust her head between two strands of wire and kept going, leaving a ten-foot trail of print material behind.

The buggy was a wreck. Little remained of Prince's harness. Miraculously, Gene suffered no more than a couple of bruises. Grandma Crow, after her bout with the fence, looked worse than he did. She must have wondered why she had ever volunteered to stay with us.

Then there was the incident with the Eynon's old car we kept in a lean-to garage attached to the barn. It was a Star, probably 1906 or 1907. The Star had flaps with only a small peephole in the center that could be buttoned down on each side to keep out wind and rain when driving. What interested Gene and me was that the flaps provided privacy. Once we buttoned the flaps down, we felt secure from outside intrusion. We loved to climb aboard the old Star and take imaginary trips, pretending that we were Raymond and Alvie, our uncles. Neither of us knew a great deal of geography, but we were learning enough to spin out some fantastic excursions.

To make our imitations conform more to reality, we smoked, just like our uncles did. Because even small amounts of cash were hard to secure in those days, we had to be very enterprising. We made a little money selling scrap iron to a Japanese collector, something not possible after Pearl Harbor. When Uncle Ossie visited, he often slipped us a nickel or dime. Hunters tipped us for showing them where they could find rabbits or quails.

Actually, it didn't take much money to get what we needed. We rarely were able to go to town, but we had Bob Taylor, our sixteen-year-old neighbor, buy a sack or two of Bull Durham tobacco, which at that time cost a nickel. We could either roll our own in the cigarette papers, which came with each sack, or we could use corncob pipes we made ourselves. We sawed out a section of a corncob, hollowed it, and fitted a wooden plug into the bottom. We made a stem from a green hickory branch by poking a hot wire through its soft center.

Gene and I traveled thousands of miles in our imaginations bouncing up and down on the old Star's springy leather seats puffing away, smoking and talking animatedly. One day, as we had gotten rather comfortable in this routine and relaxed our vigil, Grandma Crow came snooping around the lean-to. She may have chanced on us while engaged in another errand or been looking for us. At any rate she probably saw and smelled some smoke drifting out from under the side flaps. Suddenly she yanked open the door on my side, sniffed, and demanded, "You boys smoking in here?"

We both knew smoking was a no-no at our ages. "No, Grandma!" we declared, sounding as honest as we could, and stuffed our pipes in the crack between the bottom and back cushions. Suddenly the seat, stuffed with a woody, fibrous material, started billowing smoke. Grandma yanked me, and then Gene, out of the car. She then pulled the seat cushions out and put the fire out somehow. Pretty soon, *we* were on fire. That ended my smoking habit early.

Many might see incidents like these as harmless kids' stuff, but, looking back, I have to think of our out-of-control lives as products of a very bad family situation. More negative symptoms can be added. We were definitely on a rebel path, and we flaunted our reckless behavior; much of what we did was just for the hell of it. A couple of other incidents show this. One involved home brew made by local farmers and cooled in their cisterns. A second was a rampage in a melon patch that would make Augustine's behavior seem tame.[3] A third was an attack on Daddy Eynon.

During Prohibition, lots of drinkers in places like Appalachia and the Ozarks learned how to make home brew. Gene and I never saw the apparatus they put together, but we sampled their wares. Because the Rural Electrification Association had not yet reached our part of the country, farmers did not have refrigeration. When they made a batch of home brew, they bottled it in reusable beer bottles, put a cork in the top, tied a string around the neck of the bottle, and let it down into their cisterns. Gene and I and sometimes a neighbor kid or two would watch until one of the brewers left for town, sneak up to the cistern, pull up a few bottles, uncork them, drink only what was in the neck, return the cork, and let the bottle back down into the cistern. I know some of those

---

[3] Many scholars think Augustine blew his story out of proportion to the deed. Having done a dramatic wrecking job just like it, I have a different "take" on that. This symbolized character, the *imago Dei*, gone bad and in need of re-creation.

farmers must have scratched their heads and thought, "Why did it evaporate like that? I put that cork in there so tight. Still, it evaporated."

We didn't drink enough and maybe the beer wasn't strong enough to souse even eight and ten year olds, but I've often wondered whether this may not have moved Gene a step closer to the alcoholism that gripped him so tightly in later years. One of my most painful memories was seeing him battling the DTs when he came home to Sullivan for Mother's funeral in 1965. He'd evidently tried to sober up on the way home from Norfolk, Virginia. He definitely didn't want the Marshes to see him inebriated. In the middle of the night before the funeral, however, he awakened and got up unable to control his shaking. He had another attack during the funeral itself. Gene was not quite thirty-six.

It's hard now, as I think back on it, to know what possessed the two of us sometimes. The deep hurt we were experiencing in the rupture of our family doubtless played a big role, and we responded in the manner we had seen our parents exhibit, violently. All human beings have in them a capacity for violence that usually remains in check, but Dad's departure cut many restraints loose. All that held us back from getting into the kind of trouble we read about in urban newspapers today is that this farming area didn't have a great many people to hurt or a wealth of property to destroy. But we did what we could.

That brings me to Jim Landing's watermelon patch. Jim wasn't home that Sunday afternoon—Gene and I and one of the Byloe boys had been by to check. We first went to his cistern and nipped a little of his home brew, knowing that he was reputed to make the best in the county. We ambled around to his garden. Because his farm was situated in a little creek bottom, he was also one of few who could raise watermelons, for they require sandy soil. It was early for watermelons to ripen, but we were determined to find a ripe one and eat it. Well, we broke open one melon that looked like it might be ripe, but it was just beginning to turn pink. So we tried another and another and another. Then a dam that held us in check burst, and we stomped to pieces every melon in that patch.

It hurts me to think about this even now. Watermelon has probably been my favorite fruit since childhood. Mother used to tell how, at two, I had pulled a big watermelon off of the kitchen table and then sat under the tablecloth eating away. But my pain is not about watermelon as much as about the wanton way in which Gene and I had, for no reason, destroyed the watermelon patch of a gentle and kind farmer who could ill afford to lose anything he grew on his small acreage. As far as I know, he never stormed to our house and demanded that we be hauled before a judge and jailed. Maybe he never knew who did it, but I'm sure he had good suspicions.

Then there is one more incident that stands as evidence of this inner violence. I've mentioned Mummy and Daddy Eynon several times as Mother's closest friends. Gentler or kinder people never lived. One day, Gene and I accompanied Mother and Grandma Crow on one of their frequent trips to visit with the Eynons. Daddy was working in the garden, bending over hoeing or picking vegetables. Gene and I sneaked up on him from the rear. At first Gene and then I threw a small clod toward Daddy's hind end. When he didn't notice, we picked up slightly larger clods and threw harder. Finally, we pelted him as furiously as we could, very much as we had Heine Mueller. But in this case, we could not use the excuse that we were letting loose a rage for injuries we may have suffered from Dad's alcoholism. No, what started as play unleashed in us a misdirected fury that I cringe to think about today. Would that Daddy Eynon lived still to hear me beg his pardon!

In the midst of such painful circumstances, Mother decided to separate the two of us and let Gene live with Aunt Fleta and Uncle Ossie on their farm at Cuba. Grandma Crow had already moved to St. Louis to care for Donald and Patsy Crow, the children of her older son, while their mother recovered from tuberculosis.

No one could have done more to minister to our failing family, both before and after the divorce, than Fleta and Ossie Marsh. Though they wanted children, the Marshes had no children of their own in 1939. Their only daughter was born several years later, in 1943. Uncle Ossie had a special fondness for Gene, who at age ten or eleven could help with the work on the farm. The Marshes, in turn, could provide a stable and healthy home and environment as well as meet his physical needs in ways Mother could not.

When the day of Gene's departure came, carrying all of his earthly belongings tore my heart out; I sobbed uncontrollably. He did, too. In retrospect, I think our fighting may have indicated a strange sort of love and closeness rather than distance or dislike. We, of course, grew up in an unhealthy family culture in which no one knew how to practice the art of loving. We fought because we took each other seriously. At any rate I can assure you that I suffered immense pain over the departure of my brother then, and I suffer it still. Gene was killed at Norfolk while I was in England on sabbatical leave from the Southern Baptist

Theological Seminary in 1966, and I was unable to return for the funeral, so I've had no closure on a separation that began in our childhood. My every remembrance of him as I write this story causes great pain.

The next years, I suppose, did much to condition me for the solitude I've come to appreciate in later years, but the loneliness of my days at that time inflicted tremendous pain. From the time Gene left in 1939 until his death in 1966, he and I spent at most no more than a year together. He remained with the Marshes when we moved to Louisville, Kentucky, in 1942–43, where our stepfather served in the Coast Guard station at the foot of Fourth Street. John Helms had done a stint in the Coast Guard before the war and reenlisted after Pearl Harbor. In fact, part of the year Gene and I spent together occurred during the summer of 1943 when I worked fifteen weeks for the Lowry family, whose farm adjoined the Marshes', for three dollars a week and took $45 home with me to Louisville in August.

We got along pretty well that summer when we were together because both of us worked from dawn to dark putting up hay. We were too busy and too tired to fight. At that time in our lives, though, it would have been too much to expect us to go through a whole summer without a rumble of some kind, and I can think of a couple which showed that we had not yet been transformed.

Most of the time I stayed at the Lowry's farm, but one Saturday the Lowrys went to Cuba, or another nearby town, and left Gene and me at the Marshes. Uncle Ossie worked as a barber in Cuba on Saturdays. On this particular day, Aunt Fleta also went to town, but before she did, she assigned the two of us the task of cleaning the chicken house. We did what she had assigned, but then, with some time on our hands, Gene decided that we should yell obscenities at the neighbors he didn't like who lived just a couple of hundred yards up the road. So we crawled up onto the top of the chicken house, which had a very slight slope, to unleash our pretty sizeable store of scatological terms. After we tired of that, we found some nearly ripe grapes in the garden.

Both Gene and I had developed a taste for barely ripe fruit, and these grapes went down pretty well. The only trouble is, green grapes are an effective laxative. Pretty soon, both of us had an irresistible call of nature and raced for the outdoor toilet. The Marsh's toilet was a two-seater and could accommodate both of us. Unfortunately for me, however, Gene beat me to it and locked the door from the inside. No amount of pleading and screaming sufficed to cause him to relent. He laughed at my torment. After a few moments of agony I couldn't hold the pent up gas back and simply exploded. Debris from the blast covered me from head to foot. Aunt Fleta returned just in time to find me in this most embarrassing of all embarrassments. She took me down to the pond, made me wade in, and take off all my clothes. Then, she set about deciding on Gene's punishment for hurling obscenities at the neighbors, which she had already heard about by way of a phone call, and for cruelty to a little brother.

Despite his punishment, Gene continued to use his sharp mind for meanness. Just before the summer ended and I returned to Louisville, I happened to visit the Marshes again. I've always loved green peppers. Earlier in the summer the Marshes had had a lot of green peppers, which they served when I visited. Unbeknown to me but well known to Gene, in August those green peppers, while still retaining their color, turned flaming hot. Gene, well aware of my love for them, called to me, "Hey, Glenn, here are some of those great green peppers!" He pulled one off the vine and pretended to take a big bite out of it. Naïve as always, I ran to where he stood, yanked a pepper off the vine, chomped down on it, and started chewing. I gasped for air. I couldn't get my breath. I spit out all that I could and ran for the chain and cup pump at one corner of the garden. Gene doubled over laughing; anger, bitterness, and cruelty were still very much alive.

Gene came to live with his natural family only one other time, during his second year of high school. With an IQ of 128 he learned easily, but he also got into trouble easily. In mid-winter a terrible tragedy and a psychic experience occurred, shaking him to the depths. We learned later that six of his friends were on the way out to our farm to pick Gene up in a twelve-cylinder Lincoln. On the way they had to cross a train track in Sullivan. Foolishly, the driver of the car thought he could beat the oncoming train to the crossing. Four were killed. Gene waited and waited, but they never came. About midnight he finally went to bed. Deeply influenced by Mother's spiritualist ideas, at 2 a.m. he either dreamed or awakened and thought he saw an arm, which he identified as belonging to one of the four killed, reach out toward him. He leaped over the railing all the way down the stairs and spent the rest of the night shivering behind the stove in the living room. With the addition of this pain, at the end of his second year of high school, he dropped out and joined the Merchant Marine. He altered his birth certificate so he could work for Socony Vacuum Oil Company at age fifteen. After a year he entered the Coast Guard. The rest of his life, he and I never spent as much as a week together. And I was lonely.

Had you told me at age eight or nine that I'd find Grace in loneliness, I would have said, "You're crazy!" All I could discern from it then was excruciating pain. The departure of first Dad and then Gene sucked the life out of me. It hit me in my soul's solar plexus. Only from the vantage point of a long life have I been able to think of the long loneliness as a crucible of Grace. I may possess some innate contemplative leanings, but I don't believe I am innately contemplative. More likely, forced solitude gradually resulted in deeper reflection and voluntary solitude that prepared me for a life change. At this stage, *lectio divina* or other forms of meditation could not have crossed my mind. I had never seen a monastery and wouldn't have had the faintest idea what people did in one. Mother Nature, however, supplied me with wonderful contemplative moments. Even if I had never read Psalm 19, I knew that the heavens were telling the glory of God, whoever God was, and that the firmament showed God's handiwork. The long hours I would spend by myself were indeed pain-filled, but, like a crucible, their boiling and bubbling forced me to stretch my gaze beyond family ties and peer more deeply within to discover the Beyond in the midst of my life.

3

EARLY INTIMATIONS OF GRACE

How does a child survive experiences like mine and go on to have a useful and fruitful life? I can't speak for others, because I've learned not to stereotype human experience, but I will try to share with you my perceptions of what happened in my case. I attribute much of what happened to the mysterious working of grace, Immanuel God personally present, in my life. Now I can't explain to you why grace seemed to pass my brother by when it came to his alcoholism and the tragic brevity of his life. Or why it seemed to miss both of my parents, one an alcoholic and the other a victim of it who spent most of her life in grinding poverty. I'm not willing to say, like Calvinists I've known, that God has predestined some for salvation and others for damnation, some for prosperity and others for poverty, or some for fame and some for ignominy. No! No! That's too simple, and a God like that cruel. A God of infinite love shows no partiality and makes the sun to rise on both bad and good and the rain to fall on both righteous and unrighteous, just as Jesus said (Matt 5:45). There is no simple answer here, I'm sure, but part of a solution must lie, rather, in the many ways in which God channels grace into our lives and how we open ourselves to the working of grace.

My now eighty-plus years of life experience and my studies have awakened me to the endless means through which God enters mysteriously and beyond all our expectations into our lives. Means of grace are not confined to the almost universally acknowledged sacraments of baptism and Lord's supper or the Roman Catholic Church's seven—baptism, confirmation, eucharist, marriage, holy orders, penance, and anointing of the sick. If we can trust human experience all through history, we will have to conclude that God is not as limited or as neat and precise as a lot of Christian leaders have tried to make out. "All the world's alive with God," as Elizabeth Barrett Browning reminded. So we need to keep all of our sensors attuned to grace's surprises. Experience is full of grace. "Books and ideas and poems and stories, pictures and music, buildings, cities, places, philosophies," Thomas Merton observed of his experience, "were to be the materials on which grace would work."[1]

Although God—God's grace—is present in all of life, too many miss what Pierre de Caussade called "the sacrament of the present moment."[2] They may not have that special person, place, or thing enter into their lives at a critical moment when they were themselves ready and waiting and open. If I understand grace aright, it takes both *gift* and *receptivity*. That's true, even if God is the giver. God doesn't drive a bulldozer, despite what some evangelistic sermons I have heard suggest. So many things in our lives get in the way of reception: getting too turned in on ourselves; being overwhelmed by what's happening around us; anger; frustration; fear and anxiety; and a jillion other things. Yet we have to live with some confidence that the God of a universe of 150 billion galaxies loves us enough to keep trying to break through without denying our personhood.

Grace was working in my life in these years, even though I didn't know the word or understand its meaning, just as Augustine related in his *Confessions*. Grace was working through experiences in the depths, through persons, through school, yes and even through quirky religious experiences.

Please don't ask for a map or a chart of each of these. I can't give you one. My perception is, though, that in the midst of those traumatic experiences of early years ordinary saints were scratching around in the soil of my soul. I've mentioned some of them already—Ossie and Fleta Marsh, my uncle and aunt, and G.C. Busch, owner of the country store at Spring Bluff, Missouri. At this point, though, I want to focus on school. If I have any insight at all into what I have become, Cave Spring Elementary School and teacher Bertha Brown were critical factors. Very early, I think, I shifted my emotions from my heart to my head as a way of dealing with the painful and often ludicrous scenes I witnessed at home and elsewhere. In school I found a place and an activity in which I excelled, where I could avoid conflict, where I was accepted and admired and confirmed. Very early on, as a matter of fact, I began to sense a calling to teach.

As far back as I can remember I have had an inborn drive to learn. By age four I had learned to read at least a little, strongly motivated by

[1] Thomas Merton, *The Seven Storey Mountain* (New York: Giroux, 1948) 178.
[2] Jean-Pierre de Caussade, *The Sacrament of the Present Moment*, trans. Kitty Muggeridge (San Francisco: Harper & Row, 1966).

the fact that Gene started first grade that year. I couldn't let him get too far ahead in anything, least of all in something as important as reading. My basic phonetics came from names of cars on Dad's sales lot. Although there weren't as many models as we see today, there were enough to expose me to all the basic sounds in current American usage. To be sure I got the words right, I badgered salesmen who worked for Hinson Auto Sales to pronounce them for me. I probably didn't have good comprehension of what I was reading, but I could figure out how to pronounce words phonetically. Car names that called for foreign pronunciation, like Chevrolet, fascinated me and perhaps set the stage for a lifelong romance with learning languages.

When I was five, I attended kindergarten for one semester at Charless Elementary School, which was located on Shenandoah Avenue between Jefferson and Gravois in St. Louis, about two blocks from our house. It disappointed me that we spent most of our time coloring pictures rather than reading. Only two incidents cling to my mind from that semester, both about the very first day of school. One concerns a boy who wouldn't stop crying. The teacher locked him in a closet and he kicked on the door the entire period. The other had to do with a great embarrassment. One of my shoestrings came untied. Because I didn't know how to tie my shoestrings yet, I had to (blush) let a *girl* do it for me. When I got to school the next morning, I knew how to tie my shoes.

Cave Spring Elementary School was a far cry from Charless. Cave Spring was not two blocks but two miles from our house, a hefty hike for a six-year-old. So when September came, Dad hitched up old Beck and Kate to the wagon and gave Gene and me a ride to school the first day. This meant that we didn't go over the hills and through the woods as Gene and I learned to do later when we walked with the two Landing kids. We took the newly graded and graveled county road to Cave Spring Missionary Baptist Church and then the overgrown wagon trail which led from there to the school. Although a little rough, the trip posed no problem until we got to the brow of a hill, which would have overlooked the schoolyard, except that stately oak trees and brush impeded the view of it. Perched up on the wagon seat as I looked down the hill, I gulped. It seemed to plunge almost straight down. Deep ruts zigzagged back and forth across the middle of the track.

"Damn! And this goddamned wagon doesn't have a brake either," Dad swore. "I'll have to put a pole through the wheels. If I don't, the wagon will run the collars right over the mules' ears. You boys get down and walk."

He took an axe from the wagon bed, scissored over a barbed wire fence beside the road, cut and trimmed a sapling, and shoved it between the spokes on the back wheels. He clucked the mules forward. The wagon bounded back and forth over the ruts with only the front wheels turning. Even then, the mules ran the last third of the way down the hill as the collars hit their ears and the wagon careened this way and that. They kept on pulling until they topped a steep rise at the bottom. Dad yanked out the pole and let them pull the wagon the hundred yards or so into the schoolyard. On this first day of school teams and wagons took up most of the space in the yard even though Cave Spring would have only thirteen pupils in its eight grades.

Tall, stately white oaks and scrubby black oaks stood like sentinels around the schoolhouse and left room only for a small playground on one side. The playing area sloped off toward bottomland running alongside Little Boone Creek. It, too, looked nothing like Charless's level schoolyard paved with bricks. Oak and Sumac sprouts and regal goldenrods claimed most of it. But on the upper level you could see where previous generations had worn off most of the grass playing softball, dodge ball, tag, and a few other simple running games. This school, I saw right away, didn't turn out many athletes, although one alumnus whose daughter was an eighth grader, Gene Anderson, played baseball for a farm team of the St. Louis Browns. He awed us by swatting flies halfway to Boone Creek. As I soon discovered, kids here preferred to make houses out of the rails from no longer used fences rather than bang up their knees shagging fly balls.

From the outside, the white clapboard schoolhouse looked a lot like Cave Spring Church we had passed on the way. Both buildings were about the same size—perhaps 30 feet by 24 feet—and their foundations were made from sandstone, readily available in the area. Both had belfries topped by little pointed tin roofs. Tin roofs covered the rest of the buildings. On the inside, however, they differed noticeably. The school was originally a log building, which was covered outside by clapboard and inside by tongue-in-groove lumber. A well-worn blackboard stretched from wall to wall across the front. Four rows of desks of different sizes ran across the room, first and second graders on the right to seventh and eighth graders on the left. In the left front corner stood a two-section bookcase. Miss Brown's desk sat in the middle of the platform, which stretched across the front of the room. In back of the room, behind the desks, was the bench where Miss Brown did lessons with different classes while the rest of the pupils worked. The room smelled like a mixture of the compound used to sweep the floor, paste, chalk, and a variety of barnyard and body odors.

Cave Spring School was no cultural Mecca. It was mostly a room with a blackboard and a teacher. The "library," if you could call it that, had perhaps 200 books, many well worn and often missing pages. Much to my frustration, I didn't learn, for instance, how Nathaniel Hawthorne's classic *The Great Stone Face* turned out until years later because the school copy lacked the last several pages. I guessed the ending. Textbooks were never up to date and showed even more wear and tear than library books. Interestingly, the ancient eighth grade math texts included an introduction to algebra; when they were published, most students at Cave Spring didn't expect to go on to high school! Cave Spring did have a globe hung from the ceiling around which we all congregated for geography lessons. It, too, was well worn and could not have given the latest in geography, but it at least reminded us that the earth is not flat. The school had no piano or other musical instrument and no one to play it if there had been one. Once or twice during my years there a music person employed by Franklin County came and led us in some *a cappella* singing. He used a tiny pitch pipe to get us in tune. None of us could have imagined what I found at Cochrane Elementary and Halleck Hall Junior High School the year our family lived in Louisville: a music room with a piano and other instruments, a science lab with all the basic equipment, a well-appointed woodworking shop, an auditorium replete with stage and sound equipment, and quite a few other things.

You may wonder how anyone could learn enough in such a meagerly equipped place to make it through life at all, much less to attain some distinction. At Cave Spring the answer would have to be Bertha Brown. Bertha Brown was a "handsome" young woman, not yet twenty-five, although prematurely gray. She had had only a summer or two of college work at the Missouri State Teachers College, but she was an exceptional teacher—unbelievably dedicated and faithful to her calling. So far as I know, in those years she taught at Cave Spring she missed only one half-day of school. That was the day it snowed fourteen inches and the temperature dropped to twenty-three degrees below zero. But she got there at noon. None of her pupils got there; Gene and I didn't. Knowing how formidable the trip would be, Dad had put us on one of the mules and started to lead it toward Cave Spring. We didn't even get to the corner of our farm before he turned back. But I knew the next morning when we went that Bertha Brown had been there because the fire was burning in the stove. If she had not gotten there, it would have been out. She was so faithful.

Her example imprinted itself on my life in ways discursive logic never could. One of the deepest principles of my life is faithfulness. When my whole world was falling apart as my mother and father separated and then divorced during my second year of school, Bertha Brown would notice. As we trudged up that rutted hill from the schoolhouse, she would put her hand on my shoulder and say, "You can make it, Glenn. You can make it." And I knew I could because she always did.

I visited Bertha Brown in the hospital just before she died of throat cancer in 1974. She still showed that indomitable faith I'd seen in her when I was seven. "I'll make it, whatever comes," she whispered. I knew she would, too.

But "Miss Brown," as we all knew her, could teach. Oh, she wasn't preparing kids for Harvard or Yale. She focused on basics, the elements that underlie all human culture. Her limited college education notwithstanding, she knew her reading, writing, and arithmetic well enough to drill the same into the culturally deprived kids who came under her tutelage. In retrospect, I'm thankful that I went to school when the phonetic method was still in vogue. It complemented my self-teaching from the names of cars. Bertha Brown still relied on dog-eared, mouse- or child-chewed, much-used alphabet cards with the various sounds assigned to each letter to teach us the rudiments before we started reading. She drilled us over and over. Betty Lou Riske, whom I mentioned earlier, had a lot of trouble with some sounds because she had a speech impediment. Miss Brown worked ever so patiently until Betty Lou could make every sound intelligibly. Bernard Blankenship, enrolled when he was only five, had to drop out after a while because he wasn't quite ready to grasp what she was trying to teach.

Having to teach eight grades, or however many of those grades would have a pupil, would constitute an exceptional challenge for any teacher, and you may wonder how she could help her students with what they needed. Bertha Brown let a manual published by the state of Missouri set her goals for each class, most of which had only one or two pupils, and she used a variety of methods to achieve those goals. Much involved the assignment of written work, which she carefully graded and returned every day. In Gene's and my cases I think her greater challenge was to keep us busy. Both of us could do the assignments in a flash and have time on our hands. Idleness was then the devil's tool, especially for him.

Bertha Brown maintained discipline, and she did not tolerate misbehavior. In school, as at home, Gene had a genius for troublemaking. Each day, Miss Brown scheduled a "quiet time." She instructed each of us to lay our heads on our desks and take a nap or at least be "quiet as mice." One day during the quiet time Gene let out a little squeak like a mouse. "Glenn, did you do that?" she asked me. Kind of sleepily without even asking, "What?" I nodded yes. Whack! She slapped me on the cheek with her open palm. One of the eighth grade girls said, "No, Miss Brown. Glenn didn't do it. Gene did." She came over immediately to apologize, but she didn't give Gene his due either. I think she was too embarrassed, and I can't remember seeing her slap another child from that time on, though she did stand quite a few in one of the corners near the blackboard.

Contrary to what some may think, teaching six to eight grades in one school had certain pedagogical advantages. One would be reinforcement by repetition. Bright first graders could learn from eighth grade lessons, as I did. As a matter of fact, because the rows were so close, Miss Brown sometimes asked me to answer questions that students in other classes couldn't. That raised my stock with some, especially my classmate Betty Lou. When Dad helped Frank Sotebier and his family move, Betty Lou rode on the seat in Dad's wagon. As they passed our house, she pointed, "Ther'th where Glenn Hinthon liv'th. Him thmart boy," she told Dad. "Him thmarteth boy in school." It probably didn't endear me to some others whose questions I answered, but they didn't show resentment.

I wouldn't argue for a moment that we return to culturally challenged one-room schoolhouses. They wouldn't work in today's highly urbanized culture with its advanced technology. Unless outfitted differently than Cave Spring, schools wouldn't get students ready to live in our rapidly changing, cybernetic world today. But I did gain some things from my experience at Cave Spring that laid a foundation for a successful academic and teaching career, not just in the basics but in an attitude and outlook on life. Cave Spring bolstered my self-esteem.

Perhaps I should say it gave me a sense of meaning and purpose in my life that my family situation, loneliness, and poverty could not obliterate. And that was grace. How did it do that?

One element in it, I think, was the shepherding of younger children by older ones. On that very first day of school, an eighth grader named Anna (?) Anderson took me under her wing as soon as I got into the schoolyard and fussed over me like a mother hen tending her chicks. The attention embarrassed me, but it made me feel pretty good, too. I wasn't used to anyone treating me special. Mother didn't. The next day or so, Carl and Mary Landing, who were sixth or seventh graders, guided Gene and me home via their cross-country route, saving us perhaps a half-mile walk. Our farm cornered theirs. As I think back on it now, it was good that I wasn't thrown into a highly competitive situation at a time when I had so many other agendas to deal with. Cave Spring School provided a safe haven for a little, redheaded, freckle-faced boy whose world was exploding all around him.

The shepherding went on in the play during recess and at lunchtime. Some of it occurred in organized games such as I mentioned earlier. However, the playground was so uneven, rough, and rocky that we didn't have a lot of enthusiasm for that kind of play. All too often in softball games, for which we couldn't field two teams, we witnessed the skinning of knees and twisting of ankles. More of our play, therefore, took place in building. Cave Spring had an endless supply of rails at hand for the erection of houses and forts because farmers in the area had recently replaced rail with barbed or woven wire fences. Although we had to watch out for snakes, we could build without fear of the injuries we might incur on the playground.

What intrigues me even today about all of this was the comradeship, companionship, and friendship as well as creativity this common labor inspired. The older boys and girls, skilled in farm work by this time, gently directed, assisted, and encouraged the younger ones like me. Before winter arrived that first year, we had built a couple of houses that looked good enough to live in with roofs and floors covered with the thick moss which carpeted the woods.

Eating lunch together bonded us further, although it was often a cause of embarrassment for me. What embarrassed me was Mother's homemade bread. Most of the other kids brought sandwiches made with store-bought bread. Sometimes they would even have salami or bologna. I always had homemade bread spread with peanut butter or jelly, or something that did not require refrigeration. Mother baked delicious bread, and I could eat half a loaf with butter and jelly as it came out of the oven. At school, though, it was the telltale sign of the dire poverty we lived in. We couldn't afford to buy bread! Nevertheless, I can never remember another child making fun of me or calling attention to my bread. As a matter of fact, some often wanted to trade sandwiches, and that made me feel affirmed and accepted.

This one-room country school combined cooperation and competition in a manner that also equipped me to a degree for my subsequent career. I didn't have much competition in my own class at Cave Spring because much of the time I was the only pupil in it. Very often, with Miss Brown's approval, I took part in lessons with older students. School contacts and competitions, however, were not confined to single schools. Teachers arranged "meets" between schools all over the county.

I suppose competitiveness is an innate characteristic, beginning with the will to live. It grows, however, in sibling rivalries and from that in contests with other persons. At any rate, I was, and am, an intensely competitive person, and meets like these sparked the innate drive that had led to intense rivalries with Gene.

I learned quickly in these contests that I was not an athlete. If there were four contestants in a foot race, I would end up almost invariably as number four. However, there was one race in which I excelled—the sack race. This race required you to put both legs in a feed sack (called a "gunny sack") and hold it up around your waist as you covered fifty or a hundred yards. Most sack racers jumped from line to line. In this, however, I had one advantage—very small feet. I could *run* inside the sack and thus make steadier time. If I remember correctly, I came in first in every race except one, a countywide race held at Sullivan High School when I was in the eighth grade. The person who beat me was named Wilbur, who stood about six-feet-five or -six and could jump a "mile" with each jump.

The race has remained vivid in my mind. He and another boy who stood on opposite sides of me were teasing me because I was so small, just slightly over four feet. "Well, I know at least one person here I'll beat," Wilbur declared. "Me, too," replied the other one. My heart was beating a mile a minute, but I just grinned a little and kept my secret to myself. Life experience had already taught me to keep my own counsel about what I could do, do my best, and accept the outcome. I knew both of them wondered what a near midget was doing in this big race. The gun went off, and off I went. I ran as fast as my legs would carry me inside the sack. Wilbur and I left the rest of the field behind. He won by about half of a jump. The other protagonist fell and didn't finish the race. I grinned bigger still as Wilbur and I collected first and second prize and shook hands. I always hated to lose, but, somehow, that day second place seemed like first.

I won consistently in mental contests—spelling, math, and reciting poetry. We didn't receive big prizes, but, to someone as impoverished as I was, they were welcome. First prize was usually a book or a tablet, second prize a pencil, and third prize a stick of gum. I was somewhat disappointed that I never won any gum, except in one foot race, but my competitive urge drove me to come out on top, especially in math. Using a scheme I worked out for doing certain problems I could give the answer to a math problem as soon as I heard the last figure.

Rural schools like Cave Spring served as the center of their communities. Nearly everyone came to graduation exercises and the occasional plays and pie suppers put on to raise money. The plays gave children like me an opportunity to blossom. Many of the students had trouble memorizing their lines for a play, but that was something that came easily to me. As a matter of fact, I never really tried to memorize. By the time I had read through the play and we had gone through a rehearsal I usually knew almost everyone's lines and served as an on-stage prompter. When the time came for the performance and some had a little stage fright and muffed their lines, I could give them clues to get the play back on track. The plays themselves were freeing for me. They permitted me to put on a different persona and flee some of the everyday cares. It was always a great disappointment to me, however, that Mother did not come to most of these events because of her deafness. I knew she cared and was proud of Gene and me, but I wanted her to show that with her presence.

I returned to Cave Spring for the last two years of my elementary schooling, but my educational pilgrimage there was interrupted by moves to Spring Bluff, Missouri, and to Louisville, Kentucky. Within a year or so of her divorce and of Gene's departure to live with the Marshes, Mother realized that she could not afford to pay $6 a month rent on the Kleinert farm, so we moved to a farm just a quarter of a mile from Spring Bluff owned by G.C. Busch. That put me in the Spring Bluff school district and under tutelage of a new teacher fresh out of college:

Miss Matthews. Although Miss Matthews, daughter of the superintendent of Sullivan Public Schools, had better educational preparation and Spring Bluff better facilities, my year there left just one deep memory. Miss Matthews, in her first year of teaching, found herself overwhelmed by the teaching schedule and asked me, though only a fifth grader, to do math and reading lessons for the first four grades. In that she gave me my first vivid glance at what turned out to be my lifelong vocation. I've often wondered, though, how children in the first four grades felt about my tutoring.

During the year at Spring Bluff, another event affected my schooling and indeed the direction of my life. John Helms returned to his parents' farm at Cave Spring at the end of a three-year enlistment in the US Coast Guard and began coming to court Mother at the farm in Spring Bluff. They married after a brief courtship. We moved to another farm, which put me back in the Cave Spring School district for sixth grade, but I did not get to finish the year there. After the bombing of Pearl Harbor, John reenlisted and we moved to Louisville mid-year. As it turns out, I spent a semester in sixth grade at Cochrane Elementary and a semester in seventh grade at Halleck Hall Junior High in Louisville.

I need not dwell on the time I spent at either of those, except to point out that they confirmed the quality of my education, despite some deficiencies, at Cave Spring and Spring Bluff. Where I was lacking was in the arts and athletics. Louisville schools included training in art, music, woodworking, and organized sports, which Cave Spring and Spring Bluff could not provide. In academic areas, however, I was not only equal, but perhaps even a bit ahead of my fellow sixth and seventh graders. How well I did, as a matter of fact, evoked some envy from a student named Lonnie. Lonnie, a year or so older than the rest of us and sort of a class bully, picked on me and tried to start a fight shortly after I enrolled at Cochrane. Against the background of my fights with Gene and being much smaller than Lonnie I ignored his taunts. I soon discovered, however, that I didn't have to defend myself. When we played football, some of the bigger boys ganged up on Lonnie and let him know that he should leave me alone. They liked me and admired my academic gifts.

Halleck Hall offered me an opportunity to display and develop some leadership abilities. Located in Old Louisville near St. James Court and not far from the University of Louisville, it drew quite a number of students with strong cultural backgrounds in affluent and political families. Because I made the only A she gave out in geography, our geography teacher, Miss Braun, appointed me one of the hall monitors, which meant I often got out of class early. My homeroom teacher also strongly encouraged me to run for student government. Although I did, I waged an exceedingly feeble campaign because neither school I had attended had anything even remotely like that. Most political efforts I've engaged in subsequently have turned out just about as badly. It was just as well, though, in this case, for Mother decided to move back to Missouri when my stepfather was transferred out of Louisville mid-year. When she bought a farm adjoining Cave Spring Church, she assured me that I would finish elementary training in the school I began in even if under another teacher.

Much to my disappointment, Bertha Brown, having completed her college degree, now taught fifth grade in the Sullivan Public Schools, as she did for the rest of her career. Margaret Schmidt took her place at Cave Spring. She was a different person with a different style of teaching, but she did one thing that singled me out as a leader and added to my self-confidence. Immediately upon my return to Cave Spring, she asked me to serve as a sort of paid assistant, going to school early to get the fire going during the winter and staying late to clean and ready everything for the next day. Mrs. Schmidt was asthmatic and she needed extra time to walk the mile to and from the school, which provided ample opportunity to talk about many things besides school. The confidence she vested in me as her assistant bolstered my self-image and put up another road sign or two about the direction my life might take. It was another touch of grace.

I can see one particular thread running through what I have recounted thus far about my schooling, which helps to explain one very evident trait: I've never been a very assertive or aggressive person, ready to dive in and take charge. I have tended to stand back and size up a situation or a task carefully before I decide what to do. Indeed, I've usually waited for others to push me into leadership. You could see in this a lack of confidence instilled by early experience, rural background, and perhaps some doubts about my abilities, but I think there may be a deeper philosophical foundation poured by life experience. It's a confidence that things will work out somehow by God's grace or, stated in another way, a belief in God's providence. God moves in mysterious ways in our lives. If we let down like a swimmer letting down into the water, we may discover a buoyancy. But if we flail our arms around and try too hard, we will just wear ourselves out and eventually drown.

This philosophy served me well during the next phase of my schooling at Sullivan High. Living out in the "sticks," away from town, there was no way I could leap in and take charge, especially as the class with which I attended was the largest Sullivan High had ever registered. Ninety-six students enrolled in the freshman class; eighty-nine graduated in 1949. Kids who lived in Sullivan were able to play much more active roles in this big class than those of us who could only attend school happenings occasionally. What surprised me was the extent to which the central corps of them eventually tried to include me in leadership, in part because of my demonstrated academic abilities but equally because I put a lot of effort into being liked. In one-room country schools I hadn't had to work on acceptance by peers. Now I did, and that may have been the major thing I got out of high school. Surely it was more important than what I learned from classes and books.

Sullivan High was definitely not a college prep school, and I just sort of glided along without much effort. I quickly developed a reputation as a "brain," but it was that which set me up for a major lesson in human relations and made me determined to have people like me, even if I had to "dumb down." My lesson came in freshman science.

When we got our first test back, the teacher announced that only one student in the class had made a hundred. After lauding this person for a minute or two, he announced the name—Glenn Hinson. The praise started to inflate my ego, but a comment just behind me burst the balloon. Jo Ann Martin, with whom I had fallen in love at first sight when she sang at a welcome for incoming students, and who was, unbeknownst to me, almost engaged then to Carl Preston, whispered to Carl, "Yeah. He really thinks he's something." I didn't have a mirror to look into, but I probably turned several shades of scarlet. I realized that, whether out of envy or something else, she spoke the truth. Up to that time, I think I'd probably invested most of my energies in myself and my reputation and thought, "Let the Devil take the hindmost. Why should I care?" In that moment, I resolved that Jo Ann Martin and all the other kids would like me. But how? How could I get them to do that?

I may have hit on a plan immediately, but, more likely, I let her remark fester, and I lay awake several hours for a few nights worrying my way toward a solution. My plan was simple: Help those who need help with their schoolwork. During study halls, students, especially athletes, sought me out to help with homework. I was reticent about it, but I started letting some peek at my answers on exams. My generosity there, however, soon got me into trouble in the same science class in which I had received such high praise. On one of our exams I let Melvin "Meb" Brake, who was a basketball star and who sat just behind me to my left, copy one answer after another. Mr. Schwaneke watched the whole proceeding as unobtrusively as he could. When I turned in my paper, he looked it over and wrote, "100%—F." I cried. I continued to offer tutoring on homework, but I never let anyone copy again.

Although my plan had a kink in it, it seemed to work. The "sacrifice" I made for one of the school's sports stars probably enhanced my reputation with the "in" crowd. As a result, I was elected sophomore class president, receiving 89 out of 96 votes. The other seven votes were divided among two or three other nominees. I must be candid to say that, although I could make stirring speeches, I proved to be a flop as a leader. Living out of town, I participated chiefly in Student Council meetings. Near the end of the year, other class leaders pushed me to organize a class trip like other classes were taking. Because of the modest personal resources of most students, we took a trip to southeast Missouri and welcomed the invitation of high school students in Ironton, a town about Sullivan's size, to a dinner and dance. Sad to say, some of our hosts were killed after the dance. The driver of one car drank too much liquor and drove at excessive speeds on unsafe roads. I never ran or let myself be nominated for a school office again.

Schools with better academic programs would undoubtedly have prepared me better for Washington University than Sullivan High School did. Most teachers let me rest on the reputation I had gained in the first year or so, and I spent far too much time partying my last two years. There were areas, however, in which I excelled and had sufficient competition from fellow students to reach higher levels. One of those was math. Because I maintained a 100 percent average, at the end of freshman math, the teacher asked me to grade the other students' papers. Quite to my surprise, my fellow students did not quibble; they applauded. One other student, Wayne McDaniel, who went on to teach mathematics at the University of Missouri, St. Louis, and I took every advanced math class offered. He once asked me why I didn't pursue a career in that field, too. I'm not sure I answered or could answer, but, as I look backward, I think the route I have taken was within the will of God for me, though perhaps not the only route I could have taken. Besides, some other areas seemed to challenge me more.

One of those was English. I loved English, even diagramming sentences, but still more, reading and writing, composing poems. English could well have pulled me into its web had it not been for an excruciatingly painful event in my sophomore year. A pretty, petite young woman just out of college, Miss Searight, taught English Literature. She knew the literature, and she knew how to teach, but she could not maintain order. The bigger, older boys flirted with her, pulling her down on their laps, and disrupted the class. In tears she quit before the end of the year. A local Baptist pastor named A.B. Christian, who had three daughters at Sullivan High, completed the course. I've wondered ever since whether, popular as I was, I could have asserted some leadership that would have kept Miss Searight in the classroom. Here again was that deep imprint of my early family years: Steer away from conflict. Don't get involved.

English composition and creative writing set me on fire in my third year and surely nurtured a bud that has produced a full-sized plant. Here I met a really demanding teacher, one who inspired creative ideas and coached us to express them. We read creative writings. We debated. We wrote plays. We made short stories into plays. The highlight of the year for all of us in that class was our version of O. Henry's "The Ransom of Red Chief." I wrote the script and played the part of "Red Chief." Schools near Sullivan learned about it and invited us to present it in their assemblies. Everywhere we went, students gave us a rousing reception. Unfortunately, due to over exuberant "acting" on my part in one of those presentations, we never got to do it for Sullivan High. And I see here again a demon of violent family experience.

Like O. Henry's story, my script called for "Red Chief" to make his two kidnappers so uncomfortable that they were willing to pay to get rid of him. One of the nasty tricks he played was to smash a red hot potato on the back of one of his captors. Well, we didn't use a red hot potato. Just a potato. In order to give it real effect, however, I hit very hard with malice aforethought, evoking a cry of real pain from Jim Squires, who played the part. It hurt so much he refused to play the role again, and "The Ransom of Red Chief" folded. I hope I begged Jim's forgiveness. If I didn't, I'm doing so now. Like my killing of the little bird years before, this incident shows how deeply scarred I was and that I still needed a lot of healing.

So many things signaled the same conclusion. I didn't, and perhaps couldn't, develop satisfying and meaningful friendships. I did have one very close friend, Donald Hedges, whose birthday coincided exactly with mine. We were both born 27 July 1931. We were inseparable our last two years—almost like twins—and we spent much of our time running around in Mother's 1929 Model A Ford. We were very lucky not to have been involved in a serious accident because the old car seldom had good brakes. Model A's had mechanical rather than hydraulic brakes. Especially during World War II, drivers could not find brake rods. When a rod broke, they spliced it back together by welding another piece to the rod. The weld, however, made it brittle. Bouncing over a country road, brake rods often broke, so that when you pulled up to a stop sign you couldn't tell whether you would have four, three, two, one, or perhaps no brakes. Many is the time Donald Hedges and I had to jump out on the running board and drag the old Model A to a halt by digging in our heels.

Most of the time I lived in my head and relied on my intelligence to create respect and acceptance, to "impress." I couldn't trust my emotions. They were too fragile. I held most people at arm's length, fearful lest they see what I had been through or was really like deep inside where there were so many ugly scars. I longed for deeper friendships, but I was afraid to expose myself and to trust myself to another. That was true especially in my relationships with girls.

To be quite honest, I "fell in love" a number of times and didn't have the slightest idea how I might develop a healthy friendship with the person I liked. I've often wondered whether falling in love with people, especially brainy ones, is a terrible flaw, for it has happened again and again throughout my rather long life. Maybe it is a consequence of growing up in a terribly dysfunctional family. I've concluded that no one can ever explain why it happens, but I suspect that the persistent loneliness extending back to my own disrupted family beginnings had something to do with the number of times it has happened to me. Deep within my soul is a void that only love could fill. The one family model I knew, my own, could never work. The first of my infatuations was Lucille Schebaum. She was a year older than I, and one class ahead of me, when I entered Cave Spring School. Her parents were the most successful farmers in the area. She was cute and always dressed so neatly. I tried to treat her like an angel and cozied up to her younger siblings when they started Cave Spring School, but I doubt whether she would have guessed what I intended to convey. There was Virginia Blesi, my classmate at Spring Bluff. I once showed that I liked her by pushing her bicycle too fast for her to control and causing her to fall off and get skinned up a bit. I've already mentioned Jo Ann: My infatuation with her dimmed fast, however, when I learned of her deep commitment to Carl. Then, there was "Mert" Lockhart's sister, three years younger than I. Don Hedges dated one of her friends, George Wilkinson, another of our classmates, dated another. It was natural for me to ask her out, but I could never bring myself to do so. Her age may have been a factor in that, but it wasn't the real factor. She knew I liked her and she let me know that she liked me. I was articulate in everything else, but I couldn't say the words, "Would you like to…?"

The truth is, I had a very low self-image when it came to personal relationships and compensated for that by shifting to my head. School assisted me in that shift. It confirmed that I was somebody, somebody superior. My peers affirmed me. When we graduated, they asked me to write the class poem and to co-author the class "will." Teachers and administrators confirmed their estimate. Although I didn't pay that much attention to grades in my partying years, I graduated fifth in my class, the only male student in the top ten. I've never checked to confirm this, but a member of the school board told me that I had the highest score on the College Boards in the state of Missouri in 1949. Headiness helped to bolster my ego, but it could not take away my loneliness.

4

"CALL NO MAN ON EARTH FATHER"

Jesus' caution about calling anyone on earth father has always intrigued me because that's what my early life experience had taught me. By the time I was fifteen I had had both a father and a stepfather abandon ship. My father, of course, because of alcoholism, but my stepfather because he and Mother couldn't get along. John Helms was a good, hardworking, and reliable husband and father, and it tore my heart out when he and Mother decided they could not resolve their differences and called it quits after only four or five years of marriage. What these two separations taught me, above all, was to avoid close human attachments because disappointments would inevitably shatter them. Maybe that's what Jesus experienced if, as some scholars theorize, Joseph died early; no one knows for sure, of course.

My relationship with John did not begin on a high note. Like any another nine- or ten-year-old child of divorce, I had become rather possessive of my mother by the time he appeared on the scene. I didn't like it when she started to date other men about a year or so after Dad left. There was probably a mixture of fear and jealousy in my reaction. After Gene went to live with the Marshes, I was the only one around to absorb her attention, and she relied heavily on me to see that she heard people when they spoke to her and to perform most of the simple chores around the farm. Calls by suitors usually resulted in my being sent off to my attic room to do some kind of chores, or otherwise to disappear.

Suitors started turning up shortly after we moved to Spring Bluff to the farm owned by G.C. Busch during the summer of 1941. Mr. Busch moved us and let us live there rent-free. The house was small but almost new, and the farm had enough pasture to graze one or two cows Mother still owned. She had sold the rest to pay bills.

We soon discovered that the Kleinert farm had had one big advantage—location on a farm-to-market road. The Busch farm was located about a quarter of a mile off of a road maintained by the state. During the rainy season, the dirt road that ran across an open field turned into a quagmire, and deep ruts gleefully sucked car wheels into them until the axles dragged. Drivers could gun the engines as vigorously as they liked, the cars merely sank deeper and deeper into the muck. Often the gunning resulted in blowouts of the old, often-patched inner tubes still used in most tires as they heated up. Changing tires in the mud was impossible. Even the best drivers always ended up applying to the nearest farmer to come and pull the car out with a team of horses or mules.

Moving to the Busch farm enabled Mother to save twenty-five or thirty dollars to buy a 1930 Chevy coupe. Although she had worked in a car dealership, Mother, now in her late-thirties, had never learned how to drive. So she persuaded Uncle Ossie to give her the very first driving lesson on the lightly traveled country roads near Spring Bluff. Learning to drive in a 1930 Chevy was a challenge for anyone, but especially for someone her age. 1930 Chevys did not have smooth shifting automatic transmissions, power steering, power brakes, or any of those computerized features that make modern cars so easy to maneuver. Country roads were not nicely paved with concrete or asphalt either. They were graveled with coarse gravel dredged out of the nearby Bourboise or Meramec rivers. Loose gravel made it easy to lose control going around curves or up and down hills. As a matter of fact, the first accident I witnessed occurred right in front of the first farm we lived on. The driver of a fairly new 1935 Ford V-8 lost control as he took a slight curve too fast. His car ended up balancing on some tall saplings in a huge gulley at the side of the road. He lost his left ear on a broken windshield.

Mother's driving lessons supplied Gene and me with some high entertainment but also a considerable amount of anxiety as we rode with Aunt Fleta a safe distance behind.

Driving posed a physical problem for Mother. She was only 5'2", you may remember, and the old Chevy did not have adjustable seats. She solved this problem with only partial satisfaction by using a couple of thick pillows—one under and one behind her.

Because of her deafness, she couldn't tell how fast she was racing the motor when she started. She revved the motor up like she was on the front row in the Indianapolis 500. She eased the clutch out, but when it engaged, the old car lurched forward like a rabbit jumping out of its burrow. Unnerved by that, Mother responded by taking her foot off of the gas pedal altogether. That killed the engine. After a half dozen lurches and killings like that and more instructions from Uncle Ossie, she finally got the car rolling.

The next challenge was coordinating the shifting of the very stiff and cranky gears with the depressing and releasing of the clutch, something Mother never mastered. She ground the gears every time she shifted, and I could imagine the crankcase getting another load of iron filings. Feeling very unsure of herself at first, she drove too slowly to shift into high, so she kept the engine roaring. On her first lesson, however, she gradually gained enough assurance to start looking around and pointing this way and that as she talked to Uncle Ossie. She ended up in a shallow ditch as she rounded a curve. She learned from that to keep her eyes on the road. John Helms came into our lives just in time to keep us from having to put Mother's driving skills to a very extensive test.

I didn't know John well before he came calling on Mother after we moved to Spring Bluff, but Gene and I had met him. After being mustered out of the Coast Guard, he had come a couple of years before to live with his father and mother and to help them with their farming. Like my grandfather's farm at Lone Dell, the Helms farm was an early homestead located on Little Boone Creek. The house sat on top of a hill overlooking the creek. It consisted of two unfinished and weathered two-story log buildings joined by a breezeway, typical of pioneer houses. There were two rooms in each log section, one on each floor. It had no modern conveniences and remained just as it was in frontier days. The Helmses carried water about a quarter of a mile from a spring that poured its waters into Little Boone Creek.

Tom Helms had been born in that house. He, as the name indicates, was of English ancestry, but Barbara, his wife, was a full-blooded Cherokee Indian. She had high cheekbones, lovely bronze skin, brown eyes with long lashes, and uncut coal-black hair, which she gathered in a bun at the back of her head.

Gene and I passed through the Helms farm, which adjoined the Cave Spring School property, when we took the most direct route home through the woods and over the fields. One day on the way home, we picked up a hammer that the Helmses had left by a barbed wire fence and started to carry it home with us. As we skipped along our path toward home, whom should we meet but John Helms? I had seen Tom Helms at Cave Spring Missionary Baptist Church, in which he served as a deacon and key leader. But I had not seen John before. Except for the bun, he looked more like his mother than his father. He had those same high cheekbones, bronze skin, brown eyes, and black hair that she had.

My face turned several shades of red, and I quickly fumbled for an explanation as to what a hammer was doing in my hand. "Is, … is this your hammer?" I said. "We thought maybe someone had lost it. Here!"

John grinned a little. "No. We didn't lose it. We left it by the fence so we could nail it up again after we got the cows into the other field." I suspected that he knew we were intending to carry it home.

"Well, we'd better get on home. We have to milk the cows," Gene said. And we skedaddled as fast as our legs would move. Never again did we stop to pick up even a walnut on the Helms farm.

So I was a little surprised when John Helms showed up at Spring Bluff. Mother had had one other fairly serious suitor, but he faded out of the picture fast when John entered it. I could see on the very first visit that Mother liked John. She lighted up like a Roman candle as they talked about the weather, the harvest, cows, hogs, and farm business.

I must confess that I was a little cannier about "the birds and the bees" than one might expect of a ten-year old boy. Although children who grow up on a farm witness the mating of horses, cows, and other farm animals on a regular basis, I had an added source of instruction. The people who had rented the house we lived in had left huge stacks of *True Romance* and magazines of that type as well as a pile of detective magazines in the attic where I slept. Because I didn't have anything else to read and loved to read, I devoured them. Not with great depth of understanding, mind you. Many of the nuances were quite foreign to my experience and washed over me like waves lapping at the seashore. But I had a good vocabulary and understood most of what I was reading. Now I had a chance to observe some of it firsthand.

John showed up more and more frequently after that first visit. Sometimes he stayed overnight. I don't have a clear memory as to when and how it happened, but the next thing I knew Mother and John were married. They evidently "got hitched" before a justice of the peace with only a couple of witnesses present while I was visiting Aunt Fleta and Uncle Ossie at Cuba. In those days country folk did not look kindly on divorce and even less kindly on remarriage, so the quieter the event, the better for all concerned. But I was not there and not invited. Mother probably sensed the reservations I would have had and thought it best to shuttle me off for a while. It was not her nature or *modus operandi* to pay much attention to either my or Gene's feelings. And certainly not to give long explanations. The only thing I knew when I got home was that I now had a stepfather.

I rebelled. Not with a lot of fanfare, mind you. That was not my style. But I said quietly to myself, "He's not my father. I'm not going to treat him like he is. He's been imposed by a *fait accompli*, without consultation of any kind. Here I stand." Or something like that.

The first and only test came with reference to taking care of a young calf we kept at the time. John assigned me the task of feeding and watering her every morning. I didn't quite have the courage to say, "No! I won't do it." As a matter of fact, he hadn't ordered me to do it. He'd asked, "Glenn, how about you taking care of the calf? Feed and water her, okay?" Of course, he meant it as a command.

I decided that I would show my distaste for stepfathers by doing the job as fast and as carelessly as I could. I was not about to use up *my* time to please *him*. Well, my hurriedness meant sloppiness. I just dumped a little feed in the trough and a little water in the tub, scattering as much outside the receptacle as inside as I did, and scampered back to my *True Romances* or *True Detective Stories* or whatever else I was reading. I'd hardly gotten settled into my reading when John stomped up the steps and into my room.

"Glenn, I told you to take care of the calf." The tone of his voice scared me. I looked around and saw he had a switch in his hand.

"I did. I gave it food and water."

"Ha! Like Hell! Now you get down there and do it right." He whacked me across my bare legs all the way down to where the calf was tethered. He got my attention.

So much for my short-lived revolt; I wouldn't give a nickel for another whipping like that. I don't advocate the use of the rod to discipline children, but that whipping changed my attitude. I never talked to John or Mother about it. As I had learned to do from several years of being almost totally alone, I just talked to myself. I let it grind around inside me for a while and came to the conclusion that, like it or not, I would have to get along with John Edgar Helms. Better to make him like me than to wage a constant cold war. That would do neither of us any good, and it might lead to much harm.

I probably surprised him by the sudden transformation. I surprised myself a little. From that day on, I decided to like work. I don't think I had learned how to do hard, physical labor until John came on the scene, and I could not have chosen a better way to please him.

John Helms was a *"worker,"* the kind people in the Missouri Ozarks spoke about with admiration. Although he was only of average height, 5'9", growing up on a farm and service in the Coast Guard had made him muscular and strong. In the Coast Guard he had mastered his weight class in boxing, something that undoubtedly pleased Mother. Although he had limited education, moreover, he was trained as a mechanic and rose through the ranks to the level of Chief Machinist's Mate. On the farm he worked with zeal in whatever he needed to do.

The Busch farm at Spring Bluff did not have enough acreage to support a family. Very soon after Mother and John married, therefore, they decided to rent a farm owned by Chester Brown, brother of my teacher at Cave Spring, which was located about a mile from the Helms' homestead on a good farm-to-market road and only four miles from Sullivan. John would farm the Brown place and continue to help his dad farm. One other thing, however, added some urgency to the move, Mother was pregnant and needed to be closer to the hospital at Sullivan.

If Mother's remarriage delivered a small blow, her pregnancy struck a big one. Already facing doubts as to how I would fit into her life with John, now as I watched her belly puff out farther and farther I wondered if I, too, might be dispatched like Gene to live with someone else. I'd seen that happen to some other children, most notably Betty Lou Riske and her sister. My situation frightened me enough that one day I bumped Mother's swollen belly wanting to make something happen to the baby. I'm not too clear in retrospect what I thought that would be, maybe a miscarriage. Mother had had one miscarriage just after Dad left; so I knew what they were. But the baby would have been in the third trimester by that time. I can only say that in my confused state at that time I was crying out in the only way I knew how—with violence. Mother just grimaced a little. For most of my life, though, I've carried the incident in my conscience as another grim reminder of my capacity for violence.

At any rate, before the school term ended in 1942 we moved. To permit me to complete the year at Spring Bluff, Miss Matthews came by on her way from Sullivan and gave me a ride. She didn't want to lose her "star pupil," she said. John didn't even get to start farming the Brown farm, however. Still only thirty, he expected to be drafted from the moment we heard about the surprise Japanese attack on Pearl Harbor, and he reenlisted in the US Coast Guard. He was immediately reassigned and not at home when, on August 20, Mother gave birth to a baby girl, whom they named Barbara Sue after her paternal grandmother.

The birth of "Susie Q," as I nicknamed her, melted any anxieties and animosities I had harbored. Adults had fueled my anxieties about what would happen to me as they talked about the dangers of someone Mother's age, almost forty, giving birth. When the day came and the birth went off smoothly and I saw the little one for the first time, all of my worries vanished like the mist of the morning. It soon became clear that not only would Mother not give me the boot but that she needed me to help her take care of this little one in the absence of her husband. Grandma Crow came to stay with us for a couple of weeks when Mother came home from the hospital. After that, bathing the baby, changing diapers, doing laundry, and all sorts of other household chores became my responsibility, too. In addition, my responsibility increased to see that Mother properly understood what people were saying to her. She either refused to wear a hearing aid or couldn't afford to buy one. In those days they weren't the tiny units widely used today but a big button plugged into the ear and wired to a small radio carried around the waist. As I look back on these developments, I can see a measure of grace once again. I was growing fast in my sense of responsibility for others in my family. To be someone to whom others delegated responsibility was effecting a great change in my whole outlook. From this point on, that would prove telling.

Our stay on the Brown farm lasted only a few months. In the early fall we packed up and moved to Louisville, Kentucky, where John had been assigned to the Coast Guard Station at the foot of Fourth Street. War is ruthless and indiscriminate in the demands it places not only on combatants but also their families. We were fortunate, of course, that John was not in a branch of the service where he would have been at far greater risk than he was in the Coast Guard. For a family of such limited means as we had, however, moving was a tremendous strain, and it was made doubly difficult because of Mother's hearing disability. We had to dispose of livestock, furniture, car, and virtually all bulk items and take only our clothes and personal possessions. In Louisville we had to rent a furnished apartment.

Only in retrospect can I see how fortunate we were to locate a second-floor efficiency apartment at 1529 South Fourth Street, a building later torn down and replaced by an ugly apartment complex. The apartment was not great. Three tiny rooms for three persons, including one a tiny infant—four when John came home, and five for a brief time when Gene came to visit with us. What I remember most about it, however, were the bedbugs that regularly left us bleeding in the morning. The manager, who lived on the first floor, tried to fumigate regularly, but nothing seemed to get rid of the bedbugs. On a coastguardsman's income and housing allowance, however, we could not afford more.

Then there was the constant moving. When you went to bed at night, you didn't know who your neighbors would be in the morning. Apartment managers couldn't screen people too closely, and they often ended up with uncouth and rowdy types whom they had to call on the police to evict.

Moving to Louisville, however, exposed me to something I hadn't seen before first hand—segregation. In the dirt-floored basement of our apartment building lived our African-American porter. She was shocked when I spoke to her politely just like I did to everyone else and then played with her grandson. My play with Jim, however, taught me one of the most significant lessons I've ever learned. I realized for the first time that Jim didn't look like any other black person I had ever seen and that I was prejudiced, too, because until that time I always thought all African Americans looked alike.

As gross as 1529 South Fourth was, the neighborhood itself was tops. I didn't know then that it was one of Louisville's choicest residential areas, but we lived just a block from St. James Court, three blocks from Central Park, a few blocks from Louisville's premier boys high schools—Male and Manual—and a mile or so from the University of Louisville. Some of Louisville's finest homes were all around us. Louisville centered on the Fourth Street axis. A street car ran straight down Fourth Street to the heart of the downtown.

The location of our apartment set the stage for me to earn steady money, and I have supported myself almost entirely since age eleven. During the war, most people did not have cars and could not get enough gas to drive them if they did. So they had to walk to the nearest grocery. Right next door to our apartment building was a neighborhood Kroger store where most people in the area bought their groceries.

Shortly after we moved to Louisville, I was standing on the walk in front of the Kroger store when a woman asked me if I would carry her groceries home. "Excuse me. I'll have to ask my mother," I said. I didn't want to do that without letting Mother know, so I raced upstairs to tell her. That person, in the meantime, found someone else to carry her groceries. But from then on, I built a steady flow of customers who wanted me to carry their groceries to St. James Court, the Puritan Apartments, and dozens of other fine homes in the neighborhood. Some seemed to prefer me to other boys who gathered outside to do the same thing, and they tipped generously. I gave my earnings to Mother.

When I returned from my first full-time job in Cuba, Missouri during the summer of 1943, Charlie Pinto, who owned a shoe-repair and cleaning shop next to Kroger, asked me to come to work for him. He agreed to pay me and let me have tips. I picked up and delivered laundry and dry cleaning, shined shoes, and helped a little with shoe repair. Although all of these things were good for learning, I had my eyes opened wider from a friendship I developed with Pat, an African-American ironer and presser. The wages he earned from his full-time employment barely surpassed what I received in pay and tips from part-time; and I was only twelve years old!

Even though we spent just slightly more than a year in Louisville, it left enough of a mark on my life to tilt me in its direction again when I had to decide where I would get my theological training. I would have enjoyed staying longer. Early in 1944, however, John was reassigned to Alaska, and Mother didn't need much coaxing to decide to return to Missouri. By this time she and John had accumulated enough money to buy the Howse farm, which lay immediately to the west of Cave Spring Church. The original owner had ceded land for Cave Spring Cemetery. The farm also ran alongside the road to Cave Spring School.

The eighty-acre Howse farm had not been cultivated very much in recent years, and much of it was not cultivable. Mrs. Howse's son, as a matter of fact, used the largest field for a landing strip for his small plane. The three things the farm produced in some abundance were hay, pears, and irises. Most of the cultivable land grew fine red top grass, which we could use for the cows and horses. A two- or three-acre pear orchard, despite being overgrown with rough oak sprouts and trees, still bore bushels of pears. What caught the eye, however, was a row of irises of all colors that ringed the one-acre yard. Mrs. Howse, a drawling Southern matron, loved irises and had collected bulbs from all over the world.

The yard had two other distinctive features. A row of giant cedars, probably a century old, stood alongside the highway that cut through the farm. Two gargantuan maples, whose trunks were at least eight feet across, stood just behind the cedars. Each provided wonderful shade but, unfortunately, also hoisted knobby roots out of the ground all over the front yard, making it virtually impossible to mow the grass.

When we first occupied the Howse farm, it had five buildings: a log house, a smoke house, a chicken house, a barn, and an outdoor toilet. None was in good repair. We lived in the log house for two or three years, but we finally tore it down because of snakes that nested in the cracks. Black snakes were harmless and kept down mice and other rodents. What we feared were copperheads. They are poisonous and thrive in that part of the Ozarks. The smoke house was well built, but it was too small for a family to live in until John added a lean-to room on one side. That gave us one attic bedroom, a small kitchen, and a living-room bedroom combined—each about 16' by 12'. The plan was to build a bigger house to take the place of the log house, but that never came to fruition because of the divorce.

Farming like we did cannot survive today. It barely survived during and after World War II as prices kept rising. It entailed raising or growing most of the food a family would consume personally and then selling enough other things to bring in a little cash in addition. Very basic was gardening, and therein lies one of my vivid memories of our return to the farm.

We came back in the early spring, so one of our first concerns was to plough up a sizeable plot for our garden. We hired someone with a tractor to do that. Then we planted things by hand. When it came time to cultivate the rows and rows of beans, corn, tomatoes, and other things, Mother bought a team of mules. The man who sold them to us assured us that they were gentle. "In fact," he declared, "this mule is so gentle you can plough without using a line on her. Just tell her 'Gee' or 'Haw,' and she'll do what you want."

What he didn't tell us was that our mule didn't like to have a line on her and would *not* plow with one. Uninformed as we were, we figured, if she will work *without* a line, she will surely do what we want *with* a line. So Gene, who had come from Cuba to help us get settled, outfitted her with full harness and hitched her up to a shovel cultivator we intended to use. He said, "Now, Glenn, you let me do this. I can handle the plow better. You stand over there."

That sounded awfully familiar, like our escapade with the manure, and so does the rest of this story. He clucked and whacked the mule gently on the rump with the line. She took off, not in the direction she was headed *between* the rows but cattywampus *across* the rows in the garden, plowing up everything we had planted. Gene kept yelling, "Whoa! Whoa!" and sinking the shovels deeper and deeper. By the time we got the mule stopped, our garden looked like somebody had dropped a bomb on it. From that time on, we used the mule that didn't mind being guided by lines!

The farm grew enough hay to supply our five our six cows and two mules, but we had to buy other feed until the following year when we were able to grow enough corn, wheat, and oats to feed all of our livestock. Cash came chiefly from the sale of cream, as it had earlier, and shipping a few hogs and calves. So long as John remained in the Coast Guard, we fared fairly well. I can assure you, though, that farmers then, as now, did not get much return for their labor, and I could see then that farming would not be my vocation.

You can imagine my boundless joy on 8 August 1945 when Walter Helms, John's younger brother, drove down the road past our house yelling, "The war is over! The war is over! Japan has surrendered." I knew it would happen soon when I heard about the dropping of the first atomic bomb on Hiroshima on August 6.

I'd like to say that the news about an atomic bomb left me grieved and heavy of heart, but that would not be true. American propaganda had done a job on me. It had convinced me that the "Japs" deserved whatever we did to them. The only Japanese I had met were those I'd sold a little scrap iron to in 1940, and I felt guilty about that. To me, all of them were "dirty, ugly, mean Japs." The important thing was that "our boys" would not have to fight any longer or be in danger of losing their lives. More specifically, John could come home.

John did come home soon, filled with hope and enthusiasm. He immediately set out to improve our housing with the addition to the old smoke house. John and I farmed our farm and his father's farm. The manual aspect of the work was killing, but we didn't mind. Things could only get better. We used two teams—one of mules and the other of horses—but we had primitive equipment: walking plows and cultivators and a horse-drawn mower, corn planter, binder, and rake—some of which belonged to John's dad. We put up hay the primitive way, mowing, raking, shocking, and loading it onto wagons and pitching it up into the barn. When the corn ripened, we cut it row by row, shocked it, and later shucked it by hand. We stored it in bins and then fed it to hogs or hauled it to the mill to be ground for cattle feed. We were a bit more mechanized than people of biblical times who did everything by hand, but not much.

We experimented with subsidiary businesses to increase our cash flow. One of our extras was beekeeping, which we undertook because it could bring in quite a lot of cash. John had purchased a badly deteriorated aviary with about fifteen or twenty hives of bees from his brother. By "deteriorated" I mean they hadn't been cared for in a long while. There were no "separators" to keep the queens from laying eggs in the upper trays where the workers should store honey, so the honey was unusable.

The bees were wild and mean. Beehives not re-queened will become wild. When we first moved the hives to a grove of trees on our farm, we could not walk within fifty yards of them without having bees dart out and sting us. They even attacked cows, horses, mules, or dogs that dared to get too close. To work with them, we had to wear heavy clothing tied down at the sleeves and legs and don veils and gloves. Once a single bee stings, the smell incites the whole bevy, and they attack in droves. As often as not, the bees could find a vulnerable place to attack, all precautions notwithstanding. After we had re-queened all of the hives with Italian queens, we could handle the bees without wearing the extra clothing or veils.

Once we put the hives we had purchased in order, we started looking for wild bee colonies that we could hive and re-queen. We had one or two successes in this, which encouraged us to venture forth again. On one occasion, though, we learned that hiving wild bees could be costly and painful. We discovered what looked like a strong colony of bees in a tree on the Helms property near Cave Spring School. I thought I had prepared myself adequately and, once we cut the tree down, waded right into the section of the tree where the wild bees buzzed angrily around. Somehow one of those bees found an open door under my veil and led a whole troop in. I ended up with more than a hundred stings all over my head and neck and spent a couple of weeks in bed recuperating. Had I not had some inoculation by earlier stings by bees, I may well have succumbed to that fierce attack. And that was the last bee tree we tried to hive. As you can well imagine, it took a number of years for me to regain a taste for honey!

Still, despite efforts like this, we didn't have enough cash income to support more than a subsistence standard of living. John took a job as a mechanic in a garage in Sullivan. He was paid only $35 for more than forty hours a week of work. Today mechanics make more than that per *hour*! When he asked for a raise after about a year, it was denied. He quit. He and I decided that, if we were to improve our situation at all, we had to buy a tractor, and John found a good used tractor for $600. We would have to borrow money, but it seemed like our only option. Mother, always conservative when it came to money, would not go along. That triggered their separation and, in a short time, their divorce.

Fracturing of families happened a lot as a consequence of World War II. Those who returned came with hope and enthusiasm dashed on the rock of reality when they tried to pursue their dreams. Like many another returning veteran, John Helms had to pursue his dream of a better life elsewhere than on a small farm in the Missouri Ozarks. He spent the rest of his career working in the steel mills of Pittsburgh.

I'll never forget the day he came to tell me he was leaving. I was fifteen. Over the brief couple of years after his return, we had developed a very close bond—probably not of father and son but of friends. When he came to say goodbye, I was sick in bed, recovering from fatigue and heat stroke or something. Two weeks before, I had been riding one of our horses to the pond to drink at the end of a long day spent plowing when I passed out and slid off onto the ground in a heap. I remember being conscious, but I couldn't move. In a little while Gene came looking for me. He saw me lying on the ground and, evidently thinking I was *pretending* to be unconscious, started nudging me with his right foot. I watched him as if I were not in my body but outside and above it. That's the only "out-of-body" experience I've ever had.

The next thing I knew, I was at home in bed and I stayed there for two weeks, unable to summon the energy to get going. The fracas between Mother and John, followed by John's departure, undoubtedly conditioned me for or added to my malaise, and people trained in psychology will undoubtedly see the connection. Never had I felt more disheartened than seeing my family broken apart again. Never had I felt more hurt than seeing the hopes of John Helms crushed. I pressed on with the work John and I had been doing, but the disappointment weighed heavily upon me. So when John said goodbye, I cried inconsolably. And inwardly I kept crying for months afterwards. Loneliness again.

The next two years, my junior and senior years of high school, I continued as best I could with the farming operation John and I had started. I rented the tillable land on his dad's homestead and farmed

Mother's land. I worked out a fifty/fifty arrangement for both Mr. Helms and Mother. Through the sale of hay, hogs, cattle, corn, wheat, oats, watermelons, and whatever else I could raise and occasional odd jobs for other farmers I had at least as much money as most of my classmates to meet school expenses. I could buy clothes, pay for extracurriculars, and keep the old Model A Ford running, the things which seemed most essential at the time.

My regimen was mostly work, but you must not think it was all work and no play. I've enjoyed work—all kinds of work. In my mind I've made a game of just about every kind of work I've engaged in, even the tedious sort. Fishing in Boone Creek or the Bourboise or Meramec Rivers or hunting on farms in the area varied my routine. Eventually, though, I gave up hunting because I couldn't stand to kill or maim wild animals. Often I simply enjoyed sitting on the creek bank listening to it gurgle its way over stones or gravel or walking through the woods. During school sessions, I participated in many of the sports and other activities.

There are lots of tales I could tell about these two years. There were many activities to distract me, and much hard work to demand my attention. What stands out most to my inward mind, however, was the awful blow of separation from someone I had come to love, honor, respect, admire. John Helms brought to my life another touch of grace, and yet it seemed as I reached out to grasp it and pull it toward me it was whisked away. None will know how deep was the pain I suffered over both his loss and mine because I cannot put it into words. Like my dad, John, too, returned only a couple of times. He didn't write either because he wasn't a literate person. He did leave provision, however, for Barbara Sue, a trust that for many years provided her some basic support.

Early after John left, I think, I was tempted to retreat from the world, to pull into myself, to build walls around me, and to have nothing to do with people. Never again should I let myself be so open and vulnerable by entering into such a deep friendship as we had developed. I would stop trying to help Mother, whose rigidity and inflexibility had caused so much pain. The more I cried out inwardly, the more it occurred to me that John Helms' friendship was a precious gift. Better to have received and nurtured it for a time, however brief, than not to have known it at all. Yes, deep friendships may cause pain. They will pain us when they end, as they do in death unless, and until, we rediscover them in the vast ocean of divine love. They will pain us when we are alive and well because human life will inevitably skew them, twist them, or distort them. Nevertheless, it is better to love and to risk the pain than not to have loved at all. At the same time I could hear Jesus' words echoing in my mind, "Call no man on earth 'Father.' You have a Father in heaven" (Matt 23:9). My attention was turning ever more toward God.

5

RUNSWELL AND A&P

Early in June 1949, exactly one week after I graduated from high school, I set out for St. Louis looking for a job in which I could earn enough money to go to college so that I could become a lawyer. I was full of hope. Once I got my training as an attorney, I reckoned I would have money and prestige. Never again would I have to endure the poverty I had lived in most of my first seventeen years, and I would be somebody.

But I had little besides a dream. I had five dollars in my pocket—all that remained of the money I had earned in two years of farming. Von Busch gave me a ride in the G. C. Busch & Son truck in which he was hauling cattle and hogs to market and dropped me off in South St. Louis two or three blocks from the home of Raymond Crow, Mother's older brother, his wife Rose, and their two children, Donald and Patricia. Aunt Rose, a generous soul who had grown up in the hardship of a Russian immigrant miner's family in southern Illinois, had invited me to live with them. I stayed with them a week. By that time one embarrassing incident had made it clear that, no matter how sincere their desires and intentions, they didn't have enough room in their three-room "shotgun" house to accommodate a fifth person. Donald, Pat, and I bunked in the living room at the front of the house. Uncle Ray and Aunt Rose slept in the bedroom in the middle of the house. An early riser like most farmers, on my third or fourth morning I awakened at daylight with a stomachache and urgent call of nature. The sliding door between the front room and the bedroom was partly ajar, so I slipped through and tiptoed as quietly as I could toward the only toilet located on the other side of my uncle and aunt's bed. I tried not to look their way, but I realized, to my profound embarrassment, that they were involved in early morning intimacies. Later that day, Aunt Rose said, "Auntie Pete (our name for my Aunt Fleta) called and said they wanted you to come and stay with them."

So I moved into the basement of the Marshes' home and barber shop in Affton, one of the ninety-eight small communities that arched around the city of St. Louis. The basement was not elegant, but it sufficed. Actually I found it rather nice compared to the one-time smokehouse I'd lived in for the previous five years. The Marshes had just built the house/shop a couple of years before. They hadn't had time or money to furbish the basement and, a year or two after I arrived, I helped Uncle Ossie paint the walls and tile the cement floor. I didn't have a separate bath or toilet, but having only to hop upstairs to those beat walking a half block to an outdoor privy and taking baths in a washing tub behind the stove on Saturday. Compared to the three small rooms in our revamped smokehouse, the basement under the entire building seemed gargantuan, and I needed only one small section for my room. And it was warm in the winter and cool in the summer. All things considered, it had just one irksome feature: it flooded when the sewers in Affton backed up. Fortunately that happened only once or twice in my five years there. Such things seem trifling and unworthy of mention alongside the generosity of Fleta and Ossie Marsh, "inasmuchers" who took me in and shared openhandedly their home and modest possessions and, more important, their love.

The job hunt—the top item on my agenda—started out in a discouraging way. Jobs were scarce in 1949, and I didn't have much more than intelligence and energy to offer. Few skills. No experience in urban employment. Heretofore, I'd always had people seek me out and offer me jobs. For the first time in my life I was the seeker rather than the sought. I scanned the newspapers and tramped the streets. By Friday some of my hopeful optimism was fading. It turned out to be providential that I stayed with the Crows that first week. Just by chance on my last day at their house, I stumbled onto a job at Runswell Binding Company located a block or two from their flat. Had I started in Affton, I would never have found the job. It paid only sixty cents an hour, a pitiful $24 a week, but it was a JOB and the pay not as meager as it would seem today. I was glad to have it. The fact that Aunt Fleta would take only $10 a week for room and board enabled me to survive until Runswell raised my wages.

Before school began in the fall, it was clear to me that I would not have enough money to start to college. B.S. Sexton, Superintendent of Public Schools in Sullivan, assured me on a visit that summer that, because of my College Boards and grades, every college in Missouri would grant me a scholarship with the possible exception of Washington University in St. Louis. Recruiters from Central and Westminster Colleges came to visit and offer assurances of financial aid and work grants. Central, a Methodist school, had a good reputation, and Westminster, an Episcopal school, was where Winston Churchill had made his famous "iron curtain" speech a short time before. But I had no clothes. I had purchased my only suit, a heavy woolen chalk stripe, by mail from Montgomery Ward for $13. For the rest I had a couple of jeans and two or three shirts, maybe one tie, underwear, and a cheap nylon jacket. My entire wardrobe fit snugly into an 18" by 24" suitcase. I was too proud, though, to admit to either recruiter that I was that desperate and that the school would have to provide not only tuition but living expenses or a job as well. Had I gotten more advice from someone who knew something about college, I could have gone ahead, but I didn't. I'm not sure I would have acted on such advice had anyone given it. I delayed a year. What was important was that my dream was still intact. Indeed, it intensified.

My modest employment helped keep the dream in focus. I began just doing whatever odd jobs Runswell needed me to do—putting cloth on rolls to cut into different types of binding, packaging, delivering, sweeping floors. I was not good at the first of those tasks. With practically no experience in working with machinery and only five feet tall when I finished high school, it took several weeks of winding the same rolls of cloth over and over before I succeeded in getting them to come out wrinkle free. The rolls required perfection, for, when cut for a one-inch binding, even the smallest wrinkle would spoil the whole spool. Because I was very good at figures, however, I soon graduated to the job of shipping clerk, much to my personal relief. Just one thing irked me: The owner of this family-run business, Mr. Donnelly, could never remember my name. He always got my attention with "Oh, whatizzis!" elided into a single word. Or sometimes "Oh, whatchamacallit!" It's humbling not to have a name.

Somewhere near the end of my year there, I had a frightening encounter with one of the other employees, Clemon Greene. Clemon was an African American hired to replace me as the gofer and to work under my direction. He didn't like that because he was several years older than I was and a very able person. We seemed to get along okay for several weeks, but one day I pointed out that he hadn't done correctly what I'd asked or directed him to do. He exploded.

I must tell you here that Clemon was big, well built, muscular, and a St. Louis Golden Gloves boxing champion. He grabbed me by the throat and raised a pair of foot-long shears used to cut cloth with his right hand above his head like he intended to stab me. I was terrified. I knew that I might soon draw my last breath. My heart beat 150 times a minute. The one thing that occurred to me came from several years of working with animals. "Look an animal which is mad straight in the eye. Don't flinch!" I'd always heard. I'm not sure how well I managed, but, saying nothing, I glared at Clemon for what seemed like an eternity though it was probably no more than thirty seconds. He let go and put the shears down. "Bud" Donnelly, the manager, came over and told Clemon, "If you ever do that again, you're out of here."

The scary incident caused some deep reflection about my way of dealing with other people, very much as my experience in freshman science class had. I made a point of winning Clemon over after that. I could see that I hadn't been very sensitive to how difficult it must have been for a twenty-five year old man to take orders from an eighteen-year-old kid, a hillbilly at that. We became very good friends.

By the middle of the year the Donnellys wanted very much for me to stay at Runswell. They kept upping my pay, and "Bud" did me a good turn which threatened to divert me from college plans. When he bought a new car, he sold me his 1941 Chevy coupe for $100. The engine didn't run smoothly and the body had rusted out in a couple of places. I had the valves ground and some work done on the body. Like many another teenager, I began to develop car mania and reasoned with myself, "All the other kids have cars. You need a car more than you need a college education." Car mania nearly put an end to my educational dream.

Not quite, though. From somewhere deep within me came a voice saying, "That car won't last very long. It's already old. It might make you popular with your peers for a little while. But it won't help you achieve your dream. Education alone will do that." Just before I started to school in the fall, I told the Donnellys that I was leaving. Not even the promise of much higher pay could deter me. I sold the car for $600. That gave me enough cash to buy clothes and pay the $225 tuition I would pay each semester of my first year at Washington University. I quit my job at Runswell and increased my hours at A&P to thirty-five.

Twenty-four dollars a week minus taxes and social security was not much money even in 1949. Ten went for room and board and three or four for transportation. I was very insistent on paying something for board because I didn't want to be indebted to anybody for anything, but ten dollars was all Aunt Fleta would take. Radical self-dependency was my mother's doing. Early on, she drilled into me that I was never to take anything free. "If you don't owe anybody anything," she would say, "then you will have your pride." Until I was twenty-five, I can only remember one instance in which I accepted someone's offer of a piece of candy. I would always say, "Oh, no, I've just had some." Or "I'm about the eat lunch, so I'd better not take any." The real reason, of course, was one I didn't say out loud, "My mother would skin me." In many ways that was a gift, and I've seen some people who could have benefited from my mother's counsel. As I've grown older, however, I have had to recognize that she left me with a problem—the problem of accepting grace, something I could not earn or merit or deserve.

Accustomed to just scraping through during the Great Depression and conditioned by the deprivations brought on by a world war, I didn't feel stressed by a bare subsistence income. Now and then, I supplemented my piddling salary by doing odd jobs on Saturday— mowing lawns, cleaning basements, and the like—for people in Clayton that my maternal grandmother knew. I had confidence my circumstances could go nowhere but up. In excellent health and with a dream of going to college, the desire of my heart was only to put together enough money to start to college by 1950. I arrived in St. Louis, however, outfitted with scarcely more clothes than I had on my back. After a few weeks at Runswell Binding Company I scraped together enough to buy a few of the most essential clothes, mostly for work but with a decent shirt and slacks to wear to First Baptist of Affton on Sunday. The Marshes, always generous, took me with them when they had outings, and Uncle Ossie, invariably fastest on the draw with his wallet, paid for meals or movies at drive-ins, then the rage. Apart from work and church and their generosity I had no social life.

To get to Runswell Binding, I had to take a St. Louis County bus to River Des Peres and then catch a city bus down Gravois, a major St. Louis east/west artery. Skimping on the cost of travel, however, I usually walked or jogged the two or three miles from Affton to the city line. On the other end, I had to walk only a couple of blocks to get from the bus stop on Gravois to my job.

Reading these words in this era of billionaires in which CEOs take home more than 400 times what the average worker earns, you may wonder if I didn't have frequent thoughts of pulling up stakes and going back to the farm. I did contemplate it sometimes, but not because I wasn't stashing away enough money for college. What troubled my sleep at night was how my mother and half-sister Sue were faring without me to help. Sue was only seven, eleven years younger than I. Mother didn't have the strength to do heavy farming, although she had years of experience in managing on less than a little. I must confess considerable feelings of guilt about forsaking them. On this matter, the one thing that kept me going was the expectation that I would soon begin to earn enough to share some of it with them. Fortunately, a lead mining company came along about this time to contract with my mother for the right to mine under her farm. Unfortunately, mining lead may have resulted in pollution of water and soil in that area and high incidence of cancer. Mother died of colon cancer in 1965.

However strong my misgivings, it would have taken a lot more deprivation than I had experienced up to this point to pull me back to the farm. As you can well imagine, however, after about two or three months on the meager pay I got from Runswell, I grabbed the opportunity to take a part-time job at the A&P supermarket a half block from where I lived the way a drowning man grabs at a life preserver. The prospect of adding twenty-five to thirty hours to my week's work was no deterrent. During the planting and harvest seasons on the farm, I had usually toiled from dawn to dark—and sometimes after dark. Adding twenty or twenty-five dollars to the small sum I earned as a shipping clerk made me feel like I had just turned off of a gravel road onto the famous Highway 66 that ran right through Sullivan.

I'm indebted to Uncle Ossie for getting me this job. I didn't even have to apply for it. Mr. James, the manager of the store, used to get his haircut at Marsh's Barber Shop. On one visit he mentioned that he needed baggers, checkers, and stock clerks on the night shift. I wasn't there, of course, to hear the conversation, but I knew Uncle Ossie well enough to reconstruct something pretty close to it. Knowing that my $24 a week wasn't putting me on easy street, he would say, "Fleta's nephew lives with us. He's looking for a part-time job to boost the one he has. He's a hard worker." When I went to the store, Mr. James signed me up and put me to work that evening. Thence began an eight-year association with The Great Atlantic and Pacific Tea Company.

You will probably think I am stretching my understanding of grace well beyond recognized theological definitions and explanations when I say this, but I would assert that A&P was grace to me. It was grace in the first instance simply as a second job when I needed such a job. Combined with what I earned at Runswell, my pay there enabled me, long accustomed to living frugally, to amass enough money to start school. It was grace, however, far beyond that, for it was as much a critical part of my formation as a person as my college education. Coming to Washington University as a nearly empty tank with the cap off ready to fill, I will sing praises to God until the day I die for the education that I received there—and not just education, but formation that equipped me well for the rest of my life. Nevertheless, let me say loudly and clearly that the education and formation I received there would not have turned me out as the person I have become had it not been for the education and formation I got from working at A&P. I say that well aware that the combination of work at A&P and demanding study at Washington U did not turn out as well for others. At least two of my fellow clerks at A&P enrolled at the same time I did, but they found it necessary to transfer to other schools after flunking out the first semester.

How did clerking in a supermarket grace me? First, it led me gently into a more cultured and wider world than I had known to this point. You would have offended me grossly had you pointed it out to me at the time, but I was a rube, a hillbilly, a hick from the sticks. At Washington U I kept my secret by distancing myself from more culturally advantaged fellow students and by being unable to take part in many campus events. By the time I started school in the fall of 1950, however, clerking at A&P had dabbed enough polish on me that I didn't have to fear blundering every time I met professors, administrators, or fellow collegians. I'm not sure it would be so today in an age when customers can check themselves out, but in the 1950s clerking in an A&P store was a highly interactive personal experience. From the start I knew many of the people who shopped at A&P—mainly members of First Baptist Church of Affton—but, thinking back, I am surprised at how quickly I developed first-name friendships with regular shoppers.

There's something very personal about helping people with their groceries. I had already discovered that in Louisville during World War II when I carried bags for them from the Kroger store. Now, as a more grown up person who saw the same people over and over, checking them out, bagging their purchases, helping locate items they needed, and carrying on conversations about anything and everything, took on a still more personal quality. Growing up in a highly conflicted family environment, I had not developed a "gift of gab" and didn't make a serious effort to strike up conversations with shoppers, but I found many customers initiating conversation with me, often about themselves but often, too, about my hopes and dreams. No deep and abiding friendships took shape in that way, but little by little there grew in me an almost instinctive appreciation and affection for all kinds of people, even people whose outlook and ideas differed radically from my own.

A second gift had to do with concentration. It is probably accurate to say that at the time I was, by nature, highly focused, and the demands first of two jobs, and then of a job and school, turned up the concentration a few more notches. Another way to speak about this, perhaps, is to recognize that my innate competitiveness underwent testing and strengthening. I was not content simply to earn the money the store paid me; I wanted to excel or, rather, be seen as the fastest and the best at everything I did. When I bagged groceries, I was at pains not only to follow the carefully prescribed A&P plan of using cans to make a floor for the bag, then stacking boxes and packages on top of them, and placing perishables or squashables on top, but also to do the job quickly and help customers to their cars with as great dispatch as possible. In the evening, or on Saturdays when I worked, people wanted to get in and out ASAP quickly.

When called on to become a checker after a month or so, I made it a point to catch up with the recognized fastest checker in the store—in this case Grady Alsup, who, before I left to go to seminary, became a department manager. In the fifties, checking required considerable skill. You didn't pass a bar code in front of a scanner to read the price and which department it came from, you had to read, and very often know, the price printed on the can or box and then key into the register both the price and whether it represented a sale for the grocery, meat, or produce department. Although I had watched checkers negotiate all of these things while I bagged, it took a few weeks for me to be able to enter both price and department without letting the register stop in the process, which was considered the acme of efficiency. Because my line moved faster than most others, many customers chose regularly to line up in it. In addition, checkers had to handle money accurately when stores took only cash and knew nothing of cash cards or other conveniences, but my math proficiency made that part easy for me. I must confess here, though, that I was a little jealous of a high school student with extraordinary musical skills mastering the register faster than I did! My one comfort here was that he wasn't as adept at other work because he talked incessantly.

My competitive urge probably emerged most clearly in the other major endeavor of the grocery business—stocking shelves. From the beginning I could see that the full-time employees in the grocery department judged their fellow clerks by how fast and well they could unload huge trailer trucks, send goods down a conveyor belt to the basement, stack them by rows, and later get merchandise out of the basement, up the conveyor belt, and onto the shelves. During that first year at A&P, although age eighteen, I had not yet reached my full height and was still growing. What I lacked in size and strength, however, I made up for in energy. The assistant manager evidently bragged about my work to some of the full timers, who worked mostly days, so when summer came, one of them named George Drabb decided to put me to the test. He and I were assigned to stack the groceries in the appropriate places as they came down the conveyor belt from the trailer at the back of the store. George located himself by the roller conveyor and threw boxes to me. I was to catch them and put them in the appropriate slot. He threw just as hard as he could. I think that he was a little surprised that I could catch the fifty-pound boxes of cans and was feeling a little frustrated. When a case of pickles—twelve jars of 32 ounces each—came rolling around the conveyor, he gleefully grabbed it and threw it with all of his might in my direction. One corner of it slipped out of my grasp and hit the floor, bursting one or two of the jars.

George then called up over the intercom, "Hey, Earl! Your 'boy' just dropped a case of pickles!"

I grinned kind of sheepishly and didn't say anything. I just cleaned up the debris and went on with the unloading. One thing my set-tos with Gene had taught me is that some things aren't worth fighting about. I knew Earl was not going to chew me out for dropping a case and would probably surmise why and how it had happened. Had I been a tattletale there, however, I would probably never have developed a friendship with George as I did. After that, he never threw a case that I couldn't catch. He started taking me to a gym where he did weight lifting, but that didn't work too well for me. I started out pressing 110 pounds. We went several times when I had a free evening, but after a week of that I could hardly lift my arms.

I think both George and I learned in this to distinguish between good and bad or healthy and unhealthy competition. Competition is unhealthy when you do something to crow about and to put another person down. It is unhealthy when it tramples on the other person's self-esteem. Competition is healthy when you do something to challenge and to raise another person up. It is healthy when it raises the other person's self-image, even when they come in second. It has taken a lot of lessons like this one for me to put in proper perspective my inner drive to excel, but in retrospect, I look upon it as God-given. Douglas Steere suggested that this might be a haunting sense of the unknown and unfinished that lures a creative person never to be entirely satisfied. He cited a painting of Jan Van Eyck in the corner of which the great artist inscribed, "*Als Ich kan.*" Douglas interpreted this to mean, "This is not what I had hoped for, but it is the best I can manage."[1] I hope I can be forgiven for some of my unhealthy competitiveness and remembered for some of the healthy.

My years at A&P were my coming-of-age years in many respects. As I began my part-time work there, I didn't look beyond the horizon to see that I would count on this organization to see me through college and seminary, but that is in fact what happened. I worked at Runswell Binding Company and at A&P right up to freshmen orientation at Washington U. By that time I was working 35 hours a week at A&P. That provided just enough money to keep me afloat as a student. At the end of my first year of college I returned briefly to Runswell, but Mr. James hinted that he might permit me to work full-time during the summer at A&P, so I quit Runswell after only one week. Here, though, I ran into a delicate situation. Permitting me to work full time at A&P qualified me for benefits that the national company frowned on unless I intended to remain as a full-time employee ever after. When I checked the schedule on Saturday night, I discovered that Mr. James had scheduled me part time and not full time for the following week.

It threw me into a dither. I had turned down an offer from Runswell to pay me virtually any amount I asked for with the expectation that I would work a full schedule at A&P, perhaps with overtime. I phoned Mr. James at home at 11 p.m.

I tried to speak calmly, but I'm sure I communicated not only surprise but also anger when I said, "Mr. James, I understood you were going to put me on full time next week, but you've scheduled me only part time."

At this point he replied, somewhat sharply, I thought, "I can't speak to you about it tonight, Glenn. I'll talk to you in the morning."

The next morning, he summoned me to the office on the intercom and glared at me as he said, "A man shouldn't be disturbed in his home with a call like that."

---

[1] Cited by E. Glenn Hinson, *Love at the Heart of Things: A Biography of Douglas V. Steere* (Wallingford PA: Pendle Hill, 1998) 323.

I reddened, swallowed and said, "Yes, sir. I'm sorry. I apologize for that." No more.

"I'm still working on this full-time matter. The company doesn't like to give benefits unless you're permanent." A few hours later, he posted a new schedule for me, a full-time one for the summer, benefits included.

I've often wondered whether Mr. James would have taken that step had I not phoned him. It was risky for an eighteen-year-old to be that direct; I thought I had made myself almost indispensable. I felt like I had done that at Runswell, too, and they had let me know it. What I learned out of this incident, however, is that no one is indispensable, however valuable, and we are wise to approach life with a sense of modesty and even thankfulness for what we possess. It is not immodest for me to recognize that I gave Mr. James his money's worth and then some, but it would have been pure illusion to imagine that he could not replace me. The person who would replace me might not perform in the same way or even with the same drive to excel that I had, but he or she would bring some gifts that might surpass some of mine. Humility is a hard yet critical lesson.

Working at A&P in Affton injected me with quite a few humbling moments, and with them some growth in grace. As the chief neighborhood market, A&P provided employment for many local high school students. One was Grady Alsup's sister, Sally. Sally was tall, well over six feet, which was not surprising because her mother was at least a head taller than her dad, who himself was at least six feet in height. She was gorgeous from the top of her head to her toes. And, with an engaging smile and an infectious laugh, she exuded charm. Friendly and outgoing, she flirted unselfconsciously and unapologetically. A week or two after she came, my great vulnerability born of loneliness came into play. I fell in love with Sally. However much I may have yearned for it to take place, a romance with Sally never blossomed. Sally didn't fall in love with me and broke the only date we agreed to in order to visit a friend in the hospital. She always remained a warm and affectionate friend, but I was too busy with school and work and too timid to try to press a relationship. Besides, I think she danced away from too close connection with someone four or five inches shorter than she was. Sometimes, I know, she pushed attractive friends toward me in order to divert any attention from herself.

Mothers who shopped at A&P seemed to take more interest in me than their daughters did. One mother who was also a member of Affton Baptist Church succeeded in arousing her pretty daughter's interest in me. We dated a couple of times. Trying to impress her, I joined the church basketball team. If there is anything I am not, it is an athlete, although I love basketball. Why I ever thought I would impress someone by playing basketball is beyond me, but that seems to be why I did this. I entreated Mr. James to let me off on a Friday night, always the busiest of the week, so that I could play for the church team. That almost cost me my job. With little practice I played poorly. With a schedule crammed with classes, study, and work I didn't call or meet with this young lady until her birthday a week or two later. However, I did buy her a present, a nice cashmere sweater I could scarcely afford, and, without phoning in advance, took it to her house on the evening of her birthday. To my great embarrassment, she had a visitor, her latest boyfriend! Face glowing and sweat dripping inside my clothes, I sat and talked for about ten or fifteen minutes and made excuses as to why I had to hurry away. When she recovered from her embarrassment, she returned the sweater by way of Sally Alsup and probably gave thanks that she didn't get more deeply involved with a nerd like me. I sent the sweater back and resolved to keep my focus on completing my schooling before further excursions in romance, even when promoted by moms!

People who shopped at A&P sometimes provided rewarding and reaffirming moments. Many shoppers tried to tip clerks when they carried out packages, but I adhered to company policy forbidding the acceptance of tips. Sometimes, though, people gave gifts or did nice things you couldn't resist. At Christmastime one year a dear little lady who came to the store several times a week tiptoed down the aisle where I was stocking cans in the shelves. I would hesitate to guess her age, but, to a twenty-year-old, she looked ancient—spine curved, face wrinkled, hair snowy white. She was not a member of the church I attended, but I'm sure she spent lots of time in her own church. In an almost furtive way she slipped me a small white sack, gave me a hug, and then tiptoed back the way she had come. When I opened the sack, I saw confirmed immediately that she didn't belong to a teetotaler religious group, for the bag reeked of rum. It was filled with rum balls. Because my father's alcoholism threw up warning flags about "demon rum," I didn't eat the cookies, but I have always cherished memories of the love that prompted that dear little saint to do something nice for me.

I worked almost five years at A&P in Affton. As a matter of fact, I worked the day Martha and I married, 1 September 1956. Martha had to phone to make sure that I would make the wedding that night. If you knew my financial situation at the time, you would understand why. That is a story I will return to later. Here it will suffice to point out that I sought out an A&P store in Louisville when I enrolled at Southern Baptist Theological Seminary in September 1954 and worked in it another three years, save during the summers when I returned to Affton. I have to confess that the A&P store in St. Matthews, Kentucky, did not give me the genuine joy in work that I found in the store in Affton. It operated in much the same way, and I did the same work, but it didn't pay the same because Mr. James had permitted me to get the benefits of a full-time employee. Mr. Whittinghill did not. Because seminary tuition and living costs were lower, I cut back my hours of employment to twenty-five. I wanted to devote as much of my time as I could to study.

Although the stores operated in much the same way, as I said, there were some noticeable differences. The pace was slower. Because I checked out much more rapidly than other checkers, on Friday nights I was put on a register using two clerks to unload carts and two to bag instead of one for each task. The operation required much stricter concentration on my part to do speedily because the unloaders often failed to stand the prices up where I could read them. To be quite honest, I preferred to stock shelves.

One benefit I did receive from A&P in St. Matthews was that a number of professors at Southern Seminary and their spouses shopped there. These included Jesse Burton Weatherspoon, snow-topped professor of homiletics nearing retirement at age seventy. Shortly before the end of my first year I carried groceries to Dr. and Mrs. Weatherspoon's car just after receiving an invitation to serve as interim pastor of my home church, First Baptist of Affton, for the summer. I proudly announced this to the dean of Baptist preachers with a confident assertion, "I guess I'm going to learn how to preach this summer, Dr. Weatherspoon." Chuckling a little, he responded, "Well, young man, I've been trying to do that for the last fifty years or so."

My three years at A&P in St. Matthews ran through a couple of rough places. One had to do with restocking shelves after closing at 9 p.m. Mr. Whittinghill liked to drink, and he often enticed some of the high school students who worked part time to join him. At least one of those young men had trouble controlling his appetite for booze. I felt more than a little concern and even anger about it, but I never came up with a way to prevent it except to refuse to take part in the drinking. Another involved an accident. Stocking shelves one afternoon, I was pulling one of the carts used to haul boxes and heavy bags down an aisle. As I approached the end of the aisle and started to turn the corner, an elegantly attired, plump, elderly woman stepped into the path of the cart. It crowded her into an exhibit at the end of the aisle and toppled her to the floor. I helped her up and apologized. At the time she didn't seem too upset, but months later she sued. I never learned the outcome of the case, but a company lawyer deposed me for the trial.

By my third year in seminary I was getting antsy to find employment that more closely fitted my vocation and training. I welcomed a call from the Volunteers of America to serve as a sort of preacher/chaplain at Jefferson County Jail. A few weeks later as I moved toward graduate studies, I was ecstatic when Dr. Hugh Peterson, Dean of Students, asked me if I would consider an invitation to serve as pastor of a small American Baptist congregation at Eminence, Indiana. More than you might suppose, A&P had done a lot of prepare me to minister to others.

6

A SENSE OF PRESENCE

Hardly anyone who applied for admission to Washington University could have been more naïve than I. Washington University, a school founded by the Eliots of Harvard—ancestors of poet T.S. Eliot—and widely thought of as the "Harvard of the Midwest," enrolled students with far better preparation than I had received. Many of my classmates had gone to elite private schools and ranked at the top of their classes. Yet it didn't occur to me that the university might turn me down. I went through the enrollment process and orientation on autopilot. The most memorable part of orientation was a reception given to us at the stately home of university chancellor, Arthur Holly Compton, a Nobel Laureate in Physics (1927) who had played a key role in the development of the atomic bomb. Not many years after that mind-bending event, Compton enthralled us with the story that, when he traveled by train or plane, he had to check his ticket to see who he was lest he betray his connection with the Manhattan Project. Chancellor Compton was himself unassuming and not pretentious in the least, but his very presence reminded me that I was traveling in circles I had never touched before.

Testimony again of my naiveté, it also didn't occur to me that I might not be able to do the work required while working nearly full time at A&P. Neither my elementary nor my high school education had stretched my abilities. I had never really had to study and yet always managed somehow. This is not to say that what I did was easy. Moving from high school to college level work is a big step. Going from Sullivan High to Washington University was a Paul Bunyanesque step. As I look backward from the vantage point of long years spent in academia, I wonder how I did what I did. It shocked me my first year that I made only one A while maintaining only a B average. I'd always made A's in everything I wanted to make A's in. Here I couldn't do that. Knowing what I know now about the educational system, I would have sought financial aid and dropped my outside working hours to a much lower level. But none in my family could advise me; they had never gone to college.

Professors at Washington required something I hadn't had to do very often at Sullivan High—they aimed to make students think. In the small classes they probed and provoked. They gave tests that sought much more than memorization and recall. One exam in social studies in particular is seared into my memory. The questions called for us to analyze certain critical social problems and propose solutions. I had done well on that kind of test in high school and had learned how to "shoot the bull." When I got the test back, not only had I not done well but I got the first D I'd ever received. With more than a little anger and yet much trepidation I approached the professor and demanded an explanation for such a grade. He quickly pointed out that I had argued in a circle. That ended any presumption that I could just bluff my way through.

Early in each semester of the first two years, I usually made A's in most classes, but by the end, as the amount of information piled up, I felt like one of the leading runners in a race watching helplessly as others took the lead. The mix of eighteen hours of classes and thirty-five hours of A&P took its toll. By the end of my second year, I watched my grades go downhill. Zoology proved especially frustrating, for it required not only attendance at lectures but labs. With my work schedule I gradually dropped out of labs and, perhaps with a measure of grace on the part of instructors, earned a D in the course, the only one I've ever received. Worn down by the massive load I toiled under, I began to wonder if I should continue in college at all. Was I college material? Uncle Ossie even suggested at one point that I become a barber. I contemplated joining the Air Force and getting my military service out of the way. More by guts than inspiration, unwilling to admit I couldn't do it, I dragged myself through to the end. Fortunately, I had the summer, without school, to think my life through.

My sophomore year had thrown me into a double crisis—a crisis of faith and a crisis of vocation. They were connected.

You can see easily, I think, from where the vocational crisis sprang. I had gone to Washington University intending to be a lawyer. I chose a pre-law track that would have taken me into the law school in my fourth year. The legal profession is a very honorable and respectable one, but I had, with considerable naiveté, chosen that vocation for the wrong reasons—prestige and money. As much as anything, listening to Perry Mason on radio out in the Ozarks generated wondrous images of fame and fortune just waiting to shower a young man of keen mind and delicate wit. Had I sat in court and observed the proceedings, that balloon would have burst. As it was, it took a few classes at an excellent university to do that. At Washington U, professor after professor seemed to be asking, "What are you going to do with your life and education besides serve yourself?" Little by little, that question started registering in an urgent way. And I could see that I did not have an intense interest in most courses preparing me for law school.

At the same time my naïve and unreflective faith was creating another crisis. Professors in virtually every course challenged, "How can you prove that? How can you demonstrate what you believe?" The pastor of the church I attended, John F. Reagan, was too conservative to understand my struggle. Like other fundamentalists, he wanted me to compartmentalize—the religious life lived in one sphere, the life of everyday in another. His model was R.G. Lee, pastor of Bellevue Baptist Church in Memphis, where his son Nelson had served as an associate, but John Reagan lacked the oratorical skills of Lee and did more yelling than explaining. When I would take a question to him, he would say, "You believe that you'll go straight to hell!" Predictably, I didn't take many questions to him. One thing became very clear to me, namely, I had to effect some kind of integration in my thinking; I would either find a way to relate faith to empirical knowledge or it would have to go out the window.

Knowing that I've spent most of my life serving the Church, you may be asking why, up to this point, I've scarcely mentioned faith, viz. church, experience. The reason for that is because church didn't play a significant role in my life until this period when I experienced simultaneously and conjunctively a crisis both of faith and of vocation. Oh, I had had a dab of church connection from my early years, but it wasn't deep and, more to the point, it wasn't consistent or really healthy.

As I've related before, my earliest churchgoing that I remember was to the Spiritualist Church on Potomac Street in St. Louis where we lived when I was three or four. I memorized the Twenty-third Psalm, which the congregation often recited. There were times in those difficult days when I clung to the image of the shepherd leading me beside still waters. After we moved to Shenandoah, Mother occasionally shuffled Gene and me across the street to a Missouri Synod Lutheran Church. There, the teacher handed out pictures to color and told us Bible stories about Joseph, Moses, David and Goliath, Jesus, Peter, Paul, and other heroes of faith. I loved the stories because they roused my imagination and gave me some hope that God might do something to get Mother and Dad and Gene and me to like one another.

When we moved to the farm just before I turned six, Dad dragged us down to Cave Spring Landmark Missionary Baptist Church to take part in their fall revival. What I remember most about that was an out-of-tune piano, off-key singing, and a preacher yelling. Mercifully, I usually went to sleep during the sermons. I did find one hymn very touching, the one about "the little brown church in the valley by the wildwood." It brought, and still brings, tears to my eyes. We attended now and then at other times, though not regularly. Mother sometimes played the piano when we did go. Our first Christmas in the country one of our neighbors, Louella Taylor, enlisted me to recite a poem at the Christmas festivities at Cave Spring. I had the poem down pat, but when it came my turn to recite it before a full house, I got stage fright and refused to say it.

At home, meanwhile, we argued a lot about interpreting uninterpretable passages and took part in séances at the Eynon's. After hearing dispensationalist sermons at Cave Spring, Mother loved to speculate about the contemporary application of the symbols of Mark 13, 2 Thessalonians, or the Revelation of John and calculate when and how Jesus would return to set up the millennial kingdom. She spent amazingly little time looking at passages that were easier to understand. However, I received a New Testament that first Christmas, and all of the arguing inspired me to read it through.

When we moved to Spring Bluff, I went sometimes to a Sunday school at the Baptist Church there; the church did not have a worship service. The one thing I remember from that is pronouncing the name Nebuchadnezzar for the teacher, who couldn't seem to figure it out. I even took part in a camp meeting for youth. But the "testimonies" made me very uncomfortable, and I never went to another. Others recounted religious experiences very foreign to mine, and I thought it best not to tell them about séances.

My first more traditional and solid church involvement occurred the summer I worked for the Lowrys in Cuba, Missouri. Like the Marshes, the Lowrys participated actively in the Baptist church. Anytime the doors were open, they went, and they took me with them. The minister had limited theological training, but he preached good expository sermons which caused me to pay attention, maybe at first because he had a pretty daughter just a year or two older than I, and then because he was speaking to my situation. Early in August, just after my twelfth birthday, Cuba Baptist held its customary fall revival in which the pastor preached.

I can't say what prompted my decision to respond to the invitation. I knew it would please the Lowrys and Aunt Fleta and Uncle Ossie, but it was not my nature to do something because it might please others. I had no profound emotional experience. As best I can remember, I yielded to the logic of "the plan of salvation" which the pastor repeated over and over. "All have sinned and fallen short of the glory of God.... All, therefore, need a Savior.... 'All' includes *you*.... *Jesus* is such a Savior.... He died for our sins and wants to be *your* Savior." I resolved to follow Jesus and to be faithful in my discipleship. I was baptized in Brush Creek just before I returned to Louisville. Being baptized in a creek very much like I imagined Jesus was baptized was the truly memorable part of my "conversion" experience. I returned to Louisville determined to hold fast to my commitment.

Holding fast is difficult in a family environment supportive of faith. It's virtually impossible in one that isn't—and mine was not. When I returned to Louisville, I attended Southside Baptist Church week by week for the rest of our stay and even tried to tithe my income. That was an accomplishment because none of the rest of my family went. When we returned to Sullivan, however, I could not muster the same enthusiasm for Cave Spring Landmark Missionary Baptist Church and never joined, even though it stood cheek by jowl with our house. Much as I admired some of the "ordinary saints" of the church like Tom Helms and Lester Thurman, it represented a narrow fundamentalist Baptist high churchism to which I could not subscribe. According to Landmark theology, the local church is the only expression of church, of the Kingdom of God on earth. Anyone who moves from one local church to another must receive baptism into that congregation. Only members of that local congregation may partake of the Lord's Supper. Cave Spring politely dismissed all non-members when they had communion. Likewise, they would not countenance having anyone but a person of like faith and order, that is, a Baptist, preach in their pulpit. They would have seriously questioned whether any but their own were "saved." Occasionally I went to another Baptist church, the most remarkable being a snake-handling one, but most were too far away to walk, and I could not drive. My attendance at church dried up.

What resuscitated my church going was living with the Marshes when I moved to St. Louis in 1949. They didn't talk much about faith;

they just lived it. When the church held services, they went. When someone needed financial help, they gave. When the church had work to do, they worked. And I found their example compelling. My heavy work and school schedule made me tired and ready to excuse myself on Sunday mornings, but the fact that Aunt Fleta and Uncle Ossie went when they felt tired and wanted to do other things snatched away my excuses.

Communities of faith have a remarkable capacity for promoting spiritual growth. Some other people at First Baptist Church of Affton drew me further into its life. Nina Stockberger, Director of the Young People's Department in Sunday School, invited me to give "talks" and, in my junior and senior years, to teach the college class. The fact that I was invited to do that probably says more about the theological impoverishment of the church than about my qualifications. The church had five or six candidates for ministry among its youth, but none had gone to seminary or even gotten enough theological training in college to do an effective job. The other college students seemed to prefer me to other adults. Without wishing to sound immodest, I think they may have sensed in me some natural gifts for teaching. And I tried very hard to help us all relate our faith to a modern scientific picture of the universe such as I was taught at Washington University. I guess one would say that I took a "plain sense" approach. Faith, as I conceived it, needed to speak to people where they lived; otherwise, it was irrelevant.

Much to my surprise, because ministry was the farthest thing from my mind then and the church had all those other candidates, the youth elected me to preach the sermon on the church's first Youth Sunday. I preached about *agape*-love, the only idea I held strongly enough that I could make a convincing case for others. I knew that I couldn't preach what I didn't believe myself.

Helping others my age to discover a relevant faith may have heightened the urgency of answering my own questions about faith: "How do you know? How do you prove what you believe?" By the beginning of my third year I lay awake many hours at night with those questions and others like them drumming through my head. One night, after a long period of pondering, I dropped off into a fitful slumber. I remember vividly that I awakened and sat bolt upright in my bed in the pitch black of my basement room. My alarm clock read 2 a.m. I felt a powerful sense of Presence,[1] and John 8:32 was burning on my mind. "You shall know the truth, and the truth shall make you free." All of a sudden it rolled over me like a tide. "If God is truth … if Christ is truth, then nothing you discover by any other legitimate means of inquiry will negate that. The truth that matters is personal, and only *you* can decide about that. Only *you* can decide whether you will live your life from the vantage point of a relationship with God."

I *was* free. I was free, indeed! I've never had to look backwards from that decision. As Harvard University psychologist and philosopher William James pointed out long ago, such experiences have convincing authority for those who have them, though they may not convince anyone else.[2] In my case you would have a hard time convincing me that there is no God. God is as real as I am myself. Only later did I find a way to phrase what I had discovered. It's what Blaise Pascal, the brilliant seventeenth-century mathematician and philosopher, discovered: We have to wager. Better to wager that God is. If I wager that God isn't and it turns out that God is, then I've lost everything. If I wager that God is and it turns out that God isn't, I've lost nothing. But if I wager that God is and it turns out that God is, then I've gained everything. What is to tilt us in that direction?[3] He echoed Augustine's prayer, "You have made us for yourself, and our heart is restless until it rests in you."[4] So Pascal, "The heart has its reasons of which reason knows nothing; we feel it in many things!"[5] And Søren Kierkegaard, the brilliant Dane, framed the question in a compelling way: "What is a man [or woman] without Thee! What is all that he [or she] knows, vast accumulation though it be, but a

---

[1] Bernard McGinn has entitled his multi-volume *magnum opus The Presence of God: A History of Western Christian Mysticism*. In the initial volume, *The Foundations of Mysticism: Origins to the Fifth Century* (New York: Crossroad, 1997) xvi, he has cited Teresa of Avila in support of a more comprehensive definition of mysticism as "an attempt to express a direct consciousness of the presence of God." In retrospect I find it helpful to note how this falls in line with the way I have always construed this pivotal moment in my own story.

[2] William James, *The Varieties of Religious Experience: A Study of Human Nature* (New York: Collier, 1961) 73, said: Such experiences "are as convincing to those who have them as any direct sensible experiences can be, and they are, as a rule, much more convincing than results established by mere logic ever are."

[3] Blaise Pascal, *Pensées*, ed. Louis Lafuma, trans. John Warrington (London: J.M. Dent & Sons; New York: E.P. Dutton & Co., 1960) note 343, 93–94.

[4] Augustine, *The Confessions of St. Augustine*, trans. John K. Ryan (Garden City NY: Doubleday, 1960) book 1.1, 43.

[5] Blaise Pascal, *Pensées*, ed. Louis Lafuma, trans. John Warrington, note 224, 59.

chipped fragment, if he [or she] does not know Thee! What is all his [or her] striving, could it even encompass a world, but a half-finished work if he [or she] does not know Thee: Thee the One, who art one thing and who art all!"[6]

Not long after this, First Baptist Church of Affton held a revival. A young South African named Alastair Walker conducted it. During the revival, he showed a film on missions. All of a sudden, it occurred to me, "There *is* something I can do with my life besides serve myself. I can serve others." After some deliberation before the week was over I went forward during the invitation to share publicly what was going on with reference to vocation. The vocation of a lawyer is a very worthy vocation; but it is not mine. I, of course, didn't have a very clear idea what *my* vocation was. I knew only that I had to find it if my life was to have any real meaning. As best I could put it into words at that point, I wanted to do what God wanted me to do. I would follow Christ in serving other people. Two options seemed likely: to be a pastor or to be a missionary. My mind and heart were wide open. Interestingly, Alastair Walker joined me as a student at Southern Seminary a couple of years later. Both of us received the Bachelor of Divinity in 1957. His younger brother, Ian, came to the seminary as my student a few years hence!

It would be impossible to describe accurately the impact these two momentous events had on my life and work as a student. Up to this point, I was like an out-of-tune car engine in which the cylinders would not fire properly. I kept my foot on the accelerator, but the car didn't have the power it needed to climb the steep hill it had to ascend. Now, suddenly, the engine started running in tune. Although carrying the same load, it now made it up the steepest grades with power to spare.

My vocational decision required me to shift from the pre-law track to a major. I chose political science, not because I had such intense interest or had done so well in that area but because I already had the most credits in it. My heart, however, turned in a different direction—toward religion and toward classics.

Even before I resolved my problems of faith and vocation, I had enrolled as an auditor in a course on World Religions and as a student in another on the Philosophy of Religion taught by Huston Smith. I could not have made a wiser decision. Huston Smith showed me that there

---

[6] Soren Kierkegaard, *Purity of Heart Is to Will One Thing*, ed. E. Glenn Hinson, trans. Douglas V. Steere, *The Doubleday Devotional Classics* (Garden City NY: Doubleday, 1978) 3:18.

was an alternative to the narrow and oppressive options I had known up to that time. The son of Methodist missionary parents, he grew up in China, where he developed a deep appreciation for the religions of the East.[7] A mystic by temperament, he displayed in his course on world religions, as in his classic *Religions of Mankind*—which we read in manuscript in Washington University's library—an openness to direct experience of ultimate reality. He seemed to know whereof he spoke. He didn't tell us outright which philosophy he favored as a philosopher, but he seemed to lean toward the process model of A.N. Whitehead and his teachers at Chicago—Charles Hartshorne and Henry Nelson Wieman—because process philosophy served nicely as a companion to mystical experience. Wieman, in fact, was Smith's father-in-law.

I must be candid to admit that I was poorly equipped to get the most out of Huston Smith's classes. Before my 2 a.m. experience of liberation, I was clinging to the theological systems with which I was familiar like a shipwrecked sailor clings to whatever flotsam bobs around in the water. The most liberal preaching I was hearing at that time was that of Billy Graham in his 1951 St. Louis crusade. When it came time to take the final exam in the Philosophy of Religion, therefore, I cast my lot with the realism of Thomas Aquinas rather than what today makes far more sense to me, namely, process philosophy. Much in Aquinas suited my personal effort to integrate what I was learning empirically, because Aquinas himself sought to effect a new synthesis between Christian Platonism and Aristotle and has proven incredibly resilient in times of transition, but I had no exposure to modern, Catholic reinterpretations, such as those of Karl Rahner, to guide me. Teilhard de Chardin's evolutionary model, for which I have had much affinity, of course, was as yet unpublished and unknown. That did not happen until after his death in 1955. One quotation from Wieman, however, fixed itself firmly in my mind and has served since that time as a kind of axiom: "We ought to live each moment as if all Eternity converged upon it." That was an "Aha!" for me. "Yes," I thought. "All Eternity is converging upon this moment, and I must make the moment my sacrament. Maybe we can't turn our wicks up that high, for they will burn out. But we must do our utmost with who we are and what we have."

---

[7] See Huston Smith, *Why Religion Matters: The Fate of the Human Spirit in an Age of Disbelief* (HarperSanFrancisco, 2001) 74, 250, where he recounts part of his own story.

Like many another teacher, though, Smith conveyed much more in his person than I could grasp of his thought. For me *the* issue was *faith*. Could I believe in a personal reality that guides this universe toward some ultimately meaningful end? Or are things just moving at random, bumped around like billiard balls? The Korean War made this matter of faith all the more urgent. Although I got a deferral by joining the Reserve Officers Training Corps, I fully expected to go. It was not merely a charade then, when I kept asking, "Is there anything worth losing my life for in some foreign land? To what should I commit my life? What could I believe? Could I believe at all?"

What I was hearing in church did not speak to my elemental questions at all. Every sermon touted the substitutionary atonement. "Jesus died for your sins." In every invitation concluding each service the pastor quoted the same hymn: "There is a fountain filled with blood, drawn from Immanuel's veins. And sinners plunged beneath that flood lose all their guilty stains." I could not comprehend how the small amount of blood Jesus would have shed could have filled a "fountain," or how it could have washed away the sins of all humanity henceforth. There was a non sequitur about this imagery. Billy Graham's crusade didn't help much either. "Jesus is coming. He's coming back to this earth just like he left it. Are you ready? You may die tonight. Are you ready?" I could not see how I could interpret scriptures literally like Billy did when the universe I pictured on the basis of modern physics didn't look anything like the one the earliest Christians envisioned. I found a little help in Intervarsity Christian Fellowship led by one of the professors, but with my work and school schedule, I simply did not have time to attend additional meetings.

Huston Smith spoke to my dilemma personally. I can't tell you exactly why I thought so, but he communicated a deep confidence that there is something or someone at the heart of things with which we mortals can commune, a divine Mystery beyond our comprehension but nevertheless real to which the great religions bear witness. People of all faiths—not just Christians—know about the Mystery at the heart of the universe. We, too, can experience it through meditation and contemplation. When Smith lectured, he looked at us; yet, I think, with one cocked eye looking off into the distance, he seemed at the same time to be attuned to a Transcendent Personal. When I spoke to him personally, he was present and attuned to me in a way that said, "You matter. Your search matters." He inspired me to spend what little leisure time I had poring over scriptures of the world's religions—Islam's *Koran*, the *Bhagavad-Gita* of Hinduism, the *Lao Tzu* of Taoism.

Religion was not a major emphasis at Washington University in those years. There were, though, devout professors and students, especially Jewish students. And the university invited lecturers who awakened me to profound religious truths that undergirded my thinking and experience. One of those who spoke at convocation was Howard Thurman, Dean of the Chapel at Boston University. His was a mysticism shaped in the tradition of the great African-American spirituals, and he whetted my appetite to know God as intimately as he seemed to know God. The commencement address given when I graduated was by Jacob Malik, Lebanese Ambassador to the United Nations and a devout Orthodox Christian. His address helped me to see that faith could shape even political perspectives at the international level, just as we learned later through Dag Hammarskjold's *Markings*. In 1968, I was fortunate to meet Malik at the world assembly of the World Council of Churches at Uppsala, Sweden, and to let him know how his message that day touched my life.

You should not assume from these things, however, that I had become a spiritual giant. I was no more than a newborn. What was happening actually is that I was breaking out of a cave, like the one Plato spoke about,[8] which had imprisoned me and kept me from the joy of discovering the truth which sets us free. I've learned from Teilhard de Chardin, the great Jesuit palaeontologist and philosopher, to think of this as the Universal Christ, who is everywhere, in every culture and, yes, in every religion.[9] The resolution of the two crises injected into my life a new level of energy that affected everything I was doing. No longer was I just sloughing through muck and mire to get to a destination unknown.

---

[8] Plato, *The Republic*, Book 7, "Allegory of the Cave" in *Plato to E.B. White: A Book of Readings*, ed. H.C. Combs, J.J. Leonard, and R.M. Schmitz (St. Louis MO: Eden Publishing, 1949) 1–4.

[9] Pierre Teilhard de Chardin, *The Phenomenon of Man* (London: Collins, 1959), called the process of evolution "Christogenesis" (297) and asserted: "Christ, the principle of universal vitality because sprung up as man among men, put himself in the position (maintained ever since) to subdue under himself, to purify, to direct and superanimate the general ascent of consciousness into which he inserted himself. By a perennial act of communion and sublimation, he aggregates to himself the total psychism of the earth." (294) In *The Divine Milieu* (New York: Harper & Row, 1960), he proceeds to deduce from Christ's universal presence that "The Christian knows that his function is to divinise the world in Jesus Christ" (72).

Now I knew where I was headed and promptly shifted toward equipping myself to get there.

Washington University did not have courses in theology, Church history, and other subjects that might equip me for ministry. I had to search the catalogue to find classes outside of my major that might prepare me for such training in seminary. The area that seemed to come closest was classics. Greek and Roman history had fascinated me the first time I had been exposed to it as a sophomore in high school. That is why I opted for Latin as my required language, although it too fitted pre-law studies. Many found Latin very hard. Of the introductory class of thirty students in which I enrolled, only five of us remained at the end of the first semester. The four semesters of Latin that I took served as an excellent foundation for theological study. With the radical turn in my vocation I decided to take classical Greek. I had done well in Latin, but in Greek I discovered that I had an unusual gift for languages and, after graduation from Washington University, did extensive reading in Plato and other writers in a master's. program. Although the young professor, a recent graduate of Columbia University, urged me to stay on and do graduate studies in classics, I felt a certain urgency to get on with my vocation. My study, however, enabled me to sight-read the Greek New Testament when I entered seminary.

Although it did not give me the best foundation for theological studies, Washington University had equipped me for ministry far better than it would have had it supplied a whole theological curriculum. *It opened my mind. It taught me how to think.* Two incredible gifts! A tremendous amount of information is stored somewhere in my brain, a lot of it gathered during my college years. Many friends and students will know that I have a retentive memory. What I have retained in my storehouse of knowledge, however, is very small compared to what I have let slip away. Yet there is no price that can be put on a love of learning fueled by a desire for God and an ability to absorb and do something with what one learns. I have done my level best throughout my teaching career to pass these gifts on to others.

Even though my record at Washington University was far from impressive considered by itself—I ended with a 2.19 GPA on a 3.0 scale (B+), which would translate into about 3.3 on a 4.0 scale—when it is evaluated in terms of my early background and circumstances, and looked at in light of the rest of the load I carried, it looks better. I spent my first two years catching up culturally with students who had much better educational and cultural preparation. That was in itself a steep hill to climb. The climb was made steeper by the fact that I had taken the wrong road vocationally. Once I caught up and clarified my vocation, I found myself traveling on more level ground, making almost straight A's.

My experience has sensitized and tenderized me to students whose educational pilgrimage may have been conditioned by broken families, poverty, culturally deprived communities or regions, and other factors. They really do make a difference. Americans only now seem to be catching on to the impact that these things have made and slowly to make allowances. How many, I've often wondered, have fallen by the wayside because what they were doing was measured by some absolute standard without any touch of grace? In my case pride kept me from crying out for help, but I could have used some grace, and I've made a genuine effort to extend grace to others.

7

THE SOUTHERN BAPTIST
THEOLOGICAL SEMINARY

Conservative ministers in St. Louis, Missouri, who were friends of my pastor John Reagan, applied some pressure for me to get my theological training at Southwestern Baptist Theological Seminary in Fort Worth, Texas. Several factors, however, prompted me to go to the Southern Baptist Theological Seminary in Louisville, Kentucky. One was that I had lived and attended school in Louisville for about a year and felt more comfortable heading east rather than southwest. The only time I had spent in the Lone Star State was during summer ROTC training at Fort Bliss in 1953, and I did not relish more of the blistering heat I associated with Texas. More important still, I knew that I did not want to receive the kind of theological training John F. Reagan got at the precursor to Southwestern founded by B.H. Carroll. At Washington University I had begun to see how my faith could relate to the picture of the universe that modern scientific inquiry painted for me. From what I had heard about both the Texas and the Kentucky religious environments I concluded that my faith stood a better chance of growing in Louisville than it did in Fort Worth. As I was in process of thinking my decision through, moreover, Southern Seminary received a hefty boost from Washington University administrators. When they polled the student body as to whether the university should admit African Americans in 1953, they cited as their main argument the fact that the Southern Baptist Theological Seminary in Louisville, Kentucky, had integrated. I didn't learn it at that time, but Southern had granted Garland Offutt, an African-American minister, a PhD in 1946. Professors, moreover, had taught black students in their offices as early as 1900, although the Kentucky Day Laws prohibited blacks from joining whites in classrooms until 1951. Curiously, women could not take classes for a degree from the seminary until 1963.

I must confess that I didn't know much about seminaries. I frequently passed Eden Seminary, where Reinhold and H. Richard Niebuhr had gotten their basic theological training, on my way to Affton from Washington U, and thought it resembled some of the monasteries or convents that dotted the St. Louis landscape. It never occurred to me to ask where Southern Seminary stood among American theological institutions, but I had heard Duke McCall, the president of Southern, preach and liked the dignity he brought to the task. Had I known its academic reputation, I might have submitted my application with trepidation, but I don't think it occurred to me that Southern might turn me down. A couple of weeks after I applied I received a letter of acceptance from Dean Hugh Peterson. In September, I loaded my meager possessions into my 1941 Plymouth coupe and headed for Louisville with keen anticipation.

Given my limited resources, I chose to share a room in Mullins Hall, the men's dormitory. My roommate turned out to be Allen Webb from Philadelphia, Mississippi, a city that later had its reputation besmirched by murder of civil rights workers. Allen, a recent Army veteran, was going to school on the GI bill and had much more time to take part in campus activities than I did, but he and I hit it off well despite coming from different parts of the country. I did notice, however, that he and a lot of other students from the Deep South used racist language and expressed racist ideas without being conscience of doing so. That sometimes made we wince a little because we had several black students residing in Mullins and taking in classes with us, too.

One of the African Americans who went out of his way to cultivate my friendship was George Thompson, a native of Richmond, Virginia. George was short, perhaps five feet four with a string-bean build, and wouldn't have tipped the scale past a hundred pounds. When he walked down the central hallways either in Mullins or in Norton, the classroom and administration building, he sidled along the wall like he was trying to stay in the shadows. But he was bright. When his father, a prominent Baptist minister, came to Louisville to speak at Salem Baptist Church, George invited me to go with him. It was my first venture into a black church; no African Americans lived in the Missouri Ozarks. We arrived about 11 a.m. just as the service started. To my embarrassment, I was asked to join other ministers on the platform, one pink face glowing in the midst of many brown ones! George's father began preaching about noon. At first he spoke in a sort of subdued prose style, but that gradually evolved into song, sometimes joined by the whole congregation. When he finished his rousing call to freedom and hope, another minister took up where he left off. At 2 p.m. I excused myself and went back to the seminary to do my homework. George also took me with him to eat at his favorite restaurant in the west end of the city and to speak at the Lincoln Institute, a private African-American academy located just outside of Louisville at Simpsonville. This small bit of exposure sandpapered my sensitivities to the great racial disparities that existed in Louisville in 1954, the year the US Supreme Court handed down its landmark decision negating "separate but equal" in *Brown vs. Board of Education.*

Southern Seminary widened immensely the world I knew up to that time. Although the students came predominately from the Southern states, Southern Seminary attracted dozens of international student, who had forged ties to Southern Baptists through the convention's mission programs. Emanuel Dahunsi, a Nigerian branded on both cheeks with tribal markings, graded my papers in New Testament introduction. Emanuel had studied mathematics with Albert Einstein. Returning to Nigeria after completing a PhD in New Testament, he served for many years as Executive Secretary of the Nigerian Baptist Convention. Hiroshi Kanamaki, a former Japanese pilot already sealed into his plane for a kamikaze mission when the announcement came that the war was over, lived just down the hall in Mullins and sat beside me in several classes. Timothy Cho, a Korean, danced down the hall every morning, practicing exercises assigned by professors of speech. After working in Korea several years after graduating, Cho returned to pursue a PhD degree in Church history, in part under my supervision.

I'm not sure, as I look in my rearview mirror, how well Southern Seminary equipped me for the work of ministry or mission. The course of study for the basic theological degree at that time, Bachelor of Divinity, consisted chiefly of two components—the old "body of divinity" and an array of more recently developed studies in the practice of ministry. Contrary to inerrantist critics of Southern Seminary, the most notable feature of my training was its saturation with scriptures, especially of the New Testament. Not only did biblical studies claim by far the largest slice of the curriculum, but biblical perspectives found their way into virtually every other course—theology, ethics, preaching, missions, pastoral care, religious education, church administration, church music. Old and New Testament, biblical archaeology, Church history, Baptist history, theology, Christian ethics, philosophy of religion, preaching, and missions formed the core of the curriculum. By the time I came to seminary in 1954, however, a small number of courses in the nuts and bolts of ministry ringed the core: pastoral care, Christian education, church administration, church music, and speech. The missing link, and my reason for questioning how well my study prepared me as a minister, was spiritual formation. Professors or students opened classes with prayer. Occasionally a few professors slipped little sermonettes into their lectures or told stories encouraging us to steadfastness in prayer, but no one taught us how to pray the scriptures or how a life of prayer intersected with the many tasks of ministers.

Whatever concern may have existed for spiritual development, it found expression in chapel worship four days a week. I attended chapel faithfully, not out of concern to parade my piety but out of need. Like many other students, I found a lot of the sermons less than inspiring, but I went anyway with the expectation that Christ would be present in our midst as we prayed, sang, and listened. The South's largest organ and highly trained voices sometimes lifted us into the stratosphere. Often, yes very often, preachers—both home and guest—entertained and instructed and inspired and challenged us to strive to fulfill the purpose of the church and its ministry—the increase among humankind of love of God and of neighbor. My very first semester D.E. King, pastor of Zion Baptist Church in Louisville, preached, and I can still remember his text, "And Moses died in Moab" (Deut 34:5). Face black as night, Dr. King began almost in a whisper. I had to strain to hear him. Step by step, he increased his volume and the bite of his message—the cost of neglecting commitments. Thirty minutes passed in a trice. "Some day," Dr. King concluded, "invite me back when you have time to let me preach." Years later, 1961, Martin Luther King, Jr., preached from the same pulpit a sermon so precisely articulated that my wife Martha could type every syllable and punctuation mark from a tape. For that, the seminary received a salvo from an irate Georgia Baptist threatening to withhold funds or otherwise pay us back for having that "iggorant [sic] nigger."

A lot of students complained about how hard the classes were, and most were demanding. Although I did not have college classes that gave me a leg up on subjects we had at Southern, as students who had attended Baptist colleges did, I did not find my classes as demanding as those I took at Washington University. Part of the reason for that, I am sure, is that I was more highly motivated, hungering and thirsting to know God and to know what God expected me to do with my life. I don't think it would be pretentious on my part, however, to say that

Washington U had demanded more of me than most schools had asked of my fellow students, and I had worked longer hours to support myself. After finding my calling during my third year, I had stopped worrying about grades and concentrated on soaking up as much knowledge as I could in every subject, an attitude that increased at the seminary. If I had a complaint, it concerned the size of classes. At the seminary introductory classes could run as high as 200. Apart from two science classes that had general lectures two days and labs or small groups three days, the largest enrollment in my classes at Washington U was twenty-five.

Some arbitrariness did result from a grading system that required classes to maintain C averages. Graduate assistants or "fellows" rather than professors did almost all grading. As instructed by Dean Peterson, they used a cluster system. The largest cluster would receive C's and then roughly equal clusters either above or below A's and B's or D's and F's. Inevitably, the system disappointed many who hoped to attain the B average that would permit them to do graduate studies.

Southern Seminary had a young but competent faculty. It was undergoing a rapid expansion as the post-War period resulted in stunning growth of the Southern Baptist Convention and consequently an explosion in the number of persons experiencing a call to ministry. The convention's theme the year I came to Southern was "a million more in 54." As you could easily predict, the denomination did not achieve that goal, but it did increase by 283,475—from 7,886,016 to 8,169,491—in 1954, and to 8,474,741, up 305,250, in 1955, on its way to becoming America's largest Protestant denomination. As the denomination's size mushroomed, so too did seminary enrollment, and with it faculty. Distinguished older faculty members were giving way to able, younger ones. J.B. Weatherspoon, Professor of Homiletics, and Gaines S. Dobbins, Professor of Religious Education and Church Administration, retired before I completed my BD. Apart from them, every professor I had was a post-World War II hire. With the exception of Wayne E. Oates, who was one of the trailblazers in the field of pastoral care, and Eric C. Rust, a British theologian hired in 1953, they had not had time to publish extensively and to establish their reputations. It pleased me no end, however, to discover that they shared the perspective I had arrived at out of personal experience, that is, that we need not fear truth wherever or in whatever form we find it and that faith should speak to the world of today.

I will not take time to speak about each professor that I had, but I would be remiss to not highlight ways in which particular professors contributed to my formation as a person, as a minister, and as a scholar. I begin with Gaines Dobbins (1920–56). I never had a seminary class with Dr. Dobbins, but I participated in the huge class of seminarians that he taught at Crescent Hill Baptist Church, a church located just two blocks from the seminary, and learned from his dialectical method. When he had to be away, if he could not get another professor to pinch-hit for him, he would ask me to fill in.

W.W. Adams, previously professor of New Testament and president of Central Baptist Theological Seminary in Kansas City, Kansas, joined the faculty the same year I arrived. Because of my intense interest in New Testament studies, I took several classes with him in exegesis of the Greek New Testament. Although he had passed his prime as a scholar, I learned from him how to make effective use of humor in teaching, a trick he had learned from his mentor A.T. Robertson. He used irony to put biblical literalism and inerrancy to shame. Not many students who started his classes as inerrantists ended believing the Bible is literally true.

More serious scholars etched themselves and their outlook more deeply on my life and thought. T.C. Smith, who had joined the faculty in New Testament in 1950, opened to me the deep Jewish underpinnings of early Christian thought. Doing advanced study at Hebrew Union College in Cincinnati, Smith elucidated the essentially Jewish cast of the Gospel according to John and, in my third year, permitted me to participate in a seminar on rabbinic writings he offered for graduate students. Heber Peacock, who joined the Southern faculty after teaching and studying in Switzerland, taught me much not only about scholarship but about helping students to make serious biblical scholarship relevant to what they were doing. By example he demonstrated that serious scholars could be genuinely devout and put themselves unapologetically in the service of the churches. When I began doctoral work, he selected me as his graduate fellow. I felt a still closer bond to both Smith and Peacock during my first year as a graduate student when they were pulled into a controversy with President Duke McCall that I will talk about later.

Neo-Orthodoxy dominated theology in the 1950s, but, true to its Baptist heritage, Southern Seminary did not try to shape ministers in a particular theological mold. Although Dale Moody, who joined the faculty during the great surge in new hires (1948), had studied with both Karl Barth and Emil Brunner in Switzerland, he elected Brunner for our theological textbook because Brunner believed in general revelation, whereas Barth did not. In class, however, both he and Wayne Ward, added to the faculty in 1953, taught what Moody called "Bible doctrines" rather than systematic theology. With a keen interest in New Testament at that stage in my theological formation, such an approach suited me nicely and permitted me to put together a theology I could comfortably embrace. Although Ward's theology left a lot of my questions unanswered, I had a bonus in the class: John Claypool, soon to be pastor of Crescent Hill Baptist Church, served as Ward's fellow and prodded me to undertake doctoral studies, something I hadn't contemplated before.

The anomaly of the fact that I have spent most of my career teaching Church history notwithstanding, the subject did not appeal as strongly to me at this point as New Testament studies did. With Theron Price, professor of Church history from 1948 to 1958, studying at Yale during a sabbatical, I got my introduction to Church history from Hugh Wamble, then an instructor but who joined the faculty in 1956 and later taught at Midwestern Seminary in Kansas City, Missouri. William L. Lumpkin, who came on board my initial year at Southern, taught Baptist history. Sometimes he filled in for Gaines Dobbins in teaching the Sunday school class for seminarians at Crescent Hill. Although his post-luncheon Baptist history class put many of us to sleep more often than I would like to admit, I've never known a more gracious person than he or one whose scholarship and friendship I've cherished more. On returning, Price taught the History of Christian Doctrine, which I took. What I valued in Theron Price was a razor-sharp wit. One day in this class he and a student got into a protracted argument, the point of which I've forgotten. After twenty minutes of sometimes-heated debate, Price drew up to his full six feet eight inches, pointed heavenward, and said, "All right, you go *your* way, and I'll go *His*." Fortunately, it was time for the bell because that broke the class up. One day when Price had preached a rousing chapel message, one of the most evangelistic students walked with him from Alumni Chapel back to Norton Hall. Very earnestly, he said, "Say, Dr. Price, you can preach! You can really preach! You could be an evangelist. Why aren't you an evangelist?" Price stopped, looked down at him just as earnestly and replied, "Because I believe in God, son.

Because I believe in God." My all time favorite Priceism is: "If they come running like hogs after slop, it ain't the gospel."

A student could not study at Southern Seminary very long without getting caught up in an infectious excitement about missions. The air reeked of missions. Just across the valley from Norton Hall was the Carver School of Missions and Social Work, originally the Woman's Missionary Training School, where women prepared themselves for missions or social ministries and, often, found husbands among seminarians. Mission volunteers organized meetings to spread their excitement. A required course on missions taught by Cornell Goerner, professor of missions from 1938 until 1957, stirred the mission air further. A decided anti-Roman Catholic bias in the course on missions, however, distressed me enough that I once dared gently to challenge some statements made by Dr. Goerner in class that questioned whether Catholics could be Christian. He graciously corrected himself. In that pre-Vatican II era such attitudes and expressions were not surprising, however. When Southern Baptists resumed foreign mission work after the Civil War, they divided their endeavors into Pagan Fields and Papal Fields and showed which they considered more crucial by dispatching their first missionary to Italy in 1871. In the 1950s, the Foreign Mission Board concentrated a lot of its energies on Latin America.

Despite some reservations about such issues, I seriously contemplated a vocation of missions and attended meetings of mission volunteers. Those gatherings brought me into contact with furloughing missionaries from Europe, Asia, Africa, and Latin America. I often spoke to representatives from the Foreign Mission Board when they visited campus. Unfortunately, the onset of deafness before I completed graduate studies altered any plans I was devising.

I must confess that while my motivation to learn all I could about the Bible, Church history, or theology ran extremely high, I could not generate equal enthusiasm for the practice of ministry, save perhaps pastoral care. I could readily conceive of myself doing the work of a pastor, but some aspects of religious education and church administration dampened my enthusiasm considerably. *The Church Book* and *Building Better Churches* by Gaines Dobbins toned down but still operated on an idea he had framed in *The Efficient Church* when he took the Chair of Church Efficiency at Southern Seminary in 1923. Thinking of the Church as the world's greatest business and Jesus as a miracle-working entrepreneur seemed to clash with what the rest of my seminary studies taught me. At this stage, moreover, Southern Seminary had not progressed very far toward hands-on learning in the practice of ministry. Clinical Pastoral Education did not put in an appearance until I had already begun doctoral studies in New Testament. "Field education" consisted of visits to the Haymarket area to sing, preach, and "witness" to the homeless who inhabited that part of the city—our version of the Salvation Army minus their social ministry. Although many students served as pastors of churches and a few professional evangelists held revivals, most of us did not have the benefit of internships or placement under supervision of experienced ministers. This meant that, for me, my most significant opportunities to "try out" my gifts for ministry occurred during the summers when I returned to the First Baptist Church of Affton, Missouri. My first summer turned out to hold special significance in more ways than one.

I expected to take up again the task of Minister to Youth, which I had done informally before I went to Louisville, but the Rev. John Reagan asked me to serve as Interim Pastor while he took a summer sabbatical. As impressive as the name may sound, don't visualize the First Baptist Church of Affton as an awesome charge. The church still convened in a revamped farmhouse at the corner of Gravois, the town's major thoroughfare, and Heege Road. The sanctuary accommodated, perhaps, a hundred people in five rows of pews. A recently erected addition at the back supplied space for Sunday school and other activities. Although I knew that I was ill-equipped to undertake even this modest charge after putting only two semesters of seminary under my belt, would receive no remuneration for the job, and thus would also have to work full time at A&P, I accepted eagerly. I was anxious to try my wings, and they were quickly put to the test.

I will speak about my first challenging pastoral visit in the next chapter, but one or two other pastoral tasks during those six-weeks proved daunting. One long-term member succumbed to cancer, and I had to perform my first funeral and minister to the family. I made it a point to visit both before and after the funeral. Although I doubt whether I did all the things I should have, the husband and children seemed genuinely grateful. A seven-year-old boy underwent surgery at Kosair Children's Hospital to turn his feet around. For reasons I could not understand fully, the hospital did not want the parents or others to visit during the recuperation because it seemed to upset the child. Today, I think, hospitals would want at least one parent with the child around the clock. I tried my best to keep lines of communication flowing between the hospital and the parents. These two incidents alone made me aware that ministry to other persons and to families required far greater resources than I possessed in and of myself. Paul's defense of his apostolate to Corinthian critics established itself as one of my deepest convictions about ministry. "We have this confidence with God through Christ. Not that we are competent from ourselves, to be considered anything as from ourselves, but our competence is from God, who has made us competent to be ministers of a new covenant, ..." (2 Cor 3:4–6).

Preparing two sermons a week and leading a Wednesday prayer service when you have adequate training and considerable experience in the art of preparing sermons and ample time to do so is a challenging task. Preparing and leading them when you don't have such training and experience and are working full time at A&P is overwhelming. I had not sat at the feet of a master preacher, and I had not had a class in preaching yet. Consequently, my strategy for the morning worship during these six weeks was to rely heavily on exposition of one New Testament writing I had studied intensively, in this instance Paul's letter to the Philippians, which we had exegeted in advanced Greek during the spring semester. For the evening I focused on selected topics which might speak especially to youth, my chief constituency, and lure them back to church—what New Testament Christianity entails, Christian vocation, responding to a recent prediction of the end of the world, the Bible—true yet not without error, Christianity's answer to death's boast.

Rereading the sermons today causes me to blush. I wisely kept them short, no more than twenty minutes, but, even at that, they must have bored people. Yet a couple of things fall on the credit side of the ledger. They do justice to the content of scriptures. All translations are my own, and they are idiomatic and intelligible. Only here and there, however, will one find a memorable phrase or thought that those who heard might cling to, a line from John Donne or John P. Marquand. The text itself had to suffice. At the end of my time as interim, one middle-aged, thoughtful woman who had attended every Sunday, said, "Young man, I pray that you will always stay with the scriptures." The topical messages that I directed especially to questions the youth of the church were raising come nearer to being sermons, and I know that they left their mark on the twenty-five or thirty youth who attended without fail.

I served only as Minister of Youth during the next summer. Consequently, I became a supply preacher at other churches more frequently than at Affton. By that time, my preaching had improved exponentially as a result of taking a course in homiletics. Southern Seminary professors still used John A. Broadus's *The Preparation and Delivery of Sermons*, which he composed for a blind student when the Seminary reopened after the Civil War. Like Broadus, V.L. Stanfield required us to identify our subject, formulate a proposition, state an objective, identify a problem addressed, and classify the sermon as to subject and object. Regrettably they did not underscore the value of following the lectionary or emphasize worship. At Affton, as at many other Baptist churches, we still entitled the Sunday morning service a *preaching* service and not a *worship* service. Except for outstanding days in the Christian calendar, preachers usually chose user-friendly texts. I preached my first sermon using the more proper homiletic style at Affton in August 1956. Not surprisingly, one of the more objective and slightly cynical deacons in the church commented, "You are the most improved preacher I've ever heard." I hoped he was right, but I knew that I still had a steep hill to climb in order to preach effectively.

Notwithstanding the heavy load I carried otherwise, my ministry to youth at First Baptist prospered. I must confess that I had slim qualifications for this job, too, confined mostly to love for people and a certain personal charisma for relating to diverse personalities, honed mostly at A&P. The youth, from junior high through college, liked me enough to choose me to preach the sermon for Youth Sunday when I had not given even the least indication that I had an interest in ministry. At any rate, this group responded to whatever I planned. They turned out in force for serious sessions and for frivolous ones. Parents, indeed, all adults in the church, gave money, provided transportation, and rallied behind what the youth did. In retrospect, I would judge that what both the youth and their parents applauded was an effort on my part to help them understand how their Christian faith relates to the world we live in today. That is why one of my interim sermons, for instance, specifically focused on how the Bible could be true even though we cannot call it inerrant. It is why in brainstorming sessions we could discuss how one could accept evolution as a theory propounded and sustained by modern science and still believe in God directing the universe toward some ultimately meaningful end. It is why I talked about the will of God as having to do with what kind of persons we are, persons who live out our covenant with God making the very best choices we can in the circumstances.

One of my gravest disappointments in connection with this work I did among the youth of First Baptist Affton occurred years later. A pastor search committee of the church asked me to recommend someone. The person I recommended, one of my first five PhD students, although strongly favored by the search committee, had to endure a vicious tirade by a woman not a member of the church when I did youth work, accusing me of having taught it was okay for a Christian to believe in evolution, etc. She was correct about that. She was sadly mistaken, however, in thinking what I did was a negative for those youth. Some of the youth probably didn't get far beyond the Kool-Aid, cake, and ice cream we shared, but most of them grew and remain steadfast believers today because they learned how to relate faith to the scientific principles that we now know rather than conceiving of faith in a pre-scientific milieu. My student, an excellent preacher with strong interest in worship and much experience as a pastor, had a strongly favorable vote, but he withdrew his name from consideration.

Would I have done this ministry differently had I foreseen such consequences? Let me say that because of my early turbulent experience in life, I am an irenic person, one who tries to steer away from conflict. I do my best to find common ground with others. At the same time I think Christian faith calls for us to "speak the truth in love" (Eph 4:15). I would not have served those youth well had I tried to help them develop a faith that would have equipped them to live in a culture and a world that had not existed for centuries if ever. They needed help in framing a worldview consonant with a biblical faith that made room for what they were learning in school and in everyday life.

8

MARTHA

I had hardly stepped into the office at 8 a.m. on Monday morning, assuming the role of Interim Pastor of First Baptist Church of Affton in the summer of 1955, when the phone rang. A voice at the other end said, "Martha Burks has been involved in a serious accident on US 66 and is a patient at Deaconness Hospital. Will you come to see her?"

I gulped and said yes. I knew Martha slightly because she sometimes shopped at A&P with her mother or her sister Charlotte. Silently entreating God to guide someone so inexperienced, I hopped into my 1941 Plymouth and raced to the hospital. When I got to the room, Charlotte guided me in. Bandages covered much of Martha's head, and black and blue dotted what parts lacked bandages. A full cast covered one leg. It was hiked up toward the ceiling with a rope and pulley.

In those days hospitals still used ether as the anesthetic of choice. Mixed with other hospital smells and the sight of Martha, I felt myself grow woozy and sway a little as I walked up to the bed. Before I could even ask, "How are you?" Charlotte led me out of the room to catch some fresher air. I recovered enough to return and mumble that I would be back to see her when *she* felt better.

Martha's comment whenever I recount this story is, "Well, you can't say that I chased you." One leg caged in a cast and roped to the ceiling did make it unlikely for a while, but the chase may have involved more than physics—there was also chemistry.

I think that every reader of my story up to this point will recognize that I had experienced a long loneliness from childhood on—my parents' estrangement, my brother's departure, my step-father's leaving. Not all those with similar stories will have things work out in this way, but in my case the many hurts I had suffered and the assumption of adult responsibilities very early in life dampened my ability to reach out to other persons. In some curious way as a coping strategy, I stuffed the greater part of myself into my head and held the world at arms length lest getting close to others might inflict still greater hurt and cause me to fail at what I attempted. Although I delighted in the admiration others had for my intellectual gifts, it dulled my sensitivity to the wall built up between me and those persons who coveted friendship rather than showmanship and superiority. Here and there I picked up comments and vibes that exposed my mind game, and I knew that loneliness was its price.

Let me be very candid and confess a great personal weakness that has resulted from my headiness: selective inattention to reality. My philosophy has always been this: if it hurts, ignore it, run away from it, and divert your attention to pleasant things. I guess this can be both blessing and curse. It may have saved me as a little boy standing with mouth agape as his father endangered his health, his business, and his family. Yet it also shortchanged who I was and what I could mean to others. If I could avoid it, I did not visit the sick in hospitals or go to funerals. Dame Necessity alone forced me to do some things. So you can see in me some reluctance to do what a minister inevitably ends up doing—visiting people in hospitals, conducting funerals, listening to the cries of the aggrieved.

Visiting Martha in the hospital on that first pastoral visit put me on trial for all of the evasions and subterfuges I had resorted to throughout most of my twenty-three or -four years of life. Tempering and reshaping such limitations, but not eliminating them entirely, was a course in pastoral care I took my second semester at Southern Seminary. Imagine how I would have reacted had I not had a modicum of exposure to what happens in hospitals, mortuaries, homes, and churches. I might *literally* have passed out.

I don't believe I can explain to you how ministry to Martha led to my falling head over heels in love with her, but it did. After a couple of weeks' recuperation, of course, Martha began to look much more attractive than the banged up accident victim I saw at the beginning. Even with a gimpy leg, she was beautiful. Surprisingly, having to help her negotiate her way into my one-seated business coupe seemed to add to her charm and attractiveness. It at least made me conscious of some qualities I value in others, such as good humor in coping. As her life story unfolded during our conversations on the way to or from work, it became evident that we possessed quite a few compatibilities. We both grew up in wounded families. Circumstances forced both of us to accept adult responsibilities very early in life and to come to the conclusion that you express love in deed more than in word or emotion, although both of those have their part to play.

Martha was born 25 October 1930 in Jefferson City, the capital of Missouri and the hometown of both of her parents, Ralph Elmer Burks and Flossie Leora Loveall. There she attended East End Elementary School. Not long after the United States entered World War II, however, the Burkses moved to St. Louis so that both parents could work at McDonnell Aircraft, living on Cates Street. Martha enrolled in the seventh grade at Soldan (Junior and Senior) High School. Shortly afterwards, the family bought a house in Affton. Martha attended Affton High School from the eighth grade until her graduation in 1948. After graduation she enrolled at the University of Missouri at Columbia and completed two years. Limited financially, she took a position with IBM in Jefferson City, living with her paternal grandmother and step-grandfather, "Mattie" and Frank Ware. In 1953 she obtained a transfer to the St. Louis office of IBM, where she worked until we married in 1956.

When I first became acquainted with the family, Martha lived with her mother, her sister Charlotte, and her brother Ralph, usually called "Butch," on Stealey Street, a few blocks from both First Baptist Church and A&P in Affton. Her mother supported the family as a seamstress in one of the many St. Louis sweatshops that made dresses for swanky retailers such as Saks Fifth Avenue in New York. She supplemented the pitiful pay she earned in a piecework system by tailoring dresses, suits, and other clothing for a fairly substantial clientele. As the oldest child in the family, seven years older than Charlotte and fourteen than Butch, Martha helped her mother carry much of the load for the support of the household.

I'm not sure that what we did merits the designation of "courting." Chauffeuring led to dates: *Oklahoma* at Muny Opera; drive-in movies, then the craze of Steak and Shake, the harbinger of Fast Food America; occasional picnics; and trips to Jefferson City to visit Martha's grandparents. Nothing fancy or expensive on my income. In case you are concerned that our dating involved a lot of driving that we would find prohibitive today, it cost little in the post-World War II era when you could buy eight to fourteen gallons of gasoline for a dollar. Until we got really serious about our relationship, I studiously avoided taking Martha to Sullivan to visit my mother and half-sister and to see the remodeled smokehouse in which I grew up. Even my basement room at the

Marshes occasioned less embarrassment than that old shack with its tin roof and imitation rock tarpaper siding.

Fortunately for me, Martha seemed content and even eager to take part in the crowded calendar of activities I had assumed responsibility for at First Baptist Church of Affton on top of working at A&P during the summer of 1955. When removal of her cast permitted, she went to Sunday school, sang in the choir at the worship service, joined the youth group for Sunday afternoon meetings, attended evening worship, and then went with me to the youth fellowship meetings afterwards. She wouldn't have had to take part in all of those activities for me to learn that she was bright. Her employment at IBM and our many conversations were enough to confirm that. In classes that I taught at Affton and in the stream of questions she would ask afterwards, however, I discerned a keen, critical mind and eagerness to go beyond what she had learned in Sunday school up to that time. In her searching mind, I think, you may find another clue as to why I fell in love with her. Looking backwards over a half century of teaching, I see hints of a habit of falling in love with searching minds, perhaps rooted in the fact that I have valued education as the way out of poverty and its attendant limitations.

Martha and I enjoyed more intimate and romantic moments. As you might expect, most of those came at the end of full days of other activities. Still, our love blossomed like flowers in the springtime. By the end of July or beginning of August I think both of us knew that we would like to spend the rest of our lives together with the understanding that I would probably be a minister. The prospect of being a minister's wife occasioned quite a bit of discussion between us, but Martha gradually began to feel comfortable with it. In the mid-fifties, I think, most people assumed that a wife would accommodate herself and any sense of calling she may have had to her husband's calling, so I don't think we carried on any serious conversations about what I should do to encourage and aid her in *her* vocation. We surely had tons of discussions about our future, but in 1955 in our social context in America family plans revolved around the male member of the species. If and when we married, she would leave IBM in St. Louis and find employment in Louisville to support us while I completed my seminary training. Somewhat to my embarrassment in retrospect, I knew that Martha had wanted to complete her college education and that she had a serious interest in art, but it did not occur to me that she should pursue those *before* I finished my professional training. As it turned out, I completed my basic professional degree, the Bachelor of Divinity, and an advanced degree, the Doctor of Theology, and did much of my work for the Doctor of Philosophy at Oxford before she finished her BA at Bellarmine College (now University) in Louisville in 1971.

I have confessed a certain brashness or impulsiveness with reference to education, and I probably need to admit some of the same with reference to marriage. Because I've had to make adult-type decisions on my own from early on, I'm not the kind of person who is accustomed to consulting a whole array of advisors on decisions as momentous even as marriage—my mother, my pastor, my aunt and uncle, friends. Instead, I internalize and agonize privately, an approach to decision-making that has often left Martha feeling left out. After about two months of close encounters with Martha, tons of thoughts and feelings and possible scenarios and convictions and doubts were coursing through my mind and heart. I thought of a hundred reasons why I should not get married at that time: First and foremost, I was a virtual pauper still trying to get enough education to do what I thought God wanted me to do and had opted for a vocation that would never provide the money and prestige I once counted essential. The thought of relying on someone to support me ran smack dab against all those warnings about not owing anyone anything my mother had drilled into me, but how could I take responsibility for supporting another person? Running a list of yeses and nos side by side threatened to paralyze me in the same way questions about whether I would live my life from the vantage point of a relationship with God immobilized me. And I realized in this case, too, that I couldn't answer all of the questions my mind was conjuring up. Entering into a covenant with Martha entailed the same leap of faith entering into a covenant with God did. Sometime in August I decided to buy an engagement ring and propose to her.

In retrospect, I probably would propose first and then, if she accepted, ask Martha to go with me to pick out an engagement ring. That, at least today, is more apropos and less risky. So I confess to being impetuous and presumptuous. I must have assumed that she would say yes, not because I was such a great "catch," but because we had been communicating our love for one another in unmistakable ways. By this time we were virtually glued together. Knowing that her birthday would come up in October, I wanted to surprise her with the ring, and I needed to buy it before I left to return to school. Aunt Fleta and Uncle Ossie had a close friend who was a wholesale jeweler, so I had Aunt Fleta arrange for me to meet him, having little inkling as to how much diamond rings cost. As it turned out, even then they cost much more than I could afford, so I had to apply to Uncle Ossie for a loan. What great joy I felt the day I got the ring! I couldn't wait to present it to Martha and ask her to marry me come her birthday. The fact is, I *didn't* wait. The very day I purchased it, I took it with me on a date we had arranged for that evening, asked her to marry me, and gave it to her then. Thankfully, she said yes. So excited was I, I drove ten miles with my old Plymouth's emergency brake on, scarcely noticing that the car, whose brake locked around the drive shaft, ran very sluggishly.

If you think the outset of our courtship curious, you may find its continuance intriguing too. A week or so after our engagement, I headed back to Louisville and my second year in Seminary. Cultivation of our covenant now depended on phone calls, letters, and monthly visits to St. Louis until the end of the school year. Because of my Spartan finances, it meant for me also living on a restricted diet whose chief staple was the peanut butter sandwich. You won't be surprised to learn that when we married 1 September 1956, I weighed only 140 pounds.

Phoning from Southern Seminary wasn't as simple as it is today when cell phones grow out of people's ears. At that time, the seminary didn't install phones in individual rooms. I made calls from a booth on the first floor of Mullins Hall. Often callers had to stand in line to use one of the two phones and then risk something less than complete privacy. Nearly always a crowd of students congregated in the vestibule just outside the phone booth, so I never felt comfortable talking very long. In addition, long distance calls overtaxed my slim budget. On the other hand, Martha found it nearly impossible to reach me at the only phone I had access to on a first come, first served basis. Whether anyone would answer a ring even if they stood by the booths was an iffy proposition.

Our chief communication was by letter. I tried to write at least twice a week. Martha didn't write as often. She didn't save the letters I wrote to her, and I don't have clear memory about them. I suspect they contained a lot of reports and reflections on what I was learning but were also love letters. They probably contained few thoughts worth saving. Martha had warned me to expect mood swings, and I was conscious of them at times, but I didn't realize then that she sometimes battled depression. The distance that separated us certainly didn't help her equilibrium.

Then there were the trips! By I-64 today, the drive from Louisville to St. Louis takes less than four hours. In 1955 and 1956 there was no I-64. The route I usually took was US 150 north until it intersected with US 50 at Loogootee, Indiana. Then I stayed on Route 50 across Illinois to St. Louis. With light traffic it took at least six hours averaging 50 mph. For me it was a "red eye" drive. I worked at A&P in St. Matthews on Friday night until we finished restocking the shelves, usually at 11 p.m. Gifted with an unusual supply of energy, pumped up by love, and furbished with a couple of peanut butter sandwiches and a soft drink, I drove without interruption until I arrived in Affton between 5 and 6 a.m. on Saturday morning. Anxious to see Martha, I would usually get up by ten or eleven. Because Southern Seminary did not schedule Monday classes, I could stay over until Monday night, departing perhaps just after supper. The return trip would take somewhat longer, but I got in by around 1 a.m. For the most part the travel itself held few surprises. I was stopped once for rolling through a boulevard stop sign at Loogootee around 1 a.m. but was not given a ticket. I think the policeman just wanted to see if I was awake. Returning through Illinois on an icy US 50 in January, I slid off the road into a slight depression and had to ask some farm boys to push me back onto the highway. I was fortunate that did not happen when I reached the knobs in Indiana where I would have plunged into deep ditches or worse.

Those brief excursions didn't satisfy either Martha or me. We coveted more quality time together, especially when I had to fight to stay awake. Here, I think, Martha exhibited another quality that has helped our marriage to survive for more than fifty years—a sort of determination not to give up when the going gets tough. It would be presumptuous of me, of course, to articulate ambivalences she must have felt or even to repeat complaints she voiced, but what I sensed was that she loved me enough to put up with more than any bride-to-be should have to tolerate, maybe in the hope that life would not always be this way.

You probably wonder whether my grades suffered during this year. Surprisingly, they didn't. I had clarity of purpose and love-energy to push me toward my goal. I would be dishonest, however, not to admit that I looked eagerly toward the end of the spring term when I would return to St. Louis. Although I worked at least forty hours a week and resumed my role as youth minister at First Baptist Church of Affton, the summer seemed almost idyllic as Martha and I spent all the time we could together. During the year, she got more and more deeply involved in the church and, on my return, took part in my work with youth. The youth, from junior high on up, responded enthusiastically to her just as they did to me. On occasions when I had opportunities to preach at other churches I proudly took her with me. I think we were cultivating a perception of partnership in ministry. Although I claimed the spotlight, I could count on her to be present, attentive, and supportive. I learned to exercise a little caution, however, in asking her to comment on my sermons unless my ego-strength was up because she would give a critical analysis worthy of a professor of homiletics. My teaching performance always came out higher on the scale than my preaching.

By this second summer, Martha had already taken me on a round of visits to meet her extended family, especially during the Christmas season. We visited her grandmother and step-grandfather Ware several times in Jefferson City. Martha, named after her, was her grandmother's pet. At their house we met Mattie's sister, Howie, and her husband, Charles Forbis, a barber. We chatted briefly with Martha's maternal grandmother Loveall, a full-blooded Cherokee Indian, as she sat smoking her corncob pipe. We spent some time with Flossie's older and favorite sister Addie Blumer. We met Martha's uncle "Baby Earl" Loveall, a six-feet-four-inch, 300-pound excavator and trucker, and his family. We stopped by briefly to meet Martha's father, Ralph Burks, and his wife, who, at the time, sold mobile homes. Martha did not have a comfortable relationship with her father, who had abused her emotionally as a child. Some other family members we met at our wedding.

I don't remember when I first took Martha to Sullivan to meet my immediate family. She knew Aunt Fleta and Uncle Ossie from First Baptist, of course, but I did not take her to meet Mother and Sue until our relationship seemed strong enough to withstand a shock or two. To be quite frank, I'm a little embarrassed by my hesitancy, but at that stage in my life I couldn't handle open disclosure of my vulnerabilities; it has taken me a lifetime to get to that point. I'm not sure what I feared the most, perhaps exposure of all the poverty and humility of my upbringing that would become immediately evident on going to the farm my mother and sister lived on and seeing the inside of the house in which they lived, with its rough, worn floors and ugly wallpaper. Perhaps I was worried about mother's deafness, though not her intelligence. More likely, I felt some embarrassment that mother and Sue would turn out in ratty clothes, mother in worn and patched overalls and Sue in a dress mother had cut from flour sacks and sewn together. Unlike Martha's mother, mine was not a skilled dressmaker.

Whatever the cause, all my worry turned out to be for naught. Martha knew something about humble beginnings, and she knew about *my* humble beginnings and felt comfortable with Mother and Sue, and they with her. After we married, we visited often, and I always went away with a sense of gratitude for Martha's hearty acceptance of me in all of my limitations. That would come out still more vividly as we traveled life's road together.

We married 1 September 1956. First Baptist Church of Affton had celebrated other weddings, but my service as youth minister and as interim pastor gave ours a special prominence. Several of the older youth of the church served as attendants for both of us, but we also included her brother Ralph and my half-sister Sue, as well as Charlotte and Martha's close friends in high school. Martha's mother made the dresses of the bridesmaids. I teared up when I saw that my mother had scrounged around in her mysterious way and found the funds to have herself fitted with a completely coordinated ensemble including a hat that, with heels, brought her up to my shoulder. I had not seen her so elegantly dressed since I was five years old. She truly loved Martha.

I'm afraid that I created great anxiety for Martha both before and after the wedding. Concerned to get in every minute and to earn all the pay I could, I worked at A&P until nearly 6 p.m. and then hurried home to shower and scramble into my tuxedo and rush to church for the 7 p.m. service. When the service and the reception were over, Martha went to her mother's house to remove her wedding dress, pack it away, and wait. I went to the Marshes to change out of my tuxedo and into traveling clothes. Aunt Fleta and Uncle Ossie announced that they were wiping out what I owed them for Martha's ring. They also gave me an envelope filled with cash. They had done so many incredibly generous things for me and for my brother Gene since our earliest years that I broke down and cried, a display of emotion out of the ordinary for me. I babbled and burbled on for a long while until Martha phoned to ask with some exasperation in her voice, "Are you coming?" I hurried away.

Predictably, the youth had embossed our car, a 1941 Chevrolet Powerglide I managed to buy that summer, with "Just married!" and a lot of streamers, cans, and junk despite my effort to hide it. Then they chased us as we headed to our secret rendezvous. We didn't want to drive all the way to Louisville on our wedding night, so I had arranged for us to stay in a motel I had hoped they would not find, but they found us anyway.

As for the honeymoon? Martha had to have been so in love with me or been blessed with the patience of a saint—or both—to put up with one like this. The day after our wedding, we drove straight to Louisville to look for a place to live. Seminary housing for married students was full, and you can scarcely imagine the kind of apartments people had the gall to offer for the rent we could afford: In one in the Highlands of Louisville we would have had to allow another renter to traipse through our bedroom to get to his room and to have shared a bath! We finally found a livable, second-floor, three-bedroom apartment in St. Matthews just off of Lexington Road on Macon Street owned by a Southern Seminary trustee. Although it had plumbing and heating facilities dating back several decades and lacked air conditioning, it surpassed by far the other apartments we had seen. A stove and refrigerator, both in good condition, came with the apartment. During September and October we sweltered through one of Louisville's most humid and stormy periods. Virtually every night of our first month there, thunder boomed and lightning flashed around us, setting the whole building atremble.

We furnished our "honeymoon apartment" with furniture we purchased from Railroad Salvage for about $200. For the kitchen, a card table and four folding chairs. Our friends at Affton had outfitted us with everyday china, utensils, small appliances, cutlery, and other gadgets. For the living room, an early American chair, settee, coffee table, lamp stand, and lamp. For the bedroom, a double bed, dresser, and chest of drawers. Martha had put together a trousseau, but we also received a supply of linens, towels, blankets, and quilts from family and friends.

From day one we shared our chores. Martha cooked. She had had lots of experience cooking, whereas I had none. I quickly learned that she was a perfectionist about it as she was about most things. She organized menus for each week and varied meals as much as she could, although our budget didn't permit a lot of experimentation. I did much more mundane chores such as washing dishes, cleaning, keeping the car running, and building a kitchen cabinet.

In about a week I started classes and went to work again at A&P, but we knew that what I made there would not take care of the rent, buy food, pay fees at the seminary, put gas in the car, and meet other bills. Martha tried IBM in Louisville, but they could not arrange a transfer.

Like many another dutiful wife, she found a job in Administrative Services at Southern Seminary, a position she held until our son Christopher was born 27 January 1964. The pay was abysmally low, but the job had some other attractions in its connection with the seminary. Martha was eager to enter as fully as possible into what I was learning, and her work in Administrative services permitted her to do so in a significant way. Typing manuscripts for professors was one of her major responsibilities, and she didn't just type them, she absorbed what they said. Her ability to decipher often barely legible script and sometimes to make editorial suggestions led to friendships with professors, notably Eric Rust. She was the only secretary who could read Rust's script, nearly a straight line with a few squiggles. He acknowledged her assistance in all of the books he wrote during the time she served in Administrative Service. Her quickness in repartee especially delighted Rust. Once when he came into Administrative Services, he noticed that she looked exasperated. He asked, "What's the matter, Ma'atha?" She responded, "Oh, so and so is just an aass (with the broad Oxford a)." Rust said, "I don't say aass. I just say plain old American ass." The Typing Pool also typed letters dictated by professors and administrators. Martha quickly demonstrated her abilities in this and eventually became the Director of Administrative Services.

Martha and I joined Crescent Hill Baptist Church soon after we arrived in Louisville and took an active part in Sunday school and Training Union. A few weeks later, we were asked to serve as advisors to a group of 13- and 14-year-olds (I was going to say "directors," but nobody directs adolescents.) in Training Union. The youth consisted of a mix of Junior Highs from Ormsby Village, a home for abused and neglected children, and Baptist Children's Home in Middletown, Kentucky, as well as children of local families. Neither Martha nor I had experience with minstering to neglected and abused youth, but we had excellent help from the local families, especially Jim and Keyes Tate and Forrest and Nita Herren, in coping with the less domesticated children. The Tates owned and operated a chain of pharmacies in the Louisville area and lived in Cherokee Gardens, an upscale residential area near the Seminary. Forrest Herren was dean of Southern Seminary's School of Church Music.

Another opportunity for ministry turned up in the spring of 1957 when the Volunteers of America invited me to accompany a trio of volunteers who visited Jefferson County jail every Sunday morning to lead worship. Damon Runyan would have loved them. The trio consisted of Clyde (the only name I ever heard him called), a strapping country boy whose Sunday suit failed by at least four inches in reaching the tops of his shoes or the wrists as they joined his hands; a blind accordionist whose name I can't recall; and Sister Cox, the group's leader who had gone to the jail every Sunday for years and years to lead worship, counsel prisoners, and run occasional errands. The very first trip Sister Cox cautioned Martha not to get too close to the bars because some of the inmates had long arms and horny dispositions. She also whispered to me, "You will soon find out whether they will listen to your sermon. If they don't like it, they will start raking those tin cups they use across the bars. You won't be able to hear yourself think." From the first Sunday I did my best to start with something that would capture their attention, and I didn't get drowned out once. Indeed, Martha and I exercised care but managed to do some redemptive ministry to a few of those behind bars.

Pleasant and instructive as my unusual ministry at Jefferson County jail was, I welcomed a call to become pastor of First Baptist Church, Eminence, Indiana, in the late spring of 1957, learning at the same time that I had been accepted into the doctoral program in New Testament studies. By this time I had gotten most of the basic training and a modicum of the experience a minister needs, but I soon learned that, as Paul observed, we dare not place confidence in ourselves and our competencies but only in God. No matter how modest the assignment, serving as God's go-between is a tough challenge. We do indeed hold this treasure in "earthen vessels" that the "transcendent power" may be of God and not of ourselves (2 Cor 4:7).

Looking back, I feel remiss that I allowed my excitement about becoming a pastor to diminish my attention to the stress that weekend travel would place on Martha. In this age of interstate highways 135 miles doesn't sound like a great distance—no more than two hours under normal conditions—but in 1957 the two-lane roads we had to travel expanded the mileage and nearly doubled the time. We regularly drove to the area on Saturdays, so we could relax in advance of Sunday's jam-packed schedule. The "day of rest" called for teaching Sunday school, leading morning worship, afternoon visitation, youth activities, and either preaching or teaching on Sunday evening. Because Indiana was on Central Time while Louisville was on Eastern Time, we usually did not leave Eminence until 9 p.m. by Louisville clocks. With lighter traffic at night, I sometimes could slip through the many small towns and their boulevard stops a little faster, but rarely did we get to the Louisville area until after midnight. While I drove, Martha tried to sleep in the back seat of the car so as to be coherent on Monday. Naps like that aren't always restful. One night, just after midnight, as I drove through Sellersburg, Indiana, on US 31E, I had to brake vigorously to avoid rear-ending the car just ahead of me after the driver slammed on his brakes. Martha rolled out of the back seat onto the floor. Sleepy-eyed, she grasped the seat behind me, peered over the top, and asked, "What happened? We home already?"

Travel on US 31E in particular and Indiana state roads in general put us at greater risk than travel on interstates. As a matter of fact, just three or four weeks into our new pastorate, we were involved in an accident. As we proceeded north on 31E toward Austin, Indiana, on Saturday afternoon, bumper-to-bumper traffic stalled us in the middle of a narrow, two-lane bridge. A drunken driver approached the span from the opposite direction at high speed, lost control of his car, and ricocheted off cars on one side and the bridge's railing on the other. His wild ride ended as he smacked into us with full force, caving in both sides of our 1941 Chevy Powerglide. I don't remember how we got back to our apartment, perhaps by police car, but we left what remained of the car in an Austin junkyard and had to place a call to Eminence to let folks there know that they should not expect us for Sunday services. On Tuesday we received a check from those dear and thoughtful friends to help us buy another car! The driver who hit us, by the way, was uninsured, so you can imagine how overwhelmed we were. Nursing our sore spots back on Macon Street, we both cried.

In the 1950s, Baptist churches did not think of co-pastorates. Eminence Baptist Church hired me, and they got Martha as the bonus. I don't think I would stretch the truth, however, by saying that Martha and I served together as a team and that the members of the church looked to her for counsel just as they did me. As every minister does, I learned to rely on Martha to relay information and pick up cries for help or other signals I needed to respond to. Possessed of extraordinarily keen hearing, she often learned things I would have missed entirely. Although deafness did not limit me during my time at Eminence, I began to experience tinnitus in the form of cricket sounds in my ears; just a year or two after I ended my time at Eminence I had to begin wearing my first hearing aid. Martha also offered valuable counsel and criticism concerning my preaching, teaching, or other aspects of ministry. None of us like criticism, but I was sufficiently secure that I could accept her suggestions without feeling hurt and because I knew that she made them in my best interest.

Stress of travel and occasional disappointments notwithstanding, our two and a half years at Eminence Baptist Church suffuse our minds with wonderful memories. The church was full of what I call "ordinary saints," salt of the earth people whose names will not be known far beyond that small patch of earth but who etched themselves on our lives. The church could only pay $25 a week for a while. Most of them farmers, they didn't have lots of money, but they did other things to compensate. They fed us every Sunday. They gave us gifts. They treated us like family. Some loaded our car with produce every week during the growing season. The first winter, some noticed that I didn't have an overcoat heavy enough to handle Indiana weather; anonymously they sent us $70 for me to buy my first overcoat. When the engine on the 51 Chevy Sedan I bought to replace the wrecked Powerglide blew a rod, one member spent a week overhauling the engine. They replaced tires when they wore out. For years and years we kept in contact, recommending other student pastors and occasionally returning to visit. Eminence was grace abounding. So was Martha.

9

NO SUPER HIGHWAY

I did not come to Southern Seminary with any expectation that I would do graduate studies; however, the idea gradually seeped into my thinking. The prospect of being a missionary pricked my interest, for education was at that time at the heart of Southern Baptist mission work. At the time, admission to the doctoral program required only a B GPA and a minimal score of 50 on the Miller Analogies Test, and not the GRE. Applicants waited with baited breath to learn whether they had passed the MAT, and I was relieved to find that I had done so because I was eager to study in what I considered the strongest department at Southern Seminary. Little did I anticipate that, by the end of my first year, a controversy between the faculty of the School of Theology and President Duke K. McCall would result in the firing of thirteen professors, including the entire New Testament graduate faculty.

Had I known that would happen, I would almost certainly have chosen to go to Duke or one of the other schools that had accepted me. I am not sorry, however, that I chose to remain. I received excellent training in New Testament studies both from the original faculty and, to my surprise, from some who came to put a plug or two into the gaping holes they left.

Southern Seminary's tradition of New Testament scholarship dated back to A.T. Robertson (taught 1890–1934) and his colleague and successor William Hershey Davis (taught 1920–1950), but it was changing significantly when I came to Southern as a slew of bright young scholars joined the faculty soon after World War II. A prolific author with a high view of inspiration of scriptures, Robertson emphasized grammar and word studies. Robertson's most distinguished work was his *Grammar of the Greek New Testament in the Light of Historical Research*, a massive tome of more than a thousand pages, but his four volume *Word Pictures* and popular commentaries exerted much greater influence on preachers. Davis continued the grammatical emphasis but also delved deeply into evidence of Greek papyri. Both held a low view of tradition. One of Davis's former students once told me that when he said the word tradition, he scrunched up his nose and pronounced it in his most nasal tone, *tra. . . di... shun,* like a stench in the nostrils.

True to the Robertson-Davis tradition, the Southern New Testament faculty emphasized a grammatico-historical approach with careful attention to the nuances of grammar and the etymology of each word. Such an approach clearly implied that every jot and tittle of scripture was inspired. In interpretation, however, they sided with Antiochene over Alexandrian exegesis[1], as F.W. Farrar had done in his *History of Interpretation* (1886). No good word was ever said, as I might today, on behalf of the brilliant third-century biblical exegete Origen (185–254/5), a native of Alexandria who had to move to Caesarea in 231, and whose stamp imprinted itself on biblical interpretation from his day on. New Testament scholars and church historians had not yet reappraised early and medieval Christian interpretation to distinguish typology from allegory or tried to see some positive value in the four-tier method of ancient and medieval interpreters—literal, moral, anagogical, and spiritual.

This post-War faculty who taught me, however, were moving beyond their teachers as New Testament scholarship underwent significant shifts. Although A.T. Robertson had introduced graduate students to such methods as Form Criticism, which I have found even in the dissertation of inerrantist icon W.A. Criswell on the John the Baptist sect in the New Testament, he scrupulously avoided letting undergrads get whiffs of them. My professors removed this barrier and brought Southern's scholarship more closely into line with the most respected scholarship found in theological schools both in Europe and North America. Heber Peacock, who had just joined Southern's faculty in 1956 after teaching in the Baptist Theological Seminary in Rüschlikon, Switzerland, for instance, imported the more theological approach to the New Testament of Eduard Schweizer. He had studied with Schweizer in Zürich.

I will not bore you with a list of seminars that I took, but you should know that I received a competent start in this year that would end so tragically. Insofar as I can recall, the graduate faculty in New Testament

---

[1] The so-called school of Antioch emphasized the literal meaning of scriptures. The Alexandrians gave attention to the literal interpretation, but they showed more interest either in the moral (Clement) or the spiritual/allegorical meaning (Origen). Origen's primary concern was spiritual formation of those who listened to his sermons or read his treatises.

gave no hint of the storm raging between them and the president, and they did their best to lay a solid foundation of New Testament scholarship. A New Testament colloquium, in which all professors participated, introduced us novices to the most important writings in different areas—backgrounds, literature, language, archaeology, history, and theology. Trying to both improve my background knowledge and to learn theological German, I elected to do a thorough review of a hefty German tome recommended by Peacock[2]. In a seminar in New Testament archaeology William Morton and Morris Ashcraft carefully instructed us in how to frame a hypothesis and marshal a credible historical argument to support it. I wrote a paper on the menorah art found in Jewish tombs in Palestine. In a Greek seminar on 1 Peter, Estill Jones permitted me and Robert Burks to pursue a keen, Form-Critical interest in hymns from that writing. If I have a criticism of the graduate program, it is that it required no particular number of seminars but left students with the responsibility to prepare themselves for "Prelims," a comprehensive exam that would permit one to write a dissertation. That approach did assure cultivation of independence as a scholar, but many students needed more guidance and got bogged down. Quite a few failed the comprehensive twice, which meant that they could not complete their degrees.

At the heart of the controversy between professors and Dr. McCall lay his effort to shift the role of the president from chairperson of the faculty to chief executive officer of a corporation. The theology faculty resisted the new philosophy and style of administration, but the Board of Trustees sided with the president. When the group of thirteen faculty members refused to yield, the Board dismissed them.[3] Although professors let nothing about the controversy with President McCall slip out during the year, when the storm broke, they took care to communicate with graduate students, usually the students closest to them. As soon as I heard an announcement that the Seminary's Board of Trustees had voted 42 to 7 to dismiss the thirteen, I called on Heber Peacock at his home to express my dismay and support for him and the other professors. He told me that the president had tried to woo him

---

[2] J.F.W. Bousset, *Die Religion des Judentums in späthellenistischen Zeitalter* (3rd Aufl.; Tübingen: J. C. B. Mohr [Paul Siebeck] 1926).

[3] I have discussed the controversy in detail in an article on "The Southern Baptist Theological Seminary" in *The Encyclopedia of Southern Baptists* (Nashville: Broadman Press, 1971) 3:1978–83.

away from the bloc, thinking that he might be "softer" than the others, but that he was at peace with the decision. He showed neither anger nor bitterness—just a quiet confidence that what they had done was right and that God would see them through. I stopped to speak to Morris Ashcraft, one of the youngest of the group with whom I had had a seminar in archaeology that semester. He outlined for me the basic elements of the controversy from the perspective of the faculty. President McCall, in the meantime, met with students to present his case and to try to ease very considerable student anger.

Some of us did find one outlet for the pent up feelings of anger and frustration that roiled around among students. Martha and I were invited shortly after I entered the doctoral program to join Dodeka, a literary club dating back to the nineteenth century that had included some of Southern's most eminent graduates, faculty, and President McCall among them. It happened that Dodeka's annual banquet came smack dab in the middle of the controversy. As chairman of the program for the banquet that year, I sensed that we all needed some way to release our frustrations and that humor might supply that. Now the one type of humor I have had some talent at is satire, so I put together, with the help of my fellow graduate students, a satire on the administration and on the faculty left behind by the "rapture." One weakness of satire is that you can never be sure whether people will understand its subtleties, but I think all of the graduate students knew enough about the event that it could not fail. The very last thing I expected to occur was that Duke and Marguerite McCall would join our festivities. When they showed up, I put a sort of sickly smile on my face and thought, "Oh, boy! What am I going to do now?" I didn't let that deter me long or change our plans. Not only did we deliver the lines we had prepared, we exploded with every ounce of hurt, anger, and bitterness we had inside us. Would you believe it? No one laughed harder or louder than McCall himself. The more he laughed, the more we hammed it up. It doesn't take much reflection to surmise that he needed the same kind of therapy we did. The joke, at least as we saw it, was on *him*, and he could laugh at himself whether he agreed with our point of view or not. From that time on, rather than resenting what we did, he seems to have held me in higher respect even when our views clashed, as they often did. If grace is what causes us to grow toward maturity, that banquet was grace for me.

The depletion of our graduate instructors with the firings in the spring of 1958 placed students in desperate straits. A few opted for other schools. I seriously considered transferring to the University of Chicago, which quickly hired T.C. Smith for a three-year stint. I applied, was admitted, and was given a grant. Martha and I visited the campus and met with Walter Harrelson, then an associate dean. We navigated the impressive campus and then we looked at apartments. When Martha counted eight locks on the doors of most of them, she said, "You can go if you want. I'll see you when you finish." Thus ended any serious thought of transferring there. I could have picked up on my earlier offer from Duke, but our financial situation didn't encourage that option. Some other schools, such as Princeton, discouraged all students from trying to transfer. With deep ambivalence I decided to stay and make the best of the painful situation. That decision turned out happily in time.

For reasons I don't think I can fathom, my fellow graduate students put me in the forefront as a spokesperson when the American Association of Theological Schools sent a committee to investigate the vexed situation. After all, I was a first-year graduate student; others had been around for years. About all I could say was that where once we had an able faculty to teach and direct our studies, now we had none. After studying records and interviewing administration, faculty, trustees, and students, the committee called for the ATS to issue "notations" concerning faculty-student ratio, the supervision of students in the graduate program, and the adequacy of library facilities. They urged the seminary to extend financial provisions for the faculty discharged, establishment of adequate safeguards regarding tenure of faculty, improvement in faculty salaries, and a stronger sabbatical leave program.[4]

As you can well imagine, assembling an adequate graduate faculty required time. Meantime, the seminary had to put a finger in the dike. As Acting Dean of the School of Theology, Henlee Barnette (1951–78) placed some of the burden for keeping a program going on the shoulders of William E. Hull, who had just completed his doctoral work in New Testament, and hired E. Earle Ellis (1958–60) on a three-year contract. Ellis, who had studied New Testament under Matthew Black in Edinburgh, Scotland, offered a seminar in the area of his doctoral work— the Old Testament in the New. Unfortunately, he could scarcely read the Greek New Testament and was so conservative that none of us warmed to his instruction; his contract was not renewed at the end of three years. Barnette also brought Joseph A. Callaway to teach archaeology and

---

[4] Hinson, "The Southern Baptist Theological Seminary."

contracted with George Edwards, Professor of New Testament at Louisville Presbyterian Seminary and a graduate of Duke University, to conduct a seminar on the Dead Sea Scrolls. Edwards's seminar launched my publishing career. The paper I wrote for it, "Hodayoth III, 6–18: In What Sense Messianic?" was published in *Revue de Qumran*, the leading journal on the scrolls. Wayne Ward, a theology professor responsible for biblical theology, offered a seminar in biblical authority. In 1959 President McCall brought in Penrose St. Amant, a former colleague of his at New Orleans Baptist Theological Seminary, as dean of the School of Theology. St. Amant quickly set about the task of hiring new faculty. He added Jeremiah Vardaman in New Testament Archaeology and Ray Summers, formerly Professor of New Testament at Southwestern Seminary in Fort Worth, Texas, but neither addition took place in time to offer graduate seminars before I took my "Prelims."

You can well imagine how butterflies must have flitted around in my stomach during my second year. Preparing for comprehensive examinations over the five areas composing my New Testament major— archaeology, history, language, literature, and theology—meant to prepare for tests set and graded by people with whom, except for Wayne Ward, I had not done any study. How would I ready myself for the ordeal of five four-hour exams taken on successive days in one week? The graduate faculty in New Testament had handed out a bibliography with 600 titles covering these five areas. I carefully subdivided each of the five, read every book that seemed germane and provided the most complete information on a certain topic, and took careful notes. In addition, I scoured journals that might contain articles updating information on these topics. As the exam time approached, I went over the notes several times. I approached each exam with some confidence, knowing from experience that I had a retentive memory, but I also spent at least fifteen minutes quietly meditating before each exam. Not entirely to my surprise, on each exam I had almost complete recall even of obscure facts or views. At any rate my performance impressed all members of the newly constituted committee enough that I was asked to instruct in New Testament introduction and Greek for the next academic year. Graduate students usually taught only Greek, but the desperate faculty situation dictated that I do the introduction too.

Joe Callaway graded my archaeology exam, Wayne Ward New Testament theology, and Ray Summers the rest. As the only graduate-level professor in New Testament, Summers assumed the role of supervisor for my dissertation. At the time, he was supervising nineteen graduate students, so you won't be surprised to learn that I operated almost entirely on my own. More supervision may have enabled me to have worked my way through a dissertation topic with greater ease and confidence, but sloughing along on my own meshed with the way I had had to function throughout most of my life. I had the feeling, too, that standing on one's own feet really set studies at this level apart from other levels. Reading *The Chicago Manual of Style* in preparation for writing a dissertation reinforced that perception.

Several topics for a dissertation came to mind as I prepared for the comprehensive examinations. Throughout my graduate studies, however, the application of Form Criticism to writings other than the Synoptic Gospels piqued my interest. I have no idea what logical steps I may have taken toward the question, but I had an intuitive hunch come to me as I read the Pastoral Epistles in Greek in preparation for "Prelims" that one might arrive at different results about their contested authorship if one first separated the numerous formal elements and then compared the "once-words" in the remaining portions to the "once-words" in letters recognized as unquestionably by the Apostle Paul. The title I came up with was: "A Source Analysis of the Pastoral Epistles with Reference to Pauline Authorship." In the study I came essentially to the conclusion that Paul *could have* written First and Second Timothy and Titus, but I felt uncomfortable with some of my own replies to arguments against Pauline authorship—fitting them into the known life of Paul as recorded in Acts, lateness of ecclesiastical organization as depicted in them, the heresy attacked (Gnosticism), and the doctrine being Pauline rather than Paul's. Over many years of reflection I have wished that I might have had a faculty supervisor push me to look more closely into a theory of possible Lucan editorship because Luke is featured as Paul's companion in 2 Timothy 4:11 and Acts not only shares many words found in the Pastorals alone, it reflects similar organization and other signs of lateness. Why not suppose that Luke pulled together some scraps of Paul to Timothy and Titus adding a few of his own perspectives some time after Paul's death?

Teaching Greek and New Testament thrilled me, and students responded enthusiastically to me as a person and as a teacher. Southern Seminary required Greek of all students, and that made it a challenge to teach, for few had a flair for language or background in it. In "baby Greek," therefore, I attempted to introduce students to some of the key insights I had come to about learning to translate and interpret a language, above all, to analyze rather than memorize and to recall words by association rather than memorization. I even put together a basic plan for a new introductory grammar of New Testament Greek, though a shift to Church history put an end to that. In New Testament introduction I mimeographed detailed outlines that drew together the most recent and reliable New Testament scholarship. I almost got the students bogged down in study of backgrounds for interpreting the New Testament, that is, in Judaism and in the Graeco-Roman world. Teaching brought immense satisfaction.

Given the desperate need to rebuild a faculty not only in New Testament but also in several other departments, Dean Penrose St. Amant approached me about switching from New Testament to Church history, majoring in Patristics. Church history was St. Amant's own specialty, and he and Morgan Patterson had looked in vain for a Baptist who specialized in early Christian history or had the tools, especially the requisite languages, to master that period. I had demonstrated unusual language skills in both biblical languages and had shown a high level of proficiency in my two graduate language areas—Latin and German— passing both exams easily in my first year. According to Ray Summers, I showed knowledge and skill on the Greek exam that he did not possess himself, so St. Amant turned to me.

I must confess that this request placed me in a terrible quandary. I was flattered to be asked to do it. I felt it was a strong vote of confidence, not only from the dean, but also from the rest of the seminary faculty. I was not unaware, however, that a shift like this would place me under tremendous stress, and, even with that knowledge, I greatly underestimated the amount of stress. I knew my perfectionist tendencies would require me to master the field of Church history in the same way I mastered the field of New Testament. And this invitation called for me to teach classes covering the entire field, as someone said, "from Paul to Paul Tillich." While putting together a complete set of lecture notes on twenty centuries of Christian history, moreover, I would feel immense pressure to complete my dissertation on the Pastoral Epistles. The pressures I would have to cope with would not come from St. Amant or the New Testament faculty or other colleagues or from Martha. No, they would come from within, from my own drivenness. Could I handle them?

I didn't know. In my characteristic manner I spent some waking periods at night tossing the questions around. Ambition was kicking in; the dean had virtually guaranteed me a job. Little by little I felt some excitement stirring within me that I could make a more distinctive contribution in an area Baptists seemed to shun than one which drew Baptist scholars like honey draws flies. Focusing on early Christianity would not pull me completely away from my first love—New Testament. With ambivalence irresolvable I agreed to make the change. At the end of the spring semester, I laid aside my work on my dissertation and threw myself into the monumental task before me— preparing lectures for two courses in the history of Christianity.

Almost fifty years later, I have no regrets about this decision. Had I continued to teach New Testament, I would never have experienced the opportunities that opened to me because I specialized in Patristics. You may think about these as coincidences, but I prefer to think in terms of God's mysterious ways of making use of my life—God's providences, if you please, two of which I would like to cite.

Getting to Know Thomas Merton

The first instance of such providence came when I took my initial class of Church history students to the Abbey of Gethsemani in Trappist, Kentucky, on 7 November 1960. I did not take them to meet Thomas Merton, about whom I knew next to nothing. I had seen notices about *The Seven Storey Mountain*, but I had not read the book. I took them there to expose them to the Middle Ages, convinced that they would learn far more from direct contact than from an hour or two of lectures on monasticism. Protestant textbooks scarcely mentioned monastic history and then only prejudicially. Merton was our bonus.

Let me say that we all carried a lot of suspicion and prejudice. Most of the students had never met a Roman Catholic, much less a monk. Other monks took us on a tour of the monastery and then turned us over to Father Louis, as he was then known. Merton disarmed us. He enthralled us with his sense of humor and engaging manner. He spoke about the monastic life as a life of prayer, although I can't recall specifics. When he finished, he asked if we had any questions. One of the students whom I could always count on for a query asked what I feared someone would ask: "What is a smart fellow like you doing throwing his life away in a place like this?" I waited for Merton to open up his mouth and eat that guy alive. But he didn't. He grinned a little and said, "I am here because I believe in prayer. That is my vocation." You could have knocked me over with a feather. I had never met anyone who believed in prayer enough to think of it as a vocation. On the fifty-mile drive back to the seminary that afternoon, Merton's comment kept whirling around in my head along with the Protestant rubric, "God has no hands but our hands, no feet but our feet, no voice but our voice." And I began to pray that Merton and his confreres at Gethsemani might be right, that attention to God might matter more than a lot of our hyper-activism.

Two weeks after that excursion, I got a card from Merton. "Glenn, I'm coming to Louisville on Saturday. I'd like to stop in and see you." At the time we had Saturday classes, and I immediately wrote back, "Great! How about speaking to my class?" He replied by return mail, "I can't speak to groups, but if some of my friends happen to be around, I can talk to them." I got our whole faculty together, and we met with Tom in the Faculty Lounge at Southern Seminary for two hours. I then drove him down to Cunninghams in Old Louisville, his favorite restaurant—a 1930's "speakeasy."

I took students to Gethsemani every semester from that time until Merton's untimely death in Bangkok, Thailand, on 10 December 1968. An agreement with the Abbot, James Fox, about his hermitage prevented Merton meeting with the students beginning in the fall of 1964, but Merton himself always slipped around to talk to me when I brought those groups. He also included me in small groups invited to meet with him in his hermitage. As a matter of fact, I was one of the very first to meet with a small group there on 20 June 1961.[5] Please understand, my purpose in citing this is not to crow about my connection with Merton. Quite the contrary, I feel deep regret that I did not recognize and take fuller advantage of the extraordinary opportunity presented to me. Merton sent me the manuals he put together to teach novices. Daniel Walsh, Merton's mentor in his student days who had come to spend his last years at Gethsemani, gave me a copy of Merton's *Spiritual Direction and Meditation* autographed by Tom himself. I perused those, but I didn't see what relevance they had in equipping ministers who sat at my feet. Not until Merton died in 1968 did I begin systematic reading of all of his writings in such a way as to discover his message to our day, his insistence upon the importance of contemplation in a world of action.

---

[5] Thomas Merton, *Turning Toward the World: The Journals of Thomas Merton*, ed. Victor A. Kramer (San Francisco: HarperSanFrancisco, 1996) 4:129. Others included my colleagues Dale Moody and James Leo Garrett.

The truth is, in 1960 I was not ready, as most Protestants were not ready, to recover what the Protestant reformers had too hastily tossed overboard in the first flurry of reform. Here again it is possible to see why I think of my life as far more indebted to grace than to brilliance or planning on my part. I venture to say that we human beings rarely get what we aim for and are fortunate to discover that, as Douglas Steere frequently said, "Life's interruptions often turn out to be God's opportunities." I probably did achieve my *planned* purpose in taking students to Gethsemani—they learned a lot about the Middle Ages—but the *un*planned has surpassed the planned many times over, as the course of my teaching career will readily verify.

At this point, however, I need to move on to a second gift that came to me as a result of this hard decision—*expanding of ecumenical horizons*. I brought some ecumenical sensitivities with me to the seminary, but the elevation of Angelo Roncalli to the papal office on 28 October 1958 totally transformed ecumenism and generated hopes of Christian unity not imaginable up to that time. Almost immediately after his election in November he started speaking about Protestants as "separated brothers." Less than three months later, 25 January 1959, he announced the calling of a general council to which he invited other Christians to send official observers. The Second Vatican Council, the Roman Catholic Church's twenty-first ecumenical council, opened its first session on 11 October 1962. These momentous happenings coincided almost exactly with the launching of my career as a professor of Church history. I can scarcely find words adequate to express the genuine excitement, exhilaration, and joy I felt then and now in being privileged to take part in, interpret, and instruct others about those events. When I have done my three-mile walks first thing every morning, I have thanked God for permitting me to live to see such a day. Not since the reformation of the sixteenth century has Christianity experienced an event of equal importance. In his all-too-brief reign, John XXIII (1958–63) signaled a new epoch in human history, what I would label the Age of Transcendence.

What did I receive from this that I would not have received had I remained a New Testament savant? My answer is: much in every way. For one thing, as a church historian, I felt a sense of responsibility to try to get Southern Baptists to recognize a *kairos* moment, something special to which they could contribute. When the Southern Baptist Convention met in St. Louis in June 1961, Robert Alley, a professor at the University of Richmond, moved that the Convention elect an Official Observer to represent Southern Baptists at the Second Vatican Council. I realize that I didn't know Southern Baptists well at all, and perhaps understand them even less today. John's "New Pentecost" seemed so patent and powerful, I saw no way Southern Baptists could fail to respond. Although the thought of speaking to 11,000-plus "messengers" terrified me, consideration of the importance of the moment and some kind of inner urge impelled me to second Alley's motion, with his enthusiastic assent. In the two minutes allowed for such speeches, I underscored the importance of what was happening, how John XXIII had introduced a new era of Christian relationships, and pleaded with them to "lend our voices to forces of reform in the Catholic Church." The press circulated my brief remarks around the country, but reported that the convention voted the motion down 10,000 to 100. I'm pretty sure there were more than a hundred favorable votes. Convention leaders, however, undermined the vote by saying that they had not yet received a formal invitation to send an Observer Delegate. The Baptist Joint Committee in Washington, DC, dispatched an unofficial observer who reported on happenings. In an effort to assure that Southern Baptists would keep abreast of the Council I wrote articles at the end of each of the four sessions recounting major decisions.[6] Most Baptist state papers published them.

In this remarkable milieu, specialization in Patristics opened ecumenical doors for me that likely would have remained sealed had I stayed in New Testament, for much of the ecumenical dialogue involving Roman Catholics, Orthodox, Anglicans, and Protestants has revolved around what happened in the first several centuries, not just in the first century. The fact that I had obtained training in both New Testament and Patristic fields seemed to make me acceptable to all of the major Christian traditions and secured invitations to speak, write, and take part in ecumenical conversations at various levels. Down the road, this eventuated in service on the Faith and Order Commission of the World Council of Churches from 1977 until 1992 and involvement in

---

[6] "What Is the Meaning of the Vatican Council for Baptists?" *Baptist Program*, March 1963; "Vatican II, Session II: An Attempt to Improve the Image of Romanism?" *Western Recorder*, 23 January 1964; "The Development of the Papacy," *Western Recorder*, 9 April 1964; *Religious Herald*, 23 April 1964; *The Ohio Baptist Messenger*, 27 February 1964; *Alabama Baptist*, 22 October 1964. "The Ecumenical Movement: What It Is and What It Is Doing," *Christian Index*, 11 February 1965.

numerous national and international dialogues specifically because of my work in Patristics. From the outset, however, I found myself swept into whirling currents closer to home. Students immediately initiated inter-seminary exchanges in which they asked me to assume a prominent role. During the first session of Vatican II, six faculty from West Baden College in Indiana, now Loyola University in Chicago, met with me for two hours in the faculty lounge at Southern. (I seemed to be the only faculty member able or willing to meet with them at the time.) At the end of our exchange, one of the Jesuits, sounding surprised, said, "You really believe in Christ!" I admitted as much and asked why he may have doubted that. He replied, "Well, we have studied your catalogues and did not find a single course on Christology." I explained what students learned in systematic theology and other courses, notably Church history, that focused on Christ. This seemed to satisfy them, for this conversation opened the way for exchanges between students during the next several years.

As I look back over this phase of my career, the graduate student years, I'm genuinely surprised, awed would be more accurate, that things worked out as they did. I feel like I've been swimming in an ocean of grace. Let me say, however, that these gifts did not come without a price. I noticed during my New Testament year (1959–60) that I was losing my hearing. I went to otolaryngologists, first in St. Louis and then in Louisville, to see what I could do about it. In Louisville, Dr. Arthur Juers prescribed glycerine tablets to open up blood vessels to the inner ear. After a week or two, however, I saw no improvement and felt the pounding in my ears too distracting. He recommended that I get a hearing aid. One day I mentioned my dilemma to my distinguished colleague Wayne Oates. He asked, "Glenn, have you ever read the biography of Walter Rauschenbusch by Dores Sharpe?" Sharpe was Rauschenbusch's student assistant who stood by his desk and relayed questions to him from the class. I conceded that I hadn't and read it immediately. Walter Rauschenbusch lost his hearing at about the same age I was when I found mine slipping away. That forced him to resign his pastoral ministry in Hell's Kitchen and to accept an invitation to teach Church history at Colgate-Rochester, his alma mater.

I wasn't entirely unprepared for loss of hearing. There has been some heritage of deafness in my family on my mother's side. My mother was one of four children in her family to experience it, her mother one of eight. As a child, moreover, I had had terrible earaches caused by infections and no medical care. In the Ozarks during the Great Depression people managed on their own. Oil of cloves warmed a little supplied my only relief. I have a hunch that proper attention to infections would have prevented damage to the delicate instrument we rely on for hearing, but whining will not change what has happened.

During the second semester of teaching Church history, I noticed that I was also losing my voice. The loss of voice, insofar as I can see, was not connected with the loss of hearing. It was due, rather, to putting in those twenty-hour days preparing lectures in Church history and completing a dissertation in New Testament. I just wore myself down. Coping with the loss of one faculty vital to one's life work is difficult, but the loss of two can be overwhelming. I felt the floodwaters roll over me. I could see my career vanishing before me. Instead of stopping to rest my voice, I just kept on straining it and abusing it, and I cried out as we all do in such circumstances, "Why me? Of all the people in the world to whom this should happen, why should it be me? Lord, this is me, Glenn Hinson; this isn't just anybody!" Then I began to grit my teeth and clench my fist and say, "This … will … not … happen … to *me*." But I learned very quickly that the vocal mechanism is closely connected with the nervous system. The more I gritted my teeth and clenched my fist, the more I slid backward. It was like scrambling up a hill in loose gravel; the harder you scramble, the more you slide back.

I don't know how long it took or how far I sank into the dumps before it happened. Sometimes, like the psalmists discovered, you have to cry out from great depths. Little by little, surrounded by the love of my wife, encouraged by students and colleagues and friends, I began to hear those words that came to the Apostle Paul in response to his plea for removal of his "thorn in the flesh." "My grace is enough for you, for my power is perfected in weakness" (2 Cor 12:9). "Grace" has to mean more than the Protestant reformers ascribed to it, God's unmerited favor in acquitting sinners. It means, as Augustine insisted, God's gift of Godself, the Spirit, *Shekinah*. "My Presence is enough."

Let me be honest to say that this is not what we want to hear. We want to hear, "You're okay. This is not happening. This is only a dream, and when you wake up, it will have vanished like the mist of the morning." But when you are really in the pit, when you are looking up from the bottom, these are the words you need to hear: "My grace is enough." If I have learned anything from walking through a dark valley, it is how profoundly true those words are. Is that not what some unknown psalmist testified centuries before Paul? "Even though I walk through the darkest valley, I fear no evil; for *you* are with me" (Ps 23:4). When all the world shudders and shakes, you may hear the voice of the shepherd. My most significant lesson from this time of crisis was the need to let down like a swimmer to discover a buoyancy that will hold you up. The saints through the centuries remind us that we live in a sea of love, and if we trust ourselves to that like swimmers letting down into the water, we will find "everlasting arms" and "a mighty right hand" to hold us up. I fear that, all too often, we go through life like people who don't know how to swim and are afraid of water. We flail our arms and wear ourselves out, and then we drown—emotionally, spiritually.

To Paul, God also gave an explanation as to why God's grace is enough—"for my power is perfected in weakness." God's power, love power, works through weakness. Paul had trouble grasping that. He did his best to stop a movement built on the insight that God is our fellow sufferer. Vast numbers in our day will not understand either. Oh, we know a lot about power. One might say that we are obsessed with power. We want more power to put up bigger payloads into space. We want more power to run bigger electric generators so that we can have more comforts and conveniences. We want more power to terrify our enemies so that they will not try anything against us. But our power logic is not God's power logic. Our power logic runs: "The weak are weak. The strong are strong. In weakness is weakness. In strength is strength." God's power logic says: "In your human weakness you may find my power." That, a chastened Paul found, is the logic of the cross. The cross is about letting down to discover God joining us in our vulnerability. In the midst of my own agony I discovered in Dietrich Bonhoeffer's *Letters and Papers from Prison* some "Aha's!" God is not "out there" in detachment from our human weakness but "beyond in the midst of our life," Bonhoeffer insisted.[7] "The Bible directs man to God's powerlessness and suffering; only a suffering God can help."[8]

---

[7] Dietrich Bonhoeffer, *Letters and Papers from Prison*, ed. Eberhard Bethge (enlarged edition, New York: Macmillan, 1953, 1971) 282.

[8] Ibid., 361.

10

CLIMBING A MOUNTAIN

My career hung in the balance before it even got started. I suppose one always goes on hoping with reference to any physical limitation, but I soon surrendered expectations that I would recover my hearing. Recovering my voice required therapy, first at the hands of a professional speech therapist and then in singing lessons given by Inman "Prof" Johnson, who taught speech, and Hugh McElrath, who taught music. I traded with McElrath: translation of Latin documents for his dissertation at Julliard School of Music in exchange for for singing lessons. I had to learn how to speak without putting tension on my vocal chords, a goal that took much longer than I had expected because I had severely strained my vocal chords. More than anything, however, I had to learn how to let down like a swimmer letting down into the water to discover the buoyancy that is there. And I must admit that I'm still trying to learn that. I'm not a patient person. I'm the kind of driver who wants to blow the horn at the car ahead the instant the light changes.

You can visualize my dilemma. Would my voice improve enough to permit the Dean of the School of Theology to recommend my employment when I completed my dissertation? To improve significantly, I needed to get out from under stress or at least find a way to manage it. Yet teaching Church history and writing a dissertation piled stress on top of stress. What could I do to relieve it? Dean St. Amant kept reassuring me and found some funds that enabled Martha and me to take a two-week vacation early in the summer of 1961. We toured historic sites in New England and drove down Highway 1 to Virginia and back to Louisville by way of US 60, with its tortuous curves and its fabulous vistas. For me, though, the answer lay in learning, like Thomas Kelly, to discover an inner stillness in which I could say, "Nothing matters. Everything matters."

I've always thought of myself as a fast learner, but when it comes down to things that stand at the center of life, there are no quick studies. Paul, the apostle of sufferers, laid out a scheme for this kind of learning that seems to fit my own story. In a Hinson translation, he said, "suffering produces stick-to-itiveness, and stick-to-itiveness produces integrity, and integrity produces hope" (Rom 5:3–4). The Greek word I've translated as "stick-to-itiveness," *hypomone*, is sometimes translated as "patience," but in this context Paul seems to be thinking of "endurance." That certainly is what I learned here: sometimes you just have to grit your teeth and keep on keeping on.

Through my own dark night I learned that the human body has wonderful recuperative powers if you will give it a chance. Charles McGlon, my first speech teacher at Southern who succumbed to cancer far too soon in his life, suggested that I stage whisper a number of times each morning when I got up and before I spoke. "It will relax your vocal chords," he said. It did. I started jogging early in the morning, but that soon gave way to walking because I noticed that several older colleagues on the faculty had developed knee problems from jogging and that my own knees soon complained about the jarring on pavement I usually ran on. To strengthen my knees for jogging and walking, I started doing squats before I set out. "Prof" Johnson told me that to keep tension off of my vocal chords when I spoke, I needed to keep the sound bouncing off of my palate. Hugh McElrath urged me to hum. All of the sound advice I got from friends notwithstanding, when I began a lecture or sermon, I learned to expect some difficulty and not to let that resurrect anxiety. Speakers would all like to sound like Harry Belafonte, but wisdom demands that you work with the equipment you inherit. Before the end of a lecture or sermon, my voice sounded better and I spoke freely. For a long while I would feel like I made no progress, get a bit discouraged, and then suddenly and unexpectedly experience a breakthrough to a new level. That was like traveling along a fairly flat plateau with a few rises and dips and then ascending to a higher plateau for another stage of the journey. Little by little, ever so slowly, even up to the present day at age 80, my voice has continued to improve. Students were wonderfully supportive. Indeed, in 1968 they elected me "Professor of the Year," the only time such an award had been given at Southern Seminary.

Where is God in all of this? You may think I go back to Paul a bit too often to interpret and explain my own experience. I won't apologize for doing so, however, for he suffered much and learned through what he suffered. He knew the Christ who suffers with us and in us. In his letter to the Philippians he helps us to understand both what we *should* and what we should *not* expect of God in such times. On one side he seems to tell his beloved Philippians that they should act as if they were completely on their own. "Work out your own salvation (your way of living this life in Christ) with fear and trembling." "Stand on your own feet! You've got a brain and a will. Use them!" Integrally tied to that, however, like a railroad car coupled to the engine, is the causal, *"For* (Greek *gar)* it is God who is at work in you to give both the motive and the ability to do what pleases God." "You are not alone!" Please note what that does *not* say. It does *not* say, "God will make your decisions for you." I've known people virtually immobilized by their expectation that God would "zap" them. They waited, doing nothing. God gave us the intelligence and the sensitivities to make decisions. *We* must *decide.* However, God does add two things to our natural gifts: motive and ability (The Greek reads literally "the to will" and "the to do.") to do what we should do to please God. We have a lot going for us in our natural gifts; on that, fourth-century ascetic Pelagius was right and deserves more favorable treatment than the Church has often given him. But he failed to recognize that natural abilities are not enough. We need more, and we should be thankful that God adds a super-charge. Augustine called grace a *donum superadditum,* "a superadded gift."

I'm sure that Dean St. Amant had some doubts and misgivings when he decided to grant me a three-year appointment to the faculty in 1962 as Assistant Professor of Church History. Had I been in his position, I would have. My voice had improved, but it wasn't what it should be. At that time classrooms weren't equipped with amplification. Could I speak loud enough in a large classroom for students to hear me in the back of the room? Would my voice hold up when I had to speak several times a day? I know the Dean consulted with older colleagues whose judgment he trusted most, especially Wayne Oates, but he took a considerable risk with this hire. He showered me with a lot of grace. I did my best not to disappoint him.

The temporariness of my situation, as you might expect, caused Martha and me to weigh plans with extra care. With both of us already thirty, we knew we could not wait much longer to start a family. During my graduate studies, we had lived in a one-bedroom apartment in Seminary Village, about a mile from the campus. On the modest starting salary of professors at Southern in those days, around $6,000, and with a modicum of uncertainty about my future, we did not dare think big. Martha and I had both grown up during the Great Depression and did not trust the housing market or take risks with indebtedness. On the somewhat tenuous basis of my appointment to the faculty, therefore, we took what we considered a bold step of buying our first house, a two-bedroom bungalow near the end of a cul-de-sac on Gloucester Street in St. Matthews. We got it for bargain at $14,000 from one of the graduating seniors who had taken classes with me.

We settled in at 4010 Gloucester just in time to welcome Christopher Glenn into the world on 27 January 1964. I must confess that Martha handled the advent of a son with much greater calmness than I could muster. On Sunday, the day before he was born, she stayed home while I went by myself to Deer Park Baptist Church, which we had joined when I gave up my pastorate at Eminence, Indiana. On the way home through Cherokee and Seneca Parks a policeman stopped me for driving 38 mph in a 25 mph zone. I explained that I was a bit distracted and in a hurry to get home because my wife was about to give birth. He didn't give me a ticket, but he noted the offense on the back of my driver's license and kept me for thirty minutes discussing whether some New Testament commentaries he was studying were reliable or not. I assured him that they were.

During the afternoon, Martha packed her suitcase and made ready to go, and I kept suggesting that we should get her to the hospital soon. She thought not. She went to bed. Some time before midnight her water broke and she started having labor pains. Fidgety at this news, I hadn't undressed. Now I got up and sat in the doorway of the bedroom until the frequency of her labor pains increased to about a minute apart. I sat there imagining myself delivering a baby and repeating like a mantra, "Hadn't we better go?" We got to Baptist Hospital at 2 a.m., and Chris was born at 6 a.m. Yet that wasn't the end of excitement. I was scheduled to speak in chapel at 10 a.m.! The birth of our first child pumped me up enough that I managed to preach the sermon I had prepared to a packed chapel, but I could not tell you the title of it.

Let me say at this point that I wouldn't give a nickel for deafness or for the voice problems I had to cope with early in my academic career. Yet I wouldn't take a million dollars for what I have learned in and through that experience. It has humbled me. It has forced me to let myself down to where God dwells "beyond in our midst." I don't think it would be inaccurate to say that my career as a teacher benefited, even early on, from the challenges. A wretched voice did not keep students from my classes. Quite to the contrary, it seems not only to have evoked their sympathies, but also to have advance their learning. I believe my struggles may have tossed into the hopper the key ingredient in my philosophy of teaching, to which students have responded so positively throughout my career: the conviction that we teach *students*, not *subjects*. We use our subjects to teach persons, to be sure, but the focus should always be *persons*.

Far too many teachers, especially at the graduate and professional levels, fail to grasp that. They get caught up in their research and publication and push students to the periphery of their concern. Academic institutions reward faculty members for research and publication rather than for teaching. That is easy enough to understand with reference to public universities, for the Morrill Act directed the land grant colleges, now state universities, to supply "knowledge for use," and they have danced to the tune the piper played. At the same time, I fear, they have neglected the task societies most need—the training of an educated and responsible citizenry. As these public universities have grown in power and influence, they have pushed private and church-related schools, including seminaries, in the same direction. I look back with thanksgiving, therefore, that my painful beginnings in academia sandpapered my sensitivities to students. By nature and training admittedly I am a projects person, but my walk through a dark valley forced me to refocus priorities, placing persons before projects. As I have reached the fourth quarter in life, I regularly receive letters of appreciation from erstwhile students. Seldom do such letters mention a brilliant lecture I gave (and there must have been some) or an anecdote I told. No, without fail they remember me as a person connected with their formation as persons. Emphasis on persons and personalism as a philosophy of life may help to explain the rather curious path my career has taken—New Testament ... Church history ... Spirituality.

Such an observation may cause you to wonder how my two fields of specialization intersected at the outset of my career in Church history. Did I simply forget my New Testament studies, abandon my first love as it were and court this new one? Some might compartmentalize fields of study in that way, but I am not constitutionally equipped to do so. For one thing, as I learned it, New Testament studies required essentially the same historical discipline that I applied in Church history. In the case of both the New Testament and Church history, we are trying to learn all we can from Christians of another era about being the Church and carrying out its mission and purpose. As a matter of fact, my first book, *The Church: Design for Survival*, was an overflow of my New Testament studies. One colleague called it a potboiler, but it was an effort to frame a practical contemporary ecclesiology. Baptists had not written much about the nature and mission of the Church, and most of what they had written was polemical. The most serious effort at framing a Baptist doctrine of the Church was that of J.R. Graves, J.M. Pendleton, and A.C. Dayton. These "landmarkists" deliberately sought to disenfranchise all other Christian bodies that did not practice "Baptist baptism." My aim was quite different. I wanted to show how churches today, of whatever denomination, could "discard outdated institutions and practices and replace them with more relevant ones" [1] by returning ever again to an understanding of themselves as the church conceived in terms of images early Christians employed—the New Humanity, the People of God, and the Servant. From these we can draw out implications for the work of the Church in contemporary settings. *The Church: Design for Survival* grew out of a plan that Broadway Baptist Church in Louisville employed me to write to improve that church's ministry to the community and to the world. In 1978 I updated this book against the background of Alvin Toffler's warning in *Future Shock* about the effects of accelerated social change, adding a fourth image, that of the City of God.[2]

Lest you think that some continuing linkage with New Testament studies prevented me from serious attention to Church history, I would point out that I quickly expanded my range of courses in what was to be the area of my special competence—Patristics—with particular interest in the nature and mission of the church and an eye on what would serve to prepare people for ministry in it. I started my career as a professor of Church history with a conviction that the study of Church history would shed more light on the nature and mission of the Church than any other area of the curriculum. Since James Leo Garrett taught the history of Christian doctrine, I opted to develop as my first elective a course Theron Price had taught on Early Christian Institutions, an area that provided much stimulus for *The Church: Design for Survival* and also led to my DPhil Dissertation at Oxford.

Anti-institutionalism raged during the 1960s. Answering questions posed by the first generation of "Baby Boomers" about institutions incited me to want to see whether a case could be made for the contribution of institutions to the winning of the Roman Empire.

---

[1] E. Glenn Hinson, *The Church: Design for Survival* (Nashville: Broadman Press, 1967) 5.

[2] E. Glenn Hinson, *The Integrity of the Church* (Nashville: Broadman Press, 1978).

Teaching this study two or three times to sizeable classes opened my eyes to a dual contribution. On one side, institutions helped the churches to maintain their identity as a covenant missionary people as they incorporated the syncretistic peoples of the Roman Empire—no small contribution. On the other side, adapted and accommodated, they were powerfully attractive to masses looking for tangible assurances that human life mattered. Carefully prepared study based on primary sources resulted in the mimeographing (with Xerox still far down the pike) of a 287-page, single-spaced set of notes on *Early Christian Institutions: Baptism and Catechumenate, Eucharist and Liturgy, Discipline, and Ministry and Organization in Early Christianity.*

My earlier concern for Christian unity got a hefty shot of adrenalin with the election of Angelo Roncalli as Pope John XXIII just as my career began and prompted me to offer as a second elective a study of Eastern Christendom. I cited a number of reasons to justify the study by Baptist seminarians at the time (1962–63): (1) natural interest in anything relating to Christian faith, (2) growth of world awareness as a consequence of new technologies, (3) the present trend toward Christian unity, (4) the current world crisis posed by the "Cold War" as it affected the Christian mission, (5) the fact that there are Orthodox Christians in America, and (6) current interest in the subject. The class drew a large number of students, but I taught it only once because James Leo Garrett, perhaps justifiably, thought it overlapped too much with his History of Christian Doctrine. Orthodoxy does focus on developments up to the Seventh Ecumenical Council in 787. As a result, when I returned from my first sabbatical, I shifted my attention to another ecumenical topic that would not overlap, Schism in the Early and Medieval Church.

At this juncture, however, I need to speak about one more course that I created prior to my first sabbatical, Classics of Christian Devotion, which perhaps as much as any course I have taught augured the twin foci of my work in preparing women and men for ministry: solid academic preparation and deep grounding in the life of the Spirit. William A. Mueller had once offered a course on devotional classics at Southern Seminary, I think, but it attracted few students. The timing for it may not have been right. It would not seem to have been auspicious when I offered it for the first time in 1963–64 either, for the sixties welcomed and celebrated secular theology and the "God is dead" movement. What was prompting me to swim against that powerful current? Let me be honest to say that secular theology did make an important point, that is, that the churches should get out of their "smug sanctuaries" and into the "world" where the Kingdom of God is. Secular theologians followed up on some searching musings by Dietrich Bonhoeffer, and I included Bonhoeffer's *Letters and Papers from Prison* among the classics. Nevertheless, much history seemed to say that the more radical aspects of this radical theology, the "God is dead" part, would soon be dead. People needed something beyond secular humanism's insistence that "Man is on his own" and "This life is all."[3] I didn't have answers to all the questions being raised, but I thought the Classics might have some answers I did not have. More weighty still at this time were the contacts my students and I were having with Thomas Merton. In Merton, centuries of Christian contemplatives seemed to marshal a telling critique of the chorus of praises being sung for the secular city and lifestyle. Merton, in fact, was addressing at this very time a whole series of critical questions to secular theology.[4]

At any rate, response to the course itself confirmed its timing. In the first class I had twenty-three outstanding students. When I proposed it again the next year (1964–65), the registrar asked me to offer two sections with thirty students in each. The year after that (1965–66), he said I would have to offer three sections with thirty students and even that would leave 157 students on a waiting list. Such a response emitted one clear message: students, ministers, everybody were desperately seeking something—divine wisdom, truth, God—and they thought they might find help here.

I'm not trying to be ingenuous when I say that I didn't have some inspired idea as to how to teach classics of Christian devotion. At the time I had not heard of Douglas Steere's use of classics in preparing young men and women at Haverford College to work in post-World War II relief and reconstruction. So, perhaps accidentally, but to my way of thinking, also providentially, I used the methods I had learned and employed in New Testament to teach the classics. Learn all you can about the background—author, date, circumstances of writing, purpose, etc. Carefully study the message. Apply the insights addressed to people

---

[3] These are two of four points in the Humanist Manifesto framed by H.J. Blackham, a British humanist, in *The Human Tradition* (Boston: Beacon Press, 1959). The other two principles are (3) Man is responsible for his own life and (4) He is responsible for the life of humankind.

[4] He collected these in one section of *Faith and Violence* (Notre Dame IN: University of Notre Dame, 1968) 191–286.

in the author's context to us in our context. In order to give some depth to the study, we focused on ten classics. I enlisted the students as teachers. A group of two or three students prepared papers and presented a particular classic in the first half of a three-hour class. In the second half we wrestled with the insights. In that era of vigorous search as veterans returned from Vietnam, one evening class that began at 7 p.m. often had discussions going until midnight. I scheduled one class in the evenings in order to permit wives to take the course with their husbands. Sometimes that necessitated going over my limit of thirty students per class, but wives added a great deal to the discussion. They weren't content to take courses dumbed down for wives. Sometimes the excitement captured even those who took the course only to complete a requirement.

One incident stands out in my mind because it shows what impact a course like this could have and made me think that what I was trying to do mattered. In an evening session of the classics, four very conservative students enrolled and signed up to lead the class in discussion of Thomas Kelly's *A Testament of Devotion*. All four of them served as pastors of small churches and shared rides. At the beginning of the semester they sat out on the periphery of the circle we formed so as to remain as obscure and unnoticed as they could. The first several sessions of the class they did homework or occupied themselves with other business to the exasperation of other students, especially presenters. About mid-way through the course, however, one of them got fired by his church. I immediately picked up on that and secured from the seminary administration funds to help him and his family move to the campus. We discussed with him in class other things that might help. Suddenly these four came alive to what learning is all about. They made a far more thorough presentation on Thomas Kelly's *A Testament of Devotion* than they would have otherwise. After that, they could never pass me in the hall without telling me how much they loved me and the class.

Recognizing that resources for teaching classics were not readily available at the time, I spent spare time during my sabbatical in 1966–67 writing my second book, *Seekers after Mature Faith*, a guide to devotional classics. In doing so, I was slipping into a pattern that has characterized my entire career—seizing an opportunity without fully calculating the consequences and heaping my load higher and higher. Oxford, however, was a good setting in which to write a book on the classics of devotion.

B.H. Dement once taught such a class there and wrote extensively on them. A sabbatical supplied me with blocks of time to write, and I completed a manuscript before I returned from sabbatical. Sales of *The Church: Design for Survival* raised my expectation that I would easily find a publisher for *Seekers*. How wrong I was. With interest in secular theology at its apex, religious publishers didn't think a historical introduction to classics of Christian devotion would attract readers. I turned to Wayne Oates with the thought that he and I might co-author the book. After he read my manuscript he said, "Glenn, this is your book. Why don't I add some psychological commentary to what you have written and see what happens?" Our product caught the eye of a new publishing firm, Word Books, thanks to some intermediation by Kenneth Chafin, a new colleague, and it appeared in 1968. As other publishers had predicted, it didn't make the best sellers list, but it did give a nudge to the study of classics and stayed in print a long time.

My person-oriented approach to teaching drew me more and more deeply toward graduate education by way of a desire to help PhD students pass the required language examinations. Up to this time, all PhD students were required to pass examinations in two of three languages—Latin, German, or French. The failure rate was high for all three and resulted in delays in graduate studies because many students lacked both a gift and training for learning languages. To assist strugglers, I began to tutor students in Latin who hoped to major in Patristics and soon in all three languages. I was fortunate to have had excellent language training in Latin and Greek at Washington University. Although I had not studied German or French in college, I had demonstrated a high level of proficiency in the language exam in German and developed a reading proficiency in French as I wrote seminar papers. In each language I read extensively with students prepping for the exam and passed on to them the insights I had acquired. The number of passes soared skyward. When Wayne Oates was appointed Director of Graduate Studies, he established formal language classes with remuneration for the instructors. I continued Latin classes, but other colleagues then volunteered to teach German and French.

Almost from the outset of my teaching career students approached me about serving as their supervisors for the PhD. Well in advance of the steps that the faculty and administration had to take to approve me as a graduate supervisor—notably tenure and promotion to associate professor—five outstanding candidates, the maximum number, completed the entrance requirements and awaited my return from my first sabbatical. As you might expect, these are the ones who etched themselves most deeply into my consciousness not because they wrote the most outstanding dissertations or achieved the most notable success in life but because they dared to entrust their own education at an advanced level to an untried and unproven novice in a field he clearly had not had time to master. Not unexpectedly either, most wrote dissertations on subjects for which the classes on Early Christian Institutions, Early and Medieval Sects, or Classics of Christian Devotion sowed the seeds. Mark Caldwell, a philosophy major at Baylor, did a comparison of Hutterite and Benedictine ideals. Glenwood Clayton, a Furman history major who spent his career as Associate Librarian at that distinguished school, studied early Christian charity up to 400 CE. Dwayne Conner, an Oklahoman who has spent most of his career as a Methodist minister, studied the contribution of hierarchical organization to the Church's mission in the first five centuries. Thom Meigs, a Georgetown College basketball star, focused on the role of liturgical developments as they affected the evangelization of the Roman Empire. Keith Parker, native of Appalachia and graduate of Berea College who spent much of his career as a missionary in Europe, diverged from the norm in seeking to understand better some of his own roots; he wrote about "Folk Religion in Southern Appalachia."

A better than average start as a teacher and scholar and very noticeable improvement in my voice gave Dean St. Amant enough grounds to propose that I receive tenure and promotion to Associate Professor of Church History at the end of three years. Whether intentionally or not—I'm not sure—his secretary mistakenly brought the evaluations of full professors, whose support tenure and promotion required, and left them on my desk. Unaware at first what they were, I quickly scanned them and found overwhelming and unanimous support for both. Suspecting that I was not supposed to see them, but that St. Amant wanted me to do so, I quickly returned the evaluation forms to the dean's secretary and said, "I'm not sure I was supposed to see these." She grinned and said, "Oh, no, you weren't. Thanks for returning them."

Getting tenure and promotion erased most of the qualms I had had about a future at Southern Seminary. Important as they were, however, they could not have surpassed my excitement at being granted a sabbatical leave for 1966–67, after four years. Sabbaticals usually were scheduled for the seventh year, but Dean St. Amant thought that my shift from New Testament to Church history merited an earlier sabbatical that would enable me to establish a firmer foundation in Patristics.

11

OXFORD

For Oxford to have etched itself on my life, I would not have had to earn one of its prestigious degrees; just to travel there was a grace. For a person of my deprived cultural background, to live in Oxford encircled and embraced by centuries of history was in itself a sacrament.

Martha, Chris (age two and a half), and I went by ship our first time. We sailed aboard the SS Rotterdam to Southampton, England's busiest seaport. Four days at sea aboard a massive liner like the Rotterdam defies description by someone brought up the hardscrabble way I had known in early years. A comfortable cabin, waited on hand and foot, wined and dined at elegant tables alongside people of privilege, exposed to a mélange of entertainments, encouraged to play a panoply of games—how could one complain? None of us suffered from seasickness. Any tensions we brought on board evaporated quickly with the gentle roll of the ship as it plowed through calm seas under our golden globe's gorgeous summer beams. On only one night did we experience turbulence from a brief storm. I remember awakening around 3 a.m. as I felt the cabin rocking more vigorously than usual. I got up to check on Chris sleeping in the bunk above mine. He had turned crossways to brace his feet against the side railing on his bunk, but was sound asleep.

We didn't plan very wisely for the trip, I'm afraid. One colleague who had recently gone abroad counseled me, "Put the fewest clothes you think you will need in one pile and all the money you can lay your hands on in another. Then take away half your clothes and double your money." Going by ocean liner, however, we knew that we didn't need to worry about weight limits airlines imposed. Unaware that the Bodleian Library made all the books I needed readily available, I decided that I should take quite a pile of books relevant to the research and writing I would do. So we bought a huge metal trunk into which we could jam books, clothes for all seasons, toys, and a lot of American conveniences we thought we would need. One thing we didn't count on was the damage a trunk like that might suffer when longshoremen dropped it ten or twelve feet into the hold. When we met our customs agent on disembarking, he asked us to unlock and open the trunk. Rough handling had bent the trunk out of shape and jammed the lock. We couldn't get the lid up. The agent would never have gotten away with it in this age of terrorists, but after ten minutes looking at the battered trunk, he said, "Can ye just pry open a corner and let me get a wee peek in?" One corner was banged up enough to allow that, and he slapped a sticker on it. We left to British Rail the job of delivering it to 2 Ramsay Road in Headington, our home for the year, just down the street from the Quarry, where C.S. Lewis spent his last years; there was no way we could have transported a hundred-pound trunk in or on top of our little VW "bug," shipped from Amsterdam to await our arrival.

The three of us were agog from the moment we drove away from the dock and headed north toward Oxford. I had never driven on the left-hand side of the road, especially in a car equipped to drive on the right-hand side, but it didn't require much concentration to keep that in mind. What I had to catch on to quickly, however, was that some English roads didn't have lanes like American roads, and you might meet cars or trucks passing uphill or around curves with barely enough room for three vehicles to pass. I decided that the rule was, "Be prepared for anything," and hugged the left side of the road all the way to Oxford. Then there were the roundabouts. After a few months of using them I decided they were a pretty good invention, but at the beginning I had to remember to look right as cars merged around them at high speeds heading in several different directions at once.

The English countryside was magnificent that September. Just after wheat harvest, golden stubble decorated the neat, hedge-hemmed fields. Nowhere did you see the clutter and untidiness—rusted-out cars jacked up on blocks of wood, broken-down tractors and farm implements, unpainted barns and houses—or general dowdiness so characteristic of rural areas in the part of America I grew up in. As our little bug nosed its way into historic towns, only an awareness that we would have a whole year to explore kept us from stopping to gape at every thatched-roof cottage, crenulated Norman church or soaring Gothic cathedral, or geometric pathway and flowered park. We only guessed at dates on the basis of style, but everything seemed ancient by comparison with anything we had experienced in America, where antique means seventy-five years old. The word "quaint" kept slipping off of our tongues, by no means in disparagement but in awe of the culture and civilization that gave birth to ours.

We got to Oxford in the early afternoon. Driving as directly north as we could from Southampton on our way to Headington plunged us directly into the ancient city's heart—past Christ Church, its meadows and its majestic Tom Towers, east on High Street alongside the covered market, St. Mary's, the university church, and Trinity College on the left and the University Examination Schools on the right, past Magdalen College on the left and the University Botanical Gardens on the right, across the Thames, jogging slightly to the left and going up Headington Road to our destination. By 1966 Oxford had reached out to embrace newer villages like Headington, but Headington still preserved a small-town character. It had its own neighborhood shops—butcher, baker, men's and women's clothier, newsvendor, etc. Sainsbury supermarkets and superstores hadn't yet displaced family businesses in the Oxford area, as they had by the last time we spent several months there in 1992. Headington had a nice family park equipped with merry-go-round, seesaws, swings, and slides.

We felt fortunate indeed to rent Two Ramsay (pronounced *Rom-zee*) Road, about three miles from the center of Oxford, because housing was not easy to find even in 1966 in this bustling university town. My colleague in Church history, Morgan Patterson, and his family had rented the house the year before, and the owner, W.R. Francis, was happy to be assured that we planned to stay from 1 September 1966 until 1 July 1967. Mr. Francis had rented it *ad interim* to Davis and Kate Woolley, friends from Nashville. Davis headed the Southern Baptist Historical Commission. When we arrived, Mr. Francis beamed as he reported that he had installed "central heating" after the Pattersons had vacated. We soon found, however, that British and American understandings of that term differed considerably. The heat radiated from a heating element laced through a stack of bricks under the stairway leading to the bedrooms and bath on the second floor. Current fed through it three times a day warmed the bricks and they the area contiguous to the stairway, but hardly the whole house. All three of us donned thermal underwear the day we arrived, and we took it off only to bathe, usually once a week, until we departed Oxford on July 1 on our way to France. As a supplement to "central heat," we used "electric fires" to warm up whatever room we stayed in.

Please don't interpret any of this as a complaint. We loved this house. It had a teeny fenced-in yard in the front with roses and other flowers and an attractive English garden in the rear nicely laid out in geometric patterns. It had a productive apple tree or two from which we picked some tasty fruit. Besides, our excitement at living in Oxford overcame any chill we may have felt physically.

After we got settled, we became actively involved in New Road Baptist Church, a historic church founded in 1644 during the English Civil War. Eric Sharpe, the minister at that time, took pride in the church's worship and preached fine sermons, and the members, several of whom held posts at Oxford University, made us feel quite welcome and sustained. The Rev. Sharpe invited me to preach at New Road before we left for Europe, but I must confess that I did not preach the sermon I often had a "holy nudge" to preach from Romans 1:16, "For I am not ashamed of the gospel, ..." University settings seem to sap the life out of preaching. I didn't look for opportunities to speak while I was at Oxford, but one other invitation did come my way. A US Air Force chaplain asked me to give a series of lectures at the US air base at High Wycombe. My effort to critique secular theology, for which I had some appreciation but not enthusiasm, and to offer a spirituality that would meet its challenges, stretched some conservative airmen and aroused a reaction, but most responded favorably.

I lack words to describe my exhilaration at the prospect of studying Patristics at Oxford University. No other university could claim so many scholars specializing in the study of early Christianity. The Church of England ascribes to the Fathers [and Mothers] of the Church the kind of respect and authority for framing its doctrine most Protestants accord the New Testament. Thinking back, I must admit that it was presumptuous of someone who grew up in a Baptist environment and was trained in New Testament studies with a pronounced skepticism about tradition to think that I could master Patristics sufficiently to make my way among some of the world's most esteemed Patristics scholars. Baptist churches do not expose their members to post-New Testament greats such as Justin Martyr, Clement of Alexandria, Origen, Tertullian, Cyprian, Eusebius of Caesarea, the Great Cappadocians, Jerome, Augustine, *et plural*. Baptist ministers do not preach sermons based on texts from the Fathers as scholars at Oxford would do from the pulpit of Christ Church Cathedral. For a Baptist, going to Oxford to study Patristics was not like going to Oxford or other distinguished seats of learning to do biblical studies, for Baptists major in biblical studies, albeit often inadequately, from cradle to grave. Once again, eagerness and desire and grace had to trump a whole row of negatives.

However brash on my part to choose Oxford, I was heartened by several things. The Association of Theological Schools of the United States and Canada granted me one of their coveted fellowships to pursue the project I proposed. Shortly after I began research on the topic, Professor Greenslade strongly encouraged me to apply for the DPhil, confident that my research project would be "very suitable" for that degree. When I wrote Dean St. Amant on 17 November 1966, to make my case for this change of plans, he gave his enthusiastic support and secured the backing of President Duke McCall and seminary trustees. The two elements that required special negotiation were an early departure in the spring of 1968 to put in a fourth term and an additional leave to return to Oxford within about two years, the spring semester of 1969–70 to complete the fifth and sixth terms of my residency. I received formal notification of my admission as a probationer BLitt student—the customary route to the DPhil—on 25 November 1966. The next term, Professor Greenslade recommended that I be recognized for DPhil status.

At Oxford, professors and students talk about "reading for a degree." And that is what students do. There are some lectures, and few lecturers attract a significant audience. In my six terms I attended just three sets of lectures in which I had special interest. The rest of the time I spent in the Bodleian Library climbing the mountain I proposed to climb. Many comprehensive studies like this would have relied on secondary sources, but I was determined to lay aside preconceived notions and let primary sources answer the question I posed. In my sabbatical year at Oxford I read and took careful notes on all early Christian writings up to around 400 CE in addition to many contemporary sources. The answer that I came to was that these forms helped the churches to conserve their identity as a covenant missionary people while incorporating the syncretistic peoples of the Roman Empire and, adapted and accommodated to their milieu, enabled them to attract and enlist converts.

Writing a dissertation of this scope is a demanding enterprise. For me it was made more demanding by the fact that my responsibilities at Southern Seminary did not permit me to pursue it uninterruptedly. On returning to Louisville in the fall of 1967, I was expected to teach ten hours of classes at the MDiv level, offer a graduate seminar in Patristics, supervise five PhD students, serve on faculty committees, edit *Review & Expositor*, a journal published by the seminary faculty, write articles, and speak in diverse places. I fault no one but myself for such a schedule. You can see, though, that it would necessitate laying aside my Oxford dissertation for large periods of time and returning to it when I had brief interludes in which I could crank up my attention again. That is not a good formula for keeping one's focus! Dr. Greenslade wrote several times to ask if I had completed a chapter so that he could report my progress to the graduate faculty of the university.

Completion of the other three terms of my residency requirements necessitated doing some gymnastics with schedule. By departing for Oxford immediately after I finished my last class in May 1968, I was able to complete a fourth term. That, however, had an unusual complication. Martha gave birth to our daughter Elizabeth on May 10. Now I can imagine you "Tsk! Tsking!" my doing this and Martha consenting to it. "Were you out of your mind? What kind of husband and father would contemplate such a thing?" I won't try to defend myself. It bears unmistakable evidence of my single-mindedness. I had plenty of misgivings. All kinds of negatives coursed through my brain and heart. The only thing was, this scheduling alone would permit me to complete my residency at Oxford and write my dissertation within the time frame set by the university. Without Martha's blessing and active cooperation I could never have done what I did, and I will be eternally in her debt for putting up with me in my foolishness.

We arranged for one of the women students at the seminary to serve as a nanny during my absence. I learned when I got home that the nanny had not been a great help. Fortunately, Elizabeth cooperated by sleeping ten or twelve hours every night from day one. The day Martha and Elizabeth came home from the hospital I flew to New York and from New York to London to spend ten weeks in Oxford and another two weeks attending the Assembly of the World Council of Churches in Uppsala, Sweden. Those twelve weeks were among the most trying weeks of my life, reminiscent of those that followed my brother Gene's departure to live with my aunt and uncle. I have always been able to focus my attention and to shut out distractions, and I managed to write a chapter for my dissertation during my ten weeks in Oxford. Yet I experienced excruciating loneliness that I dealt with mostly by busyness. When I was not in the Bodleian, I took long walks in the university parks or around Christ Church meadow. Sometimes I browsed in Blackwell's or visited other colleges. There was no e-mail and transatlantic phone calls cost too much, so I wrote to Martha virtually every day. As you would surmise, I welcomed the end of the term when I could fly to Uppsala and from Uppsala to Louisville.

I've called attention to my ecumenical concern and outlook in earlier chapters. Pope John XXIII and the Second Vatican Council had caused a huge shift in the locus of ecumenism, but the World Council of Churches still claimed the attention of most of the world's churches. Since the Assembly in New Delhi, India, in 1961, it included Orthodox Churches and Observer-Participants representing the Roman Catholic Church. I had a special reason for attending the Assembly in Uppsala. The Assembly's theme—"The World Writes the Agenda for the Church"—epitomized the issue that inspired the subject of my dissertation. A large youth contingent attending the meeting constantly cajoled their elders to get out of their smug sanctuaries and into the world "where the action is." They chided "churchiness" and applauded "worldliness." I wasn't there as a contributor but as an observer, and I gained important insight and confirmation that I was addressing a matter of real moment to the churches.

Return to Louisville plunged me again into the hectic schedule I had pursued the year before. In order to complete the other two terms of my residency, however, I wangled from the dean a half-sabbatical for the spring semester of 1969–70. This time we went as a family. Unbeknownst to us, the Louisville travel agent who arranged our flight did us the debatable "favor" of scheduling us to fly on the first 747 to carry passengers across the Atlantic. Chris, age five, and Elizabeth, age nineteen months, were the only children on the flight. We arrived at JFK in plenty of time, checked in, and, at the appropriate time, boarded. The Hinsons had the honor of going down the ramp and into the gargantuan plane first as flash bulbs popped and cameras rolled. We had seats on the first row of the economy class cabin just behind a bulkhead, Elizabeth in a bassinette. The plane taxied out toward the runway. At Kennedy airport taxiing can take a while and, in our case, did. After about forty or forty-five minutes the captain reported that one of the engines had overheated and that we would have to return to the terminal to wait for another 747 to fly from Chicago. Meantime, the airline bussed all 345 of us through the Big Apple's snowy streets to dine at a nice restaurant. Martha and I worried about Chris and Elizabeth getting tired and cranky. In reality they fared better than the rest of the passengers. They laughed. They played. At 2 a.m. they were still full of energy when we were again asked to head the parade into the second plane.

The flight itself was quite smooth despite January weather. The one drawback from a family point of view is that it was literally the "champagne" flight. All night long, about seven hours, people traipsed back and forth up and down the aisles to replenish their supply of champagne and other free beverages. Elizabeth and Chris both slept soundly, but I doubt whether Martha or I snatched more than a wink or two of sleep. When we got to Heathrow in London, we were asked to disembark first and interviewed about the first flight of a 747. We were glad to give up our celebrity!

For this second adventure to England we planned more carefully. The airlines allowed just forty pounds of luggage per person, so we carried just enough clothes to suffice from January to August. We had had the travel agent rent a car for us to drive from the airport to our new residence in Oxford. As to a place to live, we hit it lucky. Through an Oxford travel agency we rented a lovely third floor apartment in North Oxford from the widow of a distinguished Oxford professor of classical civilization. Mrs. Harrison had taken great care to have the apartment refurbished with what even Americans could call central heating and other comforts. It was fully carpeted and attractively furnished. The only drawback was that we had to ascend a kind of circular fire escape to our apartment and worried a bit that Elizabeth might fall through the upright bars and get hurt. No such accident ever happened, however, and we often took Mrs. Harrison along with us on our outings through the Cotswolds or other places of interest. We even had opportunity to meet her son, who taught at Cambridge, and his family.

The location of our apartment about a mile and a half from the Bodleian Library prompted me to inaugurate a practice that has helped to sustain my health and perhaps to prolong my life. As anyone who has studied in Oxford can tell you, parking near the Bodleian was virtually impossible. From the first, therefore, I started walking. Walking is not only good cardio-vascular exercise; it is meditative. Immediately I noticed a decided improvement in my ability to concentrate on my project, that I thought more deeply, that I was more relaxed, that I was more fully present to others, and that I got more done. When I returned to Louisville in August 1970, I continued the practice of walking three miles a day—the distance from my house in St. Matthews to Southern Seminary. I can't calculate the effects in any precise way, but it enabled me to press forward in the writing of my dissertation.

Perhaps you will indulge me here if I sound overly apologetic. With a deadline looming just ahead I felt much pressure to get something together even if it was not what I had hoped it would be. I felt very confident about my basic idea and my research, but like many a pie, it was only half-baked. The original version of my dissertation was too long. I had to bind it in two volumes and to request an extension beyond the maximum 100,000 words. I submitted it to the Faculty of Theology on 17 June 1971, and requested the scheduling of my *viva voce* (oral) during the Sixth International Conference of Patristic Studies, September 6–11.

Active participation in the Patristics conference made me feel confident that I had gotten on top of my field of concentration. I took an active part in discussion of several papers and in a symposium, and I did not feel apprehensive about the oral examination. My examiners, Maurice Wiles of Oxford and Stephen Sykes of Cambridge, gave me only a twenty-minute exam on Friday, September 10. A twenty-minute *viva* is considered complimentary at Oxford, and I felt that both examiners responded favorably to my answers. As a matter of fact, an American friend who attended the *viva* congratulated me on having gotten such a favorable response. On the basis of their questions, however, I didn't feel as assured as he did. I thought that I had answered well and with some confidence, but they were questioning the clarity of my thesis. As I learned later on returning to Louisville, Professors Wiles and Sykes thought that I had not developed my thesis clearly enough. In accordance with their report, the faculty of theology offered me the option either of taking the BLitt or revising the dissertation with a view to clarifying and tightening up the argument.

Human life is full of failures, but human beings are not well equipped to cope with them. Barrie White, Principal of Regent's Park College, and his wife Margaret kindly invited me to dinner after the *viva*, but I was too rattled to enjoy it. Before I departed Oxford I dropped by Professor Greenslade's lodging at Christ Church to say goodbye, hoping that he might have some word for me about the dissertation and oral. He said nothing. He explained to me later that he had wanted to wait until he could clarify the decision. Flying back to Louisville surrounded by the awful loneliness that accompanies a foreboding sense of failure, I experienced one of the few times of depression I have experienced in my life. I told Martha when I got home that I felt I had failed completely. Before I received the letter from the Board of the Faculty of Theology dated 1 November 1971, Greenslade explained in his kind and gentle way what the decision was.

My sense of desolation could have caused me to throw up my hands in despair and to give up. Several things kept me from doing so, I think. One of those may be a mulish stubbornness that goes back to those rugged Ozark hills in which I grew up. I blame Bertha Brown's gentle prodding for that, "You can make it, Glenn. You can make it." Another would be a deep desire not to disappoint so many people who believed in me: First and foremost, Martha, who sacrificed so much to make it possible for me to do this. Martha typed the two-volume, 618-page first draft, and she typed the revised 514-page second draft. How could I not press on? Penrose St. Amant, who took risks to hire me when I still had voice problems and further risks to back my proposal to do the DPhil. Colleagues like Dale Moody. Dale said, "Glenn, you are not a BLitt scholar." Then there were students who were already working under my direction in the graduate studies program. Another reason would be a bit less definable. It had to do with the reason I undertook this task in the first place. I believed that not only Southern Baptists, but Christians everywhere needed seriously to wrestle with the question: How do we conserve our identity as Christians while we attempt to carry out our ministry in the world? I could see that the examiners were quite right in their criticisms and that I could produce a far more worthy piece of work if I reworked what I had had to do in considerable haste, given the many other things I had to do at the same time.

After reflecting on the examiners' criticisms, therefore, I realized that I could and should revise. Here is what they wrote:

> The basic knowledge of the patristic material used was fully adequate. The shortcomings lay in the way the material was used to constitute an argument. What will be looked for in a revision is a tightening and clarification of this argument. No new material will be regarded as requiring incorporation; indeed some excisions may be advisable.

Professors Wiles and Sykes appended to this some questions to consider in strengthening the argument. Looking backward at this rather prolonged effort, I realized that I had never freed myself entirely from my original intention to write a book and had not switched my mindset so as to focus on writing a thesis. On September 27, therefore, I wrote Dr.

Greenslade, first, expressing "my complete confidence in your guidance." I proceeded thence to say, "*I have decided to revise* in accordance with the suggestions the examiners have agreed to supply."

The revision took me longer than I expected. I had to call on Dr. Frank Stagg to fill in for me as editor of *Review & Expositor* and to drop a number of other projects. For the first time I resisted my tendency to spread myself too thin with many projects and concentrated on the revision. I asked my dear friend and colleague Dale Moody to hear me articulate my thesis and argument in support of it and see if he could spot any flaws in it. I taught a seminar on the subject to about fifteen PhD students and made copies of the revised dissertation so as to give it maximum exposure to critical reading. I sent my revision to Dr. Greenslade in February 1974. He wrote on February 8 that, after careful reading, "I adhere to my opinion that the first version should have earned the degree, in view of the historians' common way of arguing by running explication, and of its scholarship. Still, it was right and necessary to take account of the criticism about sustaining a thesis quite explicitly."[1] I responded to specific suggestions he made. Three copies of the revised dissertation arrived in Oxford on 25 March 1974. The Secretary of Faculties notified me on June 20 that the Board of the Faculty of Theology had granted me permission to supplicate for the Doctor of Philosophy. Maurice Wiles later told my former colleague Frank Tupper that I had turned a good book into a good thesis. I would like to have taken part in the commencement at Oxford and proposed initially deferring the reception of my degree until my sabbatical in 1975–76. Impatient as I am, however, I proceeded to receive the degree *in absentia* and to pick up my diploma when I attended the next International Patristics Conference in August 1975.

I may shock you when I say it, but I look back on the experience as one of life's great gifts of grace. I learned so much—about myself, about my limitations, about writing, about teaching, about everything. About *myself* I learned that, however capable, I could not immerse myself in an endless number of projects and do quality work, work that matters. I was too much a "Martha" "worried and upset about many things" and neglecting "the one thing needful" (Luke 10:41–42). Don't let busyness cause you to miss what Caussade called "the sacrament of the present moment." This experience forced me, as nothing else had, to focus my energies. About my *personal* limitations plenty of experiences had spoken

---

[1] Stanley L. Greenslade, Letter to Glenn Hinson, 8 February 1974.

loudly enough for me to hear, but they did not address *academic* limitations, and I didn't pay sufficient attention to Oxford's chief message: significant work takes time and focus. Some Oxford scholars spend their whole lives wrestling with one issue and producing one book. About *writing* I grasped for the first time the principle that has guided all of my writing since—that every essay, whether dissertation or book or article or whatnot, should have a thesis. Readers want ideas they can learn from. They are not interested in your homework. About *teaching* I learned the importance of grace. Stanley Lawrence Greenslade, already suffering from the cancer that would soon claim his life, set before me a model of gentle guidance and encouragement I can only pray that I have tried to extend to others.[2]

Before signing off on this chapter, I should mention one other role I had to play at Southern Seminary as I brought my revision of the dissertation to completion. During the early 1970s, the faculty of the seminary experienced sagging morale. A major factor behind it was the effort of Dean William E. Hull to upgrade the quality of faculty by raising standards for promotion, especially to full professor. Some associate professors had waited as long as twelve years when, normally, most expected promotion after six years. My promotion to full professor in 1973, well ahead of numerous persons with much more seniority, broke the logjam, but it did not put a quietus on faculty complaints. When invitations came to me from other schools, I felt conflicted but considered them seriously. In a 28 February 1974 journal entry, I reflected on a visit I had made to Rice University in Houston. "Golly— how affluent that school is as compared to Southern Seminary!" I wrote. "Yet I'm not sure I could go there, even if asked, which I may not be. Rice is still not the center of the Church, and I am a churchman. I'll have to wait for a specific invitation."

When Dr. McCall picked up on the morale problem in the fall of 1973, he asked the Faculty Affairs Committee to study and report on it. On 26 November 1973, the committee, headed by Hugo Culpepper, ascribed the problem to "a style and philosophy of administration of fifteen or twenty years duration." McCall wanted to know whether "fifteen or twenty years" was meant specifically or generally. Culpepper replied that some interpreted specifically, others generally. Interpreting the report, which only Dean Allen Graves voted against, as a vote of no confidence, McCall asked the faculty to elect seven persons to serve as an

---

[2] Professor Greenslade died Christmas week 1977.

Ad hoc Advisory Committee. I was one of the seven and elected vice-chairman. Culpepper chaired the committee. After meeting regularly with the committee for a year, the president put the issue back on the faculty agenda for 20 May 1974 and demanded that the faculty either rescind or reaffirm the original report. With considerable fear of a repeat of 1958, we referred his motion back to the Faculty Affairs Committee. As a member of the Ad hoc Committee, I gave this rationale: (1) that the original was subject to varied interpretations and adopted too hastily; (2) that it had subsequently been reinterpreted by the Ad hoc Committee and Joint Faculty in terms of procedures; (3) that some matters of concern had been resolved and that others would be dealt with further in standing committees; and (4) that this action was in the best interest of the morale of the total seminary community. Tension built up over the weekend. Because Culpepper was leading a retreat and could not be reached, I consulted with J.J. Owens, another committee member, and then asked Dale Moody, not a committee member, to go with me to speak to McCall. We talked to him about an alternative to rescinding or reaffirming the original statement, that is, a substitute statement with a rationale such as I gave as a preface. As the final outcome, the faculty reaffirmed confidence in McCall as president but did not rescind the original statement. It was a close call.

This faculty/administration rumble did exact a price in the resignation of Bill Hull from the offices of dean and provost. McCall had appointed him in 1969 to succeed Penrose St. Amant over considerable faculty opposition. That was understandable in view of the fact that his philosophy and style of administration coincided with McCall's more closely than St. Amant's had.[3] Unfortunately much of the faculty discontent with these focused on him rather than McCall. Shortly thereafter, near the end of the fall semester in 1974, he announced his resignation as dean and provost. On December 23, the president asked divisions to select a committee of six to serve as a search committee for dean. I was a little surprised that I was not chosen to represent the Historical-Theological Division until Eric Rust explained that he and others wanted me to be dean rather than any of the three other faculty members who coveted the office. At the time I told colleagues who asked that I would consider an invitation seriously, but time would teach me

---

[3] I have described Penrose St. Amant's tenure as dean at Southern Seminary in a *Festschrift* dedicated to him. E. Glenn Hinson, "C. Penrose St. Amant: Dean at Southern, 1959–1969," *Perspectives in Religious Studies*, 16 (Winter 1989): 41–51.

that my only qualification for serving as dean was that I had been a critic of every dean I had served under. In my journal for 23 December 1974, I wrote, "My concern is an administration without pretension and person-centered. I would move the dean's office out of the 'upper room' and put it in the midst of the faculty. The door would always be open to faculty or students. The big question is: Can I give up much teaching and scholarship at a time when I am beginning to get international recognition?" Well, I never had to answer that question. Dr. McCall did tell me that a number of colleagues were nominating me, but he wondered if I wanted to be an administrator. He would have to "train" me. I've always been happy that things did not work out that way. At the time I was grieving over the death of Charles McGlon, Professor of Speech at the Seminary, with whom I had enjoyed a close friendship from my student days. I noted in my journal that I missed Charles. "He irritated some by his perfectionism, but he had talent. And what determination! How many would have survived after open heart surgery as he did, taking 30 pills a day!"

12

A CALLING WITHIN A CALLING

Long years have taught me that most of us will experience more than one type of calling. I found that happening to me early on as I taught at Southern Seminary. "The mother of invention" began subtly to create what I would have to think of as "a calling within a calling" that eventually emerged as a major focus. I'm speaking here about the spiritual formation of ministers.

When I came to Southern Seminary as a student in 1954, few Protestant seminaries knew anything about or paid any attention to the kind of spiritual formation Catholic priests received throughout their seminary training. Like Southern, the typical Protestant school focused almost exclusively on the Body of Divinity and vocational training. To be brutally honest, if Catholics did something, Protestants didn't do it lest they seem to betray their "protest." Not many, I suspect, discerned it happening for a while, but, as Pope John XXIII prayed for his "New Pentecost," subtle changes of outlook and attitude started to open the way for Protestants, including Baptists, to do something about spiritual preparation of ministers. I don't think I can tell you why this mantle should have fallen on me. I certainly didn't plan for that to happen. Indeed, for a long time, the very thought of undertaking a task that seemed more personal and subjective than academic study aroused considerable anxiety. I planned to be the best Patristics scholar and teacher of church history I could be and worked hard at them. If I planned anything tangential to those, it was initially to nudge my students in particular, and Southern Baptists in general, toward the powerful ecumenical stream given new impetus by what was happening in the Roman Catholic Church. I defended the ecumenical movement against an attack by two Southern Baptist ministers.[1] Even in offering a course on "Christian Devotional Classics" I admit that I had an ecumenical agenda, for the classics represented the whole Christian tradition and helped students to understand and appreciate its vast

---

[1] "The Ecumenical Movement: Threat or Hope?" *Christian Century* 81 (23 December 1964): 1592–95.

variety. In the strange way God's grace works, however, I found myself tugged by a kind of subterranean tide into a role that would claim more and more of my attention and perhaps account for what others give me too much credit for.

I must confess that again I felt like I had when youth at First Baptist Church of Affton elected me to preach the sermon for Youth Sunday when, in 1969, Dr. Duke McCall asked me to respond to a paper by Camillus Elspermann, a professor at St. Meinrad Seminary, on the subject of "The Spiritual Formation of the Seminarian." The paper was to be presented at a convocation of faculties of TEAM-A, Theological Education Association of Mid-America, an organization comprised of Southern and four other seminaries in the area—St. Meinrad, Asbury, Lexington, and Louisville Presbyterian. I was a babe in comparison with respondents from the other three TEAM-A seminaries—Kenneth Kinghorn from Asbury, a United Methodist school; William Barr from Lexington Theological, a Disciples school; and Ulrich Mauser from Louisville Presbyterian. I've never asked him why he chose me, but I think Dr. McCall overvalued my readiness. It was probably a matter of choosing among the unprepared. In my favor were the contacts I had cultivated with Thomas Merton and the Abbey of Gethsemani since 1960, the astonishing success of my classes in Classics of Christian Devotion begun in 1963, and publication of *Seekers after Mature Faith* in 1968.

What my selection for that task says is that someone other than I discerned a nuance to my calling in this community of learning that I had not recognized in myself. At the time I was deeply immersed in teaching Church history, supervising my first group of PhD students, writing my Oxford dissertation, and editing *Review & Expositor*, the faculty journal. Whatever I was contributing to the spiritual formation of seminarians was response to a need, a need I perceived first in students and in churches and perhaps most of all in myself. In these circumstances it may have seemed strange, but I had growing within me a conviction that genuine piety need not conflict with excellence in scholarship or vice versa. I could see demonstration of their harmonious marriage as I read Philip Schaff's eight-volume *History of the Christian Church* or Jean Danièlou's and H.I. Marrou's *The Christian Centuries*. At Oxford, S.L. Greenslade, my supervisor, modeled a harmony of faith, love for the Church, and sound scholarship. What I was learning there was gradually purging perceptions I sometimes picked up in Southern

Baptist circles that scholarship and piety should remain far apart. It was either/or. If you were devout, you were no scholar; if you were a scholar, you had to flaunt your disdain for piety.

As I placed more and more emphasis on using my subject to educate persons, I found myself in desperate need of a deeper spiritual foundation such as I had found in Thomas Merton. If I did peek-a-boo behind my subject, hiding myself from myself and from others, I might not have had to grapple so fiercely with my own vulnerability as a human being. As soon as I let myself become vulnerable in listening to students, walking with them, and talking to them, I recognized my own need in theirs. They wanted and needed something more than information about what happened when Constantine halted persecution of Christians and then increasingly threw himself behind the evangelization of the Roman Empire. They wanted and needed not just *in*formation; they wanted and needed *formation*, and so did I, if we were to be instruments through which God would carry out the purpose of the church and its ministry. Together, we perceived that our spiritual life is "where it's at."

In this phase of my career, I must concede, I was feeling exceedingly ill-qualified for teaching others about the spiritual life. Here I was trying to offer some guidance to students in an area where, as Thomas Merton often said, "we are all beginners!" I didn't have the confidence in this field that I did when I taught the "facts," even the disputable ones, of Church history. I sometimes acted more confident than I felt, but I learned to live with questions I could not answer and to admit I could not in an era when veterans returned from Vietnam with scarcely anything but questions. My loss of hearing and then my struggle to recover my voice were grace aplenty here, for they forced me to realize that human life, my life, meant vulnerability. It is okay to be vulnerable, and it is wise to admit it in the same way the Apostle Paul did. We are "earthen vessels" (2 Cor 4:7). We have to learn to yield ourselves with all of our ineptness up to God, to share it with others, and to seek together to cope with it. In his paper Father Elspermann framed a question that I found helpful: "Formation for what kind of ministry in what kind of Church in what kind of world?" In my response I revised that just a bit: "Formation of what kinds of ministers for what kinds of ministry in what kind of Church in what kind of world?" By this point in my career I had learned through experience that I did not want to see Southern Seminary turn out ministers who thought they knew more than God did.

Far more in accord with what the Apostle Paul teaches us, I wanted ministers who could confess their vulnerability and inadequacy so that God could use them as God used the first bearers of the good tidings.

If you are familiar with the 1960s and 1970s, you will understand why "radical" or "secular" theology has had much to do with the shaping of my perspectives on spirituality and spiritual formation for ministry. There are some *kairotic* moments that have seminal importance in one's life, and this was one of those for me. To explain my perspective and any contribution I have made in this area, I need to speak about the theological cauldron that boiled and bubbled during this period as I pursued the DPhil at Oxford (1966–74) and familiarize you with my response to it.

As I was doing an apprenticeship as a Church historian during the "secular sixties" and early seventies, I also was doing an apprenticeship as a spiritual thinker and writer and attempted to respond to questions raised by the "radical" or "secular" theology that seemed to dominate it. Those who lived through that time will recall the widespread fascination with Dietrich Bonhoeffer's *Letters and Papers from Prison*, first published in English in 1953, and his musings about "religionless Christianity," a phrase first used by Karl Barth, whether our world "has come of age," whether modern people any longer have a capacity for a "God hypothesis," and whether we must now live for God in a world without God.[2] Behind all of that, of course, was an effort to make some sense of the "profound godlessness" of the age.

Scholars will debate forever how to interpret Bonhoeffer's musings, but not many construe them today in the same way that proponents of secular theology did in the sixties and seventies. At that time, there were various degrees of secularizing. Some theologians sought chiefly to recognize and affirm some values in secularity. In *Honest to God*, for instance, John A.T. Robinson, the Bishop of Woolwich, tried to get his readers to give up thinking about God as "out there" and to accept instead Bonhoeffer's felicitous vision of God as "beyond in our midst." He urged them to think of Christ as "the Man for others" and to cultivate a "worldly holiness," going "through the world to God" rather than fleeing "from the world to God."[3] In 1965, Harvey Cox, a Baptist

---

[2] Dietrich Bonhoeffer, *Letters and Papers from Prison*, ed. Eberhard Bethge (enlarged edition; New York: Macmillan, 1953, 1971) 270ff., 325, 346.

[3] John A.T. Robinson, *Honest to God* (London: SCM Press; Philadelphia: Westminster Press, 1963).

theologian teaching at Harvard,[4] celebrated prominent features of the "secular city"—anonymity, mobility, pragmatism, and profanity—as "liberating." Four years later, however, he retreated from that to dance a jig for medieval perspectives in *The Feast of Fools*.[5]

Some secular theologians ascribed the experience of the absence of God in modern society to cultural factors. Paul M. Van Buren and Gabriel Vahanian spoke of "the death of God," but they used the phrase to describe modern humans' inability to bring God into the picture. Ours is a "post-Christian era." Vahanian insisted that secularity is "a Christian obligation" and "a renewal, a reaffirmation of the Biblical doctrine about the nature of this world and the meaning of the believer's presence in it."[6]

Van Buren, too, wrote about *The Secular Meaning of the Gospel Based on an Analysis of Its Language*.[7]

Thomas J.J. Altizer, a professor of English at Emory University, and William Hamilton, a theologian, advanced a far more radical explanation. Seizing upon Nietzsche's announcement of the death of God, they found a way to attach it to Bonhoeffer's reflections in *Letters and Papers from Prison*. In their primitive state human beings needed God and religion to cope with their insecurities. Gradually, however, humankind has "come of age." In Jesus, rightly interpreted, God finally made it possible for humans to stand on their own two feet. God literally poured Godself into a human life and died. Now God is no more. What we have to do is to live with the absence of God that we are all experiencing. That means that we will have to live fully human lives. Allen R. Brockway, a Methodist minister, framed a spirituality based on the Altizer/Hamilton model. He contended that "secular saints" find little meaning in religious language in a "steady state world" such as ours. This world is "bereft of religion" and God is only a projection of our selves. Traditional ways of addressing God as Father, Son, and Spirit should be used to explain how we interact with this world. God is "definition" of the limits of human capacities; Christ is "possibility," the

---

[4] Harvey Cox, *The Secular City: Secularization and Urbanization in Theological Perspective* (New York: Macmillan, 1965) 38–84.

[5] Harvey Cox, *The Feast of Fools* (New York, Evanston, and London: Harper & Row, 1969).

[6] Gabriel Vahanian, *The Death of God: The Culture of Our Post-Christian Era* (New York: George Braziller, 1957, 1961) 61.

[7] Paul M. Van Buren, *The Secular Meaning of the Gospel Based on an Analysis of Its Language* (New York: Macmillan, 1963, 1966).

fearless stepping into the unknown; and the Holy Spirit is "decision, a man's [or woman's] own decision to receive the Christ possibility, the only life-giving possibility." The three persons of the Trinity are, for us today, "symbolic ways of apprehending the reality of their relationships with the world around them—and at the same time affirming a particular character for that relationship."[8] Secular saints can live without a God-hypothesis. Their faith is in themselves. They have everything under control at all times. They do not need the church and religious symbols, though they may put up with them. If they go down in an airplane crash, they won't think about God or their own survival but whether they paid their insurance premiums so that their families will be provided for. Shades of Nietzsche's "*Übermensch*"!

Such was the matrix in which my ideas about spirituality were gestating. You would err badly to think that I was ready to do much except let my thinking incubate as I studied and taught and preached. Nevertheless, I had some things pushing or pulling me from the womb. One of those was an invitation to give my first named lectureship. As I prepared to return to Oxford to complete my residency in the spring of 1970, I received an invitation from South Wales Baptist College in Cardiff to deliver the Edwin Stephens Griffiths Lectures.[9] I suppose I could have lectured on the subject of books I had already published—*The Church: Design for Survival* or *Seekers after Mature Faith*—but I thought a name lectureship called for something fresh. I chose instead to lay out the main lines for what would eventually appear as *A Serious Call to a Contemplative Lifestyle*. Engaging in dialogue with students in my course on devotional classics and lecturing at various colleges and universities had led me to conclude that although secular theology was enjoying a merry ride in the late-sixties, it would not remain in vogue forever. Students found far more help in searching reflections on how God is present to us even when we experience the absence of God, as in Augustine's *Confessions* or John of the Cross's *The Dark Night of the Soul*. Delving deeply into such mature writings of Thomas Merton as *Conjectures of a Guilty Bystander*, they soon grew skeptical of discordant notes in Harvey Cox's hymn of praise to *The Secular City*.

---

[8] Allen R. Brockway, *The Secular Saint* (Garden City NY: Doubleday, 1968) 92, 105.

[9] I owed this invitation to my colleague Wayne Oates, who was initially invited to give the lectures. He declined due to caution about flying after having back surgery. He kindly recommended me.

Let me be candid to admit that I thought secular theologians had put their finger on a problem with which Christianity, and perhaps all religions, have struggled through the centuries, the problem of compartmentalization, placing our religious life in one sphere, our everyday life in another. Genuine devotion, as I understood it, should encompass the whole of our lives. Compartmentalization is what the Hebrew prophets inveighed against and what Jesus of Nazareth indicted in Pharisaism—"tithing mint, dill, and cumin" but neglecting "the weightier matters of the Law" (Matt 23:23).

What I did not agree with was the answer secular theologians gave to the problem: Because you can't stop secularization, throw in the towel and join it. Up to that time, much to my regret, I had not seen Thomas Merton's critique of secular theology that would have sharpened my own analysis, although it was published in *Faith and Violence* in 1968. As I analyzed it at the time, the root problem does not rest in secularization per se but in what it has cost, a loss of transcendence. The great metahistorian Arnold Toynbee warned that this civilization we are creating poses the greatest threat to our survival as persons of any civilization that has existed since our ancestors became human precisely because of its diminishment of God-consciousness.[10] Theodore Roszak, a historian of higher education, reiterated the point, contending that scientific orthodoxy has left us with "the single vision," rational and empirical powers, and caused us to neglect the powers of transcendence.[11] Like Bonhoeffer, another martyr to the Nazis near the end of World War II, Father Alfred Delp, asked whether Westerners today are fit for religion and for God.[12] The technocratic society we are developing complicates immensely the human search for God. As many benefits as metropolis brings us, it also depersonalizes and dehumanizes. It causes a loss of self-transcendence. Princeton sociologist Ashley Montagu questioned whether we can remain human in cities larger than a few thousand people, for massive cities keep us from being involved in one another's lives. Human beings have "an instinctive need for harmony and peace, for tranquility, order and meaning," Thomas Merton insisted, but the modern lifestyle denies us these essentials. Only

---

[10] Arnold Toynbee, *Experiences* (New York & London: Oxford University Press, 1969) 316.

[11] Theodore Roszak, *Where the Wasteland Ends* (Garden City NY: Doubleday, 1972).

[12] Alfred Delp, *The Prison Meditations of Father Delp* (New York: Macmillan, 1963) 93–97.

if we discover the Ground of our Being, divine Wisdom, will we recover our sanity and our humanity.[13]

You may think me overbold to have attempted anything like this, but I took up the challenge hurled at us by Bonhoeffer and secular theology and tried to visualize God not "out there" but "beyond in our midst." Writing in the conservative South, I was keenly aware that many would simply dismiss the challenge by insisting on the "inerrancy" of the Bible, worldview and all, and repudiating the claims of science. That approach would only complete the compartmentalization—here, one's religious life, and there, one's everyday life, and ne'er the twain shall meet. It would pit sacred against secular, natural against supernatural, here against hereafter, and immanent against transcendent. It was a brash undertaking, but I was not convinced, as radical secularizers contended, that because many had trouble conceptualizing God that we should give up the effort to enable them to do so any more than I would want medical doctors to stop looking for a cure for a mysterious disease I had. A student observation put in bas-relief the problem of the secular approach.

At some time during this period, the American Association of Theological Schools (later Association of Theological Schools in the United States and Canada) sponsored Charles Whiston, a professor at Church Divinity School of the Pacific, in a series of workshops on prayer. At one of these, which Whiston conducted at Earlham College in Indiana, a student deeply influenced by "God is dead" theology of Sam Keen, who taught at Louisville Presbyterian Seminary, blurted out, "I don't know why we waste time talking about prayer. When I kiss my wife, that's a prayer. When I take out the garbage, that's a prayer." I kept it to myself at the time and let Whiston respond, but my internal reply was, "Yes, but I like to make a distinction between kissing my wife and taking out the garbage."

Once again, providentially, I think, my students and I were beneficiaries of timing. Teilhard de Chardin's theological and philosophical writings, unpublished until his death on Easter Sunday, 1955, had been appearing in a flood at this time and pointed to a way in which Christian faith could reconcile itself with an evolutionary model, enabling us to see how the Transcendent Personal touches all of life. Notwithstanding criticisms of Teilhard's theory of evolution or his

---

[13] Thomas Merton, *Faith and Violence* (Notre Dame IN: University of Notre Dame Press, 1968) 215.

seeming underestimation of the seriousness of evil, he handed out drafts of cold water to thirsty travelers in the desert with his insistence on God's ubiquity and nearness for those who know how to "see." It was not at all surprising to discover that a dialogue between Christians and Marxists at this time in Europe gave birth to the theology of hope. I will always be thankful that, during those first days in Oxford in 1966, I discovered Teilhard's *The Divine Milieu* in Blackwell's. In those searching, skeptical days as I looked for a way to bridge the gulf between everyday and Sunday lives, I needed to hear from a precocious thinker like Teilhard words like these: "God, in all that is most living and incarnate in him, is not far away from us, altogether apart from the world we see, touch, hear, smell, and taste about us. Rather [God] awaits us every instant in our action, in the work of the moment."[14] Also, "by virtue of the Creation and, still more, of the Incarnation, *nothing* here below is *profane* for those who know how to see."[15] "By means of all created things, without exception, the divine assails us, penetrates us and moulds us. We imagined it as distant and inaccessible, whereas in fact we live steeped in its burning layers. *In eo vivimus.*"[16]

Taking a cue from Teilhard, I sought first to show how we express our commitment to God through everything we do and not just through intentionally consecrated activities. One of his prayers startled me the first time I read it, but the longer I reflected on it, the more I recognized that it supplied a key to overcoming compartmentalization:

> The more I examine myself, the more I discover this psychological truth: that no one lifts his [or her] little finger to do the smallest task unless moved, however obscurely, by the conviction that he [or she] is contributing infinitesimally (at least indirectly) to the building of something definitive—that is to say, to your work, my God.[17]

In his *Letters to a Traveller*, Teilhard explained how a friend's business could effect moral progress. Our universe is not merely moving at random but is being pulled forward and upward toward the Omega Point—toward God. Because this man's business is going well, he is injecting a little more health into humankind. We do what we do with a subconscious awareness that we are contributing to the building of the

---

[14] Teilhard de Chardin, *Le Milieu Divin: An Essay on the Interior Life* (London: Collins, 1964) 64.

[15] Ibid., 66.

[16] Ibid., 112.

[17] Ibid., 55–56.

Body of Christ, the whole universe. "Because you are doing the best you can (even though you may sometimes fail), you are forming your own self within the world, and you are helping the world to form itself around you. How, then, could you fail from time to time to feel overcome by the boundless joy of creation?"[18]

In the Griffiths Lectures, therefore, I underscored Teilhard's conviction that we should seek to devote ourselves to God through our activities. I must admit that I was not quite as confident as he that we will do so through all of our activities whether we intended to do so or not. What made me demur at that point was an awareness that some persons plan deliberately to thwart divine designs or human hopes. In addition, William Law's powerful argument about intention in *A Serious Call to a Devout and Holy Life*, which students sometimes selected for classes on devotional classics, had seeped into my pores. You can see its impact in the choice of title for my own book. As I listened to secular theology's urgent call to respond to "the beyond in our midst," therefore, Thomas Merton's effort to awaken westerners to the urgency of contemplation in a world caught up in "activity for activity's sake" supplied a crucial ingredient for my own thinking and activity.

Please don't assume that at this time I had a clear picture of what contemplative lifestyle would involve. Nor would I classify myself as more than a contemplative-aborning. In 1969 and 1970 I was still reeling from the news of Thomas Merton's accidental death in Bangkok, Thailand, on 10 December 1968. When Brother Patrick Hart phoned from Gethsemani to invite me to the funeral mass, the news struck me a devastating blow. Much of the vast Merton corpus we now know—his journals, his letters, articles, and even books—had not yet appeared in print, and I did not begin to make a determined effort to read everything already in print until I started receiving invitations to give lectures about him. At this juncture I relied much more heavily on what I was learning about the life of the Spirit in today's world through the devotional classics whose insights we sought to wrest from them in these classes.

I recognized at once that, like Merton, I had to make a case for prayer in a world, even in a church, that seemed intent on pushing God out to the periphery of human life. To a considerable extent, my efforts here paved the way for a second class I offered in spirituality, "Prayer in Christian History," but ten years passed before that happened in 1980.

---

[18] Teilhard de Chardin, "To Max Bégouën." *Letters from a Traveller 1923–1955* (London: Collins, 1962) 120.

At this point I tried to answer three questions I heard secular theology posing: (1) Why pray? (2) What is prayer? (3) What can we expect prayer to do?

Many answered the first question in a predictable fashion: "Pray for what you get out of it." It was here, however, that secular theology and theologians forced serious, thinking believers to get below the surface of things. They asked: "Why pray indeed?" Their query forced me to look deep within myself, to expand the range of my reading to learn from some of the great "doctors of devotion" like Augustine and Bernard of Clairvaux, and to spend much time mulling the issue with others. What I concluded was that I prayed out of need because God had made me for God's self, to praise God, and my heart was unsatisfied until it found it equilibrium in God.

I was woefully ill-prepared to answer the question as to what prayer is, but, looking back, I think I stumbled onto the right points more or less accidentally or perhaps providentially when I summarized my answer in terms of three turnings: turning *on*, turning *in*, and turning *over*. If we were to overcome our tendency to compartmentalize, we must learn first and above all to pay attention, to see, and to listen—all immensely difficult in a culture that catches us up on a treadmill of activity and creates overpowering and all-consuming distractions. How will we overcome the forces that diminish our seeing and listening? Merton's answer, the answer of saints through the centuries, was contemplation, which I understood at that stage primarily in terms of *meditation*. When Dan Walsh gave me a copy of Merton's *Spiritual Direction and Meditation*, published in 1960, I didn't have sufficient background then to recognize that spiritual direction might be something Protestant ministers might benefit from, but I did grasp the value of meditation. Only gradually and much later, however, would I discover the foundations upon which Merton built, namely, the *lectio divina* and the four stages that lead us to God—reading scriptures (*lectio*), going from head to heart (*meditatio*), entering into conversation with God (*oratio*), and immediate communion (*contemplatio*).

As you can see, the times were inspiring quite a self-tutoring process. My Baptist upbringing had made me think of prayer as primarily telling God something or asking God for something. For the first time in a real sense I was beginning to realize that, though petition should enter into a relationship with God, our great need was to listen to God and then to put ourselves at God's disposal, as in the Lord's Prayer,

"Your Kingdom come. Your will be done on earth as in heaven." Most fortunately, teaching church history had put me at the feet of Bernard of Clairvaux and introduced me to his scheme of four stages in the love of God: (1) love of self for self's sake, where all of us begin (We can't love another unless we first love ourselves.); (2) love of God for self's sake, using God as our heavenly Bellhop; (3) love of God for God's sake, recognizing God's worthiness; and (4) love of self for God's sake, where we ask God to do with us as God wants, not as we want.

What, then, can we expect prayer to do? Even in this skeptical age not many could deny that prayer or meditation would have an effect on persons who prayed or meditated. Scientific studies of Herbert Benson at Harvard demonstrated effects. The harder question was: "Does prayer contribute something to what God is trying to get done in the world?" Here I tried to steer away from often incredible, unsubstantiated claims of "faith healers" but to affirm, with much biblical and historical support, that our outpouring of "love energies" could add something to the "love energies" with which God creates, redeems, and directs this vast universe toward some meaningful end. I was conscious then as I am conscious now that there is no greater act of faith than to pray a prayer of intercession for someone or to offer a petition for something because we cannot know what God may do with our desires. We simply trust God as the Loving Parent (*Abba/Eema*) to do everything possible to save life, effect justice, bring peace, and "work together for good with those who love God" (Rom 8:28; my version).

What might be the consequence of lifestyles informed by prayer? My focus at that time was on the simplification of lifestyles to such an extent that not only individual lives but also the world around us might be transformed. There were some in the sixties who sought "the simple life"—an idyllic life removed from the hustle and bustle of the secular city. But I could not envision retreat to a Walden Pond or a Shangri La or a mountain aerie as an option for more than a few. Rather, by discovering first what Thomas R. Kelly called "a holy Center where the breath and stillness of Eternity are heavy upon us,"[19] I thought we could simplify our use of things and our use of time. In the midst of my reflection on simplification, Jesus' word to the anxiety-ridden of his day struck me like a squall of rain in the face. At that time I had just begun to tinker with the translation, but my rendering of Matthew 6:33 gradually

[19] Thomas R. Kelly, *A Testament of Devotion* (New York: Harper & Row, Publishers, 1941) 74.

evolved into this: "Seek first God's mysterious Presence and God's okaying of you. Then these other things will fall into place." Characteristically in our pragmatic American culture we have turned the process around. We worry and fret about "many things" because we haven't discovered "the one thing" or, better "the One who is needful" (Luke 10:42).

Here is where I saw secular theology heading us toward disaster. Instead of encouraging more and more of contemporary self-indulgence, faith should call for the recovery of a philosophy of enough. I used "recovery" consciously, for Christianity has espoused such an attitude throughout its history. Our time problem, as I saw it, is closely connected to a philosophy of more and more. We have to run pantingly and frantically through crowded calendars in order to earn enough to support the kind of lifestyles we would like to become accustomed to. If we, like the Apostle Paul, could discover a "true sufficiency" (*autarkeia*), then we would be "content" (*autarkes*) in whatever circumstances we find ourselves (Phil 4:10–13). Over against secular theology's proposal that we abandon a "God hypothesis" and learn to face the world without God, I posited the very opposite. At the heart of it all was the need to experience God's okaying of us, even though we are not okay. However loudly human beings may shout that they have "come of age," deep down, existentially, they know they have not and cannot attain their potential alone. Far from it, in splendid isolation and living with the illusion that they have no need of God, they pose a grave threat to their own survival.

Once again, near the end of this period of threshing out my "calling within a calling," an unplanned and unexpected grace befell me. Douglas Steere, a Quaker philosopher who had spent much of his life trying to unravel the Mystery of communion with God, gave a kind of boost I sorely needed at the time. In 1969 he lectured at Southern Seminary on some classics of Christian devotion, widening doors I had chosen to step through a few years before. In 1972 I was asked to do Bible studies for a retreat he led at a church renewal center founded by Findley Edge, called the Vineyard. Not only did I experience the remarkable uplift I came to associate with him, he told me about the Ecumenical Institute of Spirituality that he and Fr. Godfrey Diekmann had founded at Vatican II and invited me to attend the next meeting of this group at Wainwright House in Rye, New York, in January 1973. I had never taken part in a colloquy of Catholics, Orthodox, and

Protestants where I felt such unity of spirit and purpose. In the rest of my story you will see writ large the many ways this group guided and sustained me in directing attention to spiritual formation.

13

ROME AND JERUSALEM

I was originally scheduled for a second sabbatical in 1973–74, but my pursuit of the DPhil at Oxford had required a half sabbatical in the spring semester of 1969–70 and then time to complete the revision of my dissertation in 1973. With the hefty load I had had to carry during those years you won't have trouble understanding my eagerness to go on sabbatical, this time not to work on a degree but to study the problem of teaching authority (*magisterium*) in Roman Catholicism, a project for which the Association of Theological Schools granted me a second fellowship. The ideal place for that was Rome, but the whole Hinson family also had an urgent desire to spend some time in the Holy Land, and the ideal setting for that was the Ecumenical Institute for Advanced Studies near Jerusalem, once a medieval fortress and for a time a monastery called Tantur. We spent the fall, from late August until Epiphany, in Rome and the spring, from early January until the end of May, in Tantur.

"The Problem of Teaching Authority in Roman Catholicism" may seem like a strange subject for a Southern Baptist scholar to study, even one who often veered far off the beaten track in the denomination. Some might think that these two denominations represented opposite poles of the Christian continuum. As strange as it may sound, my study of early Christian institutional development gave birth to an observation that the evolution of the Southern Baptist Convention supplied a fascinating parallel, almost a mirror image, to the development of the early Catholic Church. When it came time for me to deliver my Inaugural Address as Professor of Church History at Southern Seminary in January 1971, I presented a Hinsonized version of the famous Sohm-Harnack debate regarding "The Nature and Origin of Catholicism."[1] Rudolf Sohm, a German jurist, viewed early Christian institutional development as a

---

[1] Published in *Review & Expositor* 72 (Winter 1975): 71–89. I should make a brief note about the hiatus between delivery of the address and publication. Publication of faculty inaugurals depended on available space in issues of the journal, and the length of mine created a special challenge for the editor (Frank Stagg).

radical departure from the primitive Church as a "purely spiritual" entity and ascribed the deviation largely to a Roman power grab. Adolf Harnack, the distinguished and prolific church historian at the University of Berlin, rejected the idea that the Church was ever a "purely spiritual entity," although he too thought that Catholicism represented a radical divergence from its original nature. What reason did he give for the "fall" of the Church? Hellenization! By the third century on Greco-Roman soil, Christianity had undergone a radical transition from a Church of Gospel to one of Law and it is this that Luther and other Protestant reformers came along to rectify.

In my inaugural I rejected the idea of a "fall" of the Church either at the end of the apostolic age or about 200 CE, or as a consequence of Constantine's adoption of Christianity. My study at Oxford convinced me that the main motive for the development of Christianity in its institutional expression that Sohm and Harnack labeled "Catholicism" was the powerful missionary impulse that had spread the faith from Jerusalem to the "ends of the earth." The churches accommodated rather cautiously until the time of Constantine, then a little more freely, but never to the extent that they eviscerated their identity as a covenant missionary people. When they subsumed the pattern of Roman provinces and dioceses, in fact, they did what Baptists in the American South did as they increasingly took over the pattern of American corporate life. Critical reflection on the parallels did prompt me to question whether Baptists may have gone so far in borrowing from the business model that they imperiled their nature and mission morally precisely because of the pragmatism inherent in that model,[2] but I was not prepared to go further and deny Southern Baptists a Christian identity.

From this area of study during the remarkable events that accompanied my early teaching years, it took only an additional ecumenical impulse to see analogies between the struggle of the Roman Catholic Church with authority issues and the struggle of Southern Baptists with authority issues they confronted. What set fire to a long smoldering question in the Roman Catholic Church was Pope Paul VI's publication in 1968 of the encyclical *Humanae Vitae* forbidding the use of the "pill" as a contraceptive in the face of a positive recommendation for

---

[2] See E. Glenn Hinson, "How Far Can the Churches God with the Business Model?" *Western Recorder* (3 December 1972); *Florida Baptist Witness* (21 December 1972).

its use by a majority on a commission he had appointed. A constituency primed for a favorable decision exploded. Church attendance dropped precipitously. Some distinguished Catholic theologians, such as the leading British theologian Charles Davis, as well as scores of laypersons, left the Church, some joining other communions but others simply dropping out. The *magisterium* was under siege, and I entered empathetically into the trauma of fellow believers far more deeply than I could have imagined just a dozen years before. During the sabbatical, I actually wrote a book-length essay that was never published, but I did publish in *The Journal of Ecumenical Studies* a lengthy essay that received much commendation from Roman Catholic scholars for its fairness and depth of insight.[3]

The battle in the Southern Baptist Convention also had a long history. It went back at least as far as the controversy over evolution in the 1920s that led to the adoption of Southern Baptists' first doctrinal statement, the *Baptist Faith and Message, 1925*. It burst into flame again in 1962 when Broadman Press published Ralph Elliott's *The Message of Genesis*, a conservative but responsible interpretation of the first book of the Bible using critical methodology. The "Genesis controversy" (a characterization preferred by Elliott rather than the "Elliott controversy") led to a revision of the *Baptist Faith and Message* in 1963. Advocates of inerrancy kept stirring and fanning the embers, and when Broadman Press released the first volume of the Broadman Bible Commentary in 1970, they found fuel in G. Henton Davies's commentary on Genesis that they could keep pouring on the flames until they managed to seize control of the presidency of the Southern Baptist Convention in 1979. The "conservative resurgence" or "Baptist reformation" or "takeover of the SBC" led in 2000 to adoption of a still more conservative revised version of the *Baptist Faith and Message*.

Although some might think the Southern Baptist controversy to be quite unlike that of the Roman Catholic Church, the focus in both was on the issue of teaching authority. Inerrantists, at least the more sophisticated ones, never claimed to have copies of an inerrant Bible— that would be the original autographs. The fact that no one possesses such a document, however, did not prevent the leaders of this movement from issuing inerrant and infallible interpretations. So the issue was really about inerrant and infallible *interpreters*, the Baptist *magisterium*,

---

[3] E. Glenn Hinson, "The Crisis of Teaching Authority in Roman Catholicism," *The Journal of Ecumenical Studies* 14 (Winter 1977): 66–88.

and the revisions of the doctrinal statement brought them closer to a definition of it. You can see here what intrigued me about the problem of teaching authority in Roman Catholicism.

Rome

My time in Rome offered a bonus I did not anticipate when I laid plans for a sabbatical. W.D. "Dub" Ruchti invited me to serve as interim pastor of Rome Baptist Church while he and Helen furloughed in the United States during the fall of 1975, as their daughter got settled in Denison University.[4] We could live in their lovely apartment on Via Cassia, well located with reference to Roma Antica, and drive their Opel. Rome Baptist Church was in the Piazza San Lorenzo in Lucina just off the Via Corso, a few blocks from the Gregorian University where I intended to do most of my study.

Rome Baptist Church, I soon surmised, was like the world Church in microcosm. Friends warned me that it was "different," "unusual," "unique." "Dub" Ruchti quickly confirmed their impressions. "Most of the regulars are Americans," he observed, "but people who attend come from all over the world. A large number are business executives, but there are professors, military people, people connected with the American Embassy or some other, and tourists. The people have varied religious backgrounds: Methodist, Presbyterian, Salvation Army, Pentecostal, even Roman Catholic. They have various levels of Bible knowledge and diverse views. But they enjoy tossing theology around, and there is wonderful fellowship." The more I thought about it, the more Rome Baptist Church's situation sounded like that of the Church in Paul's day, minus persecution and harassment.

Tourists could easily miss a modest Baptist church located across the piazza from a tourist attraction like San Lorenzo in Lucina, the martyrium of St. Lawrence, who, in 258, when ordered to produce the Church's treasures, brought the poor and was roasted on a spit at this very spot. A small plaque on the door post next to a bustling bar identified Rome Baptist Church, but you had to walk thirty-five or forty feet down a hallway to reach the church itself. Prior to Pope John XXIII and the Second Vatican Council, Baptists did not think it safe to call attention to their presence in Rome. The church made me think of early Christian "house churches," such as the one discovered at Dura-

---

[4] I owed the opportunity to Dale Moody. "Dub" wrote to him and asked if he knew someone who might serve as interim. Dale recommended me.

Europos, dated 232, and the *titulus* uncovered in Rome itself under the fifth-century Church of Saints John and Paul that dated back to the early fourth century. The sanctuary of Rome Baptist Church, perhaps large enough to accommodate a hundred worshippers, was a glass-covered atrium. Alongside it was a smaller room for adult Bible study, upstairs other rooms for children's classes.

We got acquainted with the faithful of Rome Baptist Church in a Wednesday "potluck" supper at the home of Bob and Sandra Graper in Olgiata, several miles on the northern edge of Rome. Bob Graper worked for the drug giant Eli Lilly. The supper and fellowship etched three impressions of this community of believers on my brain. First, Rome Baptist Church seemed to be an extended "family." There was a bonding far more intense than any I had ever experienced, due perhaps to a feeling of isolation from Roman society that heightened their need of one another. Second, its members showed remarkable openness and sensitivity to newcomers and warm, responsive fellowship, *koinonia*, with one another. Not just the Hinsons, but all of the newcomers felt warmly embraced and welcomed like dear friends not seen for a long time. Third, they had a simple but genuine, biblically grounded faith that they tried sincerely to apply to life. In order to "introduce" his flock to me, "Dub" asked each person to tell their favorite Bible verse and explain why it was a favorite. It was a compass reading. On the way back to our apartment, we could have used a compass, for we got lost on one of the *"anulari,"* ring roads circling the city. After one or two circuits we finally spotted Via Cassia. It was almost midnight when we got to our apartment.

My first impression did not change, but at the end of four months as their pastor I had greater clarity. There was a stable cadre of families and individuals who had lived in Rome for a few months to three or four years. They were generous, and they cared about one another. They felt a keen sense of responsibility to keep the church family alive and growing. They ministered to one another and to all who cried out to them for help in time of need. Like early Christians, they preferred to be taken advantage of rather than to deny help to "the distressed Christ in his many disguises," as Mother Teresa of Calcutta called the needy. There were also "occasional attenders," some of whom had lived in Rome for a long while and came spasmodically. As you would expect in this tourist Mecca, there were many "one Sunday drop ins," some who came alone, others of whom came in groups. Groups might be large or small, depending on the tourist season. In our brief time in Rome we established strong ties with the Walton family—J.D., Jane, Rick, Jay, and Bruce—that have lasted to this very day. J.D. Walton, Jr., a research engineer at Georgia Tech, was doing research on high temperature materials and had an acute theological mind.[5] Rick, the Walton's oldest son, later came to Southern Seminary to study.

Living in Rome presented some challenges we had not met in Oxford. One might expect language to be the major one, since most Italians do not speak English. Convinced that we would establish better connections if we knew Italian, Martha and I both studied the language. After being in Italy a while, however, we found that you could get along quite well by signaling with your hands and did not use Italian as much as we would have liked to do. Chris, now eleven, enrolled in the sixth grade in the Overseas School of Rome, where most of his teachers held graduate degrees. His history teacher, an archaeologist, took her classes to the Forum to teach Roman history and triggered in him a lifelong interest in archaeology. Elizabeth, only seven, attended second grade at Marymount Academy, a Catholic girls' school, where she also received excellent instruction. The biggest challenge in both schools was to carry the 1.3 million lire required to pay tuition. We used a grocery bag!

More problematic was driving in Rome, where it seemed as though every Roman owned two cars and drove them at the same time. I had observed in 1967 that Italian drivers seemed to operate on a single rule: "Whoever is ahead has the right of way." Fortunately the Ruchti's Opel had enough power to get ahead of traffic. Unfortunately Italians drive without regard to lanes we are accustomed to in America. Driving down the Via dei Fori Imperiali or other wide streets reminded me of the Ben Hur version of a Roman chariot race. After about a week or two in Rome, Martha came down with a case of vertigo, which a doctor analyzed as being due to stress. Traveling by buses in Rome, however, did not prove less stressful, for they were jam-packed. When we first rode buses, I judged Italians extremely rude because they would push and shove to cram you into a bus before the doors closed. I decided later that they really were very considerate; if they didn't crowd you in, you might never get to your destination! The crowding distressed Elizabeth, however, because she was buried in the midst of people, and Martha had frequent dizzy spells throughout our time in Rome.

---

[5] J.D. Walton passed away on 11 February 2011.

Southern Baptist missionaries Stanley and Patsy Crabb and Bob and Flora Holifield treated us with much kindness and provided quite a lot of assistance in getting around. I was distressed, however, to discover that they had a comfortable relationship mostly with the most conservative Italian Baptists. Italian Baptists generally are socially, politically, and theologically liberal and work closely with Waldensians, and that bothered the missionaries. The brief period we spent in Rome did not permit me to foster closer ties, but I was able to establish friendships with Italian leaders through ecumenical involvement. Paolo Spanu, who visited me in the United States, and I served together in the Baptist/Roman Catholic Conversations, 1984–88. I developed close friendships with a number of Italian students when I taught at Rüschlikon in 1991 and 1994 and assisted some in studying in the States. I assisted Italo Benedetti, another leader, in writing his dissertation for the Waldensian Seminary on *The New Religious Right in the United States of America, 1979–1988.*[6]

As excited as I was about seeing Rome and serving as pastor of Rome Baptist Church, I did not delay long in getting to the Gregorian University. Because I had had no previous contact with that distinguished institution, I made arrangements through an acquaintance of Dale Moody at the Pontifical Biblical Commission. The very first morning I entered the "Greg" and made my way toward the library, I heard my name called. "Glenn, what are you doing here?" It was Jean Leclercq, a Benedictine monk from Luxembourg, the world's leading authority on Bernard of Clairvaux, and close friend of Thomas Merton. I had gotten to know him through the Ecumenical Institute of Spirituality. Jean and I had given papers at the meeting of EIOS in 1974. A much sought after scholar, he was teaching at the Gregorian in the fall semester of 1975–76. After a brief conversation I invited him to have dinner with our family. During the semester, he took me on a tour of a massive textual enterprise he and other Benedictines were engaged in.

You might find it of interest to learn that scholars at the Gregorianum do not maintain an American-style, round-the-clock, schedule. The library opened at 9 a.m., closed at 1 p.m., reopened at 4 p.m., and closed for the night at 7 p.m. During the three-hour luncheon/nap period, I sometimes toured the ancient city but usually walked down to Rome Baptist Church, had a sandwich at the bar

---

[6] Italo Benedetti, *La Nuova Destra Religiosa negli Stati Uniti d'America, 1979–1988* (Roma: Facoltá Valdese di Teologia, 1992).

adjoining and owned by the church, and then, not accustomed to napping, went to the office to continue research and writing. By the end of my stay, however, I was tempted to test the wisdom of siestas.

You will probably not have strong interest in the tedious business of research on "The Crisis of Teaching Authority in Roman Catholicism," but, as one of my most searching ecumenical endeavors, you may want to know what my labors produced. I justified the study on the grounds that "all of the churches today face a very serious challenge in attempting to influence or shape the beliefs and behavior of their own constituency, to say nothing of those who stand outside that constituency." Magnifying that challenge is "the fact that the authority crisis in the churches is merely a small scenario within a larger crisis of authority in Western society and perhaps the entire world."[7] I likened the crisis to a volcano. Under Pope Pius XII (1939–58) the volcano built up steam but was held down by the heavy hand of power. Pius was defensive toward modern non-Catholic thought and displayed an authoritarian tone that many found offensive and that severely limited participation of others in the teaching authority of the Church. John XXIII (1958–63) and the Second Vatican Council (1962–65) uncapped the volcano to relieve some of the pressures building underground. Pope John changed the Church's stance on the issue of authority and raised hopes for reform, renewal, and greater sharing of the *magisterium*. The council's actions had vastly different interpretations, however. *Strict-constructionists* wanted to return to the centralization of authority in the pope and the bishops. *Liberals* called for a new era of "co-responsibility" in all aspects of ecclesiastical life. The first and major eruption occurred when Pope Paul VI (1958–79) issued *Humanae Vitae*, prohibiting the use of the "pill" as a contraceptive, 25 July 1968. Theologians and laypersons challenged the authority and arguments of the encyclical. Why did the pope issue it? Perhaps for several reasons, but in essence he wanted to protect papal authority. Its net effect was to impair that authority and to stimulate various proposals to limit it. Hans Küng precipitated a sort of after-eruption two years later when he focused the issue on the question of papal infallibility in *Infallible: An Inquiry?* The basic issue he raised was "whether the Church's infallibility is dependent on infallible propositions." He said no, for propositions may be true and false at the same time. Thus, when I wrote this essay, a state of chaos existed

---

[7] E. Glenn Hinson, "The Crisis of Teaching Authority in Roman Catholicism," *The Journal of Ecumenical Studies* 14 (Winter 1977): 66–67.

concerning papal teaching authority. Responses to it varied widely, but I concluded that "there is little question that the papacy and thus the exercise of the magisterium will undergo vast changes in the decade ahead if it is to survive.... Yet one could only express profound regret if yielding to this concern should result in ecclesiastical anarchy and further fragmentation of Christianity."[8]

No planning on my part entered the picture here, but 1975 was a Jubilee Year. These special years of pilgrimage began with Boniface VIII in 1300, initially spaced fifty years apart but so profitable that they were reduced to twenty-five years. The special year doubtless heightened the flow of traffic and caused some inconvenience for residents, even short-term ones like the Hinsons. However, it also held some special benefits. The Church assembled relics from throughout Christendom—splinters of the Cross, blood of martyrs, rags, bones, hanks of hair. And for me a brick that had sealed one of the doors of St. Peter's for twenty-five years. It was a gift from Lorenzo, a guide at St. Peter's married to Marcia, an American Airlines stewardess. Lorenzo came reluctantly at first and then, apparently finding some sustenance in my sermons and Bible study classes, got more and more involved. The Sunday the members of Rome Baptist Church feted us as we prepared to go to Israel, Lorenzo and Marcia came. After the dinner and some games and fun, he said, "I've got a book for you, a heavy one. It weighs five pounds or more. Can you take it with you?" I assured him that I could manage somehow. He added, "But it's not really a book." "I'd love to have it anyway," I replied. He came to the last Bible study I conducted bringing me one of the bricks from St. Peter's.

Jerusalem

As our time in Rome grew short, "Dub" Ruchti asked me to spend the rest of my sabbatical year as pastor of Rome Baptist Church. It was tempting for several reasons. For one, we had all forged strong bonds with regulars at the church. As we said goodbye, we experienced the grief that usually occurs when you leave family behind as you go away for a long time. Staying in Rome, moreover, would have permitted me to dig deeper into the subject I had chosen for my sabbatical where it centered, while Jerusalem, I found out later, would take me far from it. Had I stayed where I could make use of the Gregorian library, I might

---

[8] Ibid., 88.

have cobbled together a book some publisher would have wanted to print. During our stay in Rome, too, we read and heard about distressing happenings in Israel, nothing as dramatic as the "Six-day War" of 1967, but serious enough to cause me to put a call through to Dale and Mildred Moody, who had spent the fall at Tantur. When we related events reported in Italian dailies and the *International Herald Tribune*, Dale replied, "We haven't heard anything about that here. Come on! It's as safe or safer than it is in Rome or Louisville for that matter." Not entirely reassured, we went anyway. All of us wanted to spend time in the Holy Land, and I felt an obligation to do what I had proposed for the sabbatical, but we knew that we traveled there at risk.

We spent a fortnight at Rüschlikon, January 16–31, on our way to Israel. From Zürich we flew TWA to Orly in Paris. There we changed to El Al and went through the most searching security procedures any of us had ever experienced. In 1975 neither airlines nor governments had crafted the sophisticated electronic equipment now employed. Israeli authorities strewed every piece of our luggage on the tarmac near the 707 we were scheduled to fly on. They required me to open each suitcase and watched like a hawk to see whether I would show the least nervousness or hesitation in doing so. Each of us was patted down before we boarded. I had no complaint, however, for Palestinians, both men and women, went through a far more intimidating search. During our five months in Israel, we could sense the volatility of Israeli-Palestinian relationships seething underground and learned to take precautions, for example, in sending Chris and Elizabeth to their respective schools in Jerusalem in a *cherut* (taxi) with a trustworthy Arab driver. We often witnessed intimidation of Arabs traveling from Bethlehem to Jerusalem and back and could see the effects of their humiliation.

The flight from Paris to Tel Aviv introduced us to aspects of Jewish culture we had never been exposed to. Orthodox Jewish rabbis, clearly recognizable in their black suits and wide-brimmed black hats as well as their curls, traipsed up and down the aisle saying their prayers aloud. Perhaps a sign of my own prejudice rather than their lack of authentic piety, I couldn't help but think of Jesus' chiding of "hypocrites" "who love to pray standing in the synagogues or on street corners so that they may get human attention" (Matt 6:5). American Airlines would not have permitted so much traffic in the aisles lest sudden turbulence result in falls.

Five months in the Holy Land failed to meet two of the three hopes I entertained in planning the sabbatical. Tantur proved disappointing from an academic standpoint. The institute had not had time to accumulate much of a library, certainly not the kind that would help me with the study of the crisis of teaching authority in Roman Catholicism. I was thankful that Rome had enabled me to collect adequate notes for the writing of my essay, for Tantur gave me mostly the leisure to think through what I needed to say. It did have substantial materials for biblical scholars to whom it catered. More helpful than the library was a seminar on Holocaust Theology and weekly colloquia in which sabbaticants presented research papers. Heretofore, I had not studied the Holocaust, which, more than any other event in modern history, accounted for the nation of Israel. *Yad Vashem*, the chief memorial to the Holocaust, is in Jerusalem. A visit there burned that event into my conscience as no amount of reading could have. The seminar, conducted by Frank Sherman, exposed us to a variety of interpretations and searching theological discussion. The colloquium offered a wide array of topics, some of interest only to their author but others stimulating to everyone, for instance, Mennonite biblical scholar Millard Lind's discussion of competing traditions about war and peace in the Hebrew Bible. In one, Yahweh is a warrior; in the other the king is. Dale Moody found himself sharply challenged in his effort to establish an early date for the composition of Luke/Acts. My own paper attracted quite a bit of attention, perhaps because it was an unusual topic at Tantur, and got very favorable responses from other scholars. Not many, however, could contribute knowledgably to a topic they knew little about.

Although it did not benefit me greatly from an academic standpoint, I had higher hopes for Tantur in two other areas. The one that the Holy See seems to have envisioned as its chief *raison d'être* was Christian unity. For the first time we lived and worshipped with a community speckled with a wide range of groups representing the three great religious traditions—Roman Catholic, Orthodox, and Protestant. I must confess here, though, that I did not find relationships ideal.

In what would probably be envisioned as its subordinate purpose, depth exposure to sacred sites, the Ecumenical Institute succeeded admirably, certainly with me. Like ancient pilgrims, I hoped, through firsthand exposure to those holy places, to get a firmer grip on the story of God's self-disclosure in and through the Jewish people, above all, through Jesus of Nazareth. Virtually every week, the institute conducted guided tours of both Old and New Testament sites, often under leadership of the original excavator, and missionaries living in Israel supplemented those tours. For the only period in my life I kept almost a daily journal. Heretofore most of my journaling took place "as the Spirit moved me," but visits to sacred sites seems to have inspired in me an awareness of journaling's potential for deepening insight and communicating a touch of the original event to the person who visited certain places. For the first time, I think, I grasped what Jerome's sponsor Paula and her daughter Eustochium meant when they entreated their friend and mentor the Roman matron Marcella to join them in the Holy Land as the Roman world collapsed.

> Will the day never come, they asked, when we shall together enter the Savior's cave and weep in the sepulcher of the Lord with his sister and his mother? When will we touch with our lips the wood of the cross and arise in prayer and resolve on the Mount of Olives with the ascending Lord? When will we see Lazarus come forth bound with grave clothes and look upon the waters of Jordan purified for the washing of the Lord?

After recounting visits to an array of sites, they added, "then we will sing heartily, weep copiously, pray unceasingly. Wounded with the Savior's spear, we will say together: 'I have found him whom my soul loves; I will hold him and not let him go!'" (Song of Sg 3:4)[9] I found very much as Paula and Eustochium did that being there fired up imagination and inspired desire to know God and God's purpose for humankind.

The months spent meditating in holy sites, I think, marked something of a turning point in the way I handled scriptures and in my appreciation for the way someone like Origen interpreted and applied them. By no means did I lay aside the critical skills I had developed as a New Testament scholar. If anything, I wanted greater exactness in seeking the plain meaning of biblical texts. Anyone who has read my study of Christian origins, *Jesus Christ*,[10] that aroused the ire of inerrantists in the Southern Baptist Convention, can confirm that. Writing almost immediately after returning from Palestine as the first volume in a series directed to the bicentennial of America, I did my best to convey accurately the results of objective New Testament scholarship.

---

[9] Jerome, *Epistle* 46.13. My translation. See E. Glenn Hinson, "When the World Collapsed: The Spirituality of Woman during the Barbarian Invasion of Rome," *Perspectives in Religious Studies* 20 (Summer 1993): 113–130.

[10] E. Glenn Hinson, *Jesus Christ*, vol. 1 of Faith of Our Fathers (Gaithersburg MD: Consortium Press, 1977).

I operated on the conviction that God allows the facts to stand and so should I. What did change as a consequence of exposure to these holy places was an awakening to the fact that interpreters could and should *go beyond* critical objectivity to discover the Word in the words. That was a significant step for someone who, from infancy on, had coped with life's hard moments by shifting into his head and away from his heart. On these trips we took from Tantur I found my imagination coming out in a striking way. My journals written during this period contain a great deal of factual information on every site we visited, but there is also a remarkable amount of poetry.

Reasonable reporting will not permit me to recount and share reflections on the dozens of historic sites I had occasion to visit while at Tantur that added new dimensions to my spiritual life. Tantur itself, by the way, is only a mile from Bethlehem, and our bedroom window faced east toward it. An erstwhile denizen of the Missouri Ozarks could hardly ask more from life than to live within spitting distance of the traditional site of Jesus' birth. A super-bright star hovering over it at night titillated my imagination as to whether it was the same super nova that early Christians thought guided the wise men from the East. Jerusalem and its wealth of sacred sites—the Temple Mount, the ancient walls, the Via Dolorosa, the Holy Sepulcher, the Garden of Gethsemane—are only five or six miles north from Tantur. What Jews, Christians, or Muslims could enter the Holy City without wanting to remove their shoes and touch holy ground with bare feet? In whatever direction we headed from Tantur on weekly excursions, we tread on other ground hallowed by saints who sought to make sense of this mysterious God who seeks humans out even as they seek God.

My biggest touch of grace may have been a pilgrimage through the Sinai desert. In 1976 the Sinai still remained under Israeli control. Our week's sojourn looked nothing like the forty years spent by the people fleeing Egypt on the way to taking control of the "land flowing with milk and honey" or those painful treks thousands of Christians made after Constantine's conversion. We rode on benches in the back of an open-air Israeli army truck under guidance of Ora Lipshitz, a PhD candidate at Hebrew University writing a dissertation on the exoduses (plural) from Egypt who knew the desert like the back of her hand. We ate sumptuous meals prepared by Ora and assistants rather than manna or quail. Our only "suffering" occurred a time or two the heavy truck mired down in treacherous sand, and we had to get out and push. Otherwise, we suffered little discomfort.

Ease and comfort notwithstanding, the Sinai sojourn generated some of the same excitement and anticipation it must have aroused among those pilgrims who made their way mostly on foot and without expert assistance and scratched the Prayer of the Heart on rock chimneys all over the desert in Greek or Latin. "Lord Jesus Christ, Son of God, have mercy on me, a sinner." This was no rote recitation; it came from the heart of those who faced the fearful uncertainties of life. Only the deepest and most profound faith could have sustained them as they forged ahead toward Jebel Musa, the Mount of Moses. A community of contemplatives had taken up residence a few miles from traditional Mount Sinai in an oasis on the Wadi Feiran. In the face of a cliff on one side of the dry creek bed they had hewn out cells in the sandstone. The community dubbed itself "Little St. Catherine's" to connote its link with the much larger monastery at the foot of traditional Mount Sinai built by order of the Emperor Justinian (527–65) in the sixth century, supposedly on the site of the "burning bush." No one, of course, can say for sure where Moses' mountain is. No matter, this one has played a magnificent role in keeping Christians ever on the quest for God. During the purge of icons by some Eastern emperors in the seventh and eighth centuries, St. Catherine's became a haven for icons. From the beginning it offered hospitality to the stream of pilgrims who scaled the mountain to see God in the way Moses had seen God. It also provided the great textual critic Constantin Tischendorf with one of the best manuscripts of the Hebrew Bible, Sinaiticus or Aleph!

I could not tell you what I expected to "see" on Mount Sinai, but Chris and I shared the excitement of the whole group who set out at 2:30 a.m. so as to reach the peak by sunrise. We soon came upon Dale Moody, who had chosen to start with the "fast" group, stopping to catch his breath. A little later I left Chris behind to climb at his own pace. I was thankful for the three-mile walks I took every morning that enabled me to reach the top well before sunrise just behind one of the monks from Spain who served on a rescue squad for climbers and a very athletic youth of sixteen. What did I see? An awesome sunrise and "the cleft of the rock" into which Moses had scrunched down as God passed by. I didn't "see" God, but I knew God was there just as God had been there when Moses came centuries before.

We left Israel on May 20. The Christian Arab taxi driver who had taken Chris and Elizabeth back and forth to and from school in Jerusalem drove us to the airport. He embraced me as we said goodbye. In my journal I wrote, "O God, how deeply I hurt for both Arabs and Jews here. Peace is so essential and yet so elusive. The situation has never seemed tenser. The West Bank is alive with hatred. Three Arabs have been killed—evidently by trigger-tense young troops. Could anyone, even a seasoned officer, stand taunting, name-calling?"

Martha, Chris, and Elizabeth flew TWA on the way to St. Louis via New York. I flew to Recife, Brazil, via Paris to give lectures in Recife, Rio, and San Paolo. The change in my flight plans occasioned one last reminder of the special security the situation in Palestine required. This time authorities took me into a little booth, had me strip down to my underwear, and grilled me for some time. Against the background of a semester in this agonized land I didn't have to ask why. I departed with a soul pained and praying for all whom the *shalom* they longed for seemed so far removed and so elusive.

14

BRAZIL AND BEYOND

The faculties of three Baptist seminaries in Brazil invited me to give lectures in May and June 1976. The Foreign Mission Board of the Southern Baptist Convention footed the bill for my travel. The reception Brazilians accorded me left me walking on air for a while. One special memory is the remarkable job of interpretation and translation some of my former Brazilian students did; it was inspired!

The faculties asked me to give two sets of lectures. For one I decided to focus on "Contemplative Lifestyle." Westminster Press had published *A Serious Call to a Contemplative Lifestyle* in 1974, and I thought it might address major concerns of Brazilians as it did those of North Americans. For the other I prepared a new series entitled "Horizonal Christians." I coined the word "horizonal" despite some fear that hearers would put a "tee" in it. I joked, "There are already too many horizontal people, besides those in cemeteries, I mean." In Brazil I didn't need to worry, for my hearers quickly caught on to my definition of the word in Portuguese as "persons who look beyond the horizon to see what God is trying to bring into being." To make my definition clear, I cited my own paraphrase of Romans 12:2: "persons not simply shaped in the mold of this age but who have been transformed by a recycling of understanding so that they may have a sense of what is God's will—what is good, what is acceptable to God, and what contributes to God's ultimate purpose." I used four persons to illustrate "horizonal"—Augustine, Francis of Assisi, Martin Luther, and John Woolman—and did a summary lecture on "Horizonal Perceptions Today."

In some respects both sets of lectures aimed at the same goal, pointing hearers to the importance of developing perceptions and habits that could free them from the powerful grip of culture. As illustrations of the subtle control culture exercised over American culture in the late sixties and early seventies I cited racial discrimination still holding on despite numerous court decisions and enactments of legislation, inequities regarding the role of women just beginning to be addressed in the use of inclusive language and in employment opportunities, inequalities that constantly widen in the distribution of wealth, exploitation of nature and waste of natural resources, and over-consumption and wasting of food by the few while masses die of starvation. As became increasingly evident to me from reading the writings of Thomas Merton, the major question is: How do we *acquire* perceptions not simply shaped by the age in which we live? One answer is *education*. Although education, first in our families and then in our schooling, inducts us into our culture's ways, it should also awaken us to its limitations by exposing us to the attitudes and outlooks of other ages and cultures. Unfortunately, American culture seems to be failing us in this latter task. As Theodore Roszak charged in *Where the Wasteland Ends*, American culture fosters "the single vision" of empirical observation and rational reflection and neglects what he called "the powers of transcendence." Since education has shown that we should not expect it alone to "recycle understanding," we must look to other sources for "horizonal perceptions," above all, to *contemplation*, the cultivation of attentiveness to God in everything we do. If we follow the challenge set forth by the Apostle Paul, we will desire not only to have a sense of what is God's will, but also to *act on* those perceptions. Although my own ideas were probably not fully matured at this point, I concluded my lectures with four counsels: (1) Begin where you are, and do not let the magnitude of the problems we face so overwhelm you that you throw up your hands in despair. Remember that small efforts matter. (2) Use the means at hand in institutions and programs already established and, when those do not seem to work, create new ones to do what is required. In a period of great skepticism about institutions and hostility to them, I underscored this point forcefully on the basis of my study of the contribution institutions made to the winning of the Roman Empire. (3) Exercise patience, recognizing that the wheels of change turn slowly and may not move in the direction we think best. (4) Trust God to multiply your efforts, all of which may seem small and inconsequential, straws thrown up into the wind, but which God may "work together for good with those who love God" (Rom 8:28).

The approach of the American Bicentennial in 1976 occasioned a surge in requests to do research and writing that demanded much of my time over the next several years. In April 1974 Reuben Herring, an editor of adult materials in the Church Training Department of the Southern Baptist Sunday School Board, invited me to write a book entitled *Soul Liberty* for Doctrinal Emphasis Week in April 1976. "The book would treat the doctrine of soul liberty from a historical perspective," he explained. Its due date was 1 January 1975.[1] My Oxford dissertation behind me, I jumped at the chance to publish something on a topic already roiling around in my mind despite having a heavy teaching load and other writing commitments.

Recounting the development of a doctrine of religious liberty, as distinguished from tolerance, gave me a chance to raise some warning flags about the threat posed to religious freedom by overzealous evangelism, the heartbeat of the Southern Baptist Convention. As this denomination had evolved from minority to majority status, many of its constituents had forgotten the concern that had brought Baptists into being in the first place. Rereading the final chapter of this small volume on "The Perils of Religious Liberty," I can see that I anticipated with considerable accuracy what would soon transpire.

Hot on the heels of my agreement to do *Soul Liberty*, on 1 May 1974, an editor for Consortium Press, publisher of the Catholic University of America's Fathers of the Church series, approached me about writing one volume in an eight-volume series the press proposed to publish for the Bicentennial. I told the editor, Thomas Pearl, that the volume I was best equipped to turn out on short notice was the first: *Jesus, His Antecedents, His Times, and His Followers to 400 A.D.*[2] I signed a contract November 29. The series attracted some distinguished writers, including Martin E. Marty of the University of Chicago and Dewey D. Wallace, Jr., at George Washington. Subsequently, I helped the publisher, Daniel McGrath, line up other writers, including two of my own students—Raymond H. Bailey and Jonathan A. Lindsey—and Louis Weeks, a professor of Church history at Louisville Presbyterian Seminary.

Jesus Christ was one of those books that flowed. Writing it gave me an opportunity to put into print some of the results of the extensive research and organization of materials I had done for a ThD in New Testament at Southern Seminary and for the DPhil in Patristics at Oxford, and it got excellent reviews from the academy. From an academic and literary standpoint I would judge it one of the best and potentially most useful books I have written. From two other angles, however, it turned out to be one of the most painful and costly writing ventures I have ever attempted. One of those angles had to do with the

---

[1] Reuben Herring to E. Glenn Hinson, 18 April 1974.
[2] Thomas Pearl to E. Glenn Hinson, 1 May 1974; E. Glenn Hinson to Thomas Pearl, 6 May 1974; and Thomas Pearl to E. Glenn Hinson, 16 May 1974.

publisher, who failed to get the series into print until1977—after all of the celebration ended—and did not pay what our contracts stipulated. Although I, like other scholars, had an intense desire to publish, I felt much embarrassment that I had helped to move the project forward. The other concerned the negative reaction the book received from fundamentalists in the Southern Baptist Convention.

Over many years and through many trials I've learned to accept and even to appreciate the ironies of life, and life played a colossal joke on me in this affair. For the meager $368 I was paid, I earned a million dollars worth of trouble. Looked at in terms of the ironic, I guess you could say that the book turned out to be worth more than I could have imagined as I wrote it. My heart's desire was to help thoughtful Christians, even conservative ones, wind their way through major critical issues in Christian beginnings without allowing such things to jaundice their faith. I located those origins in their Jewish and Hellenistic matrixes, but argued, against some more skeptical than I, that Jesus himself is appropriately called the "founder" of Christianity. I insisted that one cannot explain how this movement survived, much less prospered, in the Roman Empire apart from the conviction of Jesus' first followers, however well-based, that their founder, crucified by the Romans, had been raised from the dead and reappeared among them.

The whys and wherefores of Christianity's triumph in the Roman Empire are complex and debatable, too. In effect, I suggested, Christianity rode the crest of a wave of oriental religions sweeping westward at the time. To do so, it had to offer to the people of that day and sphere some of the same attractions other religions did. But it also had to offer more, for, whereas the competitors died out quickly when persecution hit them in the fourth century, Christianity survived nearly three centuries of persecution. By the time Constantine decided in favor of Christianity and against solar monotheism, 10 to 15 percent of the people of the Empire had chosen it. What was its appeal? Its charities, offered to all without restriction? Its sacraments, that gave tangible assurance of salvation? Its "good news" of forgiveness of sins and release from the power of Satan? Its moral teachings backed up by example? Its "witness" through martyrdom? Yes—all of those. Still, one must come back to its enigmatic founder for an answer.

Two or three years after it was published, the inerrantists in the Southern Baptist Convention discovered *Jesus Christ* and soon made it a *cause célèbre*, but I will return to that part of my story later. For the remainder of this chapter, however, let me talk some more of the "happy accidents" that were shaping my career after I returned from a sabbatical in Rome and Jerusalem.

Other literary opportunities came in a flood soon after my return from Brazil. William J. Fallis, Senior Editor at Broadman Press, approached me about revising and updating *The Church: Design for Survival* or producing another book on the nature and mission of the Church, and I signed a contract on 17 August 1976 for what the editors eventually entitled *The Integrity of the Church*. Broadman scheduled publication for October 1977, but my heavy teaching, writing, and speaking schedule delayed my submission of the manuscript from April to June 1977, so that it did not get in print until 1978. In *The Integrity of the Church* I mirrored *The Church: Design for Survival* in using three biblical images of the Church—the People of God, the New Humanity, and the Servant—to define its nature and mission, but added one other, the City of God. In introducing the subject a decade later, however, I set the question in the context of Alvin Toffler's best selling sociological study *Future Shock* and the challenge presented to the churches by accelerated change. Readers of my Oxford dissertation, published as *The Evangelization of the Roman Empire*, will recognize that I incorporated my chief thesis into this study of the nature and mission of the Church. Rejecting either denial or rubber-stamping of what Toffler described, I argued that, "*At one and the same time [the Church] should strive to conserve its identity while engaging in its mission in and to the world with adaptability and flexibility.*" I may have betrayed a cultivated optimism or hopefulness here, but I went on to say, "This can be done if we will keep as our point of reference who we are and what we are to do as the church—namely, if we will keep in mind the nature and mission of the church."[3]

I did something in *The Integrity of the Church* that I had not done in *The Church: Design for Survival*, namely, review the history of debate concerning the nature and mission of the Church—the Donatists, medieval sects, Protestant and Catholic reformers, Landmarkists among Baptists, Roman Catholics and Protestants today. I devoted special attention to the insistence upon inerrancy and infallibility of scriptures by Harold Lindsell in *The Battle for the Bible*. I constructed here perhaps my most tightly reasoned argument against the inerrantist viewpoint. In repudiating inerrancy, you should note that I have often accepted the application of the word "infallible" to scriptures. Properly understood,

---

[3] E. Glenn Hinson, *The Integrity of the Church* (Nashville: Broadman Press, 1978) 22.

the Latin word "infallible" (derived from *fallere*, "to deceive") means that scriptures will not deceive you, that they are trustworthy or reliable. "Inerrancy" means something quite different. It claims scientific accuracy. I made these points against Lindsell's view: (1) The Bible itself does not support such a theory. Jesus' correcting of "Moses" (the Pentateuch) (Matt 5:21ff.; 19:7–8) and Paul's distinction between "his" word and "the word of the Lord" in 1 Corinthians 7:10 and 12 deny "every jot and tittle" inspiration. (2) Lindsell's argument that if we don't hold to inerrancy of the Bible in all its parts, we will start surrendering truths it teaches one by one, can just as easily be turned around. We can make a better case from history for the reverse: If we buy into the inerrantist position, we will apostatize from what the Bible teaches by letting bigotry create an excess of zeal to make everyone believe what we believe (as happened in the Middle Ages). (3) Although one must concede that Christians held to the inerrantist viewpoint until the nineteenth century, Lindsell overlooks information about the canon, problems relating to the doctrine of inspiration, and the development of different methods of interpretation that stand against the theory. Over against the inerrantist approach I argued that we should recognize that scriptures of both Old and New Testaments are not "single-tiered," i.e., a one-layer cake. Proper interpretation requires us to recognize the diversity as well as the unity of theologies and styles of worship, etc. Acknowledgement of variety, far from constituting a problem, can benefit us immensely in being the Church today. (1) It "reminds us that we do not need to feel tied down to certain conventions and stereotypes, even those of the first century. Rather, we are free to develop programs and institutions that will achieve the purposes of the church."[4] (2) It "encourages us to respond sensitively to the social and cultural situation of the church in our own age." (3) It "teaches us not to be discouraged because we find it difficult to be the church and to fulfill its mission. We share that difficulty with early Christianity."[5]

The book received excellent reviews both inside and outside the Southern Baptist orbit. As I wrote the book, I had an opportunity to try out the ideas I have summarized above at Eagle Aerie, the state assembly ground for the Virginia Baptist General Association. During the week, I kept hearing, "He's over my head!" As I expected, attempting to relate my ideas to the society described by Toffler did stretch some minds, but

[4] Ibid., 37.
[5] Ibid., 38.

a crowd of several hundred attended very faithfully. On Friday, in introductory comments thanking the person who invited me, tongue in cheek, I said, "When I got up to speak on Monday morning and looked out into the bright faces of you Virginia Baptists, my knees quavered a bit and I said to myself, 'They're over my head!'" That brought the house down. After my lecture that morning an elderly woman came up, shook my hand, and declared, "Young man, you could charm your way out of anything!" Insofar as I can remember, I didn't experience negative vibes from other Baptist audiences, and the book remained in print for a few years.

In the wake of the Second Vatican Council the Roman Catholic publishing giant Doubleday decided to venture into a Protestant market. Randall E. Greene, one of their young editors who had graduated from the University of Kentucky, contacted Wayne Oates about writing a volume in spirituality for them. He wrote *Nurturing Silence in a Noisy Heart* and, shortly afterwards, *Making Laziness Work for You*.[6] Because I was out of town at the time, Greene asked Oates to discuss a potential book idea with me. In December 1976 he wrote to request a copy of *Seekers after Mature Faith* and promised to meet Oates and me to discuss book ideas. The proposal that we worked out entailed a three-volume edition of *Doubleday Devotional Classics: Protestant Series*.

Writing for a major publishing firm for the first time, I soon found myself under immense pressure to edit and write introductions for not *one* but *eight* Protestant devotional classics. On 19 January 1977 I sent Greene a list of eight writings, thinking initially he expected to publish one or two. April 12 he informed me that Doubleday would publish three volumes of 336 pages each and include all but one of the eight classics I listed (Lancelot Andrewes's *Private Devotions*).[7] Indicative of the urgency the publisher attached to the project, he had calculated the number of characters in each writing, instructions about obtaining permission to use copyrighted material, matters related to typescript, etc. He ended his letter with a reassuring word: "Obviously this is going to be a lot of work, but we at Doubleday sincerely believe in the inherent value of this project and encourage you in every effort to make this the best quality edition of these classics available to Protestant readers."

---

[6] Wayne E. Oates, *Nurturing Silence in a Noisy Heart* (Garden City NY: Doubleday, 1979); *Making Laziness Work for You* (1981).

[7] Randall E. Greene to E. Glenn Hinson, 12 April 1977.

I don't think I could have pulled off the project as planned had it not been for the close friendship Douglas Steere and I had developed by this time. By chance he wrote at the beginning of May to ask me if I might meet him and Dorothy at the Louisville airport when they concluded their visit to the Abbey of Gethsemani at the end of May. I quickly responded that I could and used the occasion to ask if he might help me obtain permission to use his translation of Søren Kierkegaard's *Purity of Heart* and portions of Thomas R. Kelly's *A Testament of Devotion*, both published by Harper & Row.[8] As a result of our conversation, I discovered the eighth classic I wanted to add to the omnibus in place of Andrewes's *Diary*: Douglas Steere's *On Listening to Another*. Other writings were: Richard Baxter's *The Saints' Everlasting Rest*, John Bunyan's *The Pilgrim's Progress* and *Grace Abounding* (for volume one); *The Journal of George Fox*, *The Diary of David Brainerd* edited by Jonathan Edwards, and *The Journal of John Woolman* (for volume 2). Doubleday produced a very attractive and inexpensive three-volume set that received good reviews and sold well initially.[9] Unfortunately, neither Wayne Oates's writings nor this series attracted a large enough Protestant readership to justify keeping them in print beyond a couple of years.

I must confess a feeling that someone had clobbered me in the solar plexus when I got the notification that Doubleday would let the series go out of print. Recognition that the publisher had approached me about the project, instead of me approaching them, eased the hurt a tad, but it didn't assuage it much. Doubleday also let their contract with Wayne Oates lapse. My ego was pretty fragile and perhaps inflated too much by success with my other writings. I moped around for a while until some friends in other seminaries who had used the series in classes began appealing to me to see if Westminster would reprint them. Doubleday readily surrendered the copyright, but Paul Meacham, editor for Westminster, concluded that they would have to double, triple, or quadruple Doubleday's phenomenally low price per volume ($5.95) and that the price increase would cut sales further.[10]

---

[8] E. Glenn Hinson to Douglas V. Steere, 10 May 1977.

[9] Randall E. Greene to E. Glenn Hinson, 23 January 1979, wrote that Doubleday had sold about 2,500 copies of each volume and was selling about 150 copies per month. He expected a good continuing sale on the basis of reviews.

[10] Paul L. Meacham to E. Glenn Hinson, 21 December 1981.

Any moping I may have done didn't cause me to throw away my 1923 Underwood Standard typewriter on which I wrote prior to 1992. I had scarcely gotten the Doubleday project in the mail when I found my thoughts taken over by an idea that had been fallowing in my mind ever since I had given a paper about "Prayer in an Economy of Abundance" at a meeting of The Ecumenical Institute of Spirituality in 1975. During my time at Tantur, I initiated correspondence with Joe Johnson at Broadman Press about a book I proposed to call *Rethinking Traditional Forms of Prayer*. Following further discussion, when I returned from sabbatical, I mailed a prospectus on 18 August 1976. What with publishers' wheels turning slowly and my own immersion in writing *A History of Baptists in Arkansas*, however, we did not settle on a contract for *The Reaffirmation of Prayer* until 18 May 1978.

I'm almost embarrassed to admit the brevity of the time frame within which I wrote *The Reaffirmation of Prayer*, but I could scarcely have chosen a more inspiring context for doing so. I wrote it in Banglore, India, when I attended my first meeting as a member of the Faith and Order Commission of the World Council of Churches (WCC), from August 15–31. To get the cheapest airfare, a serious concern for me, I had to stay in Bangalore four days after most others had departed. Having brought the notes I needed to do the book, I wrote in longhand almost non-stop and had virtually completed the manuscript when I returned to Louisville. The speed with which I wrote reminds me of John Bunyan's claim that *The Pilgrim's Progress* leaped from his pen "like sparks that from the coals do fly." Making prayer as the friend of humankind my chief point, I issued a call for recovery of use of the traditional forms or dimensions of prayer in corporate as well as private worship as a way to recover communion, communication, or conversation with God as the ultimate Personal Reality in the universe. Although I urged the use of traditional forms of prayer as a way to deepen relationship with God, I focused chiefly on "how this engagement with God carries over into all dimensions of our personal lives and our society." I contended that, "forms can keep us from narrow, one-sided, and self-centered perspectives which so readily intrude into our conversation with God. They can help us see the world, as it were, through God's eyes."[11] To praise, thanksgiving, confession, and intercession and petition, I added surrender on the grounds that "the most truly Christian prayer is one

---

[11] E. Glenn Hinson, *The Reaffirmation of Prayer* (Nashville: Broadman Press, 1979) 10.

which puts all things, including one's own life, in God's hands." "The central article in our prayer," I added, "is always that [God's] kingdom may come and [God's] will be done on earth as in heaven."[12] My hope in writing was to make the book, which I dedicated to Douglas Steere, "a searching, and even a disturbing, experience." We needed to ask "uncomfortable questions." "Anything less would make a mockery of prayer, nay, of faith itself."[13] Well aware that this more carefully planned approach might evoke negative reactions from non-liturgical Baptists, I raised questions as to whether Baptist prayers were really spontaneous or ended up as "liturgical prayers of very poor quality." My call, I insisted, was not for *formal* liturgies "but rather for the *deepening* of prayer through self-conscious effort."[14] To facilitate this, I underscored private prayer as preparation for public, church staff praying together for cultivation of their own relationship with God, and self-conscious preparation of prayers for public worship. The question is: "Does the Holy Spirit not work as well through a longer, self-conscious process as through a momentary one? Logic compels us to say yes indeed."[15]

In the midst of these more popular writing projects, I was hard pressed to coordinate a more scholarly endeavor in the form of *A History of Baptists in Arkansas* aimed at the celebration of the 160th anniversary of the Arkansas Baptist State Convention in 1980 that the History Committee of the Arkansas Baptist State Convention, chaired by Jerry Wilcox, one of my former students, asked me to write. This project was an especially challenging one for a scholar who did not specialize in Baptist history to undertake, and I would be the first to recognize that specialists in Baptist history might have done a better job than I did. Why did I agree to do it? Ego doubtless entered into the decision, the opportunity to add one more star to my crown, but I think the chief reason was the opportunity to write what I prefer to call a socio-institutional history of Baptists in Arkansas and perhaps change the way such histories are usually done. Baptist histories tend to be anecdotal, accounts of "great men," rather than objective explanations as to how certain groups became what they are today. As I explained in the preface, "Although I have tried to give a proper amount of credit to persons, conscious that some matter a great deal, I have sought to

---

[12] Ibid., 11.
[13] Ibid.
[14] Ibid., 12.
[15] Ibid., 13.

explain development with multiple factors in view: sociological, psychological, economic, geographical, and spiritual, as well as personal."[16] Throughout the history I called attention to the impact of social and cultural factors, particularly the business model, had on churches, associations, the convention, schools, orphans' homes, hospitals, and other institutions.

To put together a credible history was an overwhelming task, and, after a short while, I found that I needed to change radically the way I would achieve it. "Initially the Historical Committee of the State Convention employed me as 'editor' of a history of Arkansas Baptists. As the work proceeded, however, it became clear to me that I would have to do much more than assemble materials supplied by others." Besides doing research myself, I employed four graduate students—Fred Grissom, Randall Payne, Gerald Rudolph, and Robin Smith—to supplement my own research as well as articles on selected topics by others.[17]

A History of Baptists in Arkansas elicited highly favorable reviews from some, but others, perhaps expecting another "great man" account, did not think so highly of it. Charles Ashcraft, Executive Secretary of the ABSC, called it "a masterpiece" that "helped our fellowship here in Arkansas." In a letter to Duke McCall, he added, "I feel that the writing of this history is one of the best, if not the best, thing done in my ten year administration here in my native state."[18] John E. Steely, Professor of Historical Theology at Southeastern Baptist Theological Seminary, in a review for *Review and Expositor*, called it "a model for other historians of denominational work."[19] Erwin L. McDonald, Editor of *The Arkansas Baptist*, thought I gave too much attention to Congressman Brooks Hayes and neglected some other important Baptist leaders, but he went on to say that "the Hinson book is worth its weight in gold, all of its shortcomings notwithstanding. It really does show where Southern Baptists in Arkansas have come from, who they are as a denomination, and why they are like they are."[20] William Allen Poe, Associate Professor

---

[16] E. Glenn Hinson, *A History of Baptists in Arkansas* (Little Rock: Arkansas Baptist State Convention, 1979) xiv.

[17] Ibid., xv.

[18] Charles H. Ashcraft to Duke K. McCall, 15 January 1980.

[19] John E. Steeley, Review of *A History of Baptists in Arkansas, 1818–1878* in *Review and Expositor* 77 (Summer 1980): 409.

[20] Erwin L. McDonald, "New Arkansas Baptist History Is "Ivory-Tower" Version," *Arkansas Democrat* 9 (February 1908): 4B.

of History at Northwestern State University, Natchitoches, Louisiana, conceded that my narration of the story as a "socio-institutional history" was "commendable," but he faulted it for "numerous colloquialisms and grammatical problems," and concluded that, "The style of this otherwise sophisticated study will debar it from becoming the model state Baptist history."[21] Given the two-year time frame in which I wrote the book, I'm surprised I was not dealt with more harshly. At the risk of sounding defensive, however, I'm puzzled that Professor Poe spent half of his 600-word review of a 500-page book using a hatchet on three reputed "overstatements" and closing with his stylistic bomb but omitted to at least describe the content and note the book's dozens of tables, maps, charts, and diagrams depicting the development of Baptist life in Arkansas. His treatment perhaps complimented that which I received at the 1980 annual meeting of the Arkansas Baptist State Convention, at which the program committee allotted me five minutes to present their 160-year story! Alumni of Southern Seminary, however, including W.O. Vaught, Bill Clinton's pastor at Immanuel Baptist Church in Little Rock, did turn out in some numbers to hear me give a fuller presentation during their annual meeting. In this speech I thought I had complimented Vaught by mentioning his efforts on behalf of Arkansas Baptist College, an African-American school, but he later wrote a savage letter attacking me. A close friend of W.A. Criswell, I discovered later, he was playing an active role in the fundamentalist movement.

By this point you may think that I had taken on all of the writing projects anyone could possibly manage. Although that may be true, I have to report three other books that appeared in 1980 and 1981: *The Early Church Fathers* in a series of Broadman Christian Classics, *The Evangelization of the Roman Empire*, and *The Priesthood of All Believers*. *The Priesthood of All Believers* was a booklet written as the major study guide for a church training program and does not require further comment.[22]

In October 1976, Steve Bond, an editor at Broadman Press, asked me to chair an advisory committee regarding a series of Christian classics bound in leather. He and I compiled a list of persons to serve on the committee. The committee held its first meeting in May 1977 and worked out a list of twelve volumes. Because I was hard at work on *The Integrity*

---

[21] William Allen Poe, Review of *A History of Baptists in Arkansas: 1818–1878* in *Baptist History and Heritage* 15 (October 1980): 56–57.

[22] *The Priesthood of Believers* (Nashville: Church Training Department, Christian Development Division, 1981).

of the Church, The Doubleday Devotional Classics, and *A History of Baptists in Arkansas,* I had to ask to defer the submission of the volume I agreed to introduce and edit. I finally cleared my schedule enough by the end of 1978 to list the works I hoped to include in it and then trim the number. I signed a contract on 22 September 1978. The volume included the *Didache,* 1 and 2 Clement, Barnabas, Ignatius, Justin Martyr's two *Apologies,* selections from Irenaeus's *Against Heresies,* and Clement of Alexandria's *The Instructor.* The object of the collection was to help readers "see how Christianity progressed from its status as a sect of Judaism to a separate religion whose constituency consisted almost wholly of persons of non-Jewish background."[23]

Given such a glut of writing, it is not hard to understand why I delayed in getting my Oxford dissertation into print as *The Evangelization of the Roman Empire.* But there was another reason for delay, that is, some skepticism as to whether any press would publish a scholarly work done as a dissertation. I didn't want to chop up a book on which I had spent years in order to popularize it for publication. As it turned out, the answer came to me. Watson Mills, Director of Mercer University Press, came to my office one day in August 1980 to ask if I had anything Mercer might publish. I handed him my dissertation. He wrote back on September 9 enclosing a contract. Mercer intended to publish the manuscript essentially as it was except for length; it was not to exceed 320 pages. To meet their requirement about length, I had to delete two long appendixes, neither of which was integral to my basic argument. Mills wanted the manuscript by November 1 or before.

Since I have already summarized the basic thesis of my dissertation, I can focus here on the response to it. *The Evangelization of the Roman Empire* was extensively reviewed in both scholarly and more popular journals, and the favorable responses it received from every quarter assuaged somewhat the pain I had felt and perhaps repaid the energy I had expended in having to revise it. In *Church History,* William G. Rusch, Ecumenical Officer for the Lutheran Church in America, said that it "represents the highest quality scholarship and merits serious attention by patristic scholars and by all those interested in the relationship between religious movements and the institutions they create."[24] In *Interpretation,* Henry McKennie Goodpasture, Professor of Church

---

[23] *The Early Church Fathers,* ed. E. Glenn Hinson, *Christian Classics,* vol. 1 (Nashville: Broadman Press, 1980) 9.

[24] William G. Rusch, *Church History* 52 (September 1983): 349.

History at Union Theological Seminary in Richmond, Virginia, called it "a lucid and stimulating inquiry into the Patristic writings on the subject."[25] In the *Journal of Ecumenical Studies,* Jeffrey Gros, Director of the Commission on Faith and Order of the National Council of Churches (NCC), a Roman Catholic, hit very close to my earnest hopes in writing *The Evangelization of the Roman Empire* when he said,

> The book will be useful in the study of history, of missions, of church and sacrament, and of the faith and order of the community. However, its greatest contribution may be the exploration of new and reconciling methodologies for interpreting those elements in the lives of the churches which have most divided the sectarian, conservative-evangelical Christian from the churchly, confessional catholic communities.[26]

In a lengthy review for *Worship,* German Martinez, a professor at Carlow College in Pittsburgh, said:

> This is undoubtedly a most solid research, as the abundant footnotes of primary sources and research studies prove to the reviewer. It is also an admirable study for the accuracy and balance displayed by the author in dealing with a complex set of problems. In ecumenical terms, Hinson's publication is invaluable. Such unbiased exploration of a decisive epoch of the church is most wanted in interdenominational dialogue.[27]

In *Journal of Church and State,* Harry Rosenberg judged that I had demonstrated that I was "a careful historical researcher attuned to the subtlety and complexity of the social and cultural environment of the Roman Empire."[28] Martin E. Marty said of it in his newsletter *Context,* "If you really take Christian history seriously, here is one to savor."[29] Catholic New Testament scholar Raymond E. Brown once told me that he called it to the attention of Pope John Paul II during a retreat he led at the Vatican!

Somewhat to my surprise, *The Evangelization of the Roman Empire* had extensive classroom usage. The cloth-bound original soon sold out, and Mercer reprinted it in soft cover in 1987. In classes on missions and evangelism, however, conservatives soon discovered some objections they could add to the quotations drawn from *Jesus Christ.*

---

[25] Henry McKennie Goodpasture, *Interpretation* 36 (October 1983): 431.

[26] Jeffrey Gros, *Journal of Ecumenical Studies* 20 (1983): 140.

[27] German Martinez, *Worship* 57 (November 1983): 555.

[28] Harry Rosenberg, *Journal of Church and State* 25 (1983): 151.

[29] Martin E. Marty, *Context* 16 (15 February 1984): 4.

Although *The Evangelization of the Roman* Empire was out of print for a few years, I have been pleased to see its continued use in many seminaries. In January 2005, the librarian of Princeton Theological Seminary, Donald M. Vorp, wrote to ask how Princeton might obtain additional copies for classes using it. I see it listed in bibliographies of numerous courses in Christian missions, and Mercer University Press recently reprinted it.

A perusal of my bibliography during these years will reveal that books constituted only one part of my writing endeavors. By 1980 I had published more than a hundred articles and at least 250 book reviews. What accounts for such a flurry of writing? Reviewing the list, I can see that different factors prompted me to write them. Understandably I wrote many articles and book reviews for *Review & Expositor*, which I edited at this time. I also maintained a keen interest in what was happening in the denomination and published articles on such issues as ordination of women, the spiritual life, and fundamentalism. Many articles originated as addresses I was invited to give during this exciting ecumenical era, and the frequency of requests to publish my speeches made me more intentional about preparing everything for publication. In 1972, for instance, Roman Catholic colleges and universities, discovering that I had known Thomas Merton personally, invited me to share my impressions of him and understanding of his thought and contributions. From those invitations originated a series of articles on Merton: "Merton's Many Faces,"[30] "The Catholicizing of Contemplation: Thomas Merton's Place in the Church's Prayer Life,"[31] and "Expansive Catholicism: Ecumenical Perceptions of Thomas Merton."[32] Most of my articles, however, responded to requests from denominational or ecumenical publications such as *Christian Century*, for which I wrote about theological education in the SBC,[33] gave a profile of the

---

[30] E. Glenn Hinson, "Merton's Many Faces," *Religion in Life*, 42 (Summer 1973): 153–167.

[31] E. Glenn Hinson, "The Catholicizing of Contemplation: Thomas Merton's Place in the Church's Prayer Life," *Perspectives in Religious Studies* 1 (Spring 1974): 66–84; *Cistercian Studies* 10 (1975): 173–89.

[32] E. Glenn Hinson, "Expansive Catholicism: Ecumenical Perceptions of Thomas Merton," *Religion in Life* 48 (Spring 1979): 63–76; reprinted in *The Message of Thomas Merton*, ed. Patrick Hart, Cistercian Studies Series, no. 42 (Kalamazoo MI: Cistercian Publications, 1981) 55–71.

[33] E. Glenn Hinson, "Theological Education 1977: A Southern Baptist Context," *Christian Century* 94 (2–9 February 1977): 93–95.

denomination for a series edited by Martin Marty,[34] assessed a Baptist peace convocation in Louisville,[35] and reported on the annual meeting of the SBC in Houston in 1979.[36]

You are probably wondering, as I am, how I managed to do a slew of books, articles, and book reviews in such a short time because most of them did not write themselves, as *The Reaffirmation of Prayer* seems to have done. I'm not sure I can explain it myself. To my regret, I know that I often neglected my wife and children. They tolerated more than I had a right to expect of them. I have to beg their forgiveness. That I could do it at all required tremendous energy and good health, but, even more, a discipline that dated back at least to my college years when I worked at A&P and carried an eighteen-hour load at Washington University. I stretched and strengthened my academic muscles further during graduate studies and pushed myself to the limit when I moved from New Testament to teach Church history. You have seen already the price I paid for attempting the impossible, but the hard climb of those years, inuring me to hardship, produced a remarkable amount of fruit in these years. In the last analysis, however, I have to speak about grace, God at work in me to give both the motive and the ability to do what pleases God (Phil 2:13).

---

[34] E. Glenn Hinson, "The Southern Baptists: A Concern for Experiential Conversion," *Christian Century* 95 (7–14 June 1978): 610–15; later published in *Where the Spirit Leads: American Denominations Today*, ed. Martin E. Marty (Atlanta: John Knox Press, 1980).

[35] "SBC's Peacemaking Convo: How Significant Was It?" *Christian Century* 96 (14 March 1979): 268–69.

[36] E. Glenn Hinson, "The SBC—Houston, 1979," *Christian Century* 96 (18–25 July 1979): 33–36.

15

"THAT ALL MAY BE ONE"

We are all molded and shaped by the age in which we live. In some ways that is good, as it has been for me. Had Pope John XXIII and the Second Vatican Council not come along at the very beginning of my teaching career, I would not have had the heart for Christian unity and the incredible opportunities I have had to bask in the breath of God that irradiates other Christian traditions and other religions. From what I have narrated thus far, you can see why my heart and my lips want to pour out paeans of praise and thanksgiving for Pope John and his "New Pentecost."

Although I am fearful that I may seem to be bragging, I cannot render a good account of my life and work without speaking about my involvement in several important ecumenical ventures that started in the 1970s. The one with the greatest long-range import was a Consultation on Believers' Baptism held at Southern Seminary at the end of March 1979, which laid the foundation for the statement on baptism in *Baptism, Eucharist, and Ministry*, an agreed statement adopted by the Faith and Order Commission of the World Council of Churches at Lima, Peru, in January 1982, and later at the Sixth Assembly of the World Council of Churches in Vancouver, Canada, in 1983. I do not want to create the erroneous impression that I played a leading role in the Louisville Consultation. I served chiefly as the arranger and facilitator of the conference, although the Standing Commission had already nominated me to the Faith and Order Commission in 1976, and I participated fully in the discussion.

My involvement began with a letter from Stephen Cranford, a staff member of Faith and Order in Geneva, dated 1 August 1977. Noting that the Ecumenical Institute of Wake Forest University had already expressed interest in hosting a meeting, he contacted me to see if Southern Seminary would also be interested.[1] I responded on August 16 to say that we would[2] and immediately checked it out with Roy

---

[1] Stephen Cranford to E. Glenn Hinson, 1 August 1977.
[2] E. Glenn Hinson to Stephen Cranford, 16 August 1977.

Honeycutt, the Dean of the School of Theology, expressing my hope that we could host the consultation at Southern. On August 18, Honeycutt replied to say that he concurred with my suggestion of Louisville as a potential site for the consultation and would support my efforts to locate it there. Subsequently, I contacted Claude Broach and William Angell at the Ecumenical Institute and obtained their agreement to back the conference at Southern Seminary.[3] On November 4, Cranford replied that there were some in Faith and Order still holding out for Europe, but he thought that the presence of recognized Baptist scholars with interest in the issue favored Louisville. Initially Cranford and I tried to schedule the consultation for the 1978 Thanksgiving recess, but this proved unworkable for Europeans, so we moved it to the spring of 1979. Southern Seminary provided lodging and food for participants, and I sought to obtain travel subsidies for those who came from abroad.[4] Cranford estimated that we would need $11,000, so you can imagine the pressure I felt to come up with some of the funds, especially those needed by Third World participants. I arranged speaking engagements in local churches for a number of the participants and applied to foundations and wealthy persons for money. Several of our graduate students served as stewards.

As I have reviewed the thick file of correspondence, schedules, and documents from the consultation, I'm startled to see once again how many administrative details I had to attend to, especially in recognition of my relative ineptness in such matters. That I did well enough to earn commendation from Cranford[5] and others surely confirms the weight I placed on bringing Paedo-baptists and believer Baptists into a more friendly relationship and mutual understanding. No issue had created a more bitter division and caused greater suffering than baptism during the Reformation of the sixteenth century. To gather more than thirty theologians representing the two sides of the issue for an amicable discussion had tremendous emotional significance for me. Even more important, it laid the groundwork for the statement on baptism in

---

[3] E. Glenn Hinson to Stephen Cranford, 17 October 1977.

[4] In a 22 November 1977 letter to me, Stephen Cranford thought 20–22 November 1978, would be a good date, but on 16 January 1978, he wrote back to say that Morris West could not come then and suggested dates between 24 March and 11 April or 8 and 31 July 1979, as alternatives. Cranford confirmed the date of 28 March–1 April 1979, on 20 February 1978.

[5] Stephen Cranford in a letter to participants, 4 May 1979.

Baptism, Eucharist and Ministry that demonstrates "major areas of theological convergence."[6] The press release by the Faith and Order Commission probably stated the result accurately:

> The outcome of the consultation revealed that although the divide between the two practices of baptism remains, nevertheless there are signs of bridge building from both sides. Discussion indicated that for some from both groups of churches the bridge is sufficiently complete to allow mutual acceptance of each other's practice. For others the gap remaining has narrowed sufficiently to permit mutual respect and growing understanding of the reasons for the different practices.
>
> The Louisville Consultation indicated that there are grounds for optimism provided always that, as happened at the consultation, the existing disagreements are faced openly in frank discussion and are not swept under some ecumenical carpet in the cause of too superficial a consensus.[7]

The consultation brought together some distinguished theologians, both Baptist and non-Baptist. J. Robert Nelson, a Methodist theologian at Boston University, chaired it. Baptist presenters included Morris West from Bristol, England, Horace O. Russell from Jamaica, George R. Beasley-Murray from Southern Seminary, and Thorwald Lorenzen from Rüschlikon, Switzerland. Other papers were given by Joseph Eagan, a Roman Catholic from San Francisco, Lawrence Stookey, a Methodist from Washington, DC, and William Carpe, a Disciple of Christ from Lexington, Kentucky. Other church groups represented were Greek and Russian Orthodox, Lutheran, Netherlands Reformed, Episcopal, and Mennonite.[8]

---

[6] William H. Lazareth and Nikos Nissiotis, "Preface" to *Baptism, Eucharist and Ministry*, Faith and Order Paper No. 111 (Geneva: World Council of Churches, 1982) ix.

[7] Commission on Faith and Order, World Council of Churches, "Consultation on Baptism, Southern Baptist Seminary, Louisville, 28 March–1 April, 1979," 2.

[8] A full list would encumber the text, but merits notation. Besides those named, Baptists included: S.T. Ola Akande (Nigeria), Claude U. Broach (Southern Baptist, Winston-Salem, North Carolina), Arthur Crabtree (American Baptist, Villanova, Pennsylvania), Vitali Kulikov (Moscow), Emmanuel McCall (Southern Baptist, Atlanta), Norman Maring (American Baptist, Philadelphia), Dale Moody (Southern Baptist, Louisville, Kentucky), John Nicholson (British Council of Churches, London), J.S. Royal (National Baptist, Louisville, Kentucky), Günter Wagner (German Baptist, Rüschlikon, Switzerland), and Charles R. Wills (Southern Baptist, BWA, Washington, DC). Representing other denominations besides those mentioned were: John C. Bush (Disciples of Christ, Kentucky), H. Dale Crockett (United Church of Christ, Berea,

A Reuter's report created some waves among conservative Baptists to which I had to reply. It overstated what happened when it said, "The breakthrough involved a new recognition by Baptist theologians of the validity of infant baptism" and reported that Roman Catholic, Orthodox, Reformed, and Anglican theologians saw it as "'a step forward,' because the Baptist theologians accepted the validity of infant baptism and rejected a need for the sacrament to be repeated for converts to Baptist churches who were baptized in infancy."[9] Some Baptist theologians would have agreed with such statements, but the *consultation* did not. In response to one letter questioning this article, I explained that it was accurate in saying that Paedo-baptists acknowledged believers' baptism as "the most clearly attested practice for baptism in the New Testament," but noted that the writer "failed to quote the full statement in which it was merely agreed by Baptists that infant baptism 'has developed within the Christian tradition and witnesses to valid Christian insights'." I went on to say, "There is no acknowledgement at all in this statement that Baptists recognize 'the validity of infant baptism' and 'rejected a need for the sacrament to be repeated for converts to Baptist churches who were baptized in infancy.'" Although American Baptists did report that 40 percent of their churches practice open membership, "no statement of any kind was adopted which affirmed either of the statements made by the Reuter's article." What the consultation did was to help both groups understand better the viewpoint of the other.[10]

Prior even to the Louisville Consultation, I attended my first meeting as a member of Faith and Order in Bangalore, India, from 15–31 August 1978. When named to the commission in 1976,[11] I had serious doubts as to whether I could come up with the money to pay my way.

Kentucky), L.A. Hoedemaker (Dutch Reformed, Groningen, Netherlands), Nicholas Lossky (Russian Orthodox, Paris, France), John Wade Payne (Disciples of Christ, Louisville, Kentucky), Bishop David B. Reed (Episcopal, Louisville, Kentucky), Alice Schimpf (Lutheran, Columbus, Ohio), Stanley A. Schmidt (Roman Catholic, Louisville, Kentucky), Howard H. Willen (United Methodist, Hopkinsville, Kentucky), Gregory Wingenbach (Greek Orthodox, Louisville, Kentucky), and John Yoder (Mennonite)

[9] Reuters, "Theologians Hail Agreement on Meaning of Baptism," *The Blade* (Toledo, Ohio) 2 April 1979.

[10] E. Glenn Hinson to the Rev. James R. Pinkley, Jr., Director of Associational Missions, Maumee Valley Association of Baptists, Toledo, Ohio, 23 April 1979.

[11] Lukas Vischer, Director of Faith and Order, extended the invitation on 3 June 1976. I gave my acceptance in a letter dated 16 June 1976.

Although Southern Seminary provided stipends to attend professional or denominational meetings, it did not fund participation in those connected with the National or World Councils of Churches.[12] When I shared my doubts about getting to Bangalore with Stephen Cranford, Lukas Vischer, Director of the Secretariat for Christian Unity, insisted and said that, if need be, Faith and Order would pay my way.[13] Knowing the financial needs of members coming from the Third World to such meetings, however, I was determined not to burden the WCC and put out pleas to some churches and individuals who might help. Help came from Myers Park Baptist and St. John's Baptist Churches in Charlotte, North Carolina, Deer Park Baptist Church in Louisville, and two generous individuals.

You will know already how productive this trip turned out to be because of my prolonged stay in Bangalore. Far beyond the time it gave me to write a book, however, it enlarged my world and sensitized and conscientized me to the plight of people living in the southern hemisphere. Since I had never traveled so far east, I tingled both with excitement and with apprehension in anticipation. I was a little anxious that I might not have all of the inoculations I needed to go to a Third World country and had to impose on a doctor friend, Charles Gaba, to give me a malaria shot on a Sunday, the day I left. I could not have anticipated, however, the eventfulness of the flight over. Prior to my departure for Bombay (Mumbai) by way of Tehran, American newspapers featured articles on the uprising that was taking place in Iran under leadership of the Ayatollah Khomeini. When our 747 touched down, I looked out and saw fighter planes lined up along the runway. A coup had deposed the Shah. The crew announced that passengers going to Bombay should remain on board. As soon as the Tehran passengers disembarked, the mammoth plane tracked back down the runway, turned around, and took off with, by my count, twelve passengers. The crew outnumbered us two to one!

Bombay broke my heart. We arrived in the wee hours of the morning in heavy rain. A forest of little arms, mostly children's,

---

[12] In a memo dated 5 December 1977, Dr. McCall explained that "because of the position of the Southern Baptist Convention" he could not make funds available, but he had written some friends interested in the relationship of Southern Baptists to the WCC. None responded favorably. When Roy Honeycutt became president in 1984, he regularly came up with money.

[13] Lukas Vischer to E. Glenn Hinson, 19 April 1978.

stretched out and up as dozens of little voices screeched for help. This was my introduction to the dire poverty of a developing nation. I'd read about it and, at Southern Seminary, served as faculty sponsor of a World Hunger Group, but now it dashed me in the face like cold rain. Because I had about eight or ten hours before my flight to Bangalore, I took a room in the airport hotel and tried to sleep but spent most of the time thinking about those children dwarfed by malnutrition, bodies painted garishly to attract attention.

Bangalore, in India's highlands, showed far less grinding poverty than Bombay. The Commission on Faith and Order met in the Ecumenical Christian Centre at Whitefield, near Bangalore, but many of us were lodged in Kristu Jyoti College, a theological school of the Salesian Fathers twenty minutes away. I felt at home in the college when, every morning at worship, we sang "Amazing Grace." Travel back and forth by bus gave me the opportunity to get to know Raymond E. Brown, the brilliant Catholic New Testament scholar because, when we sat together, he frequently pumped me for information about early Church history. I must confess that I got more out of our conversations than I did from participation in the preparation of program sessions with the exception of further planning for the Louisville Consultation on Believers' Baptism. I did venture to question whether the phrase "unity in reconciled diversity" could be interpreted broadly enough to allow for (1) national diversity and (2) the continuation of denominations. What seems to have generated the most excitement at the Bangalore meeting was the number of people who suffered from diarrhea and dehydration or parasites. My appetite diminished steadily during my three weeks and I lost fourteen pounds, mostly because I don't like curried food, but I felt okay. The week after my return to Louisville, however, my appetite hadn't returned, and I experienced increasing nausea every day. A doctor prescribed antibiotics for parasites.

Although I gained far more from the plenary than I was able or prepared to contribute to it, the meeting did present me with an opportunity to make a small contribution toward addressing the problem of poverty in India. What happened in this case shows that little efforts matter, sometimes a great deal, and that we should not throw up our hands in despair when looking at something like world hunger in macrocosm, thus, doing nothing. Surendra Mohanty, one of our young stewards at the meeting, entreated me to help him come to the United States to study social work to prepare himself to return and carry out a ministry to his native city. I could not give strong assurances, but I promised to do what I could. On returning, I presented Mohanty's plea and suggested that the men's Sunday school class at Deer Park Church, where my family and I were members, consider sponsoring Mohanty. To my surprise, they did![14] Early in 1981, we also brought his young bride to Louisville.[15] During his time here, Mohanty proved adept at generating sponsorship for a program he called "Fishermen's Children" designed to educate the children of impoverished fishermen in Puri, near Orissa. He and his wife Bulbul started the children's home and school early in 1985 shortly after they returned to India.

Going to a second meeting of the Faith and Order Commission in the southern hemisphere stretched my already expanding consciousness and comprehension of Christianity. For one thing, the flight to Lima entailed even more risk than traveling to India. My flight, by way of Miami, went smoothly, but that of another Faith and Order member, Paul Crow's, made an unscheduled stop in the middle of the Amazon River. When I went to the Lima airport to fly home, I was told that my flight would be delayed twenty-four hours because of mechanical problems. Very anxious to get back to Louisville, I broke down and sobbed when I called Martha to tell her about the delay. As life's interruptions sometimes do, that delay turned out to be an unspeakably generous gift. A Methodist steward who had shuttled me to the airport took me to her church where I spoke at the morning worship and then to her parents' home for lunch. In the afternoon, she conducted me through the wonderful Inca museum at the heart of Lima, so that I got a firsthand glimpse of their remarkable silver craftsmanship and other evidences of their advanced civilization.

---

[14] In letters dated 27 November 1979, and 2 January 1980, I informed Mohanty that the Challengers Class at Deer Park had agreed to sponsor him but would not be able to sponsor his wife also. He married 4 January 1980. Our sponsorship, however, enabled him to obtain a visa to study in the United States in July. I cabled him 22 July that his ticket awaited him at the Calcutta airport and he was to depart for the US on 11 August. He arrived in Louisville on 12 August.

[15] On 23 February 1981, David Vaught, Southern's comptroller, informed me that Deer Park Church was guaranteeing $6,875.00 for Mohanty and his wife, that the seminary would supply $500 a month in addition to some employment for Mohanty, and that, as she arranged her visa, Vaught would work to obtain money for her air fare. By this time virtually every class at Deer Park and countless individuals not only there but in other churches as well were contributing to the Mohanty Fund. Charushree Naik (Bulbul) Mohanty arrived in Louisville a short time afterwards.

Although we met in a developing country, none of us could complain about the facilities we had at our disposal. The plenary convened in a lovely retreat and conference center on the outskirts of Lima. Although quite a few of us experienced what someone called "Montezuma's revenge"—diarrhea—a nurse quickly supplied us with Imodium, and I don't think anyone ended up in a hospital. When Montezuma put his curse on me, Wolfhart Pannenberg shared with me part of a supply of Weetabix, a dry cracker his wife had packed for him for such emergencies. With Imodium, my discomfort lasted only a day. What challenged my northern hemisphere theology more than diarrhea was the down-to-earth thinking of people who lived in more dire poverty than I had known myself, even as I grew up in the Missouri Ozarks during the Great Depression. Just a few miles from the comfortable retreat center were the barrios of Lima, with two million people subsisting without electricity, running water, sanitary facilities, or adequate housing. In another part of Lima, the wealthy lived in fortified enclaves with all of the amenities money could buy, guarded and escorted by private police. The people of the barrios in their "base churches" interpreted and applied the Gospels in simple ways; they did not have much patience for sophisticated critical study of scriptures or church tradition. They challenged us to *live* what we said we believed. One of the major shapers of liberation theology, Gustavo Gutierrez, a Peruvian, and other Latin Americans challenged us during the meeting by asking whether all of the theologizing would do something to alleviate the oppression of the poor.

The Lima meeting posed a special, personal challenge for me. A congregation founded by Southern Baptist missionaries summoned me to appear on Sunday and explain what I, a Southern Baptist, was doing in a conference sponsored by that "communist" World Council of Churches. I composed a brief speech in Spanish with the help of an interpreter, rejecting the label "communist" and explaining what the Commission on Faith and Order did. Although the congregation treated me cordially, I don't think my Spanish was good enough to convince any of them that the World Council of Churches did good work and had good intentions. Before I left Lima, I learned that a Carl McIntire disciple assumed the role of pastor the day after I spoke![16]

---

[16] Carl McIntire (1906–2002) was founder of the fundamentalist Bible Presbyterian Church and expended much of his energy attacking the WCC.

By the time the plenary of the Faith and Order Commission met in Lima, Peru, I had enough experience under my belt to benefit more from, and contribute more to, the proceedings. The greatest excitement, of course, attached to the finalizing of *Baptism, Eucharist and Ministry*, and I had done enough work on it to share a palpable excitement among most members of the Commission. Those who knew the history of the Church knew that, in this one momentous meeting, we were together atoning for 400 years of sins of which we had all been guilty and were stretching forth toward the upward call of God and a new era in our relationships. The moment we unanimously adopted *BEM*, I wept. In a preface to the document, William H. Lazareth, Director of the Secretariat on Faith and Order, and Nikos Nissiotis, Moderator of the Commission on Faith and Order, labeled it "the fruit of a 50-year process of study stretching back to the first Faith and Order Conference at Lausanne in 1927." After reviewing the steps leading to Lima, they summed up what it meant:

> In leaving behind the hostilities of the past, the churches have begun to discover many promising convergences in their shared convictions and perspectives. These convergences give assurances that despite much diversity in theological expression the churches have much in common in their understanding of the faith. The resultant text aims to become part of a faithful and sufficient reflection of the common Christian Tradition on essential elements of Christian communion. In the process of growing together in mutual trust, the churches must develop these doctrinal convergences step by step, until they are finally able to declare together that they are living in communion with one another in continuity with the apostles and the teachings of the universal Church.

Reflecting on this important statement, they went on to observe, "That theologians of such widely different traditions should be able to speak so harmoniously about Baptism, eucharist and ministry is unprecedented in the modern ecumenical movement. Particularly noteworthy is the fact that the Commission also includes among its full members theologians of the Roman Catholic and other churches which do not belong to the World Council of Churches itself." [17] To think that I was one of the latter—O God!

Momentous as the adoption of *BEM* was, the Commission was also cranking up some other important studies, notably, The Community of Women and Men in the Church, The Unity of the Church and the

---

[17] *Baptism, Eucharist and Ministry.* Faith and Order Paper No. 111 (Geneva: World Council of Churches, 1982) ix.

Renewal of Human Community, and Towards the Common Expression of the Apostolic Faith Today. Although I had a keen interest in all three studies, I was enlisted in the third in the Faith and Order Commissions of both World and National Councils of Churches. As a follow up of the initial discussion of the apostolic faith, the Commission convened a Consultation on the Apostolic Faith in the Scriptures and in the Early Church in Rome, Italy, the first week of October 1983. The consultation was composed of a distinguished group of scholars representing the whole Christian spectrum—Roman Catholic, Orthodox, and Protestant.[18] I was asked to present a paper on "The Apostolic Faith as Expressed in the Writings of the Apostolic and Church Fathers," my first formal presentation in a Faith and Order meeting. Several of the papers, including mine,[19] were published in the Faith and Order series under the title *Roots of Our Common Faith: Faith in Scriptures and in the Early Church.* I believe that I would not err in ascribing this invitation to take a leading part in a study to which Faith and Order attached such importance to my training both in New Testament and in Patristics and to the respect they accorded my work in *The Evangelization of the Roman Empire.*

The Apostolic Faith Study in the Faith and Order Commission of the National Council of Churches was launched in 1981, prior to Lima. Very much to my surprise, Jeffrey Gros and William Rusch, respectively Director and Chair of the Faith and Order Commission, asked me to chair the study during the first triennium (1981–84) and, as it turned out, to co-chair it with Roberta Bondi (United Methodist) and Lauree Hersch Meyer (Church of the Brethren) for a second. Sensitive to my deafness,

---

[18] The list is worth footnoting: Raymond E. Brown (Roman Catholic), Janet Crawford (Church of the Province of New Zealand), John Deschner (United Methodist), Kwesi Dickson (Methodist Church, Ghana), Ellen Flesseman-van Leer (Netherlands Reformed Church), Günter Gassmann (Lutheran), Glenn Hinson (Southern Baptist), Alois Klein (Roman Catholic), Georg Kretschmar (Lutheran), Emmanuel Lanne (Roman Catholic), Jorge Pantelis (Methodist Church, Bolivia), Horace O. Russell (Jamaica Baptist Union), Todor Sabev (Bulgarian Orthodox Church), V.C. Samuel (Orthodox Syrian Church in the East), Timotei Seviciu Lugojanul (Romanian Orthodox Church), Max Thurian (Reformed Church in France), Jean Tillard (Roman Catholic Church, Canada), Günter Wagner (Baptist), Geoffrey Wainwright (Methodist Church of Great Britain), Michael Wyschogrod (Jewish Community), and John D. Zizioulas (Ecumenical Patriarchate of Constantinople).

[19] E. Glenn Hinson, "The Apostolic Faith as expressed in the Writings of the Apostolic and Church Fathers," *The Roots of Our Common Faith: Faith in the Scriptures and in the Early Church,* ed. Hans-Georg Link, Faith and Order Paper No. 119 (Geneva: World Council of Churches, 1984).

my limitations in administrative skills, the considerable stress I worked under in the SBC, and especially the fact that I belonged to a non-member denomination, I accepted the honor with great reluctance. I'm hesitant to assess what the six years of study achieved and what I contributed to it, but I can summarize the chief developments.[20]

In the first triennium, the Apostolic Faith Study Group spent a considerable amount of time getting acquainted with varied perspectives on the issue in different traditions and made three important decisions that laid a foundation for the work accomplished in the second triennium: (1) that the study in the NCC stands on its own and should not be subordinated to that of the WCC; (2) that the Nicene Creed does not express all that Apostolic Faith is; and (3) that the American context has something special to offer the study, e.g., inclusive language, black churches' response, free churches' outlook, etc.

In the second triennium, the Apostolic Faith Study Group distributed the study among three sub-groups. One group focused on the Apostolic Faith in the American context. A second sought to define the criteria for Apostolic Faith as established by diverse traditions. A third produced a short study guide for the Nicene Creed. Running alongside and complementing the Apostolic Faith Study were five consultations. One dealt with language problems posed by the Creed.[21] A second elicited responses from black churches.[22] A third entailed a discussion of Christology between representative Protestant and Oriental Orthodox theologians centered on earlier WCC consultations between Orthodox and Roman Catholic theologians.[23] A fourth consultation, held at Holy Cross Seminary between representative Protestant and Greek Orthodox theologians, focused on pneumatology.[24] A fifth, convened at Fuller Seminary, expanded the discussion of pneumatology in the direction of the Pentecostal churches.

---

[20] My summary is based on a report I delivered to the full commission at Graymoor, New York, on 17 October 1987.

[21] Papers were published in the *Union Seminary Quarterly*.

[22] Gayraud Wilmore published an article based on this consultation in *Christian Century*.

[23] Papers used in this consultation have been published in a volume entitled *Christ in East and West*, ed. Paul R. Fries, and Tiran Nersoyan (Macon GA: Mercer University Press, 1987). These included "Oriental Orthodox Christology: A Southern Baptist Perspective" by me (147–54).

[24] Papers prepared for this consultation have appeared in the *Greek Orthodox Theological Review*.

For the first triennium the Apostolic Faith Study consumed a lot of my interest, energy, and time. As a matter of fact, when St. John's University in Collegeville, Minnesota, invited me to teach a course in the MA program there during the summer of 1983, I proposed the Apostolic Faith Study, thinking it would be of interest to Catholic religious and clergy. That was not a wise choice, as it turned out, however, for only two students elected it, and I've wished in retrospect that I had offered Prayer in Christian History or Classics of Christian Devotion. By the second triennium, although my interest remained high and I took an active part in the study, circumstances in the Southern Baptist Convention weighted me down and made it hard for me to continue on. On 15 December 1987, I wrote Jeff Gros to confess "a deep sense of misgiving about being overextended and not doing what I should, certainly not in quality" and asked to withdraw from the Commission. By this time, the inerrantists had seized control of the Board of Trustees at Southern Seminary as well as boards of all other agencies of the denomination. The only way to get out of the bog in which I found myself, I went on to explain, was to let someone else take my place on the Faith and Order Commission. I recommended Timothy George as perhaps "the best person, certainly more acceptable to the Fundamentalists now controlling the Home Mission Board than I am."[25] The year, 1987, also marked the end of my participation in the Roman Catholic/Southern Baptist Scholars' Dialogues.

I experienced a lot of pain in loosening this ecumenical tie. I would not claim to have handled well the stresses and strains created by a denomination undergoing a radical reorientation, but I would have coped with what was happening with far less courage and grace had I not felt sympathy and support from the wider Christian community. Although I cut the knot binding me to the work of the NCC, therefore, I was not ready to do the same with reference to the WCC and continued on the Faith and Order Commission until 1992. Due to the unexpected death of my uncle Ossie Marsh, I had to cancel my participation in the Faith and Order plenary in Stavanger, Norway, in August 1985. I did take part in the plenary in Budapest, Hungary, held 8–21 August 1989, a meeting that furthered a feeling of the impending dissolution of the Soviet Empire that I had developed during peace tours of the USSR in 1984 and East Germany in 1988. The acme of my years of involvement in Faith and Order, however, was not Budapest but my participation in a

---

[25] E. Glenn Hinson to Brother Jeffrey Gros, 15 December 1987.

"Consultation on 'Ecclesiology—Basic Ecumenical Perspectives" held in Pyatigorsk, USSR, 22–29 November 1988 in commemoration of the one thousandth anniversary of the birth of Christianity in Russia.

I can scarcely find words to express adequately the exhilaration I felt in taking part in this historic event on the very eve of the dissolution of the Soviet Union. I do not have direct evidence to confirm it, but I suspect that Premier Gorbachev himself turned some handles and spun some wheels to make this meeting happen, for, after completing our consultation in Pyatigorsk, we traveled by bus to Stavropol to worship on Sunday in the Orthodox Cathedral where Gorbachev's mother worshipped. Be that as it may, it was little short of miraculous that forty theologians from fifteen different countries in Africa, Asia, Europe, North and South America, and the Caribbean could gather to discuss ecclesiology when, for years, Russian Orthodox theologians could scarcely get exit visas to attend meetings of the World Council of Churches. That the illustrious group of theologians would happen to include a Southern Baptist who once attended Cave Spring Landmark Missionary Baptist Church in the Missouri Ozarks was *truly* a miracle!

Insofar as I can see, the consultation did not come out with any important statements. A brief press release noted that it "discussed the understanding, unity and mission of the Church in the contemporary world" without pointing to particular conclusions. With Roberta Bondi I served as a recorder for one of the study groups, but what mattered to me far more than the dialogue was the human engagement that accompanied it. On the journey northwest from Pyatigorsk to Stavropol, we passed through rich farmland whose black loam reminded me of the prairies of Illinois. Our guide, Victor Degterenko, started talking about the fine horses raised in the area. "A man here sold a horse to someone in Lexington, Kentucky, for $15 million" he said with some pride. A short time afterwards, I went up to the front of the bus where he stood and said, "I'm from Kentucky." We talked briefly for a few minutes. When we arrived at the hotel that evening, he asked me if I would take a walk with him in the town square. Public buildings were likely to be bugged.

Victor wanted to talk about faith. He asked me what he and his wife could do to help their nine-year-old daughter, Olga, respond to the teachings of atheism in the schools. "You did one important thing when you named her Olga," I said. St. Olga was Russia's first Christian. I reminded him that we can't prove the existence of God, that the Bible doesn't try to prove the existence of God; it assumes that God is. I talked about Augustine's *"credo ut intellegam"* ("I believe in order to understand"). I cited Pascal's Wager Argument and quoted his famous dictum, "The heart has its reasons, the reason cannot understand." I spoke about my own experience at age eighteen. He seemed to comprehend, and during the morning worship the next day I noticed him unobtrusively crossing himself—a bold act for someone employed by the state.

The Liturgy of St. Basil conducted by Archbishop Anthony in the magnificent cathedral in Stavropol on Sunday morning touched me deeply as I watched seventy- and eighty-year-old men and women stand for two or three hours rapt in prayer before the iconostasis. I tried to stand alongside them, but halfway through the service my knees were quivering. The church provided pews for us weak-kneed Westerners, and most of us sat. Even though I could not understand the words, I shared visually in the story of salvation and gained new insight about icons. At the conclusion a small number took communion and then brought babes in arms to receive the bread dipped in wine. A profound sense of unity with the saints of all the ages enveloped me.

The time I had spent with Victor evidently upset one of the Russian Orthodox theologians from America, always nervous about proselytism, for he grilled me about our conversation. I assured him that I was not trying to make a Southern Baptist out of Victor but simply confirming him in his faith. Before the whole group left Stavropol, Victor reported that his wife had given birth to a second daughter. Someone asked, "Well, what will you name her?" He responded, "We're thinking of naming her Kentucky." I sent word back to him, "Don't name her Kentucky! Name her after another of the Russian saints!" He sent a Christmas card with this note: "God bless you. Thanks for your openness and sincerity here in the Northern Caucasus in November 1988."

Budapest provided a good ending for my years on the Faith and Order Commission of the World Council of Churches. The Commission did not produce another notable document like *BEM*, but it took some steps forward on each of the projects launched earlier—Apostolic Faith, Unity of the Church and the Renewal of Human Community, and *BEM*—and delineated some future topics—Unity and Mission, The Unity We Seek, Ecumenical Perspectives on Ecclesiology, and The Future Role and Task of Faith and Order. At this stage I felt more engaged with a wider revolution I could see going on around me.[26] My world was in transition just like the Hungarian world, except in reverse. As the Southern Baptist Convention lapsed into fundamentalist captivity, Hungary was about to escape its captivity from the Soviet Goliath that had imposed its iron grip in 1956 during a brief try for freedom. Hungarians were already enjoying cruises up and down the beautiful Danube River, and the churches—Orthodox, Catholic, and Reformed— operated with relative freedom. Symbolic perhaps of a vast change in the city where Soviet tanks crushed a coup in 1956 were the golden arches of a McDonald's restaurant in the center of the old city. In 1957–58, one of the students wounded in the Hungarian uprising spent a year as a student at Southern Seminary. He could not understand why Americans did not come to their aid.

---

[26] In advance of Budapest I did prepare a paper on "The Ecclesiology of *Confessing One Faith*: A Baptist Response," in which I emphasized Baptist commitment to the voluntary principle in religion and careful adherence to scriptures as the two criteria by which Baptists would assess *Confessing One Faith*.

Glenn (about eighteen months) and Gene (about three)
in St. Louis, Missouri

Glenn (about age four) and Gene (age six) in backyard of house
on Potomac Street, St. Louis, Missouri

Glenn (about age seven) with cousin Carol Crow (about age three)
at farm near Cuba, Missouri

Half-sister Sue with her favorite hen in front yard of our farm
at Cave Spring, Missouri, ca. 1948

Sullivan High School

This Certifies That

Edward Glenn Hinson

has satisfactorily completed the Course of Study prescribed by the Board of Education for the High School Department and is therefore entitled to this

Diploma

Given at Sullivan, Missouri, this 20 day of May A. D. 1949

L. L. Sexton
SUPERINTENDENT

George Hayes
PRESIDENT BOARD OF EDUCATION

Olinda F. Glaser
PRINCIPAL

Mary Finell
SECRETARY BOARD OF EDUCATION

High school diploma

Glenn exiting First Baptist Church, Affton, Missouri, ca. 1951

Aunt Fleta Marsh in backyard of home in Affton, Missouri, ca. 1955

Uncle Ossie Marsh with prize tomatoes, ca. 1980

Glenn posing with anti-aircraft gun at Fort Bliss, Texas, summer 1953

Mullins Hall, Southern Seminary, 1954

Glenn at missions conference, Southern Seminary, 1955.
Professor Cornell Goerner is seated just in front to the left.

Hiroshi Kanamaki, fellow student, a former Japanese kamikaze pilot

Glenn and Martha at youth retreat, First Baptist, Affton, Missouri, ca. 1955

Glenn and Martha at a wedding reception, First Baptist, Affton, Missouri, 1955

Glenn between Albert Parish and Jesse Evans behind the pulpit
of First Baptist Church, Eminence, Indiana, ca. 1958

1951 Chevy Powerglide totaled on 31E south of Austin, Indiana

Glenn enjoying a pastoral visit with Jesse Evans at his farm

Glenn and Martha with Professor and Mrs. Otto Pieper on steps
of Alumni Chapel at The Southern Baptist Theological Seminary, ca. 1960.
Professor Pieper gave the Mullins Lectures.

Gene on a visit to St. Louis, ca. 1960

Glenn autographing copies of *Seekers after Mature Faith*, Southern Seminary, 1968

Glenn, Martha, Chris, and Elizabeth, ca. 1973

Glenn in a Kafiya on a Sinai trip, spring 1976

Glenn and Martha descending the Mount of Olives
in Jerusalem on Palm Sunday, 1976

Glenn with faculty and students of the Baptist Seminary,
Recife, Brazil following lectures in 1976

Glenn sitting next to Douglas Steere at annual meeting
of the Ecumenical Institute of Spirituality, Southern Seminary, 1988

Faith and Order Commission, WCC, consultation in Pyatigorsk, Russia, 1988

Glenn with staff and advisory board members
of *Weavings*, Nashville, ca. 2000

Glenn with Sister Miriam Schmidt at an Academy for Spiritual Formation,
Leesburg, Florida, 2003

Garrison Douglass, Elizabeth, Lee, and Emme in Hungary
with the Danube River in the background, 2010

Chris with his dog Treacle, painting by Martha Hinson

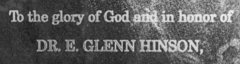

To the glory of God and in honor of

DR. E. GLENN HINSON,

Professor of Spirituality and Worship,
John Loftis Professor of Church History,
1992-1999

This window is lovingly presented
by BTSR students, alumni and friends,
April 29, 1999.

"God's love energies are continually pouring on
us. We simply need to open like a flower to the
morning sun, allowing God's love to fill us and
flow through us to others."
-E. Glenn Hinson

Dedication of the Hinson Window at Baptist Theological Seminary,
Richmond on retirement in 1999

The Hinson Window

16

BAPTIST/CATHOLIC CONVERSATIONS

In the last chapter I talked chiefly about my involvement in conciliar ecumenism of the World and National Council of Churches, what is sometimes referred to as multilateral dialogue. Although I spent a substantial amount of time in multilaterals from 1977 until 1992, and perhaps made some small contribution in nudging Christians toward one another again, I expended far more time and probably made a more substantial contribution in bilateral dialogues. A few conversations between two denominations took place prior to Pope John XXIII and the Second Vatican Council, but it was the dramatic appearance of the Roman Catholic Church on the ecumenical stage that energized dialogues. Indeed, the Catholic Church became the chief promoter and sponsor of them, and Catholic/Protestant dialogues seem to have inspired dialogues between representatives of other denominations. I took part as a Baptist, for instance, in numerous local conversations with different bodies and in national dialogues with Quakers[1] and Episcopalians.[2] My major investment of time in dialogues at the national and international levels, however, involved Roman Catholics.

In view of what was to happen shortly in the Southern Baptist Convention, you may wonder whether either the national or international Baptist/Catholic conversations mattered. Did participants not expend an unconscionable amount of time and energy in discussions that the new Southern Baptist regime would soon repudiate? What good could anyone conceive to come out of dialogues between representatives of churches seeming to stand at opposite poles on the Christian spectrum?

Let me say at the outset that neither I, nor any of the other Baptists who took part in these meetings, expected them to lead Baptists back to

---

[1] On this dialogue see *Prayer and Holy Obedience in a War-Wracked World: Papers from a Quaker-Southern Baptist Colloquy*, edited by Glenn Igleheart (Atlanta: Home Mission Board, SBC, 1982). My paper was entitled "Voluntarism and Holy Obedience" (5–25).

[2] These occurred during my two-year stint at Wake Forest University, 1982–84.

the bosom of "Mother Church." Without presuming to interpret the mind of my colleagues, I hoped, in the spirit of Pope John XXIII, to open some windows of understanding in both houses, to increase cooperation through which we might together address some of the world's pressing problems, and to grow together as the New Humanity.[3] I was delighted, therefore, when, in 1977, the Bishops' Committee for Ecumenism and Interreligious Affairs in Washington, DC, and the Interfaith Witness Department of the Home Mission Board, SBC, agreed to sponsor a series of Scholars' Dialogues, arranging for the first two sessions to meet at Mercy Center in Cincinnati, Ohio, in April and November 1978. Glenn Igleheart, Director of the Department of Interfaith Witness, shepherded the effort from the Baptist side, James D. Niedergeses, Bishop of Nashville, from the Catholic. The group agreed in the first session to hold a series of six dialogues. As it turned out, we conducted three series with six dialogues each, the Scholars' Dialogue continuing with only slight changes in the makeup until 1989, when a new conservative Southern Baptist regime replaced us. The constituency varied somewhat over the three series, but the level of scholarship and colleagueship remained high.[4]

---

[3] An *ad hoc* committee appointed in the third session stated the purpose of the dialogue in this way: "We agreed that the purpose of the RCSB Dialogue was not to issue a consensus statement on belief or practice, i.e. an Agreed Statement in the mode of the Anglican/Roman Dialogues. Rather, the purpose was that Dialogue was a model, a paradigm, a catalyst, an encouragement, a resource for dialogue at other levels between Roman Catholics and Southern Baptists, most typically for priests and ministers in local settings in the South or North." Mark Heath to James G. Niedergeses, Nashville, 27 July 1979.

[4] At the outset Baptists included: Bob E. Adams (returned missionary teaching ethics at New Orleans Seminary), Claude U. Broach (Ecumenical Institute, Wake Forest University), Francis M. DuBose (Professor of Missions, Golden Gate Seminary), William L. Hendricks (Professor of Theology, Golden Gate Seminary), E. Glenn Hinson (Professor of Church History, Southern Seminary), Fisher Humphreys (Professor of Theology, New Orleans Seminary), Doran McCarty (Professor of Missions, Midwestern Seminary), Frank Stagg (Professor of New Testament, Southern Seminary), John E. Steely (Professor of Historical Theology, Southeastern Seminary), plus Glenn Igleheart and C.B. Hastings (Home Mission Board). Catholics included: Jerome R. Dollard (Belmont Abbey), John R. Donahue (Professor of New Testament, Vanderbilt Divinity School and about mid-way through the series at Jesuit School of Theology, Berkeley, California), Richard R. Greene (Chaplain, Louisiana State University), Mark Heath (Dominican House of Studies and Professor of Theology, Catholic University of America), Donald Senior (Professor of New Testament, Chicago Federated Faculty), Joseph O'Donnell (Liaison to the SBC in Newnan,

A full review of the Scholars' Dialogue is not needed to speak about my part in it. Let me, instead, do a brief résumé. During the first series, we tried to get better acquainted and delineate some of the main points of agreement and disagreement. In line with those purposes, we devoted the first meeting to perspectives on "The Nature and Function of the Church." [5] In the second, we sought to draw "A Profile of the Two Communions in America" with papers on the history of each communion and on how each may view the other today. [6] In the third session, that met in April 1979 at Fusz Memorial Center in St. Louis, we compared the understanding of salvation in the two traditions.[7] In the fourth session, held once again at Mercy Center in Cincinnati in November 1979, the dialogue focused on the issue of authority, biblical and ecclesiastical.[8] In the fifth session, convened at Holy Spirit Monastery in Conyers, Georgia in April 1980, the conversation shifted to

---

Georgia), David J. O'Brien (Professor of History, Holy Cross University), Thomas F. Stransky (Director of the Paulist Fathers), plus James D. Niedergeses (Bishop of Nashville) and J. Peter Sheehan (American Catholic Bishops Conference).

[5] Frank Stagg, Professor of New Testament at Southern Seminary, spoke about "The New Testament Doctrine of the Church" and Fr Jerome Dollard, a monk and professor of Belmont Abbey in North Carolina, about "The Roman Catholic Experience of God in the Church."

[6] I sought to outline "The Baptist Experience in the United States," and David J. O'Brien, Professor of History at Holy Cross, sketched "The History of American Catholicism." Fr Joseph O'Donnell, Catholic liaison to the SBC with offices in Newnan, Georgia, recounted how "A Catholic Looks at Southern Baptist Churches," and C.B. Hastings, Assistant Director of the Department of Interfaith Witness, SBC, depicted "A Roman Catholic Parish through the Eyes of a Baptist."

[7] Fisher Humphreys, Professor of Theology at New Orleans Seminary, presented a paper on "The Theology of Salvation from a Baptist Viewpoint." Veering from the assigned topic, Mark Heath, Director of the Dominican House of Studies in Washington, DC, spoke about "A Catholic View of Theology." Bob Adams, Professor of Ethics at New Orleans Baptist Seminary, and Richard Green, Catholic Chaplain at LSU, compared the two traditions vis-à-vis how salvation comes to expression in the life of believers.

[8] William L. Hendricks, Professor of Theology at Golden Gate Seminary, spoke about "Southern Baptists and the Bible." In a two-part paper John R. Donahue, Professor of New Testament at Vanderbilt, delineated "The Authority of Scripture in Contemporary Roman Catholicism," and Donald Senior, Catholic Theological Union, Chicago, "The Authority and Use of Scripture in Contemporary Catholic Theology." Joe O'Donnell also presented a statement on "Authority in the Church, a Catholic Viewpoint."

spirituality and to ministry.[9] In the final session of the first series, held at Laity Lodge, near San Antonio, Texas, in November 1980, the group sought to pull together the results of three years of conversation for publication as an issue of *Review and Expositor*, of which I was editor. Thanks to the high level of excitement about interfaith conversations, *R&E* sold more than eleven thousand copies of that issue, more than double its normal printing.

The second series of dialogues had a much greater coherence because of our deliberate effort to focus on the nature and appropriation of grace in each tradition. I was asked to launch the series with a paper defining the issues.[10] One group of papers explored the nature of grace,[11] how it is received,[12] and the issue of mediation and immediacy in experiencing grace.[13] A second group focused on conversion[14] and the theology and practice of baptism.[15] A third group considered issues

---

[9] Glenn Igleheart presented "A Description of Southern Baptist Spirituality," Frank Stagg "Saints and Southern Baptists." Joe O'Donnell gave a paper on "Sacraments and Devotional Life." Thomas Stransky, Paulist Fathers, spoke informally about "Shorthand Theses on 'Apostolic Succession'." Mark Heath gave a paper on "The Development of Structures of Ministers in the Christian Church in the Fathers of the Church," Donald Senior, on "The New Testament and the Ministry of Priest/Bishop: A Roman Catholic Perspective."

[10] E. Glenn Hinson, "The Life of Grace Within Us: Defining the Issues," *Southwestern Journal of Theology* 28 (Spring 1986): 6–10.

[11] Jerome R. Dollard, "What is Grace? A Roman Catholic Perspective," *Southwestern Journal of Theology* 28 (Spring 1986): 11–14; William L. Hendricks, "The Nature of Grace: A Baptist Perspective," ibid., 15–17.

[12] J. William Angell, "The Baptist Understanding of How Grace Is Received," *Southwestern Journal of Theology* 28 (Spring 1986): 18–23; Edward Jeremy Miller, "Catholicism's View of an Ungraced Person and a Graced Person," ibid., 24–30; Richard R. Greene, "How Grace Is Received: Some Roman Catholic Perspectives," ibid., 31–34.

[13] Richard W. Harmon, "The Mediation and Immediacy of Grace in the Community of Faith: A Baptist Perspective," *Southwestern Journal of Theology* 28 (Spring 1986): 35–41; William Reiser, "The Mediation and Immediacy of Grace: A Roman Catholic Perspective," ibid., 42–44.

[14] Mary Aquin O'Neill, "Becoming a Catholic," *Southwestern Journal of Theology* 28 (Spring 1986): 45–48; William L. Hendricks, "Baptists and Children: The Beginning of Grace," ibid., 49–53; Eljee Young Bentley, "Making Converts: A Baptist View," ibid., 54–58.

[15] Jerome R. Dollard, "Roman Catholic Theology and Practice of Baptism," *Southwestern Journal of Theology* 28 (Spring 1986): 58–64; James Leo Garrett, "The Theology and Practice of Baptism: A Southern Baptist View, ibid., 65–73.

related to growth in grace—discipleship,[16] the Lord's Supper or Eucharist,[17] and communion of saints in each tradition.[18] A fourth group took up the question as to whether grace is experienced outside the Church.[19]

Our third series, conducted during the period when fundamentalists concluded their assertion of control over the SBC, did not achieve the same level of coherence as the second. At the end of the triennium, as a matter of fact, we did not have a collection of papers ready to publish. We prepared, rather, a volume designed to guide future dialogues. In it we featured some testimonies of appreciation for each other's tradition,[20] individually or jointly composed articles on Christian faith and life,[21] and suggestions about "Talking to Each Other."[22] Published both in *The Theological Educator* of New Orleans Baptist Seminary and as a book entitled *To Understand Each Other: Roman Catholics and Southern Baptists*, it brought this phase of dialogue to an appropriate conclusion. Although a more conservative regime continued

---

[16] John R. Donahue, SJ, "Discipleship and the Life of Grace," *Southwestern Journal of Theology* 28 (Spring 1986): 73–79; Fisher H. Humphreys, "Living as a Disciple," ibid., 79–84.

[17] William Reiser, "Roman Catholic Understanding of the Eucharist," *Southwestern Journal of Theology* 28 (Spring 1986): 85–89; John E. Steely, "The Lord's Supper: Theory and Practice among Baptists," ibid., 90–94.

[18] Frederick M. Jelly, "The Communion of Saints: Reflections upon the Roman Catholic Tradition in Ecumenical Perspective," *Southwestern Journal of Theology* 28 (Spring 1986): 94–100; C. Brownlow Hastings, "The Communion of Saints in Light of the Baptist Tradition," ibid., 101–04.

[19] Alan P. Neely, "Is There Saving Grace Apart from the Proclamation of the Christian Message?" *Southwestern Journal of Theology* 28 (Spring 1986): 105–111; Thomas F. Stransky, "Salvation of 'The Others'?" ibid., 112–16.

[20] James Niedergeses, "A Catholic Testimony about Southern Baptists," *The Theological Educator* 39 (Spring 1989): 8–12; Alan Neely, "I Am a Debtor," ibid., 13–21.

[21] Mary Aquin O'Neill, Jude Wiesenbeck, and Joseph Witmer, "A Primer on Religious Authority," *The Theological Educator* 39 (Spring 1989): 22–29; Eljee Bentley, "God's Gift of Salvation," ibid., 30–36; Fisher Humphreys, "Being a Christian Disciple," ibid., 37–49; Donald Senior, Donald R. Kammerdiener, Rita Forbes, and Thomas F. Stransky, "The Mission of the Church," ibid., 67–74; E. Glenn Hinson and Gerald Austin, "How We Worship," ibid., 75–87; and Robert A. Dalton and C. Brownlow Hastings, "Intermarriage," ibid., 88–96.

[22] The Scholars' Dialogue, "How We Agree/How We Differ," *The Theological Educator* 39 (Spring 1989): 97–107; C. Brownlow Hastings, "The Story of the Scholars' Dialogue," ibid., 108–123; Mary Aquin O'Neill, "Symbols that Speak," ibid., 124–29; C. Brownlow Hastings and Thaddeus Daniel Horgan, "Grass Roots Conversations: How to Have Them in Our Churches," ibid., 130–40.

conversations until 1999, Catholic participants did not consider them to be as useful because some of the Baptist participants had serious doubts as to whether Catholics were Christians.

Toward the end of the Roman Catholic/Southern Baptist Scholars' Dialogue, the Commission on Baptist Doctrine and Interchurch Cooperation of the Baptist World Alliance and the Vatican Secretariat for Promoting Christian Unity included me among those invited to take part in Baptist-Roman Catholic International Conversations. The Catholic contingent included Bede Vincent Heather, Auxiliary Bishop of Sydney, Australia; Jerome Dollard, Director of Hazelden Renewal Center in Minnesota; John R. Donahue, by this stage Professor of New Testament at the Jesuit School of Theology in Berkeley, California; Carlo Ghidelli, Under-Secretary of the Catholic Episcopal Conference in Italy; Basil Meeking, Associate Director of the Secretariat for Promoting Christian Unity; and Karl Müller, Professor of Missions in Steyler Missionswissenschaftliches Institut E.V., St. Augustin, West Germany. John A. Radano, Secretariat for Promoting Christian Unity in Rome, served as secretary for the conversations. Baptists were David Shannon, President, Virginia Union University and subsequently Provost and Professor of Old Testament at the Interdenominational Theological Seminary in Atlanta; Noel Vose, Principal of Baptist College of Western Australia and President of the Baptist World Alliance, 1985–1990; Janis Tervits, Bishop of the All Union Conference of Evangelical Christian-Baptists in Riga, Latvia; Paolo Spanu, Secretary of the Theological Department of the Italian Baptist Union; Daniel E. Tinao, President of *Seminario Internacional Teologico Bautista* in Buenos Aires, Argentina; and me. Glenn Igleheart, now Executive Secretary of the Baptist Convention of New York in Syracuse, served as Secretary. Richard Harmon, Assistant Director of the Interfaith Witness Department, SBC, in Atlanta, was an observer. This constituency also changed some during the course of the conversations.

The overarching theme for discussion was how Baptists and Roman Catholics might witness together for Christ in today's world. There were five meetings. The first, held in West Berlin 18–21 July 1984, focused on "Evangelism/Evangelization: The Witness of the Church." We met in Diakoniewerk Bethel in Berlin, a retreat center operated by an order of Baptist women deacons and located near the Dahlem Lutheran church where Martin Niemöller had the honor of being the first arrested in 1938 for his criticisms of Hitler and the Third Reich. Noel Vose presented "An

Introduction to the Baptist World Confessional Family" and Basil
Meeking spoke about perspectives of the Roman Catholic Church
toward ecumenical dialogue. Regarding the central topic, I talked about
Baptist and Karl Müller about Roman Catholic perspectives on
evangelism or evangelization.

The second, meeting in Los Angeles at the Claretian Retreat Center
during the 1985 Baptist World Congress, concentrated on the
interconnected topics of "Christology" and "Conversion/Discipleship,"
issues integral to proper understanding of Christian witness. Richard
Harmon, Baptist-Catholic liaison of the Home Mission Board, SBC, gave
a paper on a Baptist view and John Donahue, on the Catholic view of the
person and work of Christ. Carlo Ghidelli, Under-Secretary of the Italian
Episcopal Conference, and Paolo Spanu, President of the Baptist Union
of Italy, presented papers on the theme of conversion/discipleship.

The third, convened in Bishop Molloy Retreat House, Queens, New
York, in June 1986, explored some ecclesiological issues under the title of
"The Church as *Koinonia* of the Spirit." David Shannon, Academic Dean
and Professor of Old Testament, The Interdenominational Theological
Center, Atlanta, and Bishop Bede Heather each gave papers on "The
Church as Koinonia of the Spirit in the New Testament." Glenn
Igleheart, Executive Secretary of the Baptist Convention of New York,
outlined a Baptist perspective, Kilian McDonnell, a monk at St. John's
Abbey and Professor of Theology at St. John's University in Collegeville,
Minnesota, a Catholic perspective on "The Church as Koinonia of the
Spirit."

The fourth, assembled in Rome during the second and third weeks
of July 1987, directed itself to specific issues standing in the way of
improving common Christian witness, that is, proselytism and
restriction of freedom. This session introduced two new elements into
the conversations—four Bible studies relating to early Christian witness
in Rome (Acts 28:11–31 by Carlo Ghidelli, Phil 1:12–26 by E. Glenn
Hinson, Rom 13:1–7 by David Shannon, and Rom 15:1–13 by John
Donahue) and field trips to early Christian sites in Rome (Catacombs of
Priscilla, the Scavi under St Peter's Basilica, and four churches—St
Peter's, St Clement, St Mary Major, and St John Lateran). There were two
formal papers with responses: "Evangelism versus Proselytism" by Karl
Müller with response by Paolo Spanu and "Freedom and Its Limits: The
Problem of Church-State Relations" by Pablo Deiros, Professor of Church
History, *Seminario Internacional Teologico Bautista*, Buenos Aires,

Argentina, with response by Joseph Komonchak, Professor of Theology, Catholic University of America. I was deeply touched by a brief address given by Cardinal Johannes Willebrands, Secretary (1960–69) and President (1969–89) of the Secretariat for Promoting Christian Unity, before we departed. I wrote down the essence of his message.

Baptists, he said, like we Roman Catholics, belong to the Christian family. We are baptized in the name of the Father, Son, and Holy Spirit. We also share the mission. The Christian family, though divided in many points, brings us together. Our faith should unite us. We stand before Jesus Christ and are happy to meet our Savior. We, as human beings, are living in the darkness of faith. The light we have is the confession of faith we share. With it we cannot avoid meeting. We have also received Jesus' prayer that all may be one. Jesus thought about the division among his own people. The division continues with us and we must work to see how far we can go to overcome it. The Jews are also the people of Abraham, but they haven't gotten all the faith of Abraham. We must meet with those who recognize there is a law of God. In Christ we can meet together. In prayer, in all modesty, and in all respect we should go this way. We should wait until the end to meet, but we should get acquainted here on earth. As Gamaliel said, "If it is only of this world, it won't succeed; if it is of God, it can't be stopped." We look to the final coming of Christ. The veil was taken away that the light of Christ might be seen.

The last session, held in Simpsonwood, a Methodist Conference Center in Atlanta, in July 1988, sought to gather the fruits of the entire series. John Donahue and I, who had both served in the Catholic/Southern Baptist Scholars' Dialogues, were elected to prepare the final report entitled *Summons to Witness to Christ in Today's World*. The international conversations differed from the Scholars' Dialogues in that we prepared agreed accounts of each meeting. Nevertheless, John and I opted not to summarize individual sessions but "to synthesize the discussion over four years and to articulate our shared response to the revelation of God in Jesus Christ as this has been given to us in the Bible and in the faith and practice of our respective communities."[23] As you can easily imagine, effecting such a synthesis to which a disparate group of participants would agree is not an easy undertaking. Add the distance that separated John Donahue in Berkeley from me in Louisville, both with crowded calendars, and you may wonder, as I do, how we ever

---

[23] *Summons to Witness to Christ in Today's World*, typescript, 2.

pulled it off. I can see from notes that I have preserved that we agreed on a general structure for the report when we were in Rome and then divided the task of writing. Both of us failed to meet an October 1987 deadline for a first draft to be sent to Karl Müller and Paolo Spanu, a December deadline to mail a revised copy to all participants, and an April 1988 deadline for the final draft, but we met several times as our schedules permitted, and I was able to send a first draft of the report to Müller and Spanu in May 1988. Monsignor John A. Radano immediately forwarded copies to all of the others. They made a number of suggestions we were able to incorporate into the document we focused on at our meeting in Atlanta.

Summons to Witness to Christ in Today's World consists of three major sections—a résumé of the conversations, a common statement, and a review of areas needing continuing exploration. The common statement, carefully documented with biblical references, points to our witness to Christ, the call to conversion, our witness in the Church, our witness in the world, and challenges to common witness in proselytism and restriction of freedom. Areas in need of further exploration include: (1) theological authority and method, (2) concretizing *koinonia*, (3) relationship between faith, baptism, and Christian witness, (4) the different understandings of and expression of terms such as "evangelization," "evangelism," and "proselytism" in both official statements and popular understandings of our communions, (5) the place of Mary in Catholic faith and practice, and (6) concrete ways to offer a common witness of the gospel. Adoption of the document in its final form generated genuine joy and a sense of satisfaction for a task well done.

Although it got an enthusiastic reception from Roman Catholics, our work was put to a severe test in the Baptist context. When David Shannon, the chairman, presented the report to the Commission on Doctrine and Interchurch Cooperation of the Baptist World Alliance at a meeting in the Bahamas, the Brazilians vigorously objected. Brazilian Baptists are highly suspicious of Roman Catholicism, the dominant Church in Brazil. The report, nevertheless, got an okay from the larger assembly and, on recommendation of the immediate past president of the BWA (2000–05) Nelson Fanini, a *Brazilian*, a second series is under way. It received a far more enthusiastic reception from Cardinal Willebrands. When he was awarded the Bellarmine Medal in Louisville in 1989, he called special attention to the report as a model for ecumenical dialogues.

One of the most moving moments in my life occurred during the Roman leg of our international Baptist/Catholic Conversations. In a small way it epitomizes the grace I received from ecumenical dialogue, and I will never rue even one moment so spent. As you come up out of the Scavi under St Peter's Basilica, you will come face-to-face with the sarcophagus of Pope John XXIII. It is readily distinguishable from the others. It looks like an oversized, unadorned marble trunk. When I recognized what it was, tears sprang from my eyes. I knelt down and poured out a prayer of thanks for that great, humble, bold *servus servorum Dei* who dared what vast numbers thought impossible. In his opening address to the Second Vatican Council on 11 October 1962, he claimed "a sudden flash of inspiration" and that his announcement struck his hearers like "some ray of supernatural light."[24] He waxed eloquent about his dream: "For with the opening of this Council a new day is dawning on the Church, bathing her in radiant splendor. It is yet the dawn, but the sun in its rising has already set out hearts aglow. All around us is the fragrance of holiness and joy. Yet there are stars to be seen in this temple, enhancing its magnificence with their brightness."[25]

Was his view too rosy? I don't subscribe to the "Great Man" or "Great Person" theory of history, but I believe that some persons matter. They matter a great deal. And I will boldly say that I think Angelo Roncalli signaled a new epoch in human history, an age of transcendence. At its inception, it burst forth with a new "awakening." Like other "awakenings," it began with a period of disorientation, despair even, with the threat of nuclear annihilation, the war in Vietnam, violence in the cities. There followed a long period of deepened religious search. Subsequently, in great drama, we have witnessed a change of consciousness that also comes with "awakenings." What scholars have labeled "Postmodernism" rose up in protest against the rationalism of the Enlightenment and echoed Jesus' conviction that humankind could not live by bread alone. Marxism gave up the ghost in east European countries, not because they were outspent by the United States, but because Marxism left no room for transcendence. Contrary to what I had heard as an axiom of political science, viz. that Marxism would never

---

[24] *The Encyclicals and Other Messages of John XXIII*, ed. the Staff of *The Pope Speaks Magazine* (Washington, DC: TPS Press, 1964) 425.

[25] Ibid., 434.

relinquish its grip on the Soviet Union, I lived to see it come crashing down just like the Berlin Wall separating one of the world's great cities. Thanks be to God that God has permitted me not only to witness but to take part in God's new age!

17

A GATHERING GLOOM

In the late 1970s, Southern skies seemed remarkably bright for me. I was turning out one book after another, deeply engaged in ecumenical dialogue, a popular professor on campus and much in demand off campus, and active and respected in the denomination. I was not unaware of dark and threatening clouds gathering on the horizon, but they did not seem to call for a curtailment or radical revamping of my activities. One of the most personal warnings I received came from a conservative student, R.T. Kendall, now pastor of Metropolitan Tabernacle in London, the church that Charles Haddon Spurgeon built. For a while, R.T. used to take me to a Brownsboro Road Pizza Hut for lunch almost weekly to tell me that I needed to shift to the right because the fundamentalists would soon take over the Southern Baptist Convention. After a particularly stern warning one day, as I got out of the car, I said, "R.T., I accepted this call to be a professor in this seminary with one basic principle, that I would be responsible to the Truth. I will not be guided by denominational politics." I slammed the door shut and went to my office. He and I never had lunch together again.

"The Battle for the Bible" that had raged off and on since 1962 didn't seem to threaten me in a serious way. Because of my New Testament dissertation on the Pastoral Epistles I was enlisted to write an introductory essay on "The History of Early Christianity" and the commentary on *First and Second Timothy and Titus* for the Broadman Bible Commentary published in 1971. Although, or perhaps because, Henton Davies's commentary on Genesis reignited the firestorm raised by Ralph Elliott's *The Message of Genesis*, inerrantists seem not to have paid much attention to New Testament commentators. Along with many others I was invited to teach in a Nationwide Bible Conference in Dallas, Texas, sponsored by the Sunday School Board of the SBC, at which W.A. Criswell, icon of inerrancy, panned, belittled, denounced, and degraded the biblical criticism every writer for Broadman Bible Commentary had employed. I must confess that it was such a brilliant piece of demagoguery that I could scarcely remain in my seat when ten or fifteen thousand people leaped up to give him a long-standing ovation. Had I had greater sensitivity to the dynamics of huge conservative assemblies like that, I would probably have been trembling in my wingtip shoes. Like most of my colleagues, I was almost oblivious to a skillful organizing effort going on under the radar—a project of Paul Pressler, a Houston judge, and Paige Patterson, President of Criswell Bible College in Dallas.

At Southern Seminary, students called on me to sponsor a World Hunger group as a result of an article I wrote consequent to my return from India.[1] Very soon after that, I was enlisted in peace concerns inspired especially by my colleague Glen Stassen, who taught Christian ethics. Early in March 1979, Stassen and Carmen Sharp—my pastor at Deer Park Baptist Church—organized a Peace Convocation. I'm afraid I disappointed both organizers by publishing a rather critical assessment in *The Christian Century*.[2] Bill Leonard told me that Stassen was "hanging me in effigy." In my journal for March 14, however, I defended, at least for myself, what I had written. Stassen subsequently must have forgiven me, for, when he and Sharp assembled a group of us a few weeks later to publish a paper entitled *Baptist Peacemaker*, he insisted that I edit it. Quite to everyone's surprise, from the very first issue in January 1981, the journal took off. We printed six thousand copies and had to reprint. Requests for it flowed in from all over the world, and, within a year, we were printing four times that many.

By 1979 the clouds on the horizon were sending peels of thunder over the whole Southern Baptist Zion. By this time, Judge Pressler had locked his radar onto the fact that control of the presidency of the Southern Baptist Convention could assure control of the nomination of board members of Southern Baptist agencies and institutions and from thence lead to control of the Convention. At the annual meeting of the SBC in Houston in June 1979, fundamentalists, bused in droves on church buses simply to vote for the president, succeeded in electing Adrian Rogers, Pastor of Bellevue Baptist Church in Memphis, Tennessee, on the first ballot. The next year, citing pressing church and personal responsibilities, Rogers declined to let his name be placed in nomination for a second year. At the annual meeting in St. Louis in June

---

[1] E. Glenn Hinson, "The Issue behind World Hunger," *Western Recorder*, 18 October 1978; *Seeds*, February 1979, 4–5.

[2] E. Glenn Hinson, "SBC's Peacemaking Convo: How Significant Was It?" *Christian Century* 96 (14 March 1979): 268–69.

1980, fundamentalist strategists nominated and, again on the first ballot, elected Bailey Smith, pastor of First Southern Baptist Church, Del City, Oklahoma. Despite massive get-out-the-vote efforts by "moderates," the fundamentalists secured the re-election of Smith in 1981 in Los Angeles and elected their candidates year after year from that date on.

Insofar as I have ascertained from my journals and other sources, fundamentalists focused attention on me for the first time in 1979 and 1980. In an obvious effort to conciliate its severest critics, Southern Seminary hosted a "Heart of America Bible Conference" 5–7 November 1979. For the only time during my years at Southern, Alumni Chapel provided a platform for a succession of the orchestrators of the "conservative resurgence"—W.A. Criswell, Adrian Rogers, Homer G. Lindsey, Jimmy Draper, Jerry Vines, and, as a symbol of the movement, evangelist James Robison. [3] Bertha Smith, an aging career missionary, was brought in to represent a saintly presence for the conservative cause. In an intense prayer aimed at Duke McCall she pleaded for change and shocked us all with, "And if you can't *change* him, Lord, *take* him!"

McCall had picked up rumors just prior to this that Paige Patterson was criticizing *Jesus Christ*, published just two or three years before, and suggested that I meet with Patterson. So I invited him to take part in a DMin seminar I was teaching. We had an amiable discussion. Afterwards I asked him to meet with me in my office. During a two-hour chat, I related to him the rumor I had heard, handed him a copy of *Jesus Christ*, and asked him to indicate what he found problematic about it. He thumbed through it as if he were looking at it for the first time and could not name one issue. We spent about two hours in conversation and parted agreeing to disagree. He would be an inerrantist; I would not. In an interview with the editor of *The Baptist Standard*, Presnall Wood, on 14 April 1980, and in a letter to Wood on April 28, however, he came out with a list of seven "liberals" in Southern Baptist life, me among them! [4]

---

[3] In "A Special Message to the Seminary Community," *The Towers*, November 1979, Duke K. McCall explained that he had invited W.A. Criswell and James Robison to hold a Bible conference at Southern but did not take part in the selection of personnel.

[4] The remaining names were: G. Temp Sparkman, Associate Professor of Religious Education and Church Administration at Midwestern Seminary in Kansas City, Missouri; Fisher H. Humphreys, Associate Professor of Theology at New Orleans Seminary; C.W. Christian, Professor of Religion at Baylor University; Frank E. Eakin, Professor of Religion at the University of Richmond; and George L. Balentine, pastor of First Baptist Church, Augusta, Georgia.

Others included only one other colleague at Southern, Eric Rust, who had recently retired. Dale Moody felt so badly about being left off of the list that he went around in a funk for two or three months.

All of Patterson's selections from *Jesus Christ* related to the use of historical-critical methodology. In the way he quoted without regard to context, he obviously sought to raise as much alarm about my views as he could, neglecting to let readers know that, in three instances, I was criticizing views he attributed to me! Had he quoted more carefully with attention to context, readers could have easily seen what I was doing. Because I declined to respond to each of Patterson's quotations at the time, perhaps you will indulge me to quote the charges made in the interview and to highlight the distortions with quotations from the book itself.

> Patterson lifted four excerpts on the Gospels from Hinson's book *Jesus Christ*. In the first, Hinson writes that all of the sources had biases and gave their own slanted, not always factual viewpoints, which "takes away … the dogmatic certainty" with which historians operated.
>
> The second, dealing with healing miracles, states some modern scholars ascribe them to primitive mythology and Christian embellishment, which, Hinson states, "undoubtedly occurred." He adds that the primitive worldview and science of Jesus' day would have given a "different cast" to such things than would be given today.
>
> The third states the conclusion Jesus expected his return and the consummation within his own lifetime and says his "error" was due to "prophetic foreshortening. So urgent was his sense of mission, it seemed as if God had to consummate his kingdom immediately."
>
> In the fourth, Hinson wrote, "The meaning of the Last Supper has been debated by scholars and Jesus may not have commanded its repetition as suggested by Paul" (1 Corinthians 11:24).[5]

Patterson's misrepresentation of what I wrote in *Jesus Christ* is evident in the first excerpt. What he cited appears in an introductory section on sources for "The Life and Ministry of Jesus." At the outset I observed that all four Gospels "have to be seen not as biographies but as theological writings which bear witness first of all to the faith of the early

---

[5] Toby Druin, "Patterson, Seven Accused Exchange Charges," *Baptist Standard*, 14 May 1980, 8; "Six of Those Charged Dispute Paige Patterson's Charges of 'Liberalism'," *Word and Way*, 29 May 1980.

Church."[6] From thence I proceeded to review how this theological
tendency appears not only in John but also in Matthew, Mark, and Luke.
I went on to remark that each of the writings "had a theological slant
which will not allow them to be read as a dispassionate and objective
report on Jesus' life."[7] At this point, I rose to their defense. "Do
theological and historical biases such as these discredit the Gospels as
sources for the life and ministry of Jesus altogether and thus render the
'quest' impossible? *This writer would say no.*"[8] Ignoring this context
entirely, Patterson picks up at this point and, if accurately quoted, alters
what I said in a critical way. I did not say, "All of the sources," which
would tie my reference to the Gospels alone, but "all sources." I'm
making a *general* observation accepted by historians. "All sources,
however objective they claim to be, have biases. They reflect the slanted
viewpoints of their authors. At the same time most possess, in varying
degrees, some element of fact. The fact that none of these is absolutely
factual, however, does not take away all of their value. What it takes
away is the dogmatic certainty with which historians in the past
sometimes operated. He approaches all sources critically and seeks to
evaluate their accuracy from as many sides as possible." The general
observation ended here. I then referred back to my defense of writing
about the life and ministry of Jesus. "In the case of the Gospels one can
safely conclude that a kernel of historical fact underlies the early
Church's handling of the material. There is thus no justification for the
skeptical attitude which would declare the whole story nothing but a
figment of later Christian imagination. Behind the early Christian
preaching, *kerygma,* lays an historical event, the man Jesus of Nazareth
and his message."[9]

In regard to the second set of quotations, had Patterson quoted
further, the discerning reader could see that I attempted to offer a
defense of miracles. Permit me to quote more fully to illustrate his failure
properly to represent what I said.

A number of modern scholars have discounted the healing narratives
and miracle stories, ascribing them to primitive mythology and early
Christian embellishment. Some embellishment undoubtedly occurred.

---

[6] E. Glenn Hinson, *Jesus Christ* (Washington, DC: Consortium, 1977) 55.
[7] Ibid., 56.
[8] Ibid. Italics added.
[9] Ibid., 57.

Moreover, the primitive worldview and science of Jesus' day would have given a different cast to healings and other phenomena than the modern worldview and science would.

At the same time healing as a part of Jesus' ministry cannot be dismissed lightly as primitive superstition. The Gospels contain too much material concerned with healing to allow that. Furthermore, healing claims were not confined to Jesus or the early Church. Jewish rabbis reported healings. And in the third century Philostratus recounted the feats of Apollonius of Tyana as the pagan counterpart to Jesus during the first century. In recent years, moreover, the modern scientific worldview has undergone enough revision as to eliminate dogmatism. Healing is seen not merely as a physiological but much more as a psychomatic process.

Discounting somewhat for embellishment, therefore, impressive evidence for Jesus' healing ministry remains.[10]

The third citation likewise misrepresented what I wrote by truncation. The context for it is a discussion of the "little apocalypse" in Mark 13. I was arguing here, against the opinion of many scholars, that the passage may contain genuine sayings of Jesus and that he could have predicted the fall of Jerusalem. I continued,

At the same time Jesus may have used the occasion to warn his disciples again about seeing in that event the eschatological consummation. Indeed, it is difficult to avoid the conclusion that Jesus expected the return of the Son of Man and the consummation to occur within his own lifetime (Mark 13:30). His "error" [Note, please, the quotations marks!] was due to prophetic foreshortening. So urgent was his sense of mission, it seemed as if God had to consummate his kingdom immediately.[11]

The fourth quotation, once again, damns by omission. What I said here concluded a discussion of the variations in the words of Jesus in different accounts. After interpreting the statements, "This is my body" and "This is my blood," I added: 'The words in 1 Corinthians 11:24 and Luke 22:19, 'Do this in remembrance of me,' may not have been Jesus' words. They could, however, have represented his wish."[12] To me the full quotation casts what I said in a different light. During a Baptist World Alliance meeting in Zagreb, Yugoslavia, I spent an hour and a

---

[10] Ibid., 66–67.

[11] Ibid., 76.

[12] Ibid., 107.

half trying to explain to Paul Pressler, who just before had been savaging me at Glorieta, why I made that comment. I asked him, "What do you do when the traditions differ like that? Was there more than one Last Supper?" He replied, "You must accept both." I said, "If you do so, you say that they are *both* wrong." His answer to that after a long harangue as he prepared to take the elevator to the fourth floor of the hotel was, "You should not be teaching in our seminary."

When interviewed by Toby Druin, editor of *The Baptist Standard* of Texas, I insisted that the historical-critical method of interpretation of the Bible is "necessary in order to understand it, to make it relevant, to really make it come home with force as God's word to people of our time." At the same time, I said that I was "not prepared to let Paige Patterson define what our 'historic Baptist position' is." I located Patterson in a group I labeled the "rabid right" which supports such things as prayer amendment legislation "that stands smack in the face of our historic Baptist position … so I am not prepared to give him the definitive role as interpreter of what is 'Baptist'." I went on to point out that, "Baptists have always—and this is another basic principle for us—allowed freedom to interpret and that includes not only private individuals, but also churches and persons in other positions. I think one of our crucial things now is whether we are going to accord that to denominational employees."

I pointed out that, although the earliest Baptist forbears did not use historical-critical methodology because it did not develop until the nineteenth century, leading scholars such as A.H. Strong, E.Y. Mullins, W.O. Carver, A.T. Robertson, and W.T. Conner had done so in a responsible way. "Fundamentalism developed without any connection with Baptists as a reaction to the use of historical methods and some Baptists have been fundamentalists, but being a Baptist and a Fundamentalist are not the same thing. In fact, some things about Fundamentalism are quite alien to our Baptist outlook and above all is this kind of … mentality. The Paige Patterson group represents the rabid right. They do not represent our historic Baptist position; in fact I see him standing opposed to it in very, very critical points."[13]

As I look back over the Patterson attack, I feel somewhat embarrassed about the anger that intruded my reply, especially the "rabid right" tag. Patterson himself, however, was censured by leaders

---

[13] "Six of Those Charged Dispute Paige Patterson's Charges of 'Liberalism'," *Word and Way*, 29 May, 1980.

of First Baptist Church, Dallas, sponsor of Criswell Bible College. A group comprised of the current chairman and six former chairmen of deacons voted 4–3 "to require Patterson to eliminate or tone down his attacks or be dismissed." One of the group advocated firing Patterson.[14]

Bailey Smith, president of the convention from 1980 until 1982, provided the occasion for an enhancement of my visibility in the denominational controversy and to assure my toxicity to fundamentalists. On August 22, at the National Affairs Briefing in Dallas in support of Ronald Reagan's candidacy sponsored by the Religious Roundtable, an organization founded by Ed McAteer, a member of Bellevue Baptist Church in Memphis, Smith declared,

> It is interesting at great political rallies how you have a Protestant to pray and a Catholic to pray, and then you have a Jew to pray. With all due respect to those dear people, my friend, God Almighty does not hear the prayer of a Jew. For how in the world can God hear the prayer of a man who says that Jesus Christ is not the true Messiah? It is blasphemy. It may be politically expedient, but no one can pray unless he prays through the name of Jesus Christ. It is not Jesus among many, it is Jesus and Jesus only. It is Christ only. There is no competition for Jesus Christ.[15]

A few months later, Smith added insult to injury by remarking at the end of a sermon that, "Jews got funny-looking noses."[16]

High profile already, I had not entertained any thought of responding to Smith, but a few days afterwards, Sol Bernards, Director of the Anti-Defamation League of B'nai B'rith, phoned me from New York. "Glenn," he said, "I've called every Southern Baptist leader I can think of and cannot get a single one to respond to this statement."

"Try Dr. McCall, Sol," I responded. "I think he will make a statement."

Two days later, Bernards phoned me again. "Glenn, I've called McCall's office repeatedly. His secretary always cuts me off."

"Okay, Sol. I'll make a statement," I replied. I immediately plopped down in front of my 1923 Underwood Standard and dashed off "An Open Letter to Dr. Bailey Smith, First Southern Baptist Church, Del City,

---

[14] "Dallas First Leaders Ask Patterson to 'Tone Down' Attacks," *Bulletin to Towers*, 10 May 1980.

[15] From a transcription of a tape in Letter of Rabbi Solomon S. Bernards to E. Glenn Hinson.

[16] Marjorie Hyer, "Baptist Leader Is Criticized Again for a Remark He Made About Jews," *Courier-Journal*, 24 November 1980.

Oklahoma." Very conscious of the fact that Smith was not a scholar but had been elected to his office by Southern Baptists, I tried to restrain as much as I could some of the strong feelings that surged through me. I must confess that the powerful political shift to the right in connection with the Reagan candidacy aroused fears. Reading at the time Hannah Arendt's *The Origins of Totalitarianism* and Klaus Scholder's *The German Churches and the Third Reich*, I felt genuine fear about what I saw happening. One of Arendt's salient observations struck me with particular force. The Nazis succeeded by silencing the opposition. Only five percent of the members of the Nazi Party agreed with Hitler's "Final Solution," but the 95 percent did not speak. So Hitler had his way.

I will skip some prefatory statements into which I incorporated Smith's statement, but, with some apologies, I believe I should quote the substance of the letter, which others have often requested. Full quotation will enable you to discern the source of a small dust storm I created with my comment about Jesus' messianic claims. New Testament scholars galore backed me up on the point, but not all have done depth study of their Bibles.

My first reaction on hearing this [your] statement was: "Surely he didn't say that. He has been misquoted." My next reaction was: "It was a slip of the tongue. He probably spoke without notes and let some of these things slip."

My hope now is that, whether a misquote or a slip, you will prayerfully rethink what you said and make an apology to Jewish people everywhere and beg God's forgiveness for claiming to make judgments he alone should make. Let me note some problems I see in what you were quoted as saying.

1. You may have disfranchised Jesus' prayer when you said, "My friend, God Almighty does not hear the prayer of a Jew." Jesus was a Jew. He lived and died a Jew. Christianity began with the conviction of his first followers that he had risen from the dead. Though he did not "deny" he was the messiah, neither did he openly claim, "I am the messiah." Others confessed that about him.

2. You disfranchised the prayers of everyone from Abraham to Jesus—the entire Old Testament—when you said, "No one can pray unless he prays through the name of Jesus Christ." Which of the patriarchs or prophets prayed invoking his name? Neither human reason nor scriptures themselves will support the argument that they did so.

3. You cast aside our long Baptist heritage concerning religious liberty when you questioned the right of any person to pray at a political rally or

in some other political or social context. I am confident you know Roger Williams' famous analogy used to explain and defend his argument for separation of Church and State against those who argued his approach to liberty would bind the magistrate's power completely. [I quoted Williams's analogy of a ship at sea where the captain has charge of the physical welfare of passengers but cannot compel attendance at the ship's worship nor prohibit any—Catholic, Protestant, Jew, Muslim—from worshipping as they will.] May I point out how remarkably well this "lively experiment" with religious liberty has worked in the United States? Observe what has happened in Europe, where religious establishments held sway for centuries. Pluralism in America has been a major factor in the vitality of religion here.

4. The Bible teaches an unbeliever can pray and have his or her prayers answered. Cornelius, the Roman centurion, did. Observe Peter's remark on this incident in Acts 10:34–35 (a revelation for him too!): "Truly I perceive that God shows no partiality, but in every nation any one who fears him and does what is right is acceptable to him." Your "God Almighty" seems to have a bigger heart than your statement implied.

5. Statements such as this one are the stuff from which holocausts come.[17]

I asked a couple of colleagues to read my letter. Dale Moody applauded, but Findley Edge seemed hesitant. In line with my usual way of resolving ambivalence, I tucked the decision into my inmost sanctuary overnight to see whether I should proceed. That night I awakened at 2 a.m., went downstairs in our house on Heady Avenue in St. Matthews, and sat in my rocking chair. What I wrestled with like Jacob wrestling with the angel was the memory of savage conflicts in my family in early years. Those pain-filled battles had caused me to steer around and away from conflict. But at this moment, happenings in America and specifically in the American South that looked ominously like those that happened in Germany in the 1930s were saturating my consciousness; I knew that it was not a time to cut and run but a time to speak out. Rocking back and forth in my chair, nevertheless, I wanted to shove this task off on somebody else, notwithstanding my promise to Sol Bernards. Inwardly and wordlessly I whined like Jeremiah. "God, you can't expect *me* to do this. I'm an irenical person. I got sick of fighting when I was in

---

[17] E. Glenn Hinson, "An Open Letter to Dr Bailey Smith, First Southern Baptist Church, Del City, Oklahoma," *Western Recorder*, 17 September 1980, 7.

knickers. You surely don't mean for *me* to send out a letter that may cause all hell to break loose."

I can't tell you exactly how or at what time it came through. It probably didn't come in exactly these six words. But this is the message I heard loud and clear. "Yes, dammit, Glenn, hang in there!" I quietly tripped up the stairs, slipped into bed, and slept. When I got to the Seminary, I put the letter in an envelope and sent it to the Kentucky Baptist state paper. Other state papers picked it up from there, and soon the world exploded. The holocaust I had warned Bailey Smith about took place very soon; for a few days it was mine!

A couple of days after my "Open Letter" appeared in the *Western Recorder*, a Thursday, McCall called me into his office. "Glenn, you are going to have to do something about this," he almost shouted. "It's explosive!"

Fortunately, a cab was waiting for me in the circle in front of Norton Hall. So I replied honestly but with a stomach full of butterflies, "I'm sorry, Dr. McCall, but there is a cab waiting for me out front. I'm on my way to do a weekend series in a Methodist Church in Erie, Illinois. I'll have to tend to this when I get back on Monday." I didn't wait for him to say anything further. I wheeled around, grabbed my suitcase and briefcase I had left at the door, and headed for the taxi.

Boil and bubble might be a better description of what transpired that weekend. About 4 p.m. that afternoon, Frank Stagg phoned me in Erie. He said, "Glenn, you've got to call Dr. McCall. He says he's going to have to make a statement, and it will hurt you."

As soon as he hung up, I called Dr. McCall. His first words were, "Glenn, I'm not going to make a statement."

"Good," I responded with more bravado than I felt. "I'll take care of it as soon as I get back to Louisville." As confident as I sounded, my inner gyroscope wasn't working so well. Before the evening service I felt nauseous and, for only the second or third time in my life, I vomited.

By that time, however, the situation had gotten very sticky. Martha called. In the faculty lounge at Southern Seminary that afternoon McCall had said, "I'm afraid I'm going to have to make a statement, but I don't want to, for it will kick Glenn in the face." That word got to Martha in a garbled form. "If I had Glenn Hinson here, I would kick him in the face!" She was crying and wanted me to resign. Maybe a little punchy by that time, I said, "Not yet! I'm kind of enjoying the notoriety."

All day Saturday I kept receiving phone calls from colleagues, mostly supportive but a few suggesting what a threat I posed to the whole seminary. The faculty scheduled a special meeting to decide what to do with the Glenn Hinson crisis. After a whole weekend of this, on Sunday morning Wayne Ward phoned. He blurted out, "Glenn, you're a hero!"

"A hero!" I replied. "All weekend I've been a goat!"

"Well," he explained, "the *Jerusalem Post* carried your 'Open Letter to Bailey Smith' and noted that had it not been for this letter by Glenn Hinson, the Jewish Knesset would have kicked all Southern Baptist missionaries out of Israel." Nothing gets the attention of Southern Baptists like missions. Subsequently *Louisville Times* religious writer Clarence Matthews called attention especially to my letter in an article on efforts to mend fences. "The Interfaith Community instructed its staff to make copies of Hinson's letter and distribute it to its members."[18] Supportive letters easily outnumbered hate letters. Sunday evening when I returned, the air had a decidedly different quality.

The Bailey Smith incident, however, made me a marked man among fundamentalists. From that moment on, some of them started sifting my writings to dredge up damning accusations to prove how dangerous I was to ministers I taught. I was never reluctant to admit that I wanted to endanger fundamentalism, and the two incidents kept cropping up throughout the remainder of my thirty years at Southern Seminary.

What was happening in the Southern Baptist Convention aroused my concern about fundamentalist efforts to construe Baptists as "evangelicals," frequently a euphemism for "fundamentalists." On 10 November 1980 I gave an address to the South Carolina Baptist Historical Society in Columbia, entitled "Baptists and Evangelicals: What Is the Difference?" I repeated the lecture as one of the Wilkinson Lectures at Northern Baptist Seminary, Illinois, on November 13 and 14. Contrary to the interpretation of some, I did not say that Baptists couldn't be evangelicals. Much depends on what we mean by "evangelical," but we come from different wombs. What I did was to warn that, if we were to remain Baptists, we must recover our identity as Baptists, namely, in the recognition that no word handled by human beings has such an objective character to it that it can be used to coerce

---

[18] Clarence Matthews, "Remark about Jews Has Local Baptists Mending Fences," *Louisville Times*, 27 September 1980.

faith. To be valid, faith must be free and voluntary. As I construed it then and continue to construe it, that is the Baptist tradition. As I write from the vantage point of thirty years of hindsight, I would reaffirm what I said then and am not surprised that inerrantists gave it much attention, including a lengthy rebuttal by Richard Land in an interview for the *Southern Baptist Advocate.*[19]

Mercer University Press later concocted a debate between me and James Leo Garrett published in a book whose title, *Are Southern Baptists "Evangelicals"?*,[20] skews somewhat the argument I made. I would not doubt that *Southern* Baptists—at least the leadership of the Southern Baptist Convention— are "evangelicals," that is, of the fundamentalist variety. In the four chapters I wrote for this book, I took care first to establish who Baptists are historically, then to show that the word "evangelical" is used in different senses: In Europe and Latin America it is another word for Protestant, derivative from the "Great Awakening" and Pietism as an emphasis on "conversion," and in popular American usage as a euphemism for "fundamentalist." It is with reference to the third usage, which described what was happening in the SBC, that I spoke out.

Before that happened, however, Southern Seminary underwent a major administrative shift as Duke McCall asked the trustees during the 1980–81 academic year to set in motion a search for his successor.[21] He was succeeded by Roy L Honeycutt, installed on 21 April 1982. The faculty elected me to serve on the Faculty Liaison Committee to the Trustee Search Committee, and the Liaison Committee elected me as their chairperson. The search had a certain delicacy about it. The faculty had a high level of anxiety as to whom the trustees would select to succeed McCall. The viable candidates included Wayne Dehoney, Pastor of Walnut Street Baptist Church in Louisville, a former president of the Southern Baptist Convention, and one of the trustees; Bill Hull, the former dean and provost serving currently as pastor of First Baptist Church, Shreveport, Louisiana; and Roy Honeycutt, the current dean

---

[19] "Who Are We? An Interview with Dr. Richard Land," *Southern Baptist Advocate* 2 (March/April 1981): 8–10.

[20] James Leo Garrett, Jr., E. Glenn Hinson, and James E. Tull, *Are Southern Baptist "Evangelicals"?* (Macon GA: Mercer University Press, 1983) 129–194.

[21] In an interview with A. Ronald Tonks, *Duke McCall: An Oral History* (Nashville: Baptist History and Heritage Society, 2001) 327, McCall did not formally announce his retirement until the New Orleans Convention in June 1982.

and provost. The trustees, however, did not ask the Faculty Liaison Committee to name names but to write a *profile* of the person they would like to see in the office.

In a recent letter Bill Hull told me that he had heard that I was "leading a stampede" against his election. Although I exerted a considerable influence in the profile that the Faculty Liaison Committee put together, I am not by nature a stampede-type leader. The one place in which I exercised the strongest leadership was in resisting Dehoney's efforts to push himself into the picture, something the faculty definitely did not favor. This is only a personal judgment, but, as I told Hull in a response to his question about my leadership, I thought that he had the edge over Honeycutt in the factors favored by the faculty in a president with one major exception—*style and philosophy of administration*. He was inseparably linked to the McCall style and philosophy of administration that had created the morale problem in the early 1970s. Honeycutt did not suffer from that stigma. He joined the faculty after that tense period and brought with him a quite different style. When McCall lobbied for Hull to succeed him, he aroused some fears among faculty that administration of the seminary would revert to what it had been before Honeycutt. In response to those concerns, therefore, the Liaison Committee self-consciously drew up a profile that highlighted Honeycutt's obvious strong points. I tried to keep Honeycutt informed about the process, but I did not assume the trustees would necessarily adopt the faculty preference and never dropped his name to trustees. After the Trustee Search Committee made their selection public, the chairperson called me and asked, "Did we get it right?" I replied, "You did, indeed!"

Honeycutt gave a challenging address at his installation entitled "Heritage and Hope." The service, however, had what seemed to me to be one glaring omission. Charges to the President came from the Southern Baptist Convention, the Alumni, the Trustees, and the Churches, but there was none from the Faculty. Perhaps a "Resolution by the Faculty" and "Investiture by Members of the Seminary Community" rendered such a charge unnecessary, but I thought it curious and offensive.

In a journal entry for 17 December 1980, I noted that the Bailey Smith incident had strengthened "my decision to leave the Seminary when an opportunity opens." Several openings occurred at this time. One was an inquiry by Charles Talbert as to whether I would like to join the religion department at Wake Forest University. Another was the deanship of Northern Baptist Seminary, where I had given the Wilkinson Lectures November 13 and 14. A third was a contact by John Eddins about the deanship of Southeastern Baptist Seminary. By this time, however, I had begun to get a pretty clear picture of my calling, and administration did not fit into it. "I'm a scholar and teacher," I wrote. "I relish both more and more. I'd probably feel quite frustrated by administration despite the 'emoluments' of the dean's role." As it turned out, it was not the Bailey Smith affair but what happened to my colleague Dale Moody that pushed me toward Wake Forest University, where I taught for two years, 1982–84.

18

WAKE FOREST UNIVERSITY

As early as 1980, Charles Talbert, a professor in, and Carlton Mitchell, Chair of the Department of Religion at Wake Forest University, were testing whether I would have an interest in teaching at at the institution. At that time the prospect excited me, for Wake ranked in the top tier of Baptist colleges and universities in the South. The president had been one of my students. Founded in 1834, Wake had an illustrious history and had channeled numerous outstanding scholars to Southern Seminary, including Wayne Oates and Henlee Barnette. Its religion department at the time included productive scholars whose writings I admired and appreciated. Graduates of Wake Forest who came to Southern Seminary consistently excelled. Nevertheless, I wrote in my journal in December 1980, "I have reservations here in that I would make a pretty big shift in the direction of my teaching and writing." What especially troubled me was that Wake Forest did not have a PhD program in religion or plans to develop one. I thought, however, that I should always remain open to the leading of God vis-à-vis vocation.

What I finally agreed to do was to spend an upcoming sabbatical, scheduled for 1982–83, teaching at Wake to see if we meshed. Fundamentalists, I think, clapped their hands and clicked their heels when they saw this, thinking that I was abandoning ship in the face of their salvos. Quite honestly, I can tell them that they were mistaken. When I decided to join the faculty with tenure in the spring of 1983, I did not do so to secure myself against their onslaughts. It was nice to be out from under the bombardment for a while and to know that they could not affect my status; however, neither of those played a large part in my decision.

You would be mistaken to think that the decision came easily. I had taught at Southern Seminary for more than twenty years. I held the David T. Porter Chair of Church History and would not hold an endowed professorship at Wake Forest. I put together long parallel lists of positives and negatives for the two institutions, and I consulted my dear friend and mentor Douglas Steere.

After a semester, the positives seemed to favor Wake Forest. Wake's pluses included superior faculty and students, tremendous excitement about spirituality as a part of what I would do there, availability of wonderful resources and support for ecumenical involvement, the warmth of my reception in the churches and other schools in North Carolina, and the graciousness of Carlton Mitchell and the rest of the administration and faculty. If any negative factor entered into my decision, it did not have to do directly with my own controversy but that of my colleague Dale Moody.

Moody had stirred up a hornet's nest in Oklahoma in the early 1960s by insisting that scriptures taught it was possible for a Christian to fall from grace, a view that ran head on into one that evangelists espoused to assure hearers that Southern Baptists taught something competitors did not—the absolute security of the believer. "Once saved, always saved," they proclaimed, echoing the father of Landmarkism, James Robinson Graves, in his effort to show what Baptists had to offer that Methodists didn't. Possessed of a phenomenal memory for scriptures, Moody threatened their whole enterprise. Fortunately, with generous help of J. Newton Razyor, a wealthy member of the Board of Trustees of Southern Seminary during this explosive period, Moody was able to spend two years in Oxford working on *Baptism: Foundation for Christian Unity*, for which he was awarded a DPhil.

In his classes, on the preaching or lecture circuit, and in his writings, Moody did not let the issue to which he attached such importance rest. During my sabbatical year at Wake Forest, he generated another brouhaha over lapsing from grace at the annual meeting of the Arkansas Baptist State Convention. Enraged Arkansas pastors demanded his dismissal. From Winston-Salem I wrote a letter "In Defense of a Colleague" on 24 December 1982 and sent it to *Western Recorder*. In it I pointed out, first, that the Arkansas Baptist State Convention did not base charges against him on *The Abstract of Principles*, which Southern Seminary professors agreed to teach "in accordance with and not contrary to," but on the *Baptist Faith and Message* of 1963, with which Moody agreed. Actually, he helped to write that article! I noted, secondly, that Moody did not disagree substantively with the *Abstract* but simply wanted to bring it "into verbal accord with scriptures." I said, thirdly, that Baptists needed to decide what they would do with scriptures such as Hebrews 6:4–6 which Moody quoted.[1] Page Kelley also wrote a letter in support. Roy Honeycutt asked me to fly back to Louisville shortly after that to meet with a group of colleagues to determine what to do about Moody. A half dozen of us, Honeycutt presiding, met on March 5 in Old Testament Professor J.J. Owens's den and spent a couple of hours probing the options. I flew back to North Carolina the next day feeling at peace with an understanding that Honeycutt would stand by Moody, and that Moody would continue to teach at Southern until his retirement. After the meeting of trustees a week or two later I was astonished to learn that Moody was being forced to retire, with his pay continuing for two more years. News of that action devastated him and gave me a final nudge. I decided to accept Wake Forest's invitation to become a tenured faculty member.

The move to Winston-Salem came at a good time for our family. Chris had just graduated from high school and was ready to begin college. Although he scored a little low on the math portion of his SAT (always his bane), he had a high verbal score, and with timely intercession by Carlton Mitchell was admitted to Wake Forest. Chris found classes challenging and did well, but he had difficulty developing friendships and experienced a lot of pain when someone blackballed him as he applied to a fraternity. He stayed at Wake one semester after we moved back to Louisville. He then moved home and finished his degree at the University of Louisville. Elizabeth began the ninth grade in Winston-Salem. She had been in the Advanced Program in Louisville but didn't score quite high enough on placement tests to enter into the Gifted and Talented Program in North Carolina. Consequently, she found herself channeled into a school where she repeated things she had done already and was eager to return to Louisville at the end of two years there.

We all joined First Baptist Church in Winston-Salem and felt warmly embraced by members, including my retired colleague Swan Haworth and his wife Freddie. Martha soon developed some close friendships and found a lot of satisfaction in volunteering with Crisis Control Ministries.

During my sabbatical year we lived in a university apartment. We felt a little cramped by comparison with living in a house, but residing there gave us an inner glimpse of the university. When I decided to

---

[1] E. Glenn Hinson, "In Defense of a Colleague," *Western Recorder*, 2 February 1983, 3.

accept the invitation of the Religion Department to remain, we bought a house in a conveniently located subdivision and, by the sale of our house on Heady, assumed the original mortgage with an outstanding balance of less than $10,000 at a very low APR. The house had one big deficiency—little insulation; sometimes we nearly froze.

Although a small city, Winston-Salem, due in great part to the university, is culturally rich. The university itself boasts a good theater program as well as strong teams in basketball in a basketball Mecca. Wake's star was 5' 3" Tyrone Bogues, who went on to play in the NBA for several years. Largesse of the Reynolds family that brought Wake Forest University from its old location and turned it into a more affluent university also helped to sustain an orchestra, a ballet, and other cultural events.

In some respects, teaching at Wake Forest proved more satisfying than teaching at Southern Seminary. The university gave me access to many other disciplines besides religion and put me in touch with the world in which we live in ways not conceivable in a school not connected with a university. Students generally came from privileged cultural and educational backgrounds and ranked in the upper ten percent of their graduating classes, whereas Southern students ranged all across the board, many hailing from culturally impoverished backgrounds. Although Wake students didn't have as much clarity about vocation, most were more highly motivated. They did excellent research and wrote cogent papers. Where I began gradually to sense some dissonance on my part came to the fore in President Reagan's campaign for re-election in 1983 and 1984. Whereas the faculty leaned overwhelmingly toward the Democratic Party, a poll of students revealed that 83 percent would vote for Reagan, a figure probably in line with family preferences. Although I had excellent rapport with students, I felt sometimes like a citizen of another country.

What generated the keenest excitement about my stay at Wake was spirituality. I must confess that I'm still mystified as to why so many people turned to me for guidance in this area, for no one felt more like the beginner I was at this stage than I did. My main drawing card was probably *A Serious Call to a Contemplative Lifestyle*, a book I had written for college students. I suspect, however, that any awe in which Hinson groupies held me probably attests to how little Baptists in the South knew about spirituality. Here, nonetheless, was the faculty at one of the most prestigious schools with Baptist connections turning to me. Thanks in great part to Betty Talbert, Charles's wife, I came to Wake Forest with some expectation of developing an MA program in spirituality and immediately offered two classes I had taught at Southern Seminary—Classics of Christian Devotion and Prayer in Christian History—that would suit such a program. The first time I taught Prayer in Christian History at Southern, in the summer of 1980, 84 students enrolled in it, a few from as far away as New York, Virginia, and California. When I taught it at Wake, however, Ralph Wood, a Barthian, questioned whether one could teach a subject like prayer because it is, as the early Barth opined, "excessively subjective." Charles Talbert sprang to my defense there. He had read his wife's papers written for the course. "I've seen them. They are scholarly," he insisted. When I took a proposal for an MA degree program directly to a department meeting, however, Talbert ranted at me for about fifteen minutes for not going through proper channels. I hadn't the slightest idea what the channels were. Despite my clumsy handling, the program got approved, and a flock of excellent, enthusiastic students immediately applied and was enrolled.

The two years I spent at Wake Forest may have been the busiest of my career, judging by the planner/calendar in which I listed daily and weekend activities. In retrospect, I feel some embarrassment because the number of activities I engaged in surely diminished my contribution to students in some respects, although it could have enhanced them in others. I was stretched out like a rubber band by lecturing, preaching, teaching, or leading retreats virtually every weekend and often on Wednesday. North Carolina Baptists couldn't seem to do enough to welcome me and to get a touch of my modest wisdom. I apologize that I sound boastful here, but I don't know how else to call attention to my over-crowded calendar. Although I went around speaking about a contemplative lifestyle, I certainly did not practice one. The closest I came to doing so was through my three-mile walk before breakfast every morning. I didn't seem to have the word no in my vocabulary.

Looking at the schedule of weekend and mid-week engagements, two topics seem to have dominated—contemplative lifestyle and peacemaking. *A Serious Call to a Contemplative Lifestyle* attracted a lot of readers at this time, both in colleges and universities and in churches. I did numerous retreats or studies focused on the book itself. As the first editor of *Baptist Peacemaker*, I had almost an equal number of invitations to speak at peace conferences, Baptist Student Unions, and churches on different aspects of that subject—ranging from biblical and Christian perspectives to the buildup of weapons of mass destruction. Other topics included world hunger, the Southern Baptist January Bible studies for 1983 and 1984 (1 Peter and 1 Corinthians), the Church and culture, the crisis in the Southern Baptist Convention, and spiritual formation for ministry.

A résumé of churches will not hold your attention, but I should mention that they ranged well beyond the Baptist fold. Somewhat surprisingly, they included the Unitarian Universalist Fellowship of Winston-Salem. At the request of the latter I lectured on "Contemplative Lifestyle." Following my presentation, I found myself caught up in a dogfight about nearly everything I had said, particularly my assumption that contemplation has something to do with God. I went away feeling that I had run into a reverse kind of fundamentalism—of the left rather than of the right. The experience confirmed a growing impression that fundamentalism is, above all, a mentality. "I am right. Only if you agree with me can you be right or Christian or whatever else we are talking about." A very different impression rolled over me as I visited other churches, a phenomenon I had never experienced as a professor at Southern Seminary. People welcomed me almost with awe. "Oh, you teach at Wake Forest!" In its 150 years the university had etched itself ineradicably on the lives not only of Baptists but also of other Christians throughout the state.

The academy, as well as the churches, welcomed me to the eastern seaboard, too. The other Baptist schools in North Carolina, all except Meredith, which deferred its invitation, arranged for me to lecture to their faculties and/or students in 1983: Wingate College on "The Spirituality of the Teacher"; the pastors' school at Campbell University on "The Spirituality of the Minister"; Mars Hill College on "Spirituality and Peacemaking"; and Chowan College on "Christian Piety and Social Responsibility." In 1984, I also spoke to campus ministers at Southeastern Baptist Seminary on my two mainstays—"Devotional Lifestyle" and "On Being a Peacemaker." Still in North Carolina, I gave an address on "Creeds and Christian Unity: A Southern Baptist Perspective" at Duke Divinity School.[2]

Other academic engagements carried me well beyond North Carolina in 1983: the Oreon Scott Lectures at Christian Theological Seminary, Indianapolis, Indiana; a retreat for students at Virginia Tech

---

[2] E. Glenn Hinson, "Creeds and Christian Unity: A Southern Baptist Perspective," *Journal of Ecumenical Studies* 23 (Winter 1986): 25–36.

University on "Growing up in Grace"; the Staley Lectures at Union University in Jackson, Tennessee; the Fall Convocation of Mercer University in 1983; a retreat for the Baptist Student Union of the University of Tennessee; a Small Church Conference at Central Baptist Seminary in Kansas City, Kansas; lectures on "Spiritual Direction and Guidance" at Friends University in Wichita, Kansas; "Current Interpretations of the SBC" at the Pastors' School of Averitt College in Danville, Virginia.

I spent the summer of 1983, June 27 to August 7, teaching at St. John's University in Collegeville, Minnesota. That was the first of three invitations to teach in Catholic universities, and I looked forward to it, for this Benedictine school played a significant role in the Catholic Liturgical Renewal Movement from the 1930s on. I had developed a friendship with Father Godfrey Diekmann, an eminent liturgical scholar and one of the *periti* ("experts") at the Second Vatican Council, some years previously, but I probably owed the invitation to extensive ecumenical exchanges with Roman Catholic scholars. Worshipping three times a day with the monks assured me far greater profit from my time there than my seminar on "The Apostolic Faith Study" contributed to the summer school. In one respect I went to Collegeville quite unprepared. In the middle of the term a cold front moved down from Canada, which is just a few miles north of Collegeville. I had brought clothing for Southern summer comfort and nearly froze for two or three days. I was glad to escape briefly by returning south to speak at the Pastors' School at Wake Forest (July 11–15) and to lead a weekend retreat in San Antonio (July 28–31).

The way I combined peacemaking with spirituality seems to have drawn both local and national attention. A surprising number of churches in North Carolina or the surrounding area, both small and large, invited me to speak about peacemaking: an interfaith peace service held at Galilee Baptist Church near Winston-Salem in 1982; and, in 1983, an ecumenical peace service in Winston-Salem, lectures on "Prayer and Peacemaking" and "What Churches Can Do to Make World Peace" at Tryon United Church of Christ, an address on "Peacemaking" at Pullen Memorial in Raleigh, a lecture on "Peace, Justice and Economic Issues" at a Leadership Conference for North Carolina Baptists at Ridgecrest, lectures in a peace conference at Martinsville, Virginia, an address to Physicians for Social Responsibility at Wake Forest University, and a lecture series on "Christian Attitudes toward War and Peace" at First

Baptist, Winston-Salem. Then, in 1984, I did another lecture series at First Baptist Church, Florence, South Carolina.

I gave a major address on "What Churches Can Do to Help Make World Peace" at an American Baptist Peace Conference convened at Calvary Baptist Church in Washington, DC, 17–19 November 1982. I participated in numerous peace conferences such as the one at Fuller Seminary in Pasadena on "Peacemaking in a Nuclear Age" on May 26 and 27 1983. My biggest venture in that sphere, however, entailed shared leadership of a "Baptist Peace Friendship Tour" of the Soviet Union 5–19 May 1984, arranged by the North American Baptist Peace Fellowship. Because I spoke just prior to that at an American Baptist prayer conference in Columbus, Ohio (April 28–May 3), I had a very narrow connection time in my flight from Raleigh Durham airport to JFK in New York City. In Moscow I waited and waited at the luggage carrel with our Intourist guide, Ludmilla or "Milla," for my luggage. It caught up with me finally a week later in Minsk. Meantime, I either bought or borrowed a shaver, shaving soap, toothbrush and unflavored toothpaste, and a couple of other necessities. Every night I washed my underclothes and shirt and hung them up in the bathroom. About mid-week I began to feel some embarrassment about wearing the same shirt and asked "Milla" to help me buy another. She cautioned almost in a whisper, "Just buy one. Ours are no good. I buy my clothes in Italy." I took her advice, which proved prescient. The shirt literally fell apart the first time I washed it!

I won't use up space to give specifics of my two weeks in the USSR, but I should share some impressions. In a slide presentation at First Baptist Church, Winston-Salem, to a large and receptive audience on July 1, I stressed "putting faces on people." "We rely so much on US or USSR propaganda," I wrote in my journal, "we don't get the true picture. We picture one another chiefly in terms of weapons systems, hardly at all as people." The kind of response I got from Soviet people and that of the folks at First Baptist, I went on to say, argued "for continuation of efforts to create personal contacts and understanding." I thought at the time that we could make real progress if we arranged exchange visits on a large scale. "Would that I were a better organizer!!" I lamented. "I'm primarily a rouser. But someone must do the rousement, I guess, so I will continue."

In 1984 Soviet officials were manifesting much more eagerness to ease tensions than the Reagan-led American government did. A significant number of important apparatchiks met with us for more than an hour in the Kremlin. Experts on Soviet history and culture might dispute my qualifications to assess what was happening, but I could sense already some tremors that preceded the earthquake that brought the collapse of the Soviet Union in 1991. One of these tremors was the Russian people's desire to resuscitate their roots in Orthodox Christianity. When our lovely chief tour guide gave us a talk about St. Basil's Cathedral in the Kremlin, I noticed her eyes watering up as she spoke about the cathedral's icons and the Orthodox liturgy. "Do you not feel an emotional attachment to this?" I asked. As an employee of the government, she could not say yes, but she quietly nodded yes. In Leningrad, soon to be St. Petersburg again, another very bright and well-educated young woman went out of her way to lament that Westerners didn't accord Soviets enough credit for winning World War II. She then gave us a spiel about the superiority of the Marxist model, how it provided for all of the needs of all the people. "When my father was sick, the Party took care of him. When he died, the Party took care of him." I asked, "What about faith? Do some people not need faith to cope with life?" She didn't answer immediately. About five minutes later, however, she said, "My grandmother was a believer. I am not a believer, but I loved my grandmother." "What about your children?" I asked. "They may be believers, and that would be alright." I caught glimpses of a new day dawning.

Baptist churches in the Soviet Union welcomed us. Because of their commitment to separation of Church and State, they had benefited from government favors over against the previously established Orthodox Church. As I spoke in different churches, I focused on Ephesians 2:14–16, "For he is our peace, who has made us both one and broken down the wall that divides, the enmity, in his flesh, ..." When I finished speaking to a congregation in Moscow, a grizzled, snow-capped old man embraced me with tears in his eyes. Someone told me later that he had fought in the Battle of Stalingrad. He didn't know any English, but he repeated over and over, "*Mir! Mir! Mir!*" ("*Peace! Peace! Peace!*") In Tallinn, Estonia, I addressed a large congregation composed of both Baptists and Pentecostals, who shared the formerly Lutheran Cathedral. Fortunately, someone had tipped me off ahead of time that I should not use the Russian *Christos voskres!* ("Christ is risen!") because Estonians did not like anything Russian. But they, too, responded to a sermon based on the text I cited above.

Just after returning from the USSR on May 19, I led a group of five students, including my son Chris, to dig at Caesarea Maritima in Israel May 22 through June 24. A trip to the Holy Land at any time can generate an immense amount of excitement, but the prospect of taking part in an archaeological exploration at a site so important in early Christian history overcame any jet lag I may have felt from the Peace Friendship Tour. The Apostle Paul had spent two years in confinement there before being dispatched to Rome for trial (cf. Acts 26:30–32). Following the Jewish rebellions in 66–70 and 132–135 CE and the destruction of Jerusalem, the Romans governed Palestine from this city. In 232 Origen took up residence in Caesarea Maritima. He did much of his vast writing and died there in 254 or 255 after undergoing torture during the persecution under Decius (251–253). Eusebius (ca. 260–ca. 340), the first Church historian and confidant of Constantine, was bishop in Caesarea during Constantine's transition from solar monotheism to Christianity. Somewhat belatedly, I applied for a grant from the National Endowment for the Humanities, which I did not get, but Wake Forest University supplied adequate support. I tried to arrange for Martha, Elizabeth, and Martha's mother to stay at Tantur, where we had lived in 1976, but the institute did not have space.[3]

The dig itself was not too memorable. We uncovered no priceless relics of ancient Caesarea. We just plodded away at removing one stratum from the top of another and recording every find, however insignificant. More exciting for the Wake students and me, Norm Lytle, one of my former students and a missionary to Israel, led us on a trek from Jerusalem down the Wadi Qilt to Jericho. We stopped at the Greek monastery of Saint George carved out of the sandstone cliff, the supposed site of the cave in which ravens fed Elijah (1 Kings 17:3). The hospitable monks spoke no English, so I patched together a few sentences from biblical and patristic Greek.

I should interject here before closing this account of my time at Wake Forest University that, on top of this hefty schedule, I continued my ecumenical activities. These included, you may recall, twice a year meetings of the Roman Catholic/Southern Baptist Scholars' Dialogue, twice a year conferences of the Faith and Order Commission of the National Council of Churches, once a year sessions of the International Baptist/Catholic Conversations. I also took part in professional societies.

---

[3] E. Glenn Hinson to Rector, Ecumenical Institute for Advanced Studies, Jerusalem, January 2 1984.

The most sustaining group I participated in, if not the most informative, however, was not the American Academy of Religion or the American Society of Church History but the Ecumenical Institute of Spirituality founded by Douglas Steere and Godfrey Diekmann. Very special, too, was the opportunity to return to Oxford to present a paper at the Ninth International Patristics Conference in Oxford in September 1983.

You are probably wondering by this time how I could have considered leaving Wake Forest University, a position that supplied such incredible opportunities, to return to a beleaguered Southern Baptist Seminary. When asked that question pointedly by Richard Land, who now heads the Southern Baptist lobby in DC, just after I returned to Southern, I replied, "Because training ministers is my vocation!" Although my rationale ultimately boiled down to that, I can see from journal entries after I had made the decision to that I wrestled with the same question myself.

To be quite honest, I think I had developed an inflated sense of my importance in the struggle for the control of the Southern Baptist Convention. When Willis Bennett, Dean and Provost at Southern, first spoke to me about returning, Roy Honeycutt had sounded a trumpet summoning Baptist moderates to a "holy war." Contrary to what I said in my journal, I thought that, by returning to the seminary, I might help to forestall the fundamentalist takeover of that historic institution. It sounded like Honeycutt intended to stand fast and needed someone as mulish as I am to stand fast with him. It wasn't long, however, before the presidents of the six seminaries signed the "Glorieta Statement" that virtually conceded the fundamentalist charges. From that point on, it was downhill all the way. In the spring of 1984, however, I could not have anticipated what would happen at Glorieta, New Mexico, two years hence.

I have prayed ever since leaving Wake Forest University that Carlton Mitchell and other colleagues there would forgive me. Gracious as he was, Carlton did not hold it against me. Perhaps he even understood what I hoped to do in returning. When Wake Forest investigated the feasibility of starting a divinity school on in October 1989, he invited me to be one of the three consultants. The others were Joseph Hough, the President of Union Theological Seminary in New York, and Leander Keck, the Dean of Vanderbilt Divinity School.[4] I could

---

[4] Divinity School Best Practices Conference, Graylyn Conference Center, Wake Forest University, 9–10 October 1989.

make a case for such a school; the others could tell how to do it. The divinity school did come into being, and I am gratified to have had some small part in its creation.

19

BACK TO THE BAPTIST HOLY WAR

I think I experienced some of the inner turmoil soldiers must feel when, after a recuperative leave, they head back to the front. There was a certain eagerness to rejoin those alongside whom I had faced the conflict before; yet, I also shuddered at the thought of doing something so alien to whom I am.

I'm ashamed to admit it. The burden of finding a house and moving back to Louisville fell almost entirely on Martha and Elizabeth's shoulders. They returned while Chris and I scratched around in ancient Caesarea's soil almost to the end of June. We had no trouble selling our house in Winston-Salem for a small profit, but they spent many hours scouting another house located within a reasonable distance from the seminary. Their first choice, in Norbourne Estates, cost too much, and we finally settled on a house "with lots of potential," which meant in very poor repair. In my journal I noted that we could assume a $29,000 loan at 12 1/2 percent! Though the interest rate seems an astonishing figure today when a recession has forced interest rates down to around 5 percent, the going rate at the time was 14 percent. Fortunately, we had to borrow only $15,000. The state of the house, however, prompted me to ask for a half sabbatical during the fall semester of 1984–85. In addition to carrying out a substantial extracurricular schedule, I spent most of my time stripping paint, painting, repairing windows and doors, and doing myriad other things to make the house livable.

Returning to Kentucky eased my schedule in one respect: Kentucky Baptist churches did not cram my calendar like North Carolina and Virginia churches did. In other respects, however, I had an embarrassment of activities.[1] Lucky for me that I was on sabbatical!

---

[1] These included teaching a course at Wake during one summer term; participating in the International Baptist/Catholic Conversations in Berlin (July 18–22); giving the Douglas Steere Lectures at Bay View, Michigan (August 5–10)[1]; doing a series of lectures on "Deepening the Spiritual Life" at First Baptist Church, Kannapolis, North Carolina (September 9–12); addressing The American Academy of Ecumenists in Cincinnati (September 28–30)[1]; chairing a meeting of the Apostolic Faith Study of the Faith and Order Commission of the NCC (October 12–14); lecturing

In the fall of 1984 the clamor and cries of the "Baptist Holy War" engulfed the seminary, as it did other Southern Baptist entities. Honeycutt invited me to join an advisory group to discuss strategy for responding to attacks on the seminary. Phil Roberts, one of my young colleagues sympathetic with the "conservative resurgence," asked me to "debate" Richard Land, presumably as to whether Southern Seminary should capitulate to the fundamentalist demands. Land and I had given papers at a meeting of the Southern Baptist Historical Society in Nashville in April of that year, and I was quite surprised that Land had tried there to pick a fight with my paper on "Southern Baptists and the Liberal Tradition in Biblical Interpretation."[2] I had serious misgivings about getting involved in a debate and reluctantly agreed with the proviso that Roberts would see that I had a seat where I could hear Land clearly. He did his best to assure that I did *not* have such seating! He was president of Midwestern Seminary in Kansas City, Missouri, until recently forced to resign.

My cheeks have been red ever since that "debate" because I didn't take the debate seriously and focus on the real issue, as I should have. Bluntly stated, the issue was: should Southern Seminary become a fundamentalist institution? I should have argued, as I had in earlier papers, why inerrancy is not a tenable option from biblical, historical, theological, or practical perspectives. Stretched thinner than a taut rubber band with getting resettled in Louisville and discharging an array of other commitments, however, I simply repeated the paper I had given at the Historical Society meeting in April. I did inject an aside or two about Land bringing his "inerrant Bible" and that W.A. Criswell, the icon of the fundamentalist movement, did a good doctoral dissertation at Southern in which he cited approvingly such scholars as Rudolf

---

on prayer in Christian history at Alice Lloyd College in Pippa Passes, Kentucky (October 22–24); addressing a TEAM-A dinner at Southern (October 25); making presentations on spiritual growth at a South Carolina Ministers' Conference (November 1–2); speaking on world hunger at Central Presbyterian Church in Louisville (November 4); addressing the DC Baptist Convention (November 8–9); leading prayer sessions at a Sojourners' Peacemaker Retreat at Kirkridge in Pennsylvania (November 13–16); speaking to pastors in the Ohio Baptist State Convention (November 26–27); taking part in the Roman Catholic/Southern Baptist Scholars' Dialogue at Laity Lodge in Texas (November 30–December 2); and leading a retreat at Providence Baptist Church in Charlotte, North Carolina (December 6–8).

[2] E. Glenn Hinson, "Southern Baptists and the Liberal Tradition in Biblical Interpretation, 1845–1945," *Baptist History and Heritage* 19 (July 1984): 16–20.

Bultmann. Land's rejoinder was that Criswell said he had learned something after leaving seminary. During a question and answer period after our presentations, I also had opportunity to challenge Land's inerrantist perspective by asking how he would explain the distinction Paul made in 1 Corinthians 7:10 and 12 between *his* word and *"the Word of the Lord."* His reply was, "I have dealt with that in *The Criswell Study Bible."* To the students that was not an answer. Besides, he had alienated them in his presentation by attacks on various professors; they booed him roundly several times. His performance, however, does not excuse the fact that I blew an opportunity to make a case for what we were doing to train ministers at Southern Seminary.

Almost immediately after I started to teach again at Southern, fundamentalist opposition reared its head as the pastor of a small congregation near Knoxville, Tennessee, undertook a crusade to get me removed from the faculty at Southern. Jim Stroud first wrote in August 1978 to express his concern about some views I expressed in *Jesus Christ*, and I took pains to explain that he was attributing to me views I sought to refute and quoted the relevant passages. I concluded by saying that "in all fairness to any author, it is necessary to read the context in which statements are made. You can see from reading the larger quotation that I was arguing against those statements which you quoted."[3] I didn't hear from Stroud again until after Christmas in 1985. On December 31 he circulated a letter to other pastors in Knoxville to try to prevent my teaching a seminary extension course on "Classics of Christian Devotion" at Carson-Newman College during the spring of 1986.[4] He circulated with his appeal a list of five excerpts from *Jesus Christ*, four of which Paige Patterson had cited and one other about how delay of the *Parousia* forced early Christians to begin writing down stories that had circulated orally up to that time. By that time I had forgotten about my earlier correspondence with Stroud, but I pointed out again that, in most of the excerpts, he was attributing to me views I was refuting.[5]

Stroud lobbied Cordell ("Grubby") Maddox, President of Carson-Newman, to cancel the class,[6] but Maddox, once my classmate at

---

[3] E. Glenn Hinson to James R. Stroud, Third Creek Baptist Church, Knoxville, Tennessee, 4 August 1978.

[4] Jim Stroud Circular Letter to Pastors, 31 December 1985.

[5] James R. Stroud to 132 Pastors in Knoxville, 31 December 1985; E. Glenn Hinson to James R. Stroud, 3 January 1986.

[6] James R. Stroud to Cordell Maddox, 30 January 1986.

Southern, stood firm on the invitation.[7] Ten pastors took the course. As early as January 3, one of them wrote to defend the invitation and the book.[8] Others wrote later.[9] When Maddox and other staff at the college pointed out that that the selection of the course and the faculty member rested in Southern Seminary's and not Carson-Newman's hands,[10] Stroud then directed his efforts toward my removal from the faculty of Southern Seminary. He wrote Honeycutt on January 30, "greatly distressed by the heretical views of Hinson" and insisting that I was "unacceptable to Tennessee Baptists." He went on to charge that

> Both Carson-Newman College and Southern Seminary are in violation of Resolution #16 adopted by the Southern Baptist Convention, June 12, 1980 and other actions of our Tennessee and Soutern [sic] Baptist Convention. I, and a considerable number of other pastors, request that you remove Hinson from the class at Carson-Newman College, and send a suitable replacement.

He also asked whether Honeycutt would be willing to come to Knoxville with a copy of *Jesus Christ* and learn about the "'abiding and unchanging' opposition to Hinson and the views presented by him in his book."[11] In a letter to me dated February 1, Stroud indicated that he was doing his best to arrange a debate with Paige Patterson, who had agreed to do so.[12]

On February 7, Honeycutt replied to Stroud's request for a replacement. He noted that I was "a valued member of the faculty who has taught responsibly in the seminary for approximately twenty-five years." He questioned on what grounds Stroud charged me with being "heretical," and averred, "Dr. Hinson is certainly no heretic." He wanted to know whom Stroud meant when he insisted that I was "unacceptable to Tennessee Baptists" and disputed the claim that Southern Seminary was in "violation of Resolution #16" etc. Honeycutt also declined to

---

[7] In a letter to N. Richard Roach, dated 4 February 1986, Maddox thanked the Executive Committee of the Alumni Association of Carson-Newman for a resolution of support "in seeking to create an environment conducive to the achievement of the aims of a liberal arts education" and rejecting "any attempt to inhibit spiritual, academic, or ideological freedom among Carson-Newman administrators, faculty, or students."

[8] James E. Robertson to James Stroud, 3 January 1986.

[9] E.g. Rob Edwards to the Editor, *Baptist and Reflector*, 7 February 1986.

[10] As indicated by Stroud in a letter to Roy Honeycutt, 30 January 1986.

[11] Letter of James R. Stroud to Roy Honeycutt, 30 January 1986.

[12] James R. Stroud to E. Glenn Hinson, 1 February 1986.

bring a copy of *Jesus Christ* and defend it before a crowd gathered by
Stroud. He assured Stroud that the seminary would check to see if I
violated the Abstract of Principles, the one basis on which I could be
charged.

Stroud did not give up, and one can only admire his tenacity. He
merits a place with the fabled heresy-hunters of Christian history. On
February 10, he circulated a letter to all members of the Board of Trustees
of Southern Seminary to "respectfully request the administration and
Trustees to prayerfully and thoughtfully consider whether the
employment and continued employment of Dr. E. Glenn Hinson is a
violation of the trust established between Southern Seminary and the
SBC." [13] He addressed the same circular to "Dear Friend of Jesus, Carson-
Newman College, Southern Baptist Theological Seminary, and our
Tennessee and Southern Baptist Conventions." Stroud's campaign
reached its acme on February 21 when he came to the seminary to post
his "theses" against Glenn Hinson on the door of Alumni Chapel.
Although he didn't nail up his theses, he did venture into President Roy
Honeycutt's office demanding time to present his case against me.
Honeycutt said, "You go talk to Glenn Hinson." He did. We spent three
and a half hours together discussing his complaint. As I listened to him, I
could hear deep resentment over the fact that a "liberal" pastor for
whom he served as an assistant had belittled and humiliated him. Our
conversation gave him a chance to vent his feelings. On March 30 he
reported meeting with the three Tennessee representatives on the Board
of Trustees to insist on my removal from the faculty at Southern. He
explained to them, "Dr. Hinson was very kind and gracious, but he
simply does not believe in 'the divine inspiration of the *whole* Bible, the
infallibility of the original manuscripts, and that the Bible is truth
without mixture of error'."[14]

On February 23, shortly after I had begun my semester at Carson-
Newman College, 800 people gathered at First Baptist Church, Knoxville,
to hear Stroud debate my former student Wayne Nicholson regarding
the book *Jesus Christ*. The organizers had invited me to debate Paige

---

[13] James R. Stroud to all Trustees of Southern Baptist Theological Seminary of
Louisville, Kentucky, 10 February 1986. He attached Resolution #16 and three pages
of quotations from *Jesus Christ*.

[14] James R. Stroud to W. Wayne Allen, John Lee Taylor, and Steven Anderson, 30
March 1986. Steve Anderson, a member of First Baptist Church, Memphis, Tennessee,
went out of his way to offer support.

Patterson. Roy Honeycutt strongly counseled me not to take part in it,[15] and my schedule would not have permitted it anyway. By this time I was becoming increasingly aware that my deafness did not allow me to participate effectively in debate. Friends reported, however, that Wayne and other former students ably defended me,[16] although a reporter's poll estimated that three-fourths of the crowd favored Stroud.[17] For several weeks the *Baptist and Reflector*, the Tennessee Baptist state paper, carried a slew of editorial letters both pro and con. A group of about fifty moderate pastors in the Knoxville area invited me to lead a retreat at Gatlinburg the next weekend so they could affirm their support.[18]

When a student friend said to me, "Dr Hinson, I want you to know that I don't think you are a heretic. Some people do," I decided that I needed to make some kind of public response. On February 28, I spoke in chapel on the question, "Am I a Heretic?" If space allowed, I would simply quote the entire sermon because it reveals my perspective on faith more clearly than any other published writing. I will have to be content here, however, to note the chief point I made in my sermon.[19] Faith is not subscription to a certain set of propositions *about* the Bible. It is response to the living God, whom we have come to know in and through Jesus Christ. Because faith is God's gift, no human has a right to sit in judgment of the faith of another. "God alone is Lord of the conscience," as Baptists' Second London Confession asserted. "This means," I proceeded to argue, "that no mortal, whether prince or priest or Tennessee pastor, can stand in judgment over the faith of another. Faith is too deep, too mysterious, too personal, too intimate for a human being to evaluate. Who, then, can call another 'heretic' or pronounce another 'orthodox' save God?"

---

[15] Roy L. Honeycutt to Glenn Hinson, 24 February 1986.

[16] Nicholson, pastor of McCalla Avenue Baptist Church in Knoxville, had kept me informed about the brouhaha in east Tennessee. February 10, he wrote that he had defended the book to fellow pastors of the Knox County Area Pastor's Conference. February 11, Larry Alan Reeves, Pastor of First Baptist, Jacksboro, wrote a strongly supportive letter reporting the action of the Conference. February 18, J. Stafford Durham, Pastor of Woodland Baptist Church in Louisville, wrote Stroud, remonstrating him for "an all out smear-campaign against a fellow Christian."

[17] Bill Maples, "Baptists Debate Controversial Volume," *Knoxville News-Sentinel*, 24 February 1986. The *Baptist and Reflector*, 5 March 1986, carried both Stroud's and Nicholson's addresses.

[18] Dillard A. Mynatt to E. Glenn Hinson, 20 February 1986.

[19] E. Glenn Hinson, "I Am Not a Heretic!" *SBC Today*, July 1986, 14.

The Jim Stroud show turned out to be only a prelude to a bigger production put on by the "Peace Committee" appointed at the annual meeting of the Southern Baptist Convention in Dallas in June 1985. Many in the more than 45,000 people who attended that gathering entertained great hopes that the committee would bring an end to the increasingly tense, acrimonious conflict. The composition of the group, however, did not encourage optimism about compromises necessary for reconciliation. It included four persons who would serve as presidents of the SBC during the fundamentalist resurgence: Adrian Rogers, pastor of Bellevue Baptist Church in Memphis, Tennessee; Ed Young, pastor of Second Baptist in Houston, Texas; Jerry Vines, co-pastor of First Baptist in Jacksonville, Florida; and Jim Henry, pastor of First Baptist in Orlando, Florida. Among "moderates" only Herschel Hobbs had served as a president, and fundamentalists could assuredly count on more votes than moderates could.[20] Despite insistence of some members of the committee that they did not want a "witch hunt," under pressure of the conservatives, the committee focused from the start on "doctrinal purity" in Southern Baptist Seminaries.

As a professor with limited political skills in a Southern Baptist seminary, I did not grasp fully the tenuous position I was in. Although theoretically constituted of a "balance" of "fundamentalists" and "moderates,"[21] the committee's decision-making depended on strong personalities—Adrian Rogers as the chief fundamentalist voice and Cecil Sherman as the main moderate spokesperson. I will be eternally grateful to Sherman[22] that, as fundamentalists increasingly fingered me as the

---

[20] Clearly identifiable moderates included: Robert Cuttino, pastor of FBC, Lancaster, South Carolina; Bill Hull, pastor of FBC, Shreveport, Louisiana; Albert McClellan, retired program planning secretary for the SBC executive committee; Cecil Sherman; Daniel Vestal, pastor of FBC, Midland, Texas; Christine Gregory, former president of the WMU; Winfred Moore, pastor of FBC, Amarillo, Texas, and First Vice-President of the SBC in 1985.

[21] Other committee members were: Charles Fuller, chairman and pastor of First Baptist Church, Roanoke, Virginia; Harmon Born, automobile dealer, Rex, Georgia; Doyle Carlton, businessman, Wauchula, Florida; Bill Crews, pastor of Magnolia Avenue Church, Riverside, California; William Poe, attorney in Charlotte, North Carolina; Ray Roberts, retired executive director, Baptist State Convention of Ohio, Columbus, Ohio; John Sullivan, pastor of Broadmoor Baptist Church in Shreveport, Louisiana; Ed Pickering, an attorney in Laurel, Mississippi; and Jodi Chapman, Wichita Falls, Texas, wife of another fundamentalist leader later elected president of the SBC and then Executive Secretary of the Executive Committee.

[22] Cecil Sherman died 17 April 2010, in Richmond, Virginia.

number one enemy, he invited me to do a series on "Deepening the Devotional Life" at Broadway Baptist Church in Fort Worth, the church he served as pastor, the very week the trustees met at Southern Seminary. He told me later that he wanted my critics to know that I was okay with at least one member of the Peace Committee. Sherman vigorously upheld the moderate cause, but he did not have strong enough support in the committee to change the outcome and resigned before it made its final report. Among other proposals, he tried to get the committee to award moderates at least one of the six Southern Baptist seminaries.

The seminaries endured something reminiscent of the inquisitions of the Middle Ages, although the chairman of the committee, Charles Fuller, said that sub-committees made visits to the seminaries rather than summoning the seminaries to come to them in order to avoid "being designed to be *miniature inquisitions.*"[23] The team dispatched to Southern Seminary included Adrian Rogers and Cecil Sherman. This subcommittee did not meet with persons of interest individually. Instead, they sent a list of queries to which professors were to submit written responses. The responses that I prepared, however, did not go directly to the Peace Committee. Rather, they went first to a group of "editors" appointed by the Provost, Willis Bennett, who tinkered with the wording so as to make them more acceptable to the conservatives on the committee.

To the quotations excerpted from *Jesus Christ* that originated with Jim Stroud or Paige Patterson, which I answered as I indicated earlier, the committee added questions relating to my beliefs about the saving of persons of other faiths and about the resurrection. The first originated from a statement I made in *The Evangelization of the Roman Empire* regarding the early Christian attitude toward competitors. "Did the covenant have to be so narrowly defined and applied through Christianity's institutional life?" I asked. My answer to that was:

> Today, it would appear, the covenant and thus the mission of the church could be defined with a greater measure of tolerance. This would not necessitate an abandonment of monotheism nor of the conviction that some sort of special revelation occurred through Israel and Christ and the church. It might necessitate, however, the acknowledgement that the one

---

[23] Charles G. Fuller, "Report to the Executive Committee," 19 February 1986.

God has disclosed himself in particular ways through other cultures and religions besides these.[24]

Concern about my view stated there evidently originated with Charles "Chuck" Kelley, Assistant Professor of Evangelism at New Orleans Seminary and brother-in-law of Paige Patterson. Kelley called me early in 1985. He was using *The Evangelization of the Roman Empire* in a course, he explained, and spoke with muted praise about the book. But he wanted to ask me a question or two about my personal views, assuring me that he would keep whatever I said in strict confidence. I could check on his reliability with my colleagues Wayne Ward and Lewis Drummond or with his own colleagues. "Dr. Hinson," he asked, "do you believe Jews can be saved without confessing faith in Jesus Christ?" I replied without hesitation, "Yes. I only hope that, before I die, I will know God, the Father of Jesus Christ, as well as Martin Buber or Abraham Joshua Heschel."

On March 28 Kelley pursued his inquiry further in a letter in which he asked me to answer four questions: (1) "Are Christians the exclusive people of God in the world?" (2) "Can anyone have a personal relationship with God apart from the saving faith in Jesus Christ?" (3) "As a part of my dialogue with him, would I have had the responsibility to call Abraham Herchel [*sic*] to repentance and faith in Christ until the time of his death?" (4) "Are world religions other than Christianity ever an appropriate or possible way for their adherents to come to a personal, saving relationship with God?"[25] Kelley went on to explain that he wasn't being "picky" and was not "a combative type."

I answered on April 1. Citing Acts 10:34, "Truly I perceive that God shows no partiality, but in every nation anyone who fears him and does what is right is acceptable to him," I replied to the first question, "I don't think so…. God cannot be limited by institutional or cultural expressions." To the second, I acknowledged "that I think a person can have a personal relationship with God apart from a faith commitment which is related to Christianity. However, I don't think that that takes place apart from Jesus Christ, because the Christ is universal" (citing Matt 25:31–46). "My own Christology, based on a lot of study of the New Testament," I added, "would incline me to think that Christ is present

---

[24] E. Glenn Hinson, *The Evangelization of the Roman Empire* (Macon GA: Mercer University Press, 1981) 287.

[25] Chuck Kelley to E. Glenn Hinson, 28 March 1985.

everywhere and that faith directed toward God somehow is related to him." Regarding the question about Heschel, I said:

> I think there is always a place for mutual witness. I would hope that Abraham Joshua Heschel would bear witness to me as I also would want to bear witness to him. I believe we have a responsibility to call Christians to faith and repentance. All too many have neither. However, I cannot read the writings of Abraham Joshua Heschel without an awareness that he has deep faith in God, the Father of Jesus Christ. Have you read his commentaries on the Old Testament?

I conceded that the fourth question was "the one most difficult for me to answer," but the response I made shows that I did not hesitate to say yes. I quote this in its entirety:

> Based on what Paul says in Romans 1, I think it would not be possible to exclude God's revelation through other religions. In Romans 1:18 and following, Paul makes clear that God constantly manifests Himself through the creation so that other persons are without excuse. I know at least one person of Hindu faith whom I would have a very difficult time excluding from a personal, saving relationship with God. That is Mahatma Gandhi. However, I have to admit that his perception probably developed from contact with Christianity. However, he never became a professing Christian and gave reasons for that. The way he saw Christians act made it impossible for him to become a Christian. Frankly, I believe in God as one who will not be restricted by us as human beings with our sinfulness, our narrowness, our tendency to try to put a handle on Him. God is not our heavenly automat into which we can place a quarter and get out a sandwich. God is the "I Am." Therefore, for me personally, I don't really have to answer the question whether or not God can or will save through other means. Some people have come to know God simply through seeing the works of God in nature. Other religions may sometimes get in the way, but who are we to say what God can do? Only a very small view of God would lead anyone to assume that we can limit God.[26]

Kelley wrote Joseph Stopher, President of Southern Seminary's board of trustees, and demanded that I be fired. Kelley is now the president of New Orleans Baptist Seminary.

Fundamentalists charged me with universalism. Initially I didn't take their accusation too seriously, replying, "I am inclined in that direction because I don't believe a God of infinite love would ever give

---

[26] E. Glenn Hinson to Chuck Kelley, 1 April 1985.

up. But I'm not a universalist because I don't believe fundamentalists can be saved." That jest earned me a place as the centerfold in *The Southern Baptist Advocate*. When the inquiry came from the Peace Committee, I had to take it more seriously. In my response to them I distinguished between universalism, which I rejected on the grounds that it does not allow a choice, and universal revelation, which is what I affirmed in my comment in *The Evangelization of the Roman Empire*. In support I cited Romans 1:20.

A question about my view of the resurrection stemmed from what I had written in *Jesus Christ* as well as other writings. On this point I had to respond not only to the Peace Committee but to a paper entitled "The Cover-up at Southern Seminary" written by Jerry Johnson, one of Southern Seminary's trustees at the time. A graduate of Criswell Bible College and a student at Conservative Baptist Seminary in Denver, Johnson was especially upset that I had questioned the physical resurrection and identified "viewing the resurrection in literal terms as 'extreme' and 'crass,' or stupid position." At Roy Honeycutt's request I composed the following statement on the resurrection for the Peace Committee:

> I believe that God raised Jesus from the dead as the "firstfruits" of all those who believe through Jesus. When Jesus was raised, he assumed a glorified body no longer subject to limitations of space and time such as we experience. This was no resuscitation of a corpse; Jesus entered into an incorruptible state in which he would never die. The transformation of an earthly body into a heavenly body evidently explains why the disciples had trouble recognizing him (Luke 24:13–35) and how he would appear among them suddenly through closed doors (John 20:19f.) or appear to the Apostle Paul long after the ascension (1 Cor 15:8). At the same time *I believe the body which God transformed was the very body placed in the tomb on Good Friday*, for the disciples found the tomb empty and did recognize Jesus. Because the resurrection of Jesus is the only one that has ever occurred, however, we cannot "prove" it; we must *believe* it. It is the article of faith without which Christianity cannot exist.

Before the Peace Committee made its report to the Southern Baptist Convention at its annual meeting in St. Louis in June 1987, they convened a prayer retreat at Glorieta Baptist Conference Center near Santa Fe, New Mexico, with leaders of all national agencies. During the October 1986 meeting, the presidents of the six Southern Baptist seminaries drafted what became known as the "Glorieta Statement." On the day it was issued I happened to participate in a meeting of the Faith and Order Commission of the National Council of Church at Fuller Seminary in Pasadena, California. When J. Robert Nelson arrived from Houston, he reported that, according to the *Houston Chronicle*, Paul Pressler had jumped up and down and declared, "It's a miracle!" Bob added, "I thought then that what's a miracle for Paul Pressler is bad news for somebody else!" It certainly was bad news for moderates in the seminaries. In brief, the presidents threw in the towel to the fundamentalists and agreed to help them turn their institutions radically toward the right. They essentially endorsed the inerrantist view of the Bible by affirming, "The sixty-six books of the Bible are not errant in any area of reality." They admitted that, "there are legitimate concerns regarding (the six seminaries) which we are addressing." Avowing themselves "ready and eager to be partners in the peace process," they proceeded to list six actions they would take, including: reaffirm seminary confessional statements and enforce compliance by signers; foster in classrooms "a balanced, scholarly frame of reference for presenting fairly the entire spectrum of scriptural interpretations represented by our constituencies"; and "commit ourselves to fairness in selecting faculty, lecturers and chapel speakers across the theological spectrum of our Baptist constituency." To implement the shift of the seminaries to the right, they scheduled conferences on biblical inerrancy, biblical interpretation, and biblical imperatives (1987–1989).

As the points I have summarized indicate, the statement signaled a clear victory for the inerrantists. According to the "Report of the Peace Committee,"

> The Peace Committee affirmed the Glorieta Statement and ceased its official inquiry, referring unanswered questions and unresolved issues back to the administrators and trustees of Southern Baptist Theological Seminary, Southeastern Baptist Theological Seminary and Midwestern Baptist Theological Seminary, hoping the results of their actions would be satisfactory to the Convention-at-large.[27]

It's hard to find words adequate to express the forsakenness and despair many colleagues and I felt when Honeycutt reported on Glorieta in a faculty meeting early the next week. It came as a pile-driver blow. What followed hurt more. The worst news came in the form of a radical shift in the character of the Board of Trustees and, soon thereafter,

---

[27] "Report of the Peace Committee," *SBC Today*, July 1987, 10.

departures of valued colleagues replaced by persons more acceptable to fundamentalist trustees.

By 1987 the balance of the Board of Trustees at Southern Seminary had shifted. Because Southern's board had a large number of local trustees, the change had taken longer than it had in other seminaries. Fundamentalist trustees who now joined the board perceived themselves as entrusted with a mandate from the Peace Committee to deal with "unanswered questions and unresolved issues." Many came angry and suspicious. Administrators at Southern Seminary sought to ease some of the tensions and to allay some of the suspicions of new trustees by scheduling a Faculty/Trustee Cruise on the Belle of Louisville on October 12. That provided the occasion for my first meeting with Jerry Johnson, who had charged a "cover up" by Honeycutt and the staff of the seminary. I encouraged him to come to Southern to complete the theological degree he was pursuing at Conservative Baptist Seminary, but he had insulated his mind against the perceived "liberalism" of Southern Seminary. Under pressure, however, he did issue a letter of apology to Honeycutt, the Faculty, and the Board of Trustees, admitting "demonstrated lack of judgment in several respects." He admitted "ill-chosen" and "too harsh" language and failure to use the right (trustee) channels to express his concerns. He did not apologize for his views.[28]

During the annual trustee meeting in 1987, Robert M. Tenery, a new trustee from North Carolina, actually gloated as he passed me in the hallway. I had ample reason to remember him vividly. When I wrote my "Open Letter to Bailey Smith" in 1980, he had taken exception to my comment that Jesus did not openly say, "I am the Messiah." He invoked Jesus' reply to the Samaritan woman's query in John 4:25–26 as proof, but I pointed out that, whatever the English translations, the Greek has only "I am," and I noted that the "I am" in John had far greater significance than "I am the Messiah." He opened his letter with the following:

> I have just read your senseless, irrational, knee-jerk reaction to the National Affairs Briefing in the Dallas area. You are absolutely wrong and you are as far away from the historical position of Southern Baptists as you can possibly get. Your remarks are not the remarks of a learned scholar. They are the remarks of a mindless vituperative person who is

---

[28] Undated letter of Jerry A. Johnson, Central Baptist Church, Aurora, Colorado, to "Dr. Roy Honeycutt, Faculty and Members of the Board of Trustees of the Southern Baptist Theological Seminary."

lashing out in blind fury because the St. Louis Convention [that elected Smith as president] didn't go to suit him. It is shocking to know a person of your shallow concept is entrusted with the young minds of ministerial students.[29]

When I replied to Tenery's missive,[30] he responded with a second, even more sizzling tirade. He charged that I was on a "hate vendetta" against Dr. Smith and had "designs to smear him." I took Smith's statement "out of context." Linkage of his comment with the Holocaust in Germany was "perfectly asinine." The strongest supporters of Israel are inerrantists. "I know that you and a few other hotheads at Louisville are on the attack," he averred, "but I want you to be assured that some of us are going to be on the counter-attack."[31] When I spoke to a ministers' group in Greensboro on early Christian attitudes toward war and peace in the fall of 1984, Tenery and another fundamentalist spent their time heckling and harassing me until other ministers insisted that they leave.

The "Glorieta Statement" left no options for seminary administrators except to negotiate with fundamentalists who dominated the boards of trustees to change the composition of the faculties. In October 1987, Randall Lolley, President of Southeastern Seminary, and Morris Ashcraft, Dean, resigned, followed by three of 38 faculty members. That was only the start of a much larger exodus from both Southeastern and Southern Seminary and consideration of an alternative, namely, the creation of seminaries in which the tradition of theological education at Southern Seminary would continue.

At Southern in 1986 Roy Honeycutt initially had negotiated with trustees to hire Molly Marshall as professor of theology and David Dockery as professor of New Testament in a sort of tandem relationship—"moderate" and "conservative." As more fundamentalist appointees shifted the balance of the Board of Trustees, however, they sought to stifle employment of any persons with moderate leanings and to replace any who departed with fundamentalists, and they upped their criticism of me, Paul Simmons, and Molly Marshall.

Southern's administrators approached this dilemma in several ways. Alongside the series of conferences the presidents had agreed to, the seminary sponsored several conferences funded by the "evangelical"

---

[29] Robert M. Tenery, Pastor, Burkemont Baptist Church, Morgantown, North Carolina, to E. Glenn Hinson, 26 September 1980.
[30] E. Glenn Hinson to Robert M. Tenery, 6 October 1980.
[31] Robert M. Tenery to E. Glenn Hinson, 16 October 1980.

Pew Foundation designed to foster understanding of and appreciation for evangelical/fundamentalist perspectives. I found myself unable in good conscience to take part in either series of conferences. I was able to excuse myself from an invitation by Willis Bennett, the Provost, to respond to an address by George Marsden by virtue of a commitment to speak at a National Workshop on Christian Unity in Indianapolis at the same time. I did, however, reply to a presentation by Richard J. Mouw, President of Fuller Theological Seminary, on the issue of separation of Church and State at the end of the week.

Under pressure from the Board of Trustees, Honeycutt named a liaison committee to negotiate with the increasingly fundamentalist board. In the spring of 1991 this committee agreed to a "Covenant" between Trustees and Faculty that said, according to my personal interpretation, "If you don't fire us, we will work with you to help turn Southern Seminary into a fundamentalist institution." When the faculty liaison committee presented the "Covenant," I made my last speech before going on sabbatical leave. "I cannot in good conscience vote for a 'Covenant' that commits us to help turn this seminary into a fundamentalist institution. I am afraid, however, that the faculty as a whole is not in a position to vote it down. Our colleagues have agreed to it. The president has agreed to it. Thus I hope that enough of you will vote for it to see it pass." Only five of us voted against the "Covenant." It was an awful moment. By the time Albert Mohler replaced Honeycutt as president in 1993, only a few moderates remained in the School of Theology. Bill Rogers, Dean of the School of Christian Education, and Milburn Price, Dean of the School of Church Music, resigned in 1993 following the election of Mohler on March 26.[32] Three moderate trustees also resigned on April 21, saying that the moderate voice on the board scarcely existed any longer.[33]

Shortly after I returned to Southern in 1984 the faculty had elected me as chairperson of the Faculty Club. Faculty Club provided a forum in which faculty could gain perspective on the transition in progress in the denomination and in the seminaries. Perhaps in desperation as much as anything, in 1990 I proposed moving Southern Seminary to the Atlanta campus of Mercer University or the former campus of Tift College

---

[32] Mark E. McCormick, "Two Deans Resigning at Baptist Seminary," *Courier-Journal*, 17 April 1993.

[33] Mark E. McCormick, "Three of Seminary's Moderate Trustees Quit," *Courier-Journal*, 22 April 1993.

located near Atlanta. Duke McCall had said more than once that Southern would benefit from a move to Atlanta, and I thought, if there were ever a time to move, it was now. As you will know, my proposal did not bear fruit. Although there is a seminary on the campus of Mercer University in Atlanta, it is not Southern *redivivus*, but a new school, McAfee School of Theology of Mercer University.

Why didn't this work? Why didn't alumni and supporters of Southern Seminary rally to such a proposal? Numerous reasons leap out at me. In the first place, most friends and alumni who wanted the seminary to remain as they had known it did not anticipate the drastic changes inerrantists would force upon the institution. Many of them probably believed the sales pitch that the conservatives just wanted to have their views represented by adding a few conservative faculty members to give equal hearing to all points of view. When you couple the effect of this reasoning with a fear of roiling the already roiling waters, you can understand why many would think it best to do nothing. As a matter of fact, what I would call a "corporation mentality" has pervaded Southern Baptist life for a long time: "Don't make waves! Get rid of people who make waves! Don't do anything or let anyone else do anything to threaten the corporation!" Along this very line, Honeycutt, who had once called for "Holy War," did not get behind the proposal. He estimated that it would cost thirty million dollars to effect such a move. "It would be impossible to raise such an amount," he insisted. Larry McSwain, the Dean of the School of Theology and Provost, thought it would only raise false hopes.

The proposal did get aired. The faculty of Southern Seminary met at Crescent Hill Baptist Church on 28 July 1990, to discuss various options, the main one my proposal. I made a brief speech to the group in which I conceded the "foolishness" of the proposal, but went on to ask a series of serious questions we needed to face. A group of ten faculty members made a trip to the Tift campus to explore whether it might be a suitable location. That hope never got off the ground. Although Mercer was eager to unload the Tift campus, Kirby Godsey, Mercer's president, asked $10 million for it. Honeycutt, still holding out hope that the Southern Baptist Convention would do the right thing, made not the slightest signal in support. He alone could have gotten such a plan off the ground, but it was already too late. As it turned out, an alternative was in the making— the founding of a new seminary in Richmond, Virginia, in the fall of 1991 by the Alliance of Baptists.

20

SOUL SUPPORT

I have often had friends ask what kept me going during these "lean years" from 1984 to 1991. The short and easy answer would be God, and I certainly think God was present through those trying times. To maintain my footing as the earth quaked around me, I needed more than anything to be attentive to the presence of God. Much less by design or planning than by the nudges of circumstance or providence, I continued my habit of meditative walking at least forty-five minutes as the first item on my agenda every morning. When I first began that practice in 1970, we lived approximately three miles from Southern Seminary. When we moved back to Louisville from Winston-Salem in 1984 and bought a house whose back yard abutted the campus, I had to chart a new path through the knobs of Crescent Hill. As I discovered early on, walking is very meditative. It awakens you physically and improves your health, but it also boots up your attentiveness. Robins singing, flowers blooming, trees leaving, faces smiling, and a myriad other things of earth and heaven shout that "all the world's alive with God."

In this stressful period, especially as fundamentalist assaults fell upon my vulnerable spots, I gained new appreciation for the imprecatory psalms—the ones that call on God to curse people (58:6–9, 69:22–38, 109:6–19, 129:5–8, 140:10–11, 137:7–9). These prompted me to let my anger off to God. Growing up in a highly conflicted family setting, I had not learned how to cope with anger. My parents had angrily warned me, "Now don't you get angry!" I had always bottled hurts and resentments up inside myself. During these trying days, I discovered these psalms that direct us to unload even our anger on God. Neither you nor the persons you are mad at can handle raw anger. If you bottle it up inside yourself, it becomes a volcano. If you spew it out on someone else, it may forever alienate them. But God, the God of this vast universe, can handle it. Beginning my day with casting my cares on God, I'm convinced, not only got me through each day, but it extended my life.

Journaling helped, too. I can see from a review of journals I have drawn from in writing this autobiography that I journaled very consistently in this period. Journaling, at least for me, is not the same as keeping a diary. In most entries I talked to God about what was happening and about my response to the vulnerable situation in which I found myself. Having spent some time in this type of meditation, I gained perspectives that calmed me and sometimes strengthened me. Reflection often caused me to question my excess of commitments and activity or the difference between steadfastness and obstinacy in speaking out against my critics and attackers.

If my experience is a reliable guide, however, God is present not only in a direct way as a sustaining power, a calming and strengthening influence, or a bulwark against besieging forces. For me God was there, too, in the courage and support of family, students, colleagues, friends in other religious bodies, and just friends. Martha, Chris, and Elizabeth experienced more anxiety and felt more anger than I did over salvos hurtling my way. They were ready to do what they could. When all of us attended the Southern Baptist Convention meeting in St Louis in 1980, Elizabeth, only twelve years old, kept an eye out for Paige Patterson. She wanted to ask him, "Do you know my daddy?" It was obvious to her that, if he did, he wouldn't be doing what he was doing or saying what he was saying. When Jim Stroud proposed to post his "theses" against Glenn Hinson on the door of Southern Seminary's Alumni Chapel, Chris, then about twenty-one and a husky 6'4" former high school football player, took a friend about the same size to await Stroud's arrival. I have no idea what they intended to do, but Stroud did not tack anything on the chapel door.

Had I confined my world almost exclusively to Southern Baptists and to the Southern Baptist Convention, I don't think I could have kept my equilibrium in the midst of what happened during the 1980s. God was there in my connection with the Church in all of its multiple expressions—as local congregations, denominations, world assemblies, academic meetings, and endless other expressions. God was there in activities, yes even in busyness that distracted me from some of the attacks from without and some of the tremors within. Taken together, these connections kept me from feeling totally desolated by the "holy war" in much the same way such things must sustain and empower people who suffer the ravages of physical warfare. It may surprise you to hear me say this, but I found some of the stoutest soul support in *ecumenical ties* cemented through years of engagement with other

Christians, in the *peace movement,* in *academic recognition,* and even *among my fellow Baptists.*

Ecumenical Ties

I have more than a little suspicion that some ecumenical invitations were deliberately arranged as rescue operations. The one that stands out most vividly in my mind was an invitation to teach "Contemporary Spirituality" in the first two-year Academy for Spiritual Formation sponsored by the Upper Room of the United Methodist Church, which took place in February 1985 in Nashville, Tennessee. By this time, I had taken a few baby steps in spirituality thanks to contacts with Thomas Merton and Douglas Steere, teaching Classics of Christian Devotion and Prayer in Christian History, and growth through trial. But you could have fitted into a thimble what I knew about contemporary spirituality. I think those who invited me had in mind such things as New Age or Quasi-Oriental Spirituality. Accepting the invitation anyway, I gave lectures on the spirituality I knew something about—Protestant Spirituality Today,[1] Teilhard de Chardin, Dietrich Bonhoeffer, Thomas Merton, and Douglas V. Steere. When I finished my presentation on Teilhard perhaps ten minutes early, causing a slight stir among participants, one of the team who had invited me, Bert Goodwin, stepped forward to assert his solidarity with me, explaining that I was a much-besieged Southern Baptist they needed to know. To my great surprise, the shapers of the Academy invited me to teach in the second Academy in August 1987, and kept inviting me back again and again for the next twenty-five years.[2] They also asked me to teach in five-day Academies, beginning with one in South Dakota in the last week of July 1987. You won't be surprised to hear that, after one or two more academies, they changed my topic to the History of Christian Spirituality or to New Testament Spirituality, fields in which I had much greater expertise, and replaced contemporary spirituality with a study on making the transition back to one's everyday routines!

Tears drip deep inside as I think about the many ways Methodists embraced me in those trying days. One Methodist friend once told me

---

[1] An article I had published on "American Spirituality" in *Westminster Dictionary of Spirituality,* edited by Gordon S. Wakefield (Philadelphia: Westminster Press, 1983) 8–11, was the basis for this lecture.

[2] You will find a complete list of all academies in which I have taught in Appendices B, C, and D.

that I was on the prayer agenda of every Methodist conference in the United States. I smiled, but the statement made me wonder whether my situation was direr than even I knew. When the magazine that became *Weavings* was at dream stage, Maxie Dunnam, then Director of the Upper Room and a member of the Ecumenical Institute of Spirituality, invited me to write brief introductory essays on devotional classics for a journal he wanted to start. John Mogabgab, the founding editor of *Weavings*, included me in a planning consultation on 21 October 1985, and named me to the Advisory Board, where I have remained to this day.

How close our companionship is within the Body of Christ encompassing all humankind struck me quite forcefully when I served as Paul Wattson Visiting Professor of Ecumenics at the Catholic University of America in Washington, DC, in the spring of 1987. That very semester, Archbishop Hickey of Washington removed Father Charles Curran, one of the most distinguished Roman Catholic moral theologians, from his chair as Professor of Moral Theology at CUA. Curran took a liberal stance, carefully documented from Catholic tradition, on three issues heatedly debated in Catholic circles: married priests, ordination of women, and use of contraceptives. The archbishop's action incited momentary soul-searching. Should I protest by reneging on my agreement to teach in an institution that acted so contrary to the freedom that stands at the heart of the Baptist tradition? An answer came back quickly: "Ha! This is the same thing happening in the SBC? How significant would your voice be?" The startling news of Curran's banning came so late, moreover, after I had accepted the invitation and made arrangements with Southern Seminary to teach there, that I felt bound to honor my commitment and to support Curran as a colleague while I was there. I have never done anything that proved wiser or more beneficial.

A group of Father Curran's colleagues invited me to a party they hosted for him, letting me share in their bolstering an esteemed colleague. Someone had cleverly rigged up a large rat trap with a bold inscription: RAT ZINGER, a graphic protest beamed toward the Director of the Sacred Congregation for Doctrine of Faith, Joseph Ratzinger, now Pope Benedict XVI, who had ordered Curran's removal. The favorite anecdote on campus at the time, however, concerned Ratzinger's boss, Pope John Paul II. God would give the answer to three of the pope's inquiries. He asked first, "Will there be married priests in my lifetime?" "No, not in *your* lifetime." Next, he queried, "Will there be ordained women in my lifetime?" "No, not in *your* lifetime." Finally, he said, "What I really want to know is whether there will be another Polish pope." "No, not in *my* lifetime."

The Friars of the Atonement who sponsored the Paul Wattson Lectureship began as an Anglican order and were the first group to be accepted into the Roman Catholic Church as a body on 7 October 1909. They generously invited me to live in their monastery located on the campus of the Catholic University. Father Jim Puglisi, the head of the community, and the brothers treated me as one of them, letting me take Eucharist and share in the household chores, even doing a bit of cooking.

My semester at Catholic University permitted me to deepen a friendship with Jerry Austin, one of the regulars in our Roman Catholic/Southern Baptist Scholars Dialogue. In my journal for 1987 I noted numerous kindnesses he showed me when I taught at CUA. He was, among other things, a splendid cook. I got better acquainted with Avery Dulles (1918–2008), one of the most distinguished American Catholic theologians and, though conservative, a strong supporter of his colleague Charles Curran. Pope John Paul II later appointed him a cardinal. At a luncheon Avery treated me to, he explained how and why he had made the transition from the Presbyterian Church of his grandfather, a minister, and his father, John Foster Dulles, Secretary of State under Eisenhower, to the Roman Catholic Church. Although he always seemed somewhat formal, I got a different impression of him here as warm, humorous, and caring. Sidney Griffiths, professor of near Eastern and early Christian studies, whom I had gotten to know through the International Thomas Merton Society, also treated me to a meal, during which we reflected on our deep mutual appreciation for Merton.

Space does not permit me to do a résumé of the many kindnesses bestowed upon me, but I cannot bypass what was probably the pinnacle of my time at Catholic U. A part of my assignment as Paul Wattson Visiting Professor of Ecumenics was to deliver a public lecture on "The Influence of Fundamentalism on Ecumenical Dialogue." After my lecture and a time for questions, Bill Cenker, Dean of Religious Studies, bowled me over by presenting me with the Johannes Quasten Medal for "excellence" and "leadership" in religious studies. Quasten had been a noted Patrologist who had immigrated to the United States after being expelled from Germany and taught at Catholic University from 1938 until 1977. He died just a year or two prior to my lecture, and I was the second recipient.

Among the numerous ecumenical groups offering direct encouragement, none did more for me than the Ecumenical Institute of Spirituality, which, as you know already, Douglas Steere first invited me to attend in 1973. EIOS met annually on a reciprocating basis in a Catholic and then in a Protestant retreat center to expose us to diverse spiritualities.[3] The institute had a significant academic objective for its annual meetings—to keep its members abreast of groundbreaking developments in spirituality across the whole religious spectrum. In addition to presenting and discussing formal papers, however, we shared biographicals—telling what was going on in our inner as well as outer lives—and prayed together. We corresponded. Many are the times when Douglas Steere or other members wrote to follow up on a concern I alluded to in my biography. I knew that I did not walk alone through a dark and menacing valley.

Peace Movement

A glance at my extensive list of engagements in Appendix B will help you to see that churches and groups other than Baptist took notice of my situation and kept company with me. Such a strong focus on ecumenical activity, however, should not lead you to imagine that other concerns slipped away from me. Competing strongly with ecumenism for my attention during the 1980s was a peace movement spurred by the buildup of American and Soviet nuclear weaponry as Ronald Reagan moved to the White House. Sharing an important common endeavor has a way of bolstering you as you walk arm in arm with others. In 1985 my speaking schedule took off almost like *Baptist Peacemaker* did; it zoomed. Accentuation of the connection between peacemaking and spirituality widened the range of groups and churches that convened peace conferences. It brought American and Southern Baptists together in a common concern, eventuating in the creation of the North American

---

[3] Catholic centers were more readily available and hosted more of the meetings, however. On 9–12 January 1985, EIOS met in St Joseph Retreat House, Daughters of Charity, Emmitsburg, Maryland; 8–11 January 1986, in Cenacle Retreat House, Highland Park, New Jersey; 6–9 January 1987, in The Cenacle, Lantana, Florida; 6–9 January 1988, at The Southern Baptist Theological Seminary, Louisville; 4–7 January 1989, in The Cenacle, Boynton Beach, Florida; 8–11 July 1990, at St John's Abbey, Collegeville, Minnesota; 10–13 January 1991, in Scarritt-Bennett Center, Nashville, Tennessee.

Baptist Peace Fellowship.[4] Among many significant gatherings in 1985, I spoke to a Peacemaking Forum at Dayton Oaks Camp in Berne, Iowa, coordinated by a fellow student at Southern, Harold Mincey; addressed a Peace Consultation in Nashville sponsored by the Christian Life Commission, SBC, organized by Larry Braidfoot; talked to the Downtown Kiwanis in Louisville on "The Spirituality of Peacemaking"; conducted a peace conference at Ravensworth Baptist Church convened by a former student, Darryl Fleming, in Springfield, Virginia; and met with the Peace Ministry of the Kentucky Baptist Convention. From 28 June–6 July 1987, I took part in an East German Peace Tour led by my colleague Glen Stassen, living for part of the time in the Bonhoeffer Haus and in Bonhoeffer's room in East Berlin. The main venue of the tour was the small Baptist seminary at Buckow, a few miles from East Berlin, where I gave one of the main addresses, "Baptist Attitudes toward War and Peace since 1914." I ended with a reference to troubling nationalistic attitudes among Southern Baptists and noted in my journal for July 2 that "The E. Germans knocked on the tables as I concluded with considerable feeling." In 1989 I gave the Dahlberg Lecture on Peacemaking at First Baptist Church, Phoenix, Arizona. Edwin Dahlberg, long time pastor of Delmar Baptist Church in St Louis, was an ardent advocate of peacemaking and instrumental in the founding of the original Baptist Peace Fellowship.

Academic Recognition

Scholars have fragile egos. We are all prima donnas. So it was probably a happy accident that I ascended to new heights academically as the most savage attacks on me occurred, for academic recognition undoubtedly helped to bolster me with some assurance that I had at least a modicum of credibility. I've wondered sometimes what the impact would have been had I experienced rejection on both fronts. That's purely speculative, however, for recognitions kept flowing my way. Although not acceptable to those who now controlled the Southern Baptist Convention, I seem to have gained increasing acceptability in the Academy. Response to the publication of *The Evangelization of the Roman Empire* in 1981 and other writings in church history resulted in my nomination to the Council of the American Society of Church History,

---

[4] At the end of my decade as editor, I confessed in one journal entry for 17 October 1989, that I felt some embarrassment about my reaction to "surrendering *Baptist Peacemaker* to the NABPF and Ken Sehested," the new director.

1986 to 1988. In April 1986, I presented a paper at the spring meeting of
the ASCH on "Charismatic Gifts in the Evangelization of the Roman
Empire" in Fort Worth, Texas, a follow-up of my Oxford dissertation. As
further icing on my Roman Catholic connections, I taught the History of
Protestant Worship at the University of Notre Dame during the summer
of 1989. I also did a DMin seminar at Canadian Theological Seminary in
Toronto in January 1990. I received invitations to deliver lectures at a
number of colleges, universities, and seminaries.[5]

Although I published only one book, a fresh translation of early
Christian sources on the nature of the Church entitled *Understandings of
the Church,*[6] a look at my bibliography will show that I had the attention
of the Academy. Early on, I made it a habit to prepare public lectures
with a view to publication, for editors usually requested permission to
publish them. A number of papers or addresses ended up being printed
in more than one journal, often in translation,[7] book,[8] or in condensed
form.[9] During this period of notoriety, I found myself increasingly called
on also to write for dictionaries, encyclopedias, symposia, and
Festschriften. The eighties and nineties seemed to mark the heyday for
dictionaries and encyclopedias, and the diversity of my publications or
perhaps my own beleaguered situation brought a raft of invitations. In
my specialized field of Patristics I contributed articles to *The Encyclopedia*

---

[5] See the list in Appendix B under Endowed Lectureships and Lectures at
Colleges, Universities, and Seminaries.

[6] E. Glenn Hinson, *Understandings of the Church* in Sources of Early Christian
Thought (Philadelphia: Fortress Press, 1986). In retrospect I believe I would do this
book differently, giving more attention to early Christian institutions such as baptism,
worship, eucharist, discipline, and the like.

[7] My paper given at Catholic University on "The Influence of Fundamentalism on
Ecumenical Dialogue" appeared in condensed form in three different publications: in
English in *Ecumenical Trends* 16 (December, 1987): 192–95; in Dutch in *Voorlopig
Magazine* 44 (16 January 1988), in French in *Oecumenisme,* September 1988, 16–18; in
German in *Una Sancta* 47 (1992): 12–18. The full text was published in *The Journal of
Ecumenical Studies* 26 (Summer 1989): 468–82, and later in *Oekumenische Rundschau* 41
(Oktober 1992): 449–63, with the title *"Christlicher Fundamentalismus: Hoffnung oder
Katastrophe für Cristentum?"*

[8] "Spiritual Preparation for Apocalypse: Learning from Bonhoeffer," for instance,
appeared first in *Cistercian Studies* 84 (Fall 1987): 156–68, and then in a symposium
edited by Tilden Edwards.

[9] "Southern Baptist and Medieval Spirituality: Surprising Similarities," *Cistercian
Studies* 20 (1985): 224–36, and several times in various publications.

of Religion, edited by Mircea Eliade,[10] *Encyclopedia of Early Christianity*, edited by Everett Ferguson,[11] and the *Mercer Dictionary of the Bible*, edited by Watson E. Mills.[12] I fear that I betray myself as a "jack of all trades and master of none" here, or at least someone who doesn't know how to say no, but I would defend myself meekly by saying that experts who invited me to contribute to other dictionaries and encyclopedias must have thought my writings reflected some expertise or they would not have asked. I wrote two items for the *Harper's Dictionary of Religious Education*, edited by Iris V. Cully and Kendig Brubaker Cully[13] and three for the *Dictionary of Pastoral Care and Counseling*, edited by Rodney L. Hunter.[14] Invitations to contribute to such volumes continued to multiple in the 1990s, as fundamentalists increased their attacks.

The gradual increase in my publications in spirituality led to a number of requests to contribute to symposia. Essays I wrote for works edited by others included: "Puritan Spirituality" in *Protestant Spiritual Traditions*, edited by Lutheran Frank Senn[15]; "The Contemplative View" in *Christian Spirituality: Five Views of Sanctification*, edited by Methodist Donald L. Alexander[16]; and ten entries in *Christian Spirituality*, edited by

---

[10] *The Encyclopedia of Religion*, ed. Mircea Eliade (New York: Macmillan; London: Collier Macmillan, 1987): "Constantinianism" (4:71–72), "Irenaeus" (7:280–83), "Justin Martyr" (8:220–23), and "Tertullian" (14:406–08).

[11] *Encyclopedia of Early Christianity*, ed. Everett Ferguson (New York: Garland Publishing, 1990): "Fasting" (344–45), "Infant Baptism" (461–62), and "Missions" (605–09). To the second edition (1997) I added an entry on "Marcella" (713).

[12] *Mercer Dictionary of the Bible*, ed. Watson E. Mills (Macon GA: Mercer University Press, 1990): "Canon" (130–35), "Clement, First" (159–60), "Diognetus, Epistle to" (214–15), "Egerton 2 Papyrus" (235), "Eusebius" (273), "Ignatius" (401–02), "Interpretation, History of" (408–10), "Irenaeus" (410–11), "Justin Martyr" (484), "Mandaeans, Mandaeism" (544–45), "Mani, Manichaeism" (545–46), "Patristic Literature" (654–57), and "Roman Empire" (769–72).

[13] *Harper's Dictionary of Religious Education*, ed. Iris V. Cully, and Kendig Brubaker Cully (San Francisco: Harper & Row, 1990): "Meditation, Forms of" (403–05) and "Prayer" (494–97).

[14] *Dictionary of Pastoral Care and Counseling*, ed. Rodney L. Hunter (Nashville: Abingdon Press, 1990): "Literature, Devotional" (654–56), "Ministry (Protestant Tradition)" (734–37), and "Spirituality (Protestant Tradition)" (1222–23).

[15] *Protestant Spiritual Traditions*, ed. Lutheran Frank Senn (New York/Mahwah NJ: Paulist Press, 1986) 165–82.

[16] "The Contemplative View" in *Christian Spirituality: Five Views of Sanctification*, ed. Methodist Donald L. Alexander (Downers Grove IL: InterVarsity Press, 1988) 171–89.

Frank N. Magill and Ian P. McGreal.[17] Retirement of older colleagues at Southern initiated a stream of articles for *Festschriften*. The first celebrated the life and thought of Eric Rust, Professor of Philosophy of Religion.[18] The next, published by the National Association of Baptist Professors of Religion, honored Dale Moody, Professor of Theology.[19]

Fellow Baptists

The extent of my ecumenical and academic involvement may leave the mistaken impression that the Baptists, save for my local congregation, deserted me or that I deserted them. Although the inerrantist leadership of the Southern Baptist Convention did their best to demonize those who did not subscribe to their view of inspiration, their attitude did not sway all Southern Baptist churches or organizations, infect other Baptist denominations, or prevail in the Baptist World Alliance. As a perusal of Appendix B will substantiate quickly, a large number of Southern Baptist churches invited me to speak about spirituality, peacemaking, Baptist or Church history, the SBC controversy, and quite a few other issues. Fundamentalist attacks probably made the invitations more selective among Southern Baptists, but I spoke almost as often as my schedule would permit. Alongside the dozens of brief stints, I should single out a heartening eighteen-month stint as interim pastor of Glendale Baptist Church in Nashville in 1988 and 1989. In addition to regular contacts with churches, I still received frequent invitations from Baptist or ecumenical ministers' groups. College chaplains and campus ministers invited me to give lectures or lead retreats for students. In January 1989, I led a retreat for Baylor University faculty, under President Herbert Reynolds a stalwart moderate force in Texas, focusing on the controversy in the Southern Baptist Convention.

American Baptists must have caught on to the tenuous circumstances I was in and frequently called on me during this period. Until inerrantists took control of it, Southern Seminary graduated more

---

[17] *Christian Spirituality*, ed. Frank N. Magill, and Ian P. McGreal (San Francisco: Harper & Row, 1988).

[18] "Eric Charles Rust: Apostle to an Age of Science and Technology," in *Science, Faith and Revelation: An Approach to Christian Philosophy*, ed. Robert E. Patterson (Nashville: Broadman Press, 1979) 13–25.

[19] "Dale Moody: Bible Teacher Extraordinaire," *Perspectives in Religious Studies* (Macon GA: Mercer University Press, 1987) 14:3–18.

American Baptist ministers than any American Baptist seminary, so it was natural to hear often from alumni. On 20 March 1985, the General Board of the American Baptist Churches invited me to Valley Forge to speak about the SBC—how it functions, the problems it faced, and how American Baptists might help. A task force drafted a resolution regarding dual alignments with SBC congregations. Regional bodies and churches called on me to lecture and lead retreats. Occasions included an American Baptist Convention Regional Prayer Conference in Manhattan, Kansas, on in February 1986 and an ABC regional conference in Toledo, Ohio, the following month. The latter was especially memorable, for the day I returned to Louisville the commuter to Cincinnati bounced up and down like a yoyo in winds up to 75 mph that did their darndest to keep the plane from landing. With only three passengers aboard, the scheduled flight to Louisville had to land in Lexington after more than an hour aloft. Desperate for earthly security, we three terrified souls rented a Lincoln Town Car from Budget, the heaviest car they had in their fleet, and drove the rest of the way. When the driver let me out in front of my house, golf-ball sized hail covered our front yard. The one plus from the storm was that State Farm had to help pay for the replacement of our roof. Other venues included the Ohio Young Pastors Conference (March 1987), a weeklong Prayer Conference in the American Baptist National Assembly at Green Lake, Wisconsin (July 1989), and a retreat for the staff of the American Baptist General Board at Valley Forge, Pennsylvania. (February 1991). Churches ranged as near as Cannelton, Indiana, and as far as Buffalo, New York.[20]

Numerous former students remembered me in my trials. Bahamian George Cumberbatch invited me to preach at the consecration service for a newly erected sanctuary for First Baptist Church in Freeport, Grand Bahamas (March 1985). Bill (William H. III) Elder invited me to give the "Brooks Hays Lectures" on "Spiritual Formation in Social Transformation" to Pulaski Heights Baptist Church in Little Rock, Arkansas (February 1987). I developed a special friendship with Brooks, the Arkansas congressman whom President Eisenhower called on to assist in the integration of Little Rock schools in 1957, when he headed the Ecumenical Institute of Wake Forest University. Brooks served two terms as President of the Southern Baptist Convention between 1957 and 1959. His son Steele, a judge, and his wife attended each lecture. Steele choked up when he tried to thank me for remarks I made about Brooks

---

[20] See Appendix B for the full list.

and for the lectures. His wife thanked me for my emphasis on women's equality; she planned soon to enter an Episcopal seminary, either General in New York City or Yale.

My semester at Catholic University provided a slate of invitations from churches in the area. At Gordon Cosby's invitation I spoke twice at the Church of the Savior and once to its satellite, the Potter's House. Other churches included Kensington Baptist and Chevy Chase in DC, and Broadview Baptist in Temple Hills, Maryland. At Chevy Chase, Jody Powell, Jimmy Carter's Press Secretary, hosted a large group of friends and me at luncheon in a posh restaurant on Sunday. That is as close as I've ever come to national power brokers.

Paulo Siepierski, a former PhD student and at the time Professor of Church History and Missions in a Baptist seminary in Recife, Brazil, scheduled a lecture tour for me in August 1991. Unfortunately my travel agent did not inform me that I had to have a visa (something my trip in 1976 did not require), and I ended up languishing in Miami for three or four days trying to secure one before finally having to cancel. My luggage, already aboard the Pan Am flight I was scheduled to fly, went to Recife without me. Among other things, I missed giving the inaugural address for the new president of the Baptist Seminary. Paulo, however, had translated a number of my articles and published them in a book along with some of his own essays.[21]

As I look back over the years immediately after my return to Southern Seminary from Wake Forest University, I believe that I truly grasped the meaning of membership in the Body of Christ, the People of God, the New Humanity. As you can see from review of my writings, at the outset of my teaching career, my mind and heart were intensely engaged in a search to understand the Church and how it carries out its mission in the world. I thought that Church history was the discipline that would help most in my search. I can say with certainty that following the deaths of my father, my mother, and my only brother within about a year, 1965–66, the Church—first, Deer Park Baptist in Louisville but beyond that, the worldwide fellowship of humankind—became my extended family, a family somewhat wounded like my natural family, but a family nonetheless. The larger part of my ecclesial family rallied round me, embraced me, and lifted me up even as a smaller segment of that family disowned me. Here, surely, I had every

---

[21] E. Glenn Hinson and Paulo Siepierski, *Vozes do Christianismo Primitivo* (São Paulo: Temática Publicações, ca. 1991).

reason to give thanks to God for the search for Christian unity prayed for in us by Christ ("that all may be one, just as you, Father, are in me and I am in you, that they may all be in us"—John 17:21) and made reality by the Holy Spirit. The "one great fellowship of love" is real!

21

RÜSCHLIKON

Little did I know what was in store for me during my eagerly awaited sabbatical in 1991–92. Actually, when thinking about taking another sabbatical as early as 1987, I didn't foresee teaching at the International Baptist Theological Seminary in Rüschlikon, Switzerland. In November 1987, Professor James Y. Holloway, on behalf of the Department of Philosophy and Religion, explored with me the prospect of spending a year as Lilly Professor at Berea College in 1988–89.[1] The prospect excited me greatly because I had much respect for Berea, where I had spoken a number of times, and its mission to Appalachian students whose backgrounds paralleled my own as a denizen of the Missouri Ozarks. Unfortunately the timing was wrong. My colleague Bill Leonard was scheduled for sabbatical at that time, and I was not eligible for a full sabbatical until 1991–92, since I had taken a half-sabbatical in the fall of 1984–85. Berea had already filled the slot for that year.[2] I mention this as something of an ironic twist in my personal story: had I taught at Berea, the Rüschlikon brouhaha might never have happened.

When it became clear that I could not take my sabbatical at Berea in 1991–92, I turned my attention to Oxford, by far the best place to work on the three projects I contemplated: completing the history of Christianity up to 1300 I had agreed to write for Broadman Press, editing a volume on John Bunyan for the Classics of Western Spirituality, and initiating the writing of a volume on prayer in Christian history. In a letter addressed to the Board of Trustees dated 5 January 1990, I requested a sabbatical "to pursue at Oxford University in England" those three projects during the period from 1 August 1991 to 31 July 1992. Rüschlikon did not figure in my plans at that time. When and how did that fateful change of plans take place?

During my sabbatical in 1975–76, Penrose St Amant—who served as President of the International Baptist Theological Seminary from 1972 to

---

[1] James Y. Holloway to E. Glenn Hinson, 5 November 1987.
[2] Alfred Perkins to E. Glenn Hinson, 15 December 1989.

1976—invited me and my family to spend two weeks in Rüschlikon.[3] We arranged our visit to coincide with our transition from Rome to Jerusalem in January 1976. I spoke in chapel and lectured in several classes. Much to my surprise, while I was there, the faculty elected me to succeed St Amant as president, an honor that I declined a few weeks later after reflecting on it.[4] At that time, my stock was quite high in Southern Baptist circles, although I later heard rumbles from the Foreign Mission Board about the violation of normal procedures. From that time onward, however, I enjoyed a close friendship with Günter Wagner, Thorwald Lorenzen, and other members of the faculty, several of whom had been my students. In January 1991, Kandy Queen-Sutherland, Coordinator of Academic Affairs, wrote to say that the Academic Affairs Committee had voted to invite me to teach in the fall semester.[5] In my response, I listed Oxford and one other option but saw nothing standing in the way and welcomed the possibility.[6] The faculty had already invited me to give the Hughey Lectures on "Baptists and Religious Liberty" March 6–7.[7] In a confirmation letter to President John David Hopper, I commented, "I think there is something providential in your invitation." [8] I had no idea how prophetic those words and the subjects of my lectures would prove to be. The three titles were: "The Pain that Brought Religious Liberty to Birth," "The Long Awaited Birth of Religious Liberty," and "The Peril to Religious Liberty Today." The last lecture focused particularly on what was happening in the Southern Baptist Convention.

---

[3] Penrose St Amant to E. Glenn Hinson, 3 December 1975.

[4] Penrose St Amant to E. Glenn Hinson, 7 April 1976, said: "We still regret but understand your decision."

[5] Kandy Queen-Sutherland to E. Glenn Hinson, 25 January 1991.

[6] I noted in this letter that I had planned for some time to spend the year in Oxford and that "someone there has proposed me for Regius Professor of Ecclesiastical History." I thought any such appointment highly unlikely because the monarch appoints Regius Professors! The other option had to do with someone's nomination of me for the George Foster Cherry Award given by Baylor University for excellence in teaching. I did not expect this honor to happen, however, for most went to non-Americans.

[7] America celebrated its bicentennial in 1991. In anticipation of that, a former student asked me to revise and update *Soul Liberty* (Nashville: Convention Press, 1974). It appeared under the title *Religious Liberty: The Christian Roots of Our Fundamental Freedoms* (Louisville: Glad River Publications, 1991).

[8] E. Glenn Hinson to John David Hopper, 7 February 1991. The reference was to teaching medieval church history, but it had broader implications.

Accepting the invitation to teach at Rüschlikon entailed jumping through some hoops with the Foreign Mission Board, one of which was to make a written statement "attesting to agreement with the *Baptist Faith and Message* [of 1963]."[9] Had the 2000 *BFM* been in force, I would not have passed. Mission Board staff took care to guide Martha and me through the certification process and to inform us on anything we could expect to encounter during our time in Switzerland. On July 12, the Coordinator of the International Services Department informed me that we had been approved. I arranged to attend and give a paper at the Eleventh International Conference on Patristic Studies in Oxford, August 19–24, en route to Zürich. Martha and Elizabeth planned to fly from Louisville and meet me in London on August 24. The three of us then flew from Heathrow to Zürich.

Returning to Oxford on the twenty-fifth anniversary of my first sabbatical generated both nostalgia and special pleasure, for on this visit I stayed in Christ Church College. One of Oxford University's oldest and most distinguished colleges, Christ Church was where I met with my DPhil supervisor, S.L. Greenslade. The path around Christ Church meadow has always been my favorite place to stroll and meditate. My paper, well attended and received, was about "Women among the Martyrs."[10]

The rudeness of a passenger on the flight from London to Zürich made me a little cranky, but our welcome in Zürich quickly wiped away my peeve. The campus, once the estate of the Bodmer family, whose name graces one of the most important collections of early Christian papyrus manuscripts, is spectacular. Southerners could not have improved on the kindnesses extended to us by seminary staff and faculty.

I considered it a great honor to teach at an institution that had earned a distinguished reputation for outstanding scholarship and the preparation of ministers and teachers, in the past especially for Eastern Europe but increasingly for Africa and Asia. In those areas, Baptists are too few to maintain educational facilities that could train ministers adequately, so they send some of their most promising students to Rüschlikon. The faculty had asked me to teach three courses: Medieval Church History, Introductory Latin, and Classics of Christian Devotion. I wondered whether I could keep ahead of my class in medieval history as

---

[9] Tom E. Prevost to E. Glenn Hinson, 8 May 1991.

[10] E. Glenn Hinson, "Women among the Martyrs," *Studia Patristica*, 25:423–28.

I wrote the textbook. We could not find a reasonably priced textbook, so I photocopied my manuscript and handed it out to the 24 students. That was good because some of them had difficulty taking notes due to language limitations, but it overtaxed the seminary's meager budget. At the end of the semester I had to beg friends in the States for money to reimburse the photocopying account! The bookstore finally managed to secure copies of the *Primer of Ecclesiastical Latin* for the nine students who elected to take Latin I. I brought copies of all of the devotional classics we used in that elective, which also enrolled nine students.

From our first week at Rüschlikon, Martha, Elizabeth, and I made it a point to get acquainted with this small, Alpine country. Every morning, I did my preprandial morning walk through a section of Zürich. On Sunday, September 1, we took part in an ecumenical service celebrating the 700th anniversary of Switzerland as a confederation at the *Halbinsel* (half island) of Au, a few miles from Rüschlikon. The seminary choir sang two or three selections. Sermons in English, German, and Italian emphasized water, *Gemeinde* (community), and *esperanza* (hope). The next Saturday we took the train to Basel, where we went first to the Kunst Museum with its outstanding collection of Reformation painters—notably Rembrandt, Holbein, and Dürer—and modern artists such as Picasso, Matisse, and Chagall. I liked best the Münster, a wonderful example of Gothic in red sandstone. Buried in it are Oecolampadius (1482–1531) and Erasmus (1469–1536). Excavations show that the church dates back to the Celtic period. On Saturday, September 14, we took the train to St. Gallen, about an hour from Zürich. The present church there dates back to the eighteenth century, but Saints Columban (c. 543–615) and Gall (c. 550–645) founded the monastery around 600.

Teaching in the European setting permitted me to do something I had been able to do in only a modest way in Louisville, that is, expose students firsthand to events, places, and people we talked about. Soon after the term began, I scheduled a trip to Ravenna, Assisi, and Rome, plus intermediate points, for October 17–21. Students were agog at the prospect. But just as plans were starting to fall together a cataclysm struck: the Foreign Mission Board of the Southern Baptist Convention defunded Rüschlikon on October 9.

Defunding Crisis

The bottom dropped out of my stomach when John David Hopper gave me the news. What happened over the next couple of months revives a memory of one of my favorite Abe Lincoln anecdotes. A ne'er-do-well inhabitant of some small town on the prairie was tarred and feathered and ridden out of town on a rail. A bold reporter ventured to ask him how he felt about this treatment. "Wa'l," he replied after giving the question a little thought, "if it warn't for the honor o' the thing, I'd just as soon 'uv walked."

In *The Baptist Reformation: The Conservative Resurgence in the Southern Baptist Convention*, Jerry Sutton, pastor of Two Rivers Baptist Church in Nashville, detailed the "conservative" rationale for the action taken by the Foreign Mission Board. First, the seminary had offended Judge Paul Pressler, energetic leader of the "conservative resurgence." When he visited the seminary in 1984, he "noted that there were few students present and that those who were present were instructed to stay away from him."[11] Second, in 1985 three Rüschlikon professors—Thorwald Lorenzen, Hans H. Mallau, and Günter Wagner—defended Eduard Schutz, President and Professor of the Baptist seminary at Hamburg, when he questioned the doctrine of the virgin birth. Third, I entered the picture. "The straw that broke the camel's back, however, was the invitation by John David Hopper to professor Glenn Hinson from Southern Seminary to teach at the Rüschlikon Seminary. Coupled with this was what the trustees considered a disappointment over the seminary's statement of beliefs, or in reality the lack thereof."[12]

Sutton had gone to considerable lengths in the earlier part of his book to establish me as exhibit A as to why the "Baptist reformation" had to take place, reprising the offensive statements from *Jesus Christ*[13] and *The Evangelization of the Roman Empire*.[14] In reference to the former, he quoted the pericopes Paige Patterson cited in 1980 and summed up:

> So here was Glenn Hinson, professor of church history at Southern Baptist Theological Seminary, teaching, in essence, that the Bible could

---

[11] Jerry Sutton, *The Baptist Reformation: The Conservative Resurgence in the Southern Baptist Convention* (Nashville: Broadman & Holman, 2000) 274.

[12] Ibid., 274–75.

[13] Ibid., 18–20. See also p. 434.

[14] Ibid., 23–24.

not be trusted and that Jesus Christ was not who the Bible claimed that He was. No wonder conservatives were up in arms.

Concerning the latter, he remarked:

> In this book Hinson was clearly outside the bounds of normative Southern Baptist theology. He failed to hold to the authority of Scripture, and with that he failed to see the necessity of conversion in order for a person to be rightly related to God. Again, this is clearly outside the bounds of what is considered normative Southern Baptist theology.[15]

He reiterated Jerry Johnson's charges in "The Cover-up at Southern Seminary."[16] He digested my Paul Wattson lecture at Catholic University in March 1987 in which I suggested that a "divorce" might be the better solution to the controversy in the SBC.[17] Following his review of the defunding of Rüschlikon by the Foreign Mission Board, he summarized James Stroud's case against me and the case for me made by Roy Honeycutt and others.[18] He cited the effort of Southern trustee John R. Michael, just before I came to Rüschlikon, to persuade me to sign "an affirmation of main evangelical truths," pledging "to teach in accordance with and not contrary to *several main evangelical tenants* [sic]."[19] He identified me several times as one of the leading interpreters from the moderate side, always intent on blaming me for the denomination's tilt toward "liberalism" or "modernism."[20]

It suffices here to summarize briefly the action of the Foreign Mission Board on October 9 and its decision to reaffirm that action on December 6 after a meeting with representatives of the European Baptist Federation. On October 9, despite an impassioned plea by Keith Parks, President of the FMB, the Board voted 35–28 to withdraw the $365,000 allocated for operating expenses of Rüschlikon seminary, almost 40 percent of its budget. The FMB had transferred ownership of the seminary to the European Baptist Federation in 1988, but it had agreed to continue funding through 1992, gradually scaling down its contributions thereafter. According to an Associated Baptist Press report, the Board appeared ready to approve that arrangement when they assembled on

---

[15] Ibid., 24. See also pp. 420, 422, 424

[16] Ibid., 27.

[17] Ibid., 168.

[18] Ibid., 346–47.

[19] Ibid., 353, citing John R. Michael to E. Glenn Hinson, 25 April 1991; John R. Michael to Roy L. Honeycutt, 8 May 1991. Italics mine.

[20] Ibid. 458, 465–67, and 472.

October 7, but "that support quickly evaporated when news of Hinson's teaching assignment at Rüschlikon circulated among board members the next day."[21] After rejecting an effort of administrators to have a line item for the money left blank to allow for study of the legal ramifications of the action, the Board voted instead to divert the $365,000 to Eastern Europe.

European Baptists, even East European Baptists,[22] did not react as the trustees of the FMB anticipated. The Executive Committee of the European Baptist Federation, meeting at Rüschlikon on October 11, responded with a sharp, "Think again!" In a letter to Keith Parks, Karl Heinz Walter, General Secretary of the EBF, said:

> This is not a breach of trust primarily with the Seminary in Rüschlikon, but with the EBF and the 32 Baptist unions affiliated with it. The European Unions immediately registered their view that the Board's action is unfair. Furthermore, European Baptists question the trustworthiness of the Foreign Mission Board, especially in view of pending partnership agreements between the Board and European unions.[23]

Numerous European leaders underscored the trust issue. The outgoing EBF president, Peter Barber of Scotland, said, "To have 40% of your income cut off at less than 2 months' notice is a cruel blow, whatever the reason. It makes it all the harder to know it is the result of a decision by the leaders of a mission board whose support has been guaranteed in a carefully framed agreement."[24]

---

[21] Robert Dilday, "FMB Eliminates Funding for Rüschlikon Seminary," Associated Baptist Press, 10 October 1991.

[22] That included Romanian Baptists. The Board did get a supportive letter from Iosif Ton, Chancellor of the Oradea Bible Institute and Pastor of Second Baptist Church of Oradea, Romania. Ton wrote to William Hancock on 1 November 1991 to "congratulate" the Board of Trustees of the FMB "for the decisive action taken to discontinue the financial support of the Baptist Seminary in Rüschlikon, Switzerland." He proceeded to recount how the seminary had undermined the faith of different persons who went there to study. He blamed the seminary as "one of the causes of the deadliness that settled in the Baptist churches of most of Western Europe in the last forty years." He thanked God "that liberal theology did not penetrate so far in Eastern Europe." Paige Patterson had a hand in founding this institute.

[23] European Baptist Press Service, "European Baptists Tell Foreign Mission Board to 'Think Again' after Rüschlikon Seminary Defunding," 11 October 1991.

[24] Ibid.

Such strong statements notwithstanding, the trustees of the FMB refused to rescind their action. They invited European leaders to meet with them on December 5 and 6. William Hancock, Chairman of the Board of Trustees of the FMB (and once one of my students), proposed a three-point solution to the problem: (1) That Karl Heinz Walter, Wiard Popkes (Chairman of the Rüschlikon Board of Trustees), and John David Hopper "acknowledge their insensitivity to conservative concerns" of trustees regarding Rüschlikon's theological direction. (2) That the seminary provide the Europe and Middle East Committee of the trustees with advance "awareness" of the selection of professors to teach there, but "not to determine or dictate policy." (3) That the seminary give an accounting of funds received from US sources other than the Foreign Mission Board. A couple of trustees noted that trustees of the FMB should ask forgiveness for their insensitivity, too. On behalf of the Europeans, Wiard Popkes replied: "This will not be an acceptable solution, and I want to be quite open on this." He observed that European Baptists were quite concerned about Southern Baptists' twelve-year-old controversy. He had no fear of "sincere conservative theology," but "militant fundamentalism is what we are afraid of and do not want." After the meeting, Walter told reporters that he was not optimistic about the future relationships between the Foreign Mission Board and European Baptists. "We need to have this partnership, and I hope we will find a way," he said. But he added that, "at the moment I don't see a practical way to restore fellowship and trust. October 9 is a date from which we have to start anew." Any sign of changes in FMB policy about "the autonomous and indigenous nature of the work in Europe" or about personnel, would require him to convene a meeting of all general secretaries of the European Baptist unions. "We could not survive if the theological struggle you have here in this country would come to our continent."[25]

When Looking Up to See Bottom

You are probably wondering by this time what kept me going as I looked up to see bottom. I prayed. I counted on God. As before, though, I counted too on help of my fellow human beings. Where did such help come from? I'm happy to report in this instance that it came in a rushing

---

[25] European Baptist Press Service, Report on Meeting of Trustees FMB with European Baptist Leaders, 6 December 1991; Ed Briggs, "Seminary Fails to Get $365,000," *Richmond Times-Dispatch*, 7 December 1991, B-5.

torrent from my own, from Southern Baptists even, and I believe I can understand why. Southern Baptists have a mania for missions, as I wrote years ago in an essay for *Christian Century*,[26] and the defunding of Rüschlikon was an arrow aimed at the Southern Baptist heart and soul. Individuals, churches, conventions, and all the rest threw up their dukes to defend their reason for existence. Some, to be sure, came directly to my defense, but even they realized that pushing the mission button could throw a guard around the most vulnerable. The fundamentalists had succeeded in creating enough suspicion about me by tarring and feathering me with images of a "liberal," but now they had overplayed their hand as they threatened the mission enterprise far more than a little squeak of heresy could ever do.[27]

Support came from many sides. It began with the faculty and staff and students at Rüschlikon and the faculty and staff and students of my own seminary, and the constituency of our home congregation (Deer Park in Louisville), and extended to alumni and friends of both seminaries, Baptists throughout America and in other countries, Christians with whom I had worked toward Christian unity throughout the world, and even friends of other faiths.

On October 12, the Rüschlikon faculty drafted a statement directed to the Board of Trustees of the Foreign Mission Board addressing the moral, missiological, and theological aspects of the board's action to defund. Early drafts used much stronger language, but the final document, dated October 16, averred:

> Faculty, administration and students accept full responsibility for asking Dr. Hinson to lecture and teach at Rüschlikon. He is a Christian scholar of integrity, a man of faith, and of deep commitment to the Word of God and to the church. As a Baptist historian, he knows that the liberty

---

[26] E. Glenn Hinson, "The Southern Baptists: A Concern for Experiential Conversion," *Christian Century*, 95 (7–14 June 1978), 610–15; reprinted in *Where the Spirit Leads: American Denominations Today*, ed. Martin E. Marty (Atlanta: John Knox Press, 1980) 137–48.

[27] John Merritt, a missionary elected president of the European Baptist Federation, has detailed the damage inflicted in a carefully documented study entitled *The Betrayal of Southern Baptist Missionaries by Southern Baptist Leaders, 1979–2004* (Asheville NC: John W. Merritt, 2004).

of conscience and the courage to express one's conviction belongs to the treasures of our Baptist heritage.[28]

The same day, the student body of the seminary sent me a strongly affirmative letter autographed, often with a personal note, by every student.

> We, the Student Body, wish to express to you our concern in what must be an extremely difficult time for you and your family. We would like you to know that your presence here at the seminary is very enriching to us, and we feel privileged that you chose to spend part of your sabbatical teaching here at Rüschlikon. We also want to express how terribly upset we are that you have been made to look and feel responsible for the FMB's decision of last week. We realize it is only their need for a scapegoat that you were brought into the situation. We want to affirm that you are indeed an asset to the institution in many ways. Please know that we are keeping you in our prayers. It will not be easy to return to the States in light of what is happening, but we know God will give you and your family the courage and strength to continue your work.[29]

Personal notes brought tears to my eyes. Francesca Nuzzolese inscribed in her native Italian, *"Anche Gesù era un 'liberale'"* ("Jesus was also a 'liberal.'") Some of the students in the Latin class wrote, "Glenn's *Magister Spiritus est*" ("Glenn's teacher is the Spirit.") Wiard Popkes, Chairperson of the Board of Trustees, Rüschlikon, conveyed "the affirmation of the Board of Trustees of you as an individual and of the worth of your contribution to the Seminary," assuring me of support "in prayers and in Christian love offered to you and your family at this time."[30]

Honeycutt and my colleagues in Louisville rose to the occasion, too. Consequent to the action on October 9, Honeycutt expressed shock at the decision to defund the seminary and "in the process to malign the reputation of a renowned Christian scholar. He added:

> This action effectively tries and convicts a respected Southern Baptist leader without a hearing and without recourse. I am dismayed by the unnecessary pain this assault will inflict on Dr. Hinson, and I continue to wonder how much longer Southern Baptists will tolerate the devastating

---

[28] "Statement of the Faculty of the Baptist Theological Seminary, Rüschlikon, Switzerland," 16 October 1991.

[29] The Student Body, Baptist Theological Seminary, Rüschlikon, to E. Glenn Hinson, 16 October 1991.

[30] Wiard Popkes to Glenn Hinson, 1 November 1991.

effects of partisan politics which have been inflicted on our Baptist way of life.[31]

Honeycutt called me later to reassure me. Bill Leonard faxed both a personal letter and a statement of the Faculty Club of Southern Seminary drafted October 10 endorsing Honeycutt's statement and adding, "We unequivocally support our colleague E. Glenn Hinson, a faithful Baptist witness, who for over thirty years has taught in accordance with and not contrary to Southern Seminary's Abstract of Principles."[32] Hundreds of Southern students signed a strong letter of support for me addressed to the trustees of the Foreign Mission Board.

Churches soon joined the protest. On October 23, our family congregation, Deer Park Baptist Church in Louisville, directed "A Memorial" to the Trustees of the FMB. In it they expressed "grief" at the board's "unwarranted abuse of our brother" and affirmed their strong belief in "his character and commitment" based on personal acquaintance. In sum, they said, "We attest to the integrity of the life and teaching in this congregation of Glenn Hinson as marks of faithful discipleship. He has not only encouraged but modeled personal piety, spiritual maturity, and Christian charity. He has supported cooperative mission endeavors within our community and around the world with his time, means, and wisdom."[33] On November 20, the Denominational Identity Committee of Crescent Hill Baptist Church addressed a similar letter to Bill Hancock, Chairman of the Board of Trustees, FMB. They expressed their "profound disappointment" about the defunding and "outrage" at their treatment of me. "We love and respect him as an exemplary follower of Christ, a renowned Christian scholar, a life-long student of the Bible, an effective teacher, and a devoted churchman."[34]

Personal letters addressed to the trustees of the Foreign Mission Board, to William L. Hancock, to Rüschlikon, to denominational papers, to local newspapers, or to me are too numerous to mention. All of the letters sent to me by their writers or by friends spoke favorably, although I'm confident the trustees had their backers. It was especially touching to

---

[31] Robert Dilday, "FMB Eliminates Funding for Rüschlikon Seminary, 10 October 1991.

[32] Bill J. Leonard, Fax transmission, 17 October 1991.

[33] "A Memorial to the Trustees of the Foreign Mission Board of the Southern Baptist Convention," adopted in regular business session, 23 October 1991.

[34] Denominational Identity Committee, Crescent Hill Baptist Church, to William L. Hancock, 20 November 1991.

me that some, for example, long-term missionaries,[35] spoke out despite the risk to themselves and their careers. One thing jumps out at you in the exchanges. *For the inerrantists* everything hinges on *doctrinal purity,* and doctrinal purity hinges on belief in inerrancy of the Bible. *For my defenders* everything hinges on personal character, piety, spirituality, or whatever else you may call it. *There are quite different concepts of faith here.* For the inerrantists, faith means subscription to a certain set of propositions; for non-inerrantists, faith means trust in God, the Mystery of the universe; it means commitment to a reality beyond our comprehension whose life we try to make manifest through what Paul called "the fruit of the Spirit"—love, joy, peace, patience, kindness, goodness, gentleness, and self-control.[36]

Writing is one thing. Taking action is another. Isam Ballenger, Director of the Foreign Mission Board's work in Europe, and Keith Parker, Associate Director, resigned. Isam became my colleague at Baptist Theological Seminary at Richmond in the fall of 1992. Keith Parks, President of the FMB, also resigned on 20 March 1992. As reported by Robert O'Brien, Parks reaffirmed his belief in the Bible and his conservative theology. But he told trustees he could not endorse the conservative movement "in good conscience … because my basic concept of the Bible is what I think Baptists have always stood for"—to

---

[35] Roy and Joyce Wyatt, long-time missionaries in Spain and Colombia, who had spent some time at Rüschlikon, addressed a strong letter of protest to Hancock and of support to John David Hopper and me at Rüschlikon.

[36] Confirmation of the point can be found in exchanges between student leaders of the two seminaries and fundamentalist trustees. Michael C. Cat, Pastor of Sherwood Baptist Church, Albany, Georgia, to Dianne L. Oliver, Student Body President, Southern Seminary, 30 October 1991, and Dianne L. Oliver to Michael C. Catt, 12 November 1991; Simon Gebs, Student Body President, Baptist Theological Seminary, Rüschlikon, to Trustees of the Foreign Mission Board, SBC, 13 November 1991, and Ron Wilson, Pastor, First Baptist Church, Thousand Oaks, California, to Simon Gebs, undated. Catt identified himself "as a trustee, elected by Southern Baptists who are overwhelmingly committed to Biblical inerrancy," who could not "in any way, support a school that questions the sayings of Jesus as authentic." He added a P.S.: "As a seminary student, I often thought I knew more than others who were in positions of authority. I now know that to be arrogant ignorance. You have a *right* to your opinion, however uninformed it is. *We* have a *responsibility* to act as Trustees consistent with the historical position of Baptist [sic]. Your politically motivated letter writing campaign and petition will only further seal the fate of Rüschlikon by those who may have been on the fence but do not appreciate such obviously organized assaults on the trustees."

cooperate in a non-creedal manner.[37] The Cooperative Baptist Fellowship later hired Parks as its first mission's director.

The crucial issue for Rüschlikon at this juncture was alternative funding. Before going to Rüschlikon, actually, I wrote a letter dated 15 April 1991, appealing for funds "to help save a great institution" in view of the agreement between the FMB and EBC gradually to diminish support. I pointed to Rüschlikon's strategic importance in Europe, where it had trained 85 percent of European Baptist leaders, and its growing importance for Asia and Africa. There were not enough Baptists in Europe to fund it. I expressed hope that the Alliance of Baptists and the Cooperative Baptist Fellowship would recognize an opportunity here, but I hoped that much more support would come from "persons of wealth who can catch a vision of what Rüschlikon is doing and can do." I planned to introduce John David Hopper to friends at the Atlanta meeting of the CBF on May 9–11. The defunding of the seminary by the Foreign Mission Board, however, created a more urgent need, and I was happy to see a large contingent of individuals, families, and churches ante up. A number of churches redirected part of their Cooperative Program and Lottie Moon Christmas offerings to Rüschlikon. For the remainder of the year the seminary fared well, I think. More important than particular offerings, however, the crisis gave the fledgling Cooperative Baptist Fellowship a clear *raison d'être*. When I taught again at Rüschlikon in the spring of 1994, Cecil Sherman, elected Coordinator of the CBF in April 1992, perhaps half-seriously, gave me some credit for its existence.

Italian Interlude

There may have been something providential about the timing of our church history excursion to Italy. It was fortunate certainly that we could get out from under the dark clouds hanging over this beautiful but vulnerable Eden. Obsessing over our fragile situation for a week was plenty. We needed to divert our minds from the negative and refocus them on what Rüschlikon existed to provide—education.

In planning the trip, I learned something about geopolitics. Much to my disappointment, a Bulgarian and a Romanian student could not get visas even to an incredibly open country such as Italy. Twenty from the class of 24, however, could go, and we easily filled up the other

---

[37] "Parks Explains Decision to FMB Staff," *Western Recorder*, 31 March 1992.

seventeen places on our bus with other students, staff, Martha, Elizabeth, and a faculty wife, Jill Lorenzen. From day one, of course, we had to worry about cost because the bus, food, admissions, and everything else were dear, and students had little money. One dear Italian student, Giuseppe Miglio, however, did an incredible job of arranging places for us to spend the night and to eat at minimal cost. We ended up with enough money to tip our bus driver fairly generously.

I've done quite a lot of traveling in my lifetime, but no journey I have taken has provided greater pleasure than this one did. Departing with true Swiss punctuality at 8 a.m. Thursday, we ate a sack lunch courtesy of the seminary en route to Ferrara, where we spent the night hosted by two pastor alumni of Rüschlikon. Ferrara is the birthplace of Girolamo Savonarola (1452–98), the ill-fated pre-reformation reformer. A statue of Savonarola stands in front of the Norman-looking castle.

Friday morning we headed to Ravenna, the western link with the Byzantine Empire after the Germanic invasions. We toured San Vitale to view its wonderful mosaics and the mausoleum of Galla Placidia (c. 390–450), daughter of the Emperor Theodosius I. San Vitale was undergoing extensive restoration, but the mausoleum remained intact. Our Yugoslav driver, Toni, initially turned down a request to stop in Florence as we headed westward and then southward toward Rome, but he backtracked when he noticed that we were ahead of schedule. We had to make a more hurried stop in Assisi than I wanted, but we had a nice pizza lunch and toured the Chiesa di S. Franceso. From Assisi we headed to Rocca di Papa, where the Italian Baptist Union had prepared dinner for us and arranged lodging. Rocca di Papa is where the pope resides much of the time, but we didn't expect to meet him there; Italian Baptists wouldn't have liked it.

It rained nearly all day Saturday. Monsignor John Radano, Associate Director of the Secretariat for Christian Unity, who served as the Catholic coordinator of our International Baptist/Catholic Conversations (1984–88), arranged a tour of the Vatican Library and the Scavi (excavations under St Peter's). We got wet going to and fro, but we loved every moment of our time. Later we made a brief stop at Santa Maria Maggiore, a fifth-century church with exceptional mosaics.

Sunday we got to the ancient city around 9:30 a.m. to tour the Forum and visit the Mamertine Prison before we went to the Trastevere Church, an Italian-speaking Southern Baptist congregation whose pastor, Bob Holifield, had been my classmate at Southern Seminary. The church was conducting a revival, so they could not keep a commitment to feed all of us at noon. Seventeen of us thus went to a Chinese restaurant owned by a Trastevere Church member. Thanks to the charm of Giuseppe Migliore, she refused to let any of us pay for our lunch. In the afternoon we visited San Clemente and Saint John Lateran, the Bishop of Rome's cathedral. San Clemente features numerous levels of the religious history of Rome—a Mithraeum, the *titulus* of Titus Flavius Clemens, a fourth-century church, several expansions in the Middle Ages, and finally the present twelfth-century church. The outstanding attraction of Saint John Lateran, where the famous Lateran councils met, is sculptures of the Twelve Apostles. The most eye-catching of these is Bartholomew, reputedly flayed-alive, who stands holding the folds of his flesh in his hands. Universal claims of the papacy are based on Saint Peter's burial under Saint Peter's, but the church of the Bishop of Rome features the whole apostolate.

On Monday morning, we had breakfast at Rocca di Papa and headed north toward Switzerland. Toni's adept driving permitted us to have lunch in Florence. It is a long ways from Rome to Zürich, but we arrived back at the seminary about 6 p.m.

Dousing Doldrums

Returning to Rüschlikon felt like coming down to earth with a thud after a walk in the clouds. I'm by nature more an "up" than a "down" person, but at this point I had to let myself confront reality. In my journal for October 30 I confessed, "I now expect SBTS trustees to press for my removal." November 9, I sounded pretty morose, believing that "my own career is near its end" and wondering if, at age sixty, I had much hope of securing another job.

Fortunately, my "down" period did not last long. Writing the history of Christianity in the Middle Ages and making copies ready for students to read demanded my full concentration and didn't allow me to keep feeling sorry for myself. In addition, my colleagues and students buoyed me. Rüschlikon was a lovely place to teach.

While the Foreign Mission Board decided whether they would rescind their action, Martha, Elizabeth, and I took a trip to München, Dachau, Nürnberg, and Salzburg. I jotted in my journal: "It is one of those times when I can't do anything. No one asked me to come to Richmond to defend my views. That would probably not faze any of the Fundamentalists, but one of these days I should have a chance to reply to all the attacks." We departed December 5 and didn't return until December 9.

When I received a report on our return, I jumped up and down clicking my heels five times. In my journal on December 9 I applauded a 13–10 vote of the European Committee of the FMB *not* to restore funding lest it create confusion among people or in churches who had rallied to support the seminary. I also felt elated that Karl Heinz Walter and Wiard Popkes had spoken forcefully in meeting with the Board in Richmond. Popkes declared that Europeans did not want "Militant Fundamentalism," which he compared to Communist countries where people are afraid to say anything lest they say something wrong. What the Board had done, I thought, gave moderates "a golden opportunity to initiate support for work in Europe, set up a Board, and make Europe their first field, hiring current missionaries."

This same December 9 entry reveals another reason why my spirits lifted—a job offer from Baptist Theological Seminary at Richmond. This was not my first contact regarding the new school. In the initial stages of planning, in 1990, just after I proposed moving Southern to the Atlanta area, Allen Neely phoned to ask me if I would consider the role of president. I explained that I wanted first to see how my proposal for Southern might play out. The Alliance of Baptists then turned to Tom Graves, Pastor of St John's Baptist Church in Charlotte, North Carolina. On one other occasion I had opportunity to bless the effort. In May 1990 I gave lectures in Richmond to the Virginia chapter of the Southern Baptist Alliance under the title "The Barbarian Invasion of the Southern Baptist Convention." When I finished, Elmer West asked me, "What do you think about establishing a new seminary?" I replied, "It is of God." I proceeded to underscore how urgent it was to get on with the development of an alternative to the six Southern Baptist schools. The seminary opened in the fall of 1991 with three faculty members—Tom Graves, Tom Halbrooks, and Linda Bridges—and thirty-two students. In speaking to me at this point, Graves underscored how important it was for me to come and develop a new model for education of ministers with focus on spiritual formation.

I didn't give an immediate yes. Even in dire circumstances such as I found myself in at the time, my musings in my journal reveal some internal wrestling. I thought I might help get the seminary off the ground and make a creative contribution in spiritual formation for ministry, but I worried that I might have to reimburse Southern

Seminary for my sabbatical. I wondered, too, how financially viable the new seminary would be. Could it provide enough salary to keep the Hinson family going? We were ready to make some sacrifices, but how much could we handle?

Arrivederci!

The rest of our stay at Rüschlikon bubbled with joy and hope. The Lorenzens and the Wagners treated us to wonderful Christmas parties. I preached at Rüschlikon Baptist Church the last two Sundays of December.[38] John David Hopper expressed hope that I might continue to teach at Rüschlikon, perhaps under sponsorship of Baylor University. Neither Martha nor Elizabeth nor I looked forward to departing. The hullabaloo notwithstanding, we had never experienced a closer bond with any Christian community. Saying goodbye to faculty, staff, and students for whom we had developed such deep affection was as wrenching as leaving home and family was for so many of the students coming from other countries and continents. It hurt. Would that we had not made other plans! What sustained us at that moment was a glimmer of hope that we might return as we did just two years hence.

---

[38] On behalf of the Preaching Planning Committee, Doris Wagner asked me to preach December 22 and 29. Letter of Doris Wagner to E. Glenn Hinson, 10 July 1991.

22

OXFORD AND THE RUBICON

We headed to Oxford on Tuesday, 7 January 1992. Financial considerations prompted us to travel by train and ferry rather than by plane. We soon found out that train travel carrying a surplus of heavy luggage is a chore. The first leg of the journey was the easiest. Kent Blevins, Professor of Theology at Rüschlikon and once my student at Southern Seminary, took us by station wagon to the Zürich *Bahnhof* and, at 6:15 a.m., we didn't have to fight traffic. The *Bahnhof* also had plenty of carts to help with luggage. Thereafter, the trip toughened.

At Basel we had to lug our things through French passport control. This meant carrying all of it up stairs in a hurry as we changed from Swiss to French transport. Once on the way across France, we expected to find Metz the hardest because we had only eight minutes to transfer, but the train we took out of Metz parked on the track next to ours, so we had only to walk a few feet to it. When we got to the ferry at Calais, we found no carts and had to wrestle our bags through a long, slow line at passport control. Fortunately, the ship's personnel took the bags at dockside, permitting us to take a bus. The ferry docked late at Dover, however, and, after waiting for luggage to come off the carousel, we had to run like crazy to catch the train to Victoria Station. This time, though, we had a cart to the bus and another from the bus to the train. We got aboard with two or three minutes to spare. A raft of people got left behind.

We enjoyed, or perhaps endured, a noisy, bumpy train ride to Victoria Station. The station has been modernized, but the "Royal" train was dirty and in no way comparable to Swiss trains. At VS we could not find a cart. Someone told Elizabeth that they once had 300 but now had only three. The rest had been stolen! We were all pooped, so we deposited two bags in the overnight will call, ate some pizza, and took the underground to Paddington Station. If the train was bad, the subway was horrendous—dirty, noisy, rickety, and on its last leg. At Paddington Station, however, the atmosphere improved noticeably, and we got a train to Oxford at 10:20 p.m.

I've alluded several times to our shaky financial situation. For the first time on a full sabbatical I had not applied for a grant from the Association of Theological Schools of the United States and Canada such as I had received twice before (1966–67 and 1975–76). I had obtained a $5,000 grant from the Louisville Institute toward the biography of Douglas Steere, and Southern Seminary gave us an additional $2,000. However, we did not rent our house in Louisville because Martha's mother lived with us at the time, and Chris had moved back from Chicago when the death of his major professor foiled completion of his PhD work in Syro-Palestinian archaeology at the University of Chicago. He had taken a night job at UPS and was teaching as an adjunct at the University of Louisville, but we had to pay normal household expenses. On our end, Elizabeth accompanying us added to our costs. Consequently we sweated the addition of £600 a month plus utilities to our stay in England; we had had free housing at Rüschlikon. Food seemed to cost less in Oxford than in Zürich, though not much. Already we had had to draw money from the grant for the Steere biography.

Quite frankly, as I noted in my journal on 9 January 1992, we had "felt taken advantage of about the cost of housing." The Nicholsons, however, completely demolished any resentment. They "could not have been more thoughtful or nicer," I added. Tuesday night they hosted us in the Provost's Lodgings at Oriel College and fed us breakfast the next morning. Wednesday, Hazel insisted on fixing sandwiches to take with us to eat on the way to London to retrieve the bags we had had to leave there. While we were gone, she shopped and prepared a meal for our return. Unaware of her thoughtful surprise, we stopped at a Chinese restaurant when we got back to Oxford, so we had a lovely meal the next day.

Although cost of housing burdened our budget, we made a most fortunate arrangement with reference to transportation. We traded the use of Elizabeth's Ford Escort to George and Ruth Beasley-Murray during a semester he planned to live in Louisville and teach at Southern for the use of their brand new Rover sedan. He originally planned to meet us in London, but he called before we left Rüschlikon to say that he could not do so due to an important meeting. I didn't feel very kindly about that when we arrived late at night. When we took command of the car on Wednesday, however, we felt immensely grateful. The use of the car gave us freedom and permitted us to enjoy Oxford and England much as we had on previous occasions.

SBTS or BTSR?

From the first day we set foot on English soil, the cauldron stoked by the defunding of Rüschlikon bubbled and boiled with the question: Will you return to Southern Seminary or will you go to Richmond? Any hesitation I may have felt at this time evaporated when I received the letter from Roy Honeycutt a month later conveying a "warning" from the Personnel Committee of the Board of Trustees of Southern Seminary, the end product of trustee John Michael's vendetta against me.

The meeting with John Michael on 25 April 1991 remains very vivid in my memory. It was only the first step in a determined effort to have me fired. Curiously, he opened our conversation with a couple of interesting admissions. First, he said he had talked to every student who would talk to him and could not find a one who would "blow the whistle" on me. Then he asked me, "Do you know why we want you out of here?" I said, "No. I'm a little surprised by it." "Because you have too much influence," he replied. He then presented me the letter asking me to agree *not* to teach five things:

1. That any portion of scripture is not accurate, factual, and historically reliable (despite allowances for parables, metaphor, textual criticism, and the differences in Bible versions).

2. That Jesus Christ did not rise literally and bodily from the grave, with "flesh and bones," and within historical space and time, as testified in the Gospel accounts.

3. That Jesus Christ lacked any consciousness of divinity or deity, or that Jesus Christ is not fully God as well as fully man.

4. That Jesus was ever in error.

5. That non-Christian religions are to be affirmed or encouraged.[1]

Michael indicated in a letter to Roy Honeycutt that I told him at that meeting and in a letter dated May 2 that I "would not be willing to refrain from teaching those views."[2]

Actually, I did not say that in so many words, but he could have deduced it from my unwillingness to sign his document. As I pointed

---

[1] John R. Michael to Roy L. Honeycutt, 24 July 1991. Michael did not leave with me the letter he asked me to sign. He detailed his charges in this eleven-page letter with quotations from *Jesus Christ* and *The Evangelization of the Roman Empire*. I responded from Oxford on 26 January 1992, to the particulars.

[2] John R. Michael to Roy L. Honeycutt, 24 July 1991, A-1.

out the many difficulties created by the inerrantist view of scripture, he responded, "Well, I'm only a layman." "But you are trying to tell me what I can teach," I said. Regarding the resurrection of Jesus, I noted that Michael's debate was with the Apostle Paul and not with me. On the divinity of Jesus, I affirmed my agreement with the Nicene Creed and underscored Jesus' addressing God as "Abba." Concerning Jesus' "error," I insisted that the use of quotation marks meant so-called. About other religions, I said, "Jesus was a Jew. He never became a Christian. How can I not say anything positive about Judaism?" The upshot of our conversation was, "John, I signed one statement when I joined the faculty, the Abstract of Principles. I will not sign any other."

Following my unwillingness to submit to his demand that I sign a letter agreeing not to teach certain things, he spent the next three months fashioning a case to prove that I probably stood in violation of the Abstract of Principles. On July 24, he sent Honeycutt an eleven-page, single-spaced letter detailing the five "concerns" he had specified in his meeting with me, making an effort to prove that, in my writings, I violated the Abstract of Principles.

Concern #1: Regarding Scripture. What disturbed him particularly, as it did other inerrantists, were my references to "embellishments" in the Gospels, which he construed as negative. The Seminary's use of the Abstract rather than the *Baptist Faith and Message* 2000 confronted him with a challenge in making his main point, about inerrancy of the Bible, because its article on scriptures did not use the term. It even avoided the word "infallible" used in the Second London Confession from which it drew. Article I of the Abstract reads: "The Scriptures of the Old and New Testaments were given by inspiration of God, and are the only sufficient, certain and authoritative[3] rule of all saving knowledge, faith and obedience." Michael used this logic. "If the scriptures are embellished and must be treated with caution, or might otherwise be discredited or questioned, then they cannot also be 'given by inspiration of God, and (be) the only sufficient, certain and authoritative rule of all saving knowledge, faith and obedience.' Dr. Hinson's teaching could be seen as a departure from the Abstract of Principles on this point."[4]

---

[3] The Second London Confession, chap. 1. *Of the Holy Scriptures*.1, reads: "The Holy Scripture is the only sufficient, certain, and **infallible** rule of all saving Knowledge, Faith, and Obedience."

[4] John R. Michael to Roy L. Honeycutt, 24 July 1991, A-3.

Concern #2: Regarding the <u>Resurrection</u>. He focused here on my discussion of Paul's rejection of the "crass and literal" view of Jesus' resurrection and emphasis upon the risen Christ possessing "not a physical but a spiritual body." He cited, too, a distinction I made between definiteness of the death of Christ and less certainty about his resurrection as proof that I didn't believe the resurrection as he conceived it. I wrote: "The most definite fact about Jesus is the crucifixion. No Christian, surely, would have invented a tale of the ignominious death of the founder of Christianity. Of his resurrection perhaps, of his death no."[5] Michael added, "Dr. Hinson's position on the resurrection seems not only to violate the Abstract with respect to Article I: THE SCRIPTURE, but it might also be a violation of Article VII: THE MEDIATOR. This article of the Abstract says that Christ took on the human nature, then suffered, died, was buried, and rose again the third day. What kind of resurrection was it? Christ died **in the flesh**, and he was buried **in the flesh**. The scripture makes it clear that He **also rose again in the flesh**.... Therefore, Dr. Hinson's rejection of the literal, physical resurrection might be seen as a departure from the Abstract of Principles, Articles I and VII."[6] Michael was taking some liberty in casting his own interpretation of resurrection on the Abstract. Article VII reads:

> Jesus Christ, the only begotten Son of God, is the divinely appointed mediator between God and Man. Having taken upon Himself human nature, yet without sin, He perfectly fulfilled the law, suffered and **died upon the cross** for the salvation of sinners. **He was buried, and rose again the third day**, and ascended to His Father, at whose right hand he ever liveth to make intercession for His people. He is the only Mediator, the Prophet, Priest and King of the Church, and Sovereign of the Universe.

Note, please, "flesh" is not mentioned either about death or resurrection.

Concern #3: Regarding the <u>Divinity of Christ</u>. Michael ascribed to me here a view I was disputing, i.e., that Jesus had only a "prophetic consciousness" and that the early church attributed divinity to him. He glossed over the main point I tried to make, even though he quoted this part of my argument: "When full allowance has been made for the early Church's backward look, however, it is still necessary to concede that

---

[5] *Jesus Christ* (Gaithersburg MD: Consortium Press, 1977), 97.
[6] John R. Michael to Roy L. Honeycutt, 24 July 1991, A-5. Bold print mine.

Jesus' self-understanding possessed a uniquely authoritative character."[7] Had he continued, he would have noted the evidence I cited for his "unique filial consciousness" "in Jesus' confession of and prayer to God the Father." I added, "That such thinking went back to Jesus and not just the early Church is demonstrated by several things." I elaborated especially on Jesus' addressing God as "*Abba*" and argued for the legitimacy of what is known as "the Johannine bolt from the blue" (Matt 11:27=Luke 10:22). "It is not beyond belief that Jesus may have let his consciousness of being God's special instrument of revelation shine through."[8] From his restricted quotation, however, Michael went on to say: "Dr. Hinson's position on the divinity of Christ might be a departure from Article I: THE SCRIPTURE (previously cited), and it may also be a departure from Article III: THE TRINITY: 'God is revealed to us as Father, Son and Holy Spirit, each with distinct personal attributes, but without division of nature, essence or being'."[9] There is another *non sequitur* here.

Concern #4: Regarding the "Error" of Jesus. The issue for Michael here was my designation of Jesus' expectation of the return of the Son of Man and consummation of the age within his own lifetime (Mark 13:30) as "error" "due to prophetic foreshortening."[10] In Michael's view, Jesus, of course, could not err just as scripture could not err. He discounted my interpretation of the quotation marks as "so-called error" and proceeded to cite my discussion of Albert Schweitzer's conviction that Jesus left no room for the church as my own and omitted my refutation. He added, "It is clear from the context that Dr. Hinson indeed believes that Christ made a mistake, that He was in error…. This position puts Dr. Hinson at risk of violating the Abstract with respect to Article III, THE TRINITY (previously cited), as well as ARTICLE II, GOD: "There is but one God, the Maker, Preserver and Ruler of all things, having in and of himself, all perfections, and being infinite in them all; and to him all creatures owe the highest love, reverence and obedience."[11] ARTICLE II does not refer to Jesus, so you have another *non sequitur*.

Concern #5: Regarding Other Religions. Michael here objected to some comments I had made in an epilogue to *The Evangelization of the*

---

[7] *Jesus Christ*, 84.
[8] Ibid., 85.
[9] John R. Michael to Roy L. Honeycutt, 24 July 1991, A-7.
[10] *Jesus Christ*, 76.
[11] John R. Michael to Roy L. Honeycutt, 24 July 1991, A-9.

Roman Empire in which I asked whether the mission of the church "could not be defined with a greater measure of tolerance." He underscored especially statements I cited in Chapter 19.[12] Michael commented:

> In that the Abstract of Principles is a synopsis of Christian doctrine and faith, Dr. Hinson may be teaching contrary to the whole Abstract when he advocates the legitimacy of other world religions and suggests that we cooperate with non-Christian religions rather than convert their adherents. It is impossible to faithfully teach the unique doctrines of Christianity while also advocating the legitimacy of other ways of faith. By their very nature, other religions stand in opposition to Christianity.[13]

Huh? Can you explain the logic: that teaching "the unique doctrines of Christianity" would preclude "advocating the legitimacy of other ways of faith"?

Michael met with Honeycutt on two more occasions to prompt him to respond to his request that the trustees issue a "warning." While waiting for Honeycutt to respond to his July 24 letter, Michael decided to go public by sharing his request for a "warning" to me with the *Indiana Baptist*, news journal of the ultra-conservative State Convention of [Southern] Baptists in Indiana. The paper published the story on November 5. During a faculty-trustee retreat on November 8, Honeycutt criticized the editors of the *Indiana Baptist* for airing publicly accusations "dealt with in full some years ago by the seminary's board of trustees." Michael himself formally apologized.[14]

On 8 January 1992, Honeycutt reported to the Trustee Committee on Academic Personnel his response to Michael's "Request for trustee warning to Professor Glenn Hinson." He made these points: (1) The evidence John Michael submitted "essentially duplicates the concerns which the Board of Trustees considered in 1986." (2) Honeycutt had discussed with John Michael the "quandary" he felt "in considering the recommendation of a formal trustee warning of a faculty person whom the President believes to be functioning within the seminary's confessional statement and therefore innocent of charges of dismissal." (3) Since the seminary's personnel policies governing faculty discipline contain no category of official trustee warning, "any warning of a

---

[12] *The Evangelization of the Roman Empire* (Macon GA: Mercer University Press, 1981) 287, 288.

[13] John R. Michael to Roy L. Honeycutt, 24 July 1991, A-10.

[14] Herb Hollinger, "Trustee Seeks 'Warning' but Apologizes to Faculty," Baptist Press, 8 November 1991.

professor should be confined to administrative action rather than involving the Board of Trustees. At most, the trustees might properly direct the President to caution or warn a faculty or staff person." (4) He evaluated the relationship between John Michael's request and the adoption of the Covenant in April 1991 and the trustee action in 1990 not to revisit the trustee action of 1986 "which concluded there was no evidence justifying the termination of any member of the faculty about whom anyone had expressed concern to the President or the Trustees." (5) He reviewed my current theological position in relation to the concerns raised by John Michael in his letter and "concluded Professor Hinson is functioning within and not contrary to the Abstract of Principles and there are no grounds for disciplinary action." On the basis of these considerations, he forwarded John Michael's request "as information for the committee but recommends no action on the request that the trustees issue a formal warning to Professor Hinson."[15]

On 22 November 1991, I had replied to John Michael's charges as published in the *Indiana Baptist* on November 5. On January 29, about three weeks after my arrival in Oxford, Larry McSwain faxed to me a reorganized version of my response to four points in John Michael's letter of July 24. On February 3, I completed my response to Michael's fifth concern and faxed it to Southern Seminary for distribution to the Academic Personnel Committee. To avoid encumbering the text, I relegate them to an appendix. They represented essentially a repeat of the responses I prepared for the "Peace Committee" in 1986. The document shows how nearly impossible it is to communicate accepted historical methodology to someone who subscribes to the inerrantist viewpoint. I have the feeling that I may have alienated John Michael from the start by failing to acknowledge his *authority* as a trustee, something that seemed of utmost importance to him. The foundation for the authoritative position he held was belief that every jot and tittle of scripture was inerrant, and I should not question it. From this vantage point I can see why things I wrote got his hackles up; they threatened the only foundation on which he could stand and hurl thunderbolts at me.

The key matter of interest at this point is that the action of the Academic Personnel Committee determined my decision to leave Southern Seminary and join the faculty of Baptist Theological Seminary at Richmond. On February 5, Honeycutt wrote that "on February 3, 1992,

[15] Roy L. Honeycutt to Trustee Committee on Academic Personnel, 8 January 1992. He attached Michael's letter and my statement on the Resurrection.

the Trustee Committee on Academic Personnel acted to bring closure to concerns or charges against you" and that he expected the full Board would adopt their report. At the same time he added that, "bringing closure to concerns or charges did include a warning." In receiving the President's report dated January 8, they approved the following statement:

> The Academic Personnel Committee shares the concern expressed by Mr. John B. Michael in his letter to the President of July 24, 1991, regarding the writings of Dr. E. Glenn Hinson. We acknowledge with appreciation the explanations and clarifications offered by Dr. Hinson. We accept his commitment to teach in the future in accordance with and not contrary to the Abstract of Principles. Furthermore, the Academic Personnel Committee directs the President to warn Dr. Hinson that if in the future he should teach the positions which Mr. Michael in his letter of July 24, 1991, interpreted him to have expressed, he might be in violation of the Abstract of Principles and thus in jeopardy of dismissal.[16]

Honeycutt indicated that Michael had originally sought dismissal, but a meeting with Wayne Allen, Chair of the Board of Trustees, and Rick White, Chair of the Trustee Committee on Personnel, had persuaded him to withdraw the call for dismissal in favor of the "warning." To his credit and my deep thanks, Honeycutt did prepare for the plenary of the Board a response not only to John Michael's but also to James Stroud's charges against me. He did not leave me blowing in the wind. Nevertheless, I didn't need long reflection to decide my course of action. "Warning" and "closure" reminded me of a rattlesnake coiled and ready to strike. As soon as I read the letter, I thought, "Shades of the medieval inquisition! How grateful to God I am that in America we have separation of Church and State. I don't need to put up with this kind of abuse." Tom Graves and Tom Halbrooks urged me to fly to Richmond to meet with them, but I thought that would be an expense the fledgling seminary did not need to bear. We arranged to meet when I was scheduled to lecture in the Pastors School of the University of Richmond, July 6–10.

Fruitful Days

Financial worries and the Southern debacle notwithstanding, our three-month stay in Oxford proved fruitful. Regarding the money

---

[16] Roy L. Honeycutt to E. Glenn Hinson, 5 February 1992.

situation, I applied for additional funds through the Education Commission of the Southern Baptist Convention before I severed my ties with Southern,[17] but I did not receive them because of my decision to leave the seminary. We struggled to make ends meet. Elizabeth took a tutorial with Morris West, the former principal of Bristol Baptist College, and had to pay a modest fee. Regent's Park would have charged me about $500 as a visiting member of the Senior Common Room and for use of the college and university libraries,[18] but Paul Fiddes had me give two lectures in lieu of these fees. In the first of those, addressed to a group of British Baptist ministers, I adapted a lecture published in several periodicals under the title "Southern Baptist and Medieval Spirituality: Surprising Similarities,"[19] deleting "Southern." In the second, delivered to a university audience, I prepared a fresh lecture in my special field of competence entitled: "When the World Collapsed: The Spirituality of Women during the Barbarian Invasion of Rome."[20] By this time, my hearing aids did not function adequately. During the question and answer session following the first lecture, it became evident that my hearing did not permit me to respond well to questions, and Paul Fiddes quickly closed the session. So after the next lecture, Larry Kreitzer, one of the tutors and once my student at Southern, wrote down the questions and handed them to me. That worked much better.

Two other lectureships did not alleviate our financial distress, but they did bolster my self-esteem. In October 1991, John Morgan-Wynne, whom I had gotten to know when he served as a tutor at Regent's Park, invited me to preach at the weekly Lord's Supper service at Bristol Baptist College and to give a lecture on some aspect of spirituality March 4–5.[21] In December, Hugh Matthews, Principal of South Wales Baptist College in Cardiff, invited me through my former colleague Karen Smith[22] to give, for the second time, the Edwin Stephen Griffiths lectures on February 26 and 27. In an evening lecture to a sizeable University of

---

[17] Larry McSwain to Glenn Hinson, Fax, 14 February 1992.

[18] Paul S. Fiddes to E. Glenn Hinson, 15 February 1990.

[19] Originally published in *Cistercian Studies* 20 (1985): 224–36.

[20] *Perspectives in Religious Studies* 20 (Summer 1993): 113–30. I later revised and used this as the Bainton Lecture at Yale.

[21] John Morgan-Wynne, Bristol Baptist College, to E. Glenn Hinson, Rüschlikon, 23 October 1991.

[22] Karen Smith to E. Glenn Hinson, 5 December 1991.

Cardiff audience I focused on "Ecumenical Spirituality,"[23] featuring Thomas Merton and Douglas Steere. To a mainly Baptist group the next morning I spoke about "Ministers as Midwives and Mothers of Grace,"[24] a topic I had addressed several times in speaking to ministers' groups.

Our budget crunch required me to do something I found a little embarrassing, perhaps both to me and to the college—carry a sack lunch and eat it wherever I could find privacy. At first I ate on the steps in one of the hallways. When the principal's secretary saw me there one day, she found a room I could use.

Money woes didn't keep us from making the most of our stay in England. Thanks to George Beasley-Murray's new car, we managed to travel quite a lot during our three months in Oxford. Besides going to Cardiff and Bristol, we re-visited some of our favorite historic sites such as Salisbury Cathedral and Stonehenge. Unfamiliarity with driving and parking on the left side of the road resulted in a minor mishap on a visit to Gloucester on March 5 following my lecture in Bristol. As I parked near Gloucester Abbey at lunchtime, I checked my rearview mirror for cars as I opened the door, but I failed to see two cyclists who peddled between cars stopped at a traffic light and the curb. One of them hit the door as I swung it open and then tumbled into his partner. Neither cyclist was hurt, but the spill bent the frame of one of the bikes. Many in England evidently settle such small liabilities (£129.50) personally, but I feared that I might get caught in a legal snare or be taken advantage of, so I left the matter in the hands of Beasley-Murray's insurer.[25]

The turbulence of this period may have diminished the amount of work I achieved on the sabbatical, but it did not disrupt it entirely. At Rüschlikon, all the ruckus notwithstanding, I completed a draft of a history of Christianity up to 1300. I felt pessimistic about its publication by Broadman Press. Feeling duty-bound to honor commitments, however, I planned to submit it and let Mike Smith, the chief editor, decide what to do with it.

---

[23] "Ecumenical Spirituality," *Ecumenical Trends* 20 (July/August 1991): 97–104; *Spirituality in Ecumenical Perspective*, ed. E. Glenn Hinson (Louisville KY: Westminster/John Knox Press, 1993) 1–14.

[24] Published in several places, it appeared first with the title "Midwives and Mothers of Grace," *Theological Educator* 43 (Spring 1991): 65–79; as "Ministers as Midwives and Mothers of Grace," in *Handbook of Spirituality for Ministers, Volume 2*, ed. Robert J. Wicks (New York and Mahwah NJ: Paulist Press, 2000) 642–55.

[25] E. Glenn Hinson to K.G. Ackerley, Boylan & James Ltd, South Croydon, Surrey, England, 24 March 1992.

At Oxford, I planned to focus on the second project I had laid out for this sabbatical, preparation of a volume on John Bunyan for the Classics of Western Spirituality. While I taught at the Catholic University of America in the spring of 1987, I laid out a proposal for a volume on Bunyan in that distinguished series in a letter to John Farina, the editor at Paulist Press. I hoped to locate an early copy minus the addendum about Christiana, to use some of the sketches printed in early editions, and to print selected passages from *Grace Abounding* alongside *The Pilgrim's Progress* to illustrate Bunyan's personal journey as the basis for the pilgrim's. [26] At that time I expected, unrealistically I would say, to submit my Church history manuscript to Broadman Press in the summer of 1987, but did not promise the Bunyan volume before 1 July 1988. In the best of times, these dates would have been overly optimistic. In the worst of times, which I entered into from 1985 on, they were beyond imagination.

Despite distractions, I did concentrate a lot of energy on the Bunyan project. After spending two or three weeks in the Bodleian Library writing my paper on the spirituality of women during the barbarian invasion of Rome in 410, I spent day after day researching Bunyan materials in the Angus Collection at Regent's Park. I read and took notes on all of Bunyan's writings in preparation for writing an introduction to a volume on John Bunyan for the Classics of Western Spirituality. I can blame partly on circumstances my failure to carry through with my promise, but I must place most of it on my own shoulders.

If you have followed my story to this point, I'm sure you have caught some glimpse of my most besetting sin. My *glaring* fault is the one that has afflicted every human being since Adam and Eve—failure to recognize human limitations or pretensions to "be as God" (Gen 3:5). In my case, this manifests itself in the form of taking on more than I can handle. The consequence of that is that I have given God and other people less than my best. I look back with embarrassment on particular instances when I dropped the ball. One of those involved my dissertation at Oxford, and I think I have kept going back to Oxford to let the spirit of that great center of learning seep more deeply into my soul, so that I would produce more "gold, silver, and precious stones" and less "wood, hay, and stubble" (1 Cor 3:12). But here again I was "biting off more than I could chew." I never seemed to learn.

---

[26] E. Glenn Hinson to John Farina, Paulist Press, Mahwah, New Jersey, 10 March, 1987.

Our sojourn in Oxford ended abruptly at the beginning of April. Chris called to say that Martha's mother, Flossie Burks, better known at our house as "Momo," had had a stroke. She had had good health up to this point, but she was eighty-five, so we felt we would have to return home. Fortunately, American Airlines secured seats for us in this emergency. The Nicholsons, generous souls that they were, did not hold us to the arrangement we had made to stay in their house until July. We flew out of Heathrow the morning of April 7. Martha and Elizabeth both found seats on the aisle. I had to take a seat in the middle of the center section, but I did not complain. To get a seat at all on a flight where the airline promised $600 and other amenities for volunteers to delay until the next flight nixed any urge to complain.

The long day's journey gave me opportunity once again to ruminate on my situation vis-à-vis this people rent by strife. In my journal I voiced some optimism. "If the Cooperative Baptist Fellowship and the Alliance can get properly organized, they would have a golden opportunity to pick up ties with other Baptists in the US and around the globe and to develop a new style of mission work." I reflected, too, on some pragmatic personal decisions I had to make, notably about taking early retirement from Southern in order to secure health insurance, an insurance policy, and a burial plot in Cave Hill Cemetery.[27]

Realigning

Going on sabbatical had swept away a lot of the engagements that usually crowded my calendar. With my early return to Louisville, however, it didn't take long for the empty spaces to fill. The Cooperative Baptist Fellowship summoned me to speak twice about my Rüschlikon experience to large "break out" groups at the annual meeting in Fort Worth, April 30–May 1. I was introduced at a luncheon sponsored by Baptist Theological Seminary at Richmond. For four days at the beginning of May, I taught in the Academy for Spiritual Formation at

---

[27] I wrote to the Seminary Vice President for Business Services, T.J. McGlothlin, Jr., about the benefits of early retirement. In a letter dated 3 April 1992, he advised me to take it. "You could begin drawing a benefit from your annuity fund (or delay that until a future date). Southern Seminary would provide family health insurance and a $20,000 life insurance policy on yourself only. The seminary would pay the cost of the life insurance policy and the retiree cost for health (you would continue to pay health coverage for your dependents). At age 65 the Seminary's health plan would convert to a Medicare Supplement with you paying the cost of Medicare."

Camp Sumatanga in Alabama. May 20–21, I took part in the meeting of the Advisory Board of *Weavings* in Nashville, and on May 24, I received the Cuthbert Allen Award for contributions to ecumenism given by the Ecumenical Institute of Wake Forest University and Belmont Abbey in Belmont, North Carolina. Surely there was some irony in the award coming to someone who had called for a "divorce" among Baptists in the South! The second week of June, I took part in the Executive Board meeting of the International Thomas Merton Society at Bellarmine University in Louisville, and a week later, I attended the annual meeting of the Board of Consultors of the Society of the Atonement in Graymoor, New York. In July, I gave four lectures on "Mature Faith" in the Pastors School of the University of Richmond. The week I spent there furnished me with an opportunity at last to be interviewed by Tom Graves, Tom Halbrooks, and Linda Bridges.

Severing ties after more than thirty years in a community of learning, weeping when it wept, and rejoicing when it rejoiced, is never easy. Roy Honeycutt and Larry McSwain hosted me at luncheon to see if I might have second thoughts about going to Richmond. Still holding out some hope of the "Covenant" ending the fundamentalist assault, I think, they had hoped I would not go to BTSR. We had a cordial luncheon and parted amicably, but I had to repeat what I had said in April 1991 when the faculty voted for the Covenant: "I cannot in good conscience assist in turning Southern Seminary into a fundamentalist institution."

Page Kelley was moving with me to Richmond. He planned to teach only a short time and had fifteen boxes. I had 115 and seven four-drawer filing cabinets. We both miscalculated the weight. We rented a U-Haul truck with a 7,500-pound weight limit. The truck ran downhill fine, but it seemed to run sluggishly ascending hills on I-64 in West Virginia and Virginia. On some hills we crept along at fifteen or twenty miles an hour by the time we got to the top and watched as huge semis zipped past us. When we stopped for supper at White Sulphur Springs, West Virginia, we pulled the truck into the Shell station next to the diner where we ate and asked a grizzled-looking mechanic to check the tires. "They look kind of low," we said. "And the truck is sluggish." He put some air in the tires without checking first. When he checked, he said, "Whew! Sixty pounds! You got plenty of air. What you got in that truck? Moonshine?" We had a good laugh, but we breathed sighs of relief when we got past the last steep grades at Charlottesville and coasted into Richmond.

Tom Graves and Tom Halbrooks signaled the new regime we had chosen to join. They helped us lug those heavy book boxes and wheel filing cabinets into the offices we would occupy. Southern Seminary would have hired a mover, and I couldn't imagine either Duke McCall or Roy Honeycutt wrestling those cartons and cabinets. I prayed that Richmond would do well, but I knew that it would not forget its vulnerable beginnings.

23

RICHMOND

We were all vulnerable. The Baptist Theological Seminary at Richmond was vulnerable. I was vulnerable. My family was vulnerable.

On the basis of a decision made by the Alliance of Baptists in Greenville, South Carolina, in March 1989, BTSR had opened its doors in the fall of 1991 with three faculty members—Tom Graves, Tom Halbrooks, and Linda Bridges—and thirty-two students with little more than $225,000 given by West End Baptist Church from the sale of their property as they went out of business under leadership of their interim pastor, Elmer West. It was the seminary's good fortune that the Presbyterian School of Christian Education was nearing the end of its life and about to merge with Union Theological Seminary at Richmond. PSCE put one of its buildings at the disposal of the fledgling school and rented two of its faculty houses next door to me and to Page Kelley when we moved there in August 1992. A considerable part of the new seminary's meager budget, more than $60,000 ($1,800 per student and faculty), went to UTS for the use of its outstanding library. The remainder had to pay faculty salaries and benefits.

Following a sabbatical in two expensive venues and a switch from Southern Seminary to the Baptist Theological Seminary of Richmond, the Hinson budget hit rock bottom. I had to ask the Cooperative Baptist Fellowship for expense money to fulfill their request that I speak at the annual meeting in Fort Worth at the end of May, since I didn't want to make such a request from Southern after announcing my resignation in March. By the time school began on September 15, I had earned enough honoraria to alleviate our worst distress, but not enough for comfort. Much to my regret and embarrassment, I didn't have enough money to entertain Paul Fiddes, Principal of Regent's Park College, Oxford University, when he visited Richmond August 29 to September 1, hoping to raise some funds for Regent's Park. He stayed with me in the, as yet, scantily furnished house on Palmyra, and I introduced him to some key moderate leaders in Richmond whom I thought might offer help and guidance in fund raising—Ray Spence at Second Baptist, Jim Flaming at

First Baptist, and Jim Slatton at River Road—but, except for their generosity in paying for a breakfast, he had to pay his own way. Martha remained in Louisville with her mother, Chris, and Elizabeth until January 1993. Thanks to a generous arrangement of a scholarship by President John Mulder, Elizabeth, in the meantime, enrolled in Louisville Presbyterian Theological Seminary. Chris, however, was in a kind of limbo with reference to his work at the University of Chicago. We had not yet become aware that he had already been doing battle with severe depression. He eventually resolved the school problem several years later by completing a PhD in Old Testament studies at Baylor University.

I moved Martha and her mother with the essentials into our rented home next door to BTSR's office and classroom building during the hiatus between semesters. The colonial style house itself was spacious and well kept, but we soon discovered a deficiency. The heating system relied on a heat pump that seemed to circulate more cold air than warm, and, during the winter months, we nearly froze. Martha and I engaged a realtor to help us locate another house, preferably in the area, but we found that we would have to pay a third more for anything comparable to the house we owned in Louisville. Ultimately, we decided to keep our home in Louisville and stay in the rental. When Martha and I went to Switzerland in the spring of 1994, we were fortunate to enlist Donna Hopkins, one of our students and a dear friend, now pastor of Calvary Baptist Church in Roanoke, to stay with Martha's mother, who was already approaching ninety.

Very soon after moving to Richmond, we discovered a few things about the capital of the Confederacy that we didn't know. In 1991 Richmond vied with New Orleans for per capita murders. We lived on the edge of one of the nation's busiest drug markets, and Virginia made it easy to acquire guns. The Virginia state legislature worried that they might put too much of a damper on gun sales when they prohibited the purchase of more than one handgun a month! Martha and her mother never felt comfortable in Richmond, and were relieved to move back to Louisville in 1995 in order to prepare for Elizabeth's wedding. Martha's mother was a skilled dressmaker and made all of the dresses for the bridesmaids as well as for Martha and herself. They did not return to Richmond. I rented part of the house to one of the students the next year, but I then secured an apartment from Union Theological Seminary for the remainder of my time in Richmond. Colleagues and students took good care of me in those four years, and I took advantage of opportunities to return to Louisville as often as I could. Loneliness is a part of my story.

A Third Beginning

A tenuous financial situation was only one element in my personal vulnerability. Coming to Richmond thrust me in the middle of a career change of considerable magnitude. Remember, I prepared for and began my career as a New Testament scholar. Restriction of my days in that pursuit to one year kept me from falling so deeply in love with it as my first love that I could not learn to love another, Patristics. Equipping myself at the highest level in the study of early Christianity at Oxford, I seemed set to enter into a lifelong relationship with this new love. But, alas, as so often happens in the most promising of lives and marriages, the best-laid plans took another curious turn. In speaking to Tom Graves and Tom Halbrooks, I had insisted that I should retain the title of a professor of Church history if I came to Richmond, but I had an intense enough interest in spiritual formation of ministers that I would consider trying to teach spirituality. However great my concern for spiritual formation for Christian ministry, I did not want scholars in theological education to think less highly of spirituality than of Church history, a field in which I had established a substantial reputation up to this time.I must confess that, all through the years I taught at Richmond, I felt some ambivalence about my competence to teach in a field in which I did not have and could not obtain the preparation I had gotten in New Testament studies at Southern Seminary or in Patristic studies at Oxford University. The high esteem that both specialists and lay people accorded me in spirituality literally shocked me—for training in the spiritual life would probably best be pursued by spending years in a Trappist monastery.[1] Only one or two Catholic universities and the Graduate Theological Union offered PhDs in spirituality. The most significant training I have had has probably come from exposure to those I call "ordinary saints" and my deliberate study of classics of Christian devotion along with some touches of God's Presence in my own life.

---

[1] This may seem a curious proposal, but a United Methodist professor in St Paul's Theological Seminary in Kansas City, Missouri, W. Paul Jones, became a Family Brother of the Trappist Order in 1989 and took life vows in 1992. He joined the Roman Catholic Church and alternated between a communal life in a Trappist monastery and a hermitage in the Missouri Ozarks.

In their initial approach, while I taught at Rüschlikon in November 1991, Graves and Halbrooks invited me to BTSR as "Professor of Worship and Spirituality." They sent me a job description that called for me to help develop a curriculum and teach courses in worship and spirituality, work with Richmond Hill and/or other retreat centers to deepen the experience of students in spirituality, offer leadership in chapel worship, train students to transfer what they learned to the churches, help students develop spiritual resources, serve as a resource person for local churches in the area of spirituality, be a liaison between the seminary and Richmond Hill or other schools in the Richmond Theological Consortium, and play an active role in the faculty. Daunting demands! And I will be quite honest to say that I was not up to such a far-reaching request and am grateful that they never held me to it. The truth is, as Graves told me on numerous occasions, they considered simply my coming to Richmond a key ingredient in the seminary's survival and success. They thought that I, as a person with strong academic credentials who also had a strong interest in spiritual formation for ministry, could help. I would give the seminary "credibility."

As I undertook to fashion a plan for the spiritual formation of men and women for Christian ministry, I looked particularly to models employed in Roman Catholic seminaries, which required classes in spirituality every semester and a spiritual director throughout seminary, but with a keen awareness that a Baptist seminary could do only a partial adaptation. Four out of thirty credits toward a degree would not permit a class in spirituality each semester, and by 1992, Baptists, like most Protestants, had not yet developed a sufficiently positive attitude toward spiritual direction to make it a requirement, although some might have considered it as an option. My repertoire, you know already, included the two courses I had taught for many years—"Classics of Christian Devotion" (since 1963) and "Prayer in Christian History" (since 1980). In all modesty I think those two courses *had* furnished many ministers with some basic grounding in the spiritual life, as letters I receive nearly every week today would confirm. They could constitute two of the four credits. To do a creditable job of preparing women and men for Christian leadership, however, I decided that I had to add, for the students' first semester, an "Introduction to Christian Spirituality" and, as an "exit" course, "Ministers as Spiritual Guides."

One of the first things I learned about myself in trying to prepare people for this impossible task of Christian ministry is that I am not a "methods" person. Early on in my career, in fact, I realized that my students learned more from my life than they did from my lectures, assignments, and tests. I found that even more true in teaching spirituality. Neither of my main teachers and mentors—Thomas Merton and Douglas Steere—were "methods" persons. In line with what I absorbed from them little by little, I designed a course operating under the rule of thumb that *simple is better*. As I undertook this assignment, a ray of light broke through to me from the manuals Thomas Merton sent me shortly after my first visit to the Abbey of Gethsemani: *As you have learned, teach your students to learn from the saints in Christian history*. That would begin with saints in the scriptures, but it would continue with their long march through history. From the saints I learned that *the main thing is the covenant God chose to enter into with humankind*. The spiritual life, whether of ministers or of any other person, has to do with how we live out our lives in light of this covenant. Our chief focus should be on *deepening our covenant relationship*, much as spouses try to deepen their marriage covenant. Deepening our covenant relationship depends on *increasing our attentiveness. Attentiveness to God is in essence what prayer is.* In quest of increasing attentiveness, I began each class with ten minutes of silence, employed the extraordinary Teilhardian *Prayers* of Michel Quoist[2] as guides, had students compose ten Quoist-like prayers, and required journaling as a form of prayer. Since our covenant with God should touch all of life, I discussed spirituality and sexuality and added a social dimension to Baron Friedrich von Hügel's model of balancing experiential, intellectual, and institutional elements. I also made much of the need to simplify our lives. As aids in sustaining the spiritual life, I encouraged adaptation of *lectio divina* to other reading, listening, and seeing and arranged retreats at Richmond Hill to foster a practice of solitude and silence.[3]

In "Ministers as Spiritual Guides" I did not seek to outfit persons as spiritual directors, an impossible goal in a single semester. Spiritual

[2] Michel Quoist, *Prayers*, trans. Agnes M. Forsyth, and Anne Marie de Commaille (New York: Sheed and Ward, 1963).

[3] At the request of The Upper Room I incorporated the basic substance of my teaching in this course in *Spiritual Preparation for Christian Leadership* (Nashville: Upper Room Books, 1999). The book has been widely used in seminary classes and was translated into Korean very soon after publication.

direction would require much more intensive and intentional spiritual direction and specialized study, as in the two-year Shalem program developed by Tilden Edwards. I did assist Richmond Hill in the development of a parallel program called RUAH (Hebrew "spirit"), in which some students enrolled. My modest objective in this class was to help ministers and churches recognize how spiritual guidance is an essential aspect of everything they do. We did make Tilden Edwards's *Spiritual Friend*, a thorough exposition of Shalem's approach to individual spiritual guidance, the axle around which the course turned.[4] As in the "Introduction," I began each class with ten minutes of silence, and here, too, we learned from the saints, spiritual masters such as the fourteenth-century English mystics—Walter Hilton, the author of *The Cloud of Unknowing*, and Julian of Norwich; sixteenth- and seventeenth-century guides—Ignatius Loyola, Francis de Sales, and Martin Luther; and twentieth-century masters—Baron Friedrich von Hügel, Douglas Steere, and Thomas Merton. Students had to write a paper on one spiritual master. Only after gleaning key insights from the masters did we turn to the art of spiritual guidance—matching guide and guidee, assessing aptitude for spiritual guidance, and learning the process. The study moved, inevitably, from there to re-imagining ministry in terms of its relation to spiritual guidance—in the person of the minister, in leading worship, in pastoral ministry, in administration, and in group spiritual guidance.

I remained hopeful during my seven years at BTSR that the seminary would eventually require students to take one class in spirituality each semester, much as Roman Catholic seminaries do. Despite the enthusiasm for this element in the curriculum, that did not happen. Many ministers from the Richmond metropolitan area and students from Union Theological Seminary and Presbyterian School of Christian Education elected to audit or to take the classes for credit. To keep class size from getting out of control, I limited each to twenty persons, which required me to offer at least two sections each semester. Near the end of my tenure, I decided to require some other options besides Classics and Prayer in Christian History—The History of Spirituality, Theology of Religious Experience—which I now think may have been a mistake. Scarcely any other study can surpass in importance the Classics and Prayer in Christian History.

---

[4] Tilden Edwards, *Spiritual Friend: Reclaiming the Gift of Spiritual Direction* (New York and Ramsey NJ: Paulist Press, 1980).

A Very Hospitable Reception

The inhospitableness of Southern Seminary in my last years there may have magnified my sense of heartfelt welcome in Richmond, but words simply cannot describe the loving embrace I received on moving to the Baptist Theological Seminary at Richmond. Much as I had felt on going to Wake Forest University, colleagues and students, both at the Baptist Seminary and at Union/PSCE, couldn't do enough to say, "Welcome!" Whereas Baptist churches in Kentucky were beginning to treat me as a foul odor, the churches in Virginia, DC, Maryland, and other seaboard states, Baptist and others, went out of their way to get a whiff of this fresh breeze from the hinterlands. Very quickly, I faced once more the problem of a calendar jam-packed with engagements.[5] Yet better by far to be too busy than to be rejected and repudiated!

The seminary was a very hospitable place. Joining this small faculty at the same time I did were Elizabeth Barnes, who had taught at Southeastern Seminary and stirred the Alliance crowd in Greenville to risk launching the seminary, as Professor of Theology, and Isam Ballenger, who had resigned from the Foreign Mission Board in protest of the defunding of Rüschlikon, as Professor of Missions. Isam's son, John, had been my student at Louisville. The staff received me with open arms. Linda McNally—Receptionist, Secretary, and Assistant to Everybody—made me feel that Richmond was a very special place and this new seminary a very special school shortly after I arrived when she donated a kidney to her eleven-year-old granddaughter. Going above and beyond the call of duty, she typed manuscripts for me until I learned to use a computer. Up to that point, I had typed all my manuscripts on my 1923 Underwood Standard and handed them to a pool of expert typists at Southern. The new seminary outfitted me with a computer, a beginner's model perhaps, and said, "You are now your own typing pool." Tom Graves asked me to lead the Faculty Retreat September 1–2 and to speak at student orientation September 10–11. Enrollment had jumped from 32 to 94! A week later, Presbyterian School of Christian Education invited me to lead their fall retreat at Ginter Botanical Gardens.

---

[5] See Appendix C.

The Spirituality Phenomenon

I'm not sure how to depict "the spirituality phenomenon" that cast a nimbus around my seven years in Richmond. By labeling it a "phenomenon," I am interpreting it as a happening much greater than anything I may have contributed during these seven years. As l look back on that time, I see a mysterious and unexplainable vortex of excitement that pulled me toward itself and sucked me in. Novice in spirituality that I was and will be always, I tried primarily to encourage and entice people to do one thing—open like flowers to the morning sun in order to let God's love energies flow into them. An artist captured my aim in the stained glass window friends had installed in my honor when I retired at the entrance to Watts Hall, the building Baptist Theological Seminary at Richmond purchased from Presbyterian School of Christian Education and refurbished in 1995. A dancer leaps Godward, arms uplifted, stretching skyward toward the sun above. God is there, declaring, "I love you with infinite, unconditional love!" I said often, the bottom line of spirituality is to hear God say those words.

I am convinced that what took place in those years was connected with something much larger than what inerrantists call "the conservative resurgence" or "the Baptist reformation" and moderates "the takeover," something much larger than a moderate movement seeking to form institutions suitable for a denomination within a denomination, certainly something much larger than the founding of a new seminary forming ministers in a new style to lead churches linked to the Baptist tradition. Spirituality, to be sure, fit the "moderate" ethos better than it did the doctrine-obsessed "evangelical" ethos. The larger something may have been an "awakening," the fourth such awakening scholars have identified since the Puritans first came to the American shores.[6] It probably connected with the *aggiornamento* that emerged during the pontificate of Angelo Roncalli as Pope John XXIII (1958–63), but I scarcely know how to describe my own experience and participation in it. What many evidences seem to point to are a hunger and thirst for spiritual guidance manifest in invitations to me to teach, preach, promote, nurture, or just model the life of the Spirit in the world of today.

---

[6] I follow here W.G. McGlothlin, *Revivals, Awakenings, and Reform* (Chicago: University of Chicago Press, 1960).

On my arrival in Richmond, churches served by friends, or former students perhaps, extended invitations to me to express their affirmation of me in reaction to the negations I had experienced at Southern Seminary and in the Southern Baptist Convention. Baptists in Virginia, more cognizant of their Baptist heritage than Baptists elsewhere in the South, liked to let me know that they were *Virginia* rather than *Southern* Baptists. Hence I had invitations to speak on other subjects than spirituality. Such requests, however, soon fed into spirituality as the consuming concern, based on an assumption that I could help people get in touch with the working of God in their lives.

One reason I feel impelled to connect the spirituality phenomenon with something much wider is not only its geographical range up and down the eastern seaboard but also its connection with a wide array of institutions or groups—churches, colleges and universities, seminaries, retreat centers, ministers' groups, para-church organizations, *et plural*. Inevitably, Virginia would account for the heftiest part of the schedule. My first year in Richmond, I served as Interim Pastor of West End Baptist Church in Petersburg, twenty-five miles south of the seminary, for almost six months in 1993. Meanwhile, churches and other groups in Richmond and beyond kept me busy. I will not try to detail those, for you can see a complete list of my engagements during my time at BTSR in Appendix C. Perhaps it will suffice to underscore what is fairly obvious in that list. (1) My role on the faculty of the Academy of Spiritual Formation increased. (2) I lectured extensively in colleges, universities, and seminaries, mostly about spirituality and spiritual formation, but often too on some aspect of Baptist or Church history. (3) Lectures on spirituality or retreats in Baptist churches far outstripped other engagements. (4) I did a substantial number of presentations, however, in churches other than Baptist. (5) I also did a surprising number of lectures or retreats for denominational gatherings, especially those connected with the Virginia Baptist General Association, American Baptist Churches, Alliance of Baptists, or Cooperative Baptist Fellowship. (6) I lectured a substantial number of times to ministerial associations and preached at several ordinations or installations. (7) My active involvement in peacemaking declined as the peace movement wound down during the Clinton administration. (8) Judging by invitations to lecture or give retreats, the spirituality phenomenon extended far beyond the eastern seaboard, as far northeast as Rochester, New York, and as far southwest as Laity Lodge near Kerrville, Texas. (9)

It also cropped up in professions or institutions related to the health-care industry.

Tom Turner, who first contacted me in 1980 shortly after completing a theological degree at Vanderbilt[7] and had returned to Greenville, South Carolina, to found Pilgrim's Rest Retreat Center, enlisted me to help launch what we decided to call simply "A Gathering of Baptists Interested in Spirituality." More than 150 people attended the initial "Gathering" at Mars Hill Baptist College in the mountains of North Carolina in August 1994, and the numbers increased year after year. I gave a major address at the first meeting. I was scheduled to speak about "The Wisdom of Douglas V. Steere" on the fifth anniversary of the "Gathering," in August 1998, but an episode with elevated heartbeat while sanding floors in our house precluded my attendance. Someone read the address, which I faxed. "Gatherings" have continued to this day but not always at Mars Hill College.

The Message

You won't gain much from a résumé of more of my crowded calendar, but you may want to know what I tried to do during weekend, mid-week, week-long engagements at churches, schools, and gatherings of any kind. Predictably, many churches and college or university groups asked me to speak about contemplative lifestyle. *A Serious Call to a Contemplative Lifestyle* appeared in a revised and updated version in 1993. Instead of teaching the book, I focused on key themes and biblical texts, always basic for Christians, which help us to understand and develop a contemplative lifestyle.

On the basis of Paul's prayer for the Philippians (Phil 1:9–11), for instance, I spoke about "The Trajectory of Spiritual Growth." Ultimately, we want to see God, as Jesus said in the Beatitude (Matt 5:8), to participate in the life of God, but penultimately, as Paul says here, we desire purity of heart and fruit of righteousness. The way to that goal is "to have a sense of things that really matter," but the gateway to the way lies in the first petition—that God's love may constantly grow in us in understanding and in every sensitivity.

I construed Paul's exhortation to the Thessalonians to "pray without ceasing" (1 Thess 5:17) as best fulfilled by "Making All of Life a Prayer" in the way Brother Lawrence suggested. We can *Practice the Presence of*

---

[7] Thomas B. Turner, Saxon Baptist Church, Spartanburg, South Carolina, to E. Glenn Hinson, 15 February 1980.

God if we learn how to "see" and to "listen" to God in all of life. Once again, the *Prayers* of Michel Quoist prove most helpful. Quoist prefaced one section of prayers with this observation: "*If we knew how to look at life through God's eyes, we would see it as innumerable tokens of the love of the Creator seeking the love of his creatures.*"[8] He prefaced the second section: "*If we knew how to listen to God, if we knew how to look around us, our whole life would become a prayer.*"[9] Jesus' counsel to the anxiety-ridden in the Sermon on the Mount supplied the most basic text for "Prayer and the Simplification of Life." In a Hinson paraphrase, "Seek first God's mysterious presence and God's okaying of you; then these other things will fall into place" (Matt 6:33). Jesus spoke about the "kingdom" as like a seed growing mysteriously, leaven in a lump of dough, a thief in the night. We must be awake, alert, attentive, and watchful to see God's mysterious Presence. Because we are not okay, God alone can okay us. Once this inner transformation takes place, life is lived from a holy Center. It becomes simplified.

In teaching "Prayer in Christian History" I focused on questions people most often ask about prayer: How do we "pray without ceasing" (1 Th 5:17)? What should we expect prayer of intercession or petition to do (James 5:16)? What does prayer have to do with the will of God (Phil 2:12–13)? What do we do when we not only do not get the answer we want but do not get *any* answer to prayer (Luke 8:1–8)?

Save for the spring of 1994 when I taught again at Rüschlikon and a few gaps during the summers when I returned to Louisville, my schedule remained crowded throughout my time in Richmond. In looking back, you probably wonder, as I do, how and why I could maintain such a schedule. In it you see exposed once again one of my most serious faults—an inability to say no and, because of over-busyness, diminishment of my effectiveness, ensnared like a curious kitty in a ball of twine. All too often, quantity pushed quality to the side. I am fearful that over-busyness caused some lapses and miscues in what should have been my main business—the care of souls. One incident in particular haunts me.

Joe Burton, one of my former students at Southern Seminary, came to BTSR and asked me to help him plan a sabbatical and to meet with him at selected times to discuss his ministry. I rejoiced in his decision and readily agreed. According to the plan, he visited different churches

---

[8] Quoist, *Prayers*, 17.
[9] Ibid., 29.

each Sunday to gain new perspectives on worship, read all of Henri Nouwen's writings,[10] and spent several days each week in a cabin in the Blue Ridge loaned for that purpose by a family in First Baptist Church, Radford, Virginia. During a weekend I spent with his congregation, September 20–22, 1996, I could see that Joe was highly respected and deeply loved, and his sabbatical seemed to have rejuvenated him. At my request, we had him lead us in a chapel service dedicated to Henri Nouwen, who died suddenly of a heart attack at age 64 on September 21. Joe entitled his tribute: "He So Longed to Be Loved." I suspect that could describe Joe, too. A few weeks later, he went out to the cabin where he had retreated during his sabbatical and took his own life. I've often wondered if, in the hectic schedule I maintained, I missed a clue to some inner agony, whether I failed to listen Joe to "a condition of awareness of the Eternal Listener,"[11] which is what a discerning spiritual guide should do.

Ups and Downs

Even in the most idyllic climates, rain inevitably falls. I should mention two occasions when I was responsible for some uncomfortable moments in this usually harmonious community of learning. Once, when the president and dean were away attending a meeting and it came my turn to preach in our weekly chapel, I chose to send up a warning flare about the danger of what I call a "corporation mentality," in which concern for the institution pushes aside every other concern. What prompted my warning were signs of abandonment of the Alliance of Baptists, who had founded BTSR, and alignment with the Cooperative Baptist Fellowship, which supplied more money. I cited the growth of the corporation mentality in the Southern Baptist Convention, illustrating it with the way in which Midwestern Seminary handled "the Genesis controversy" sparked by the publication of Ralph Elliott's *The Message of Genesis*. For a time, the administration supported Elliott, but, when they felt a threat to the institution, they fired him for

---

[10] Nouwen died unexpectedly of a heart attack at age 64 on 21 September 1996.

[11] A phrase I draw from Douglas Steere's classic *On Listening to Another* in *Doubleday Devotional Classics*, ed. E. Glenn Hinson (Garden City NY: Doubleday, 1978) 3:209–24.

"insubordination" in refusing to agree not to republish his book![12] I quoted James L. Sullivan, longtime President of the Sunday School Board, SBC: "In a corporate structure, like a Southern Baptist Institution, the worker must either carry out the directives or seek employment elsewhere. It is just that simple."[13] As evidence of the danger to the newly developed Cooperative Baptist Fellowship, I noted Duke McCall's lamentation in a speech to the Whitsitt Society. McCall had spent almost his entire life building up the Southern Baptist corporation and warned that if people in the CBF weren't careful, in twenty years it would be where the SBC is. I added, "He was right except in the length of time. It has already happened."[14] Then I asked whether the corporation mentality had not already made an appearance in BTSR. What I had reference to was the movement of the seminary in its sixth year, after finally inaugurating Tom Graves as its president, to weaken its ties with the Alliance of Baptists who founded it. I closed with a lamentation of my own about possible departure from our vulnerable beginnings.

The speech evoked a standing ovation from the students and others in attendance. When Tom Halbrooks and Tom Graves returned the next day, Halbrooks complimented me highly about it. I had requests for copies from far and wide. A few days later, however, Tom Graves, at someone else's suggestion, I think, interpreted it as an attack on him. Dan Bagby, who had come recently from Seventh and James Baptist Church in Waco, Texas, to teach pastoral care, convened a meeting of faculty twice to deal with the president's wounded feelings. I assured Tom Graves that I was not attacking him. Actually I had not thought of him at all as I addressed the issue. I pointed out that the growth of the "corporation mentality" had entered strongly into my thinking throughout my career, dating from a widely circulated article I wrote for Baptist state papers in 1972.[15] The intensity of my concern had grown as I had watched what happened in the Southern Baptist Convention. I am fearful, though, that I did not convince him, and my speech that day

---

[12] Elliott had recently published his story in *The "Genesis Controversy" and Continuity in Southern Baptist Chaos: A Eulogy for a Great Tradition* (Macon GA: Mercer University Press, 1992).

[13] James L. Sullivan, *Baptist Polity as I See It* (Nashville: Broadman Press, 1983) 172.

[14] E. Glenn Hinson, Unpublished sermon, "Courage and the Corporation," 6.

[15] E. Glenn Hinson, "How Far Can the Churches Go Using the Business Model as a Pattern for Church Life?" *Western Recorder*, 16 December 1972, 3, 14; *Illinois Baptist*, 3 January 1973, 8.

introduced an element of mistrust into our relationship during the rest of my years in Richmond.

I've wondered if the change in our personal relationship figured in a second painful incident. As I looked toward retirement from the Baptist Theological Seminary at Richmond, I was concerned to ensure that the person who succeeded me in teaching spirituality would know more about it and have better preparation to teach it than I did. Equipping at a higher level could best be done, I thought, by pursuing PhD work in spirituality either at the Catholic University of America in Washington, DC, or the Graduate Theological Union in Berkeley, California, the two most notable institutions with PhD programs in spirituality. Because of the proximity of CUA to Richmond and my connections with the school, I was able to assist some outstanding students to enroll in the PhD program in spirituality there in hopes that one of them would take my place when I retired. The first to enroll was Stephanie Ford, a graduate with a 4.0 GPA. Although Halbrooks and Graves asked me specifically to assist in securing my successor when I announced my retirement, I showed my ineptitude for administration and perhaps erred in not checking with Tom Graves earlier on what I had planned—specifically to appoint Stephanie Ford—because, despite my strong backing for her and a unanimous faculty vote, he vetoed her appointment. That stunned me and hurt very badly, and I declined to participate further in the search process. What cut deeply was that I would not see spiritual formation for Christian ministry advance beyond where I had led it. Yet it was presumptuous of me perhaps to think that *my* plan was the only one and to forget how important it was to give Tom Graves a real choice.

A Grand Sendoff

However great my disappointment regarding my successor, Tom Graves, my colleagues, students, and friends from everywhere arranged a grand sendoff on 29 April 1999. They brought Martha from Louisville. Quite to my surprise, they unveiled the "Hinson Window" at the entrance to Watts Hall with a suitable ceremony. I had noticed carpenters removing the original window a few days prior as they completed the renovation of a small room for a prayer chapel, but they kept the new window carefully covered. Before noon came the unveiling followed by a huge outdoor meal for a throng of people. In the afternoon, Tom Graves; Lewis Weeks, President of Union Theological

Seminary/Presbyterian School of Christian Education; Rebecca Weaver, Professor of Church History at UTS; Stephanie Ford, PhD student at The Catholic University of America; and Theresie Houghton, my teaching assistant at BTSR who had much to do with the Hinson Window, gave extravagant tributes about my teaching, scholarship, person, etc. In the evening, my colleagues treated me to a faculty sendoff, replete with a roasting. Tom Halbrooks sang a song composed by Dave Hunsicker, a friend of many years and one of my former PhD students at Southern, ribbing me about my reluctance to give up my 1923 Underwood for a Dell. Dan Bagby did a bit of satire. Some other colleagues expressed thanks more graciously. When called on to respond at the end of the evening, I had no prepared speech. Instead I spoke extemporaneously from the heart, laying aside all negative feelings and focusing on the remarkable leadership Tom Graves and Tom Halbrooks had provided and on the high expectations I had for the future of the Baptist Theological Seminary at Richmond. I would need a long time to resolve feelings of hurt or disappointment, but I had learned long before to look on the bright side of life.

24

CHURCH HISTORIAN PLUS

Lest I distort the story I'm telling, let me hasten to say that stepping into this whirlpool of concern for the spiritual life did not lead to abandonment of my vocation as a Patristics scholar and church historian. As I've noted before, when Graves and Halbrooks approached me about coming to Richmond, I insisted that Church history must remain a part of my title and work. Although Halbrooks planned to teach the required courses in Church history and Baptist history, I would offer some electives in my special field and retain the title Professor of Church History as well as Professor of Spirituality and Worship. The only matter requiring clarification was the order of the two titles, and, after some discussion, we agreed on the title Professor of Spirituality, Worship and Church History.

A tragedy opened the way for me to be named to the first endowed chair of Baptist Theological Seminary at Richmond. In Birmingham, Alabama, shortly after the seminary opened, an eighteen-wheeler ran a red light, crushed the car, and snuffed out the lives of John F. Loftis and his young daughter. I had taught John at Southern and served on his PhD committee. John and his wife Deborah, a music major at Southern, attended the same church my family and I belonged to for a year or two—Beechwood Baptist in Louisville. I had written in support of John's election as director of the Baptist history collection in Alabama. When Deb, a native of Richmond, received a settlement from the trucking company in 1995, she, her family, and John's family established the John F. Loftis Chair of Church History with the stipulation that I would be the first holder of it. My title became Professor of Spirituality and John F. Loftis Professor of Church History.

As things worked out, I continued to devote a substantial amount of my teaching to Church history. I taught a course on "The Early Church Fathers" to students at BTSR and Union Theological Seminary. When Rebecca Weaver, Professor of Church History at Union, went on sabbatical, she asked me to teach early Christian history in her absence. She and I later teamed up to teach a course she had already entitled "The

Other Story," a study of women in the early and medieval periods of Christian history. Each school accounted for about twenty students, making this a large elective class. I team-taught a course on ecumenism also with the current and former deans of Presbyterian School of Christian Education, James Brashler and Isabel Rogers.

Rüschlikon 1994

By an arrangement agreed on in 1992, I returned to Rüschlikon in the spring of 1994 to teach early Church history and classics of Christian devotion. The return to Rüschlikon had a special poignancy, for European Baptists were already discussing sale of the valuable property and moving the International Baptist Seminary to Prague, the Czech Republic. Martha and I took part in a reconnaissance visit to the expected site where Rüschlikon's faculty met with the theological faculty of the University of Prague. Two special sidelights of this semester merit mention: (1) Our daughter Elizabeth, now a student at Louisville Presbyterian Seminary, visited, bringing with her Lee Hasty, who is now her husband, and his mother. (2) Thanks to my service as interim pastor in Petersburg, Virginia, I was able to help an Estonian student, Tarmo Toom, one of the brightest I have taught anywhere, to secure financial assistance of the Titmus Foundation in Virginia to bring his wife and children to Richmond. Later, I helped him to leap some hurdles and to get enrolled in the PhD program in Patristic Studies of the Catholic University of America, where he now teaches.

As a highlight of my course in early Christian history, I again arranged a tour of Italy February 21–26. On the way to Ferrara, we made an unscheduled stop at Chiaravalla, a monastery founded by Bernard of Clairvaux and named after him. The men stayed this time in a Cappuchin monastery in Lendinare, the women in a convent at Rovigo. In Rome, we were hosted once more by Italian Baptists at Rocca di Papa and met again with the Secretariat for Promoting Christian Unity. We toured the Catacomba di S. Priscilla, which features some of the most loved early Christian frescoes—the good shepherd, the three children in the fiery furnace, the Madonna and child, the Magi, Noah in the Ark of Torah, etc. A bright young American priest conducted our group through the Scavi under St Peter's. He sought with some enthusiasm to promote the idea of Peter's burial in the necropolis. A trip to Ostia, the seaport of ancient Rome, also set this tour apart from our earlier one. An inscription commemorating the death of Monica gave it special meaning for those who, in Classics of Christian Devotion, studied Augustine's *Confessions*.

Writing

Even before I returned to Rüschlikon, I had brought to a close my long, arduous, and complicated effort to write a history of Christianity up to 1300.[1] As you would expect, Broadman Press declined to publish my completed manuscript, which I submitted in 1992.[2] Consequently I turned to Abingdon and to Mercer University Press, and both wanted to publish it, Abingdon only the patristic part but Mercer the entire manuscript. Both books received highly favorable reviews[3] and had substantial sales. The National Association of Baptist Professors of Religion featured *The Church Triumphant*, published by Mercer University Press, in their spring meeting on 15 March 1996 with a careful and complimentary review by George Shriver. Shriver especially commended the ecumenical outlook of the book, assessing it in light of principles set out in a study entitled *Telling the Churches' Stories: Ecumenical Perspectives on Writing Christian History*.[4] In my preface to *The Church Triumphant*, I indicated several other concerns that informed my historiography as I wrote it, which could perhaps be summed up in the word "inclusiveness." They included rejection of the idea of a "Fall" of the Church espoused in the Free Church tradition, more objective treatment of groups traditionally labeled heretical, incorporation of more of the story of women in the Church's history, use of a socio-institutional approach focused more on "ordinary saints" and less on "great men," and special attention to the use of coercion by Christians.[5]

---

[1] I signed a contract with Broadman Press on 25 February 1981. When Harold Smith returned a copy of the contract on May 19, Broadman scheduled publication for June 1984. (Harold S. Smith to E. Glenn Hinson, 19 May 1981.) Had the denominational waters not been so roiled, I might have met the deadline. Given my own situation at the center of the storm, however, any expectation of completing such a book in that period of time was out of the question.

[2] Trent C. Butler to E. Glenn Hinson, 22 December 1992.

[3] An exception is a review by Mark Gustafson, Calvin College, in the *Journal of Early Christian Studies* 6 (Spring 1998): 327–29, who used most of his space picking at stylistic matters.

[4] I happened to chair the Apostolic Faith Study of the Faith and Order Commission of the National Council of Churches when it commissioned that study, but I did not take part in the working group.

[5] E. Glenn Hinson, *The Church Triumphant: A History of Christianity up to 1300* (Macon GA: Mercer University Press, 1995) xi-xii.

Trends in the Southern Baptist Convention spotlighted such perspectives as these and motivated me to give them priority in my continuing research, speaking, and writing. One area of particular concern at this time was the diminishment of the roles of women in the SBC. Before leaving on sabbatical in 1991, I had organized and chaired a graduate colloquium in Church history on the role of women in early Christianity. In the International Patristics Conference in August of 1991, I presented a paper highlighting the remarkable role of women among Christian martyrs.[6] During my sabbatical in Oxford in the spring of 1992, I followed up with a study of the spirituality of women as they watched the advance of barbarians toward Rome at the end of the fourth century.[7] In November 1993 I made use of that research to give the Roland Bainton Lecture at Yale Divinity School entitled "Inclusiveness in Teaching and Writing Church History: The Case of Marcella."[8] In August 1995, I attended and presented a paper at the Twelfth International Patristics Conference in Oxford on women biblical scholars in early Christianity.[9]

Another issue was the Southern Baptist Convention's redefinition of religious liberty and repudiation of the separation of church and state as a Baptist doctrine. On 8 October 1992, I gave a paper on "The Background to the Moderate Movement in the Southern Baptist Convention"[10] in a conference convened by Buddy Shurden at Mercer University in Macon, Georgia. On 6–7 October 1995, I took part in a "Baptist/Humanist Dialogue" at the University of Richmond, challenging the tendency of both the Religious Right and atheists to equate humanism with secularity.[11]

---

[6] E. Glenn Hinson, "Women among the Martyrs," *Studia Patristica*, ed. Elizabeth A. Livingstone (Leuven: Peeters Press, 1993) 25: 423–28.

[7] E. Glenn Hinson, "When the World Collapsed: The Spirituality of Women during the Barbarian Invasion of Rome," *Perspectives in Religious Studies*, 20 (Summer 1993): 113–30.

[8] See also my entry on "Marcella" in the *Encyclopedia of Early Christianity*, ed. Everett Ferguson, et al. (revised edition; New York & London: Garland Publications, 1997) 2:713.

[9] "Women Biblical Scholars in the Late Fourth Century: The Aventine Circle," *Studia Patristica* (Leuven: Peeters, 1997) 33:319–24.

[10] Published in *The Struggle for the Soul of the SBC: Moderate Responses to the Fundamentalist Movement*, ed. Walter B. Shurden (Macon GA: Mercer University Press, 1993) 1–16.

[11] E. Glenn Hinson, "Must Humanism Be Secular?" in *Freedom of Conscience: A Baptist/Humanist Dialogue*, ed. Paul D. Simmons (Amherst NY: Prometheus Books, 2000) 182–93.

Not surprisingly, my reputation as a historian concerned about spirituality brought invitations in which the historian's craft converged with and blended into the topic of spirituality. I presented a paper entitled "Rootedness in Tradition and Global Spirituality" to a "Scholars' Retreat" held at the Abbey of Gethsemani in January 1993, to discuss "post-modernism."[12] The Abbey brought me back to Kentucky to take part in an event at the Center for Study of Ethics and Culture in October. On 4–5 June 1993, I delivered a keynote address commemorating the 100th anniversary of Thomas R. Kelly's birth at his alma mater, Wilmington College.[13]

I invested much of my Richmond research time, six and a half years altogether, in the writing of a biography of Douglas V. Steere.[14] As I indicated in the Preface to *Love at the Heart of Things*, I tried to enable readers to gain from Douglas Steere some of the fundamental insights I had learned from close association with him. As one of the eminent American religious leaders of the twentieth century, he touched many lives as a key figure in the founding of Pendle Hill, as a Quaker global minister, as organizer of relief for war torn Finland at the end of World War II, as ecumenical pioneer, as extraordinary peacemaker, as Quaker visionary and guide, as contemplative scholar, as midwife of saints, as a consummate letter writer, and as an existential realist philosopher. He had a gift for coining or popularizing memorable phrases: "Life was lent to be spent," "being present where you are," "mutual irradiation," "that love which is at the heart of things."

Colleges and universities called on me to lecture on a wide variety of topics, for virtually all of which I drew chiefly from my historical studies. My new accent on spirituality sounded with greater clarity. In retrospect, I feel somewhat embarrassed that I spoke so often and wrote so prolifically. I had no unspoken or unpublished thoughts. The schools honored me by asking; I wonder if I honored them with the quality of my lectures

[12] Published in *The Merton Annual: Studies in Culture, Spirituality, and Social Concerns*, 6:6–22.

[13] E. Glenn Hinson, "The Impact of Thomas Kelly on American Religious Life," *Quaker Religious Thought* 27 (July 1995): 11–22.

[14] E. Glenn Hinson, *Love at the Heart of Things A Biography of Douglas V. Steere* (Wallingford PA: Pendle Hill; Nashville: Upper Room Books, 1998).

Professional Connections

Shifting my main teaching responsibilities did not lead to an abandonment of involvement in professional societies I had attended or held membership in for many years. I continued membership in the American Academy of Religion, the American Society of Church History, the North American Patristics Society, the National Association of Baptist Professors of Religion, and the Baptist History and Heritage Society. A crowded calendar did not permit me to participate actively in all of these groups, but I attended the AAR annually because most other societies met in conjunction with it. I served a term as President of the National Association of Baptist Professors of Religion in 1994. In my presidential address in Chicago on 20 November 1994, you can see evidence of the effect teaching spirituality was having as I challenged my colleagues to provide not only *in*formation but to accept responsibility for *formation*. I concluded the address with this personal statement:

> I confess that I have often tried to dodge this aspect of my vocation as a teacher. During my early years, I was more comfortable confining my work to the processing of information for the head. Over many years, however, I have begun to hear those who were or are my students talk about experiences in my class which were "life-changing." I have watched them function in ways which have convinced me that we teach not subjects but persons and that the reward of the teacher rests in the profoundly personal impact you have made as you have wrestled with certain subjects. More and more, I am feeling comfortable trying through my own special studies to teach students how to see and how to listen, to discern the Transcendent transecting time. The present awakening and the revolution from a typographic back to an iconic and tactual culture may lend us some help. The future of humankind in the new millennium may depend on it.[15]

A wry twist on my shifting role at this time … I could not stay for dialogue when I finished the address because I had agreed to respond to two papers presented to the Society for the Study of Christian Spirituality, which met simultaneously with the NABPR!

Instead of dropping the old and putting on the new, over several years I had been drawn into the widening academic concern for spirituality. I joined the Society for the Study of Christian Spirituality in

---

[15] E. Glenn Hinson, "The Educational Task of Baptist Teachers of Religion on the Edge of a New Millennium," *Perspectives in Religious Studies* 22 (Fall 1995): 237.

1993, serving for three years on its board, and was named one of the Advisory Editors of *Spiritus*, a scholarly publication of the SSCS that succeeded its *Christian Spirituality Bulletin*. Having my appetite and thirst for spirituality whetted in secular theology's brief reign, the birth and growth of deep and authentic interest in spirituality in academia aroused in me a subtle sense of satisfaction at the direction in which things have moved since I published *Seekers after Mature Faith* (1968), *A Serious Call to a Contemplative Lifestyle* (1974), and *The Doubleday Devotional Classics* (1978).

Where my investment in *Spiritus* has concerned chiefly the penning of a couple of articles,[16] I have invested heart and soul in a twenty-five year journey with *Weavings*, a celebrated bi-monthly focusing in each issue on focal concerns in spiritual growth and development, as a writer and as a member of its Advisory Board.[17] *Weavings* took off like a rocket, gaining 45,000 subscribers at one point. As the digital revolution has created serious challenges for newspapers, periodicals, and journals of all kinds, forcing such outstanding papers as *The Christian Science Monitor* to go strictly online, I have endured an agonizing period of soul-searching with the *Weavings* staff about its future and rejoice with unspeakable joy to see it live still with a redesign commensurate with the challenge.

The Ecumenical Institute of Spirituality, of course, continued to play a central role both in personal sustenance and professional stimulus. Groundbreaking topics on which the institute focused in this period and sharing of personal stories and insights by this extraordinary group helped to chart my course at Richmond. Themes and meeting places included: the power of myth in Christianity (Pendle Hill, Pennsylvania 1992); contemplation in Islam, Buddhism, Hinduism, and Carmelite spirituality (St Mary's Seminary and the Carmelite Monastery, Baltimore, 1994); the city as a context for biblical faith (Servant Leadership School, the Church of the Savior, Washington, DC, 1995); Thomas Merton (Abbey of Gethsemani, Trappist, Kentucky, 1996); spirituality and urban violence (Richmond Hill, Richmond, Virginia, 1997); and how

---

[16] E. Glenn Hinson, "Trends in Baptist Spirituality," *Christian Spirituality Bulletin* 7 (Fall/Winter 1999): 1, 3–7; "The Progression of Grace: Re-Reading of *The Pilgrim's Progress*," *Spiritus* 3 (2003): 251–62.

[17] Missing only in 1994 when I taught at Rüschlikon, I noted the following dates for other meetings: May 17–18, 1993; May 22–23, 1995; June 3–4, 1996; June 1–2, 1997; June 8–9, 1998; and May 24–25, 1999.

learning/formation and interpreting deep texts take place today (Pendle Hill, 1999).[18] The last meeting was to me an especially memorable one not so much for the subject as for subsidiary reasons.

On January 14, 1999, I set out for Wallingford from Richmond. In the Washington, DC, area I met Stephanie Ford, a PhD student at Catholic University, and Dorothy Devers, one of the original members of EIOS. About halfway between Baltimore and Wallingford a severe winter storm struck. Icy rain and sleet soon covered the windshield of my old 1979 Oldsmobile 88 with a blanket of ice. The defroster worked well, but it couldn't heat the windshield enough to keep ice from forming on it. I had to stop under overpasses and scrape the windshield. Thankfully, with many prayers silently uttered, we made it. So, too, did ninety-three-year-old Dorothy Steere. Although only eight of our members got through the storm, she was there. In her honor Pendle Hill Publications distributed cloth-bound copies of my recently published biography of Douglas to all who got through. I mailed copies to others.

Out of my appointment as Paul Wattson Visiting Professor at the Catholic University of America in 1987 grew a continuing relationship with the Friars of the Atonement and service on their Board of Consultors. I attended meetings of the Consultors at Graymoor, the Motherhouse of the Friars, in Upstate New York[19] and published articles in *Ecumenical Trends*,[20] a journal published by the Friars.

ITMS

Because Thomas Merton figured so prominently in the way spirituality gained a foothold and little by little increased in importance in my career, I need to say a special word about my involvement in the International Thomas Merton Society, something that brought both blessing and a measure of pain. Following Merton's death, I was called on to speak about him in Merton symposia. Several of my papers were published.[21] In May 1978, on the tenth anniversary of his death, I gave a

---

[18] A meeting scheduled for Mt Savior Monastery, Elmira, New York, in 1998 had to be cancelled due to severe weather.

[19] One meeting during the Richmond period is listed in my calendars: 21–23 June 1993. I attended others before that.

[20] "Ecumenical Jubilee," *Ecumenical Trends* 19 (December 1990): 169–70; "Ecumenical Spirituality," ibid., 20 (July/August 1991) 97–104.

[21] "Merton's Many Faces," *Religion in Life*, 42 (Summer 1973): 153–67; "The Catholicizing of Contemplation: Thomas Merton's Place in the Church's Prayer Life,"

major paper on Merton's ecumenical outlook at a symposium sponsored by the Vancouver School of Theology.[22] I was also one of the Program Consultants for the Merton Commemoration at Columbia, 27 November–10 December 1978.

At the invitation of Bill Shannon, Professor at Nazareth College of Rochester, New York, I joined a representative group of Merton scholars at Bellarmine College (now University) on 29–30 May 1987, to found the International Thomas Merton Society and to prepare an observance for the twentieth anniversary of Merton's death.[23] Much to my surprise, before the first biennial meeting of the society at Bellarmine on 25–28 May 1989, a Nominating Committee chaired by Mary Luke Tobin, asked me to succeed Bonnie Thurston as treasurer. Bonnie was named Vice-President and Bob Daggy, Director of the Merton Studies Center at Bellarmine, as President.[24] On Bonnie Thurston's assurances that the job was not difficult,[25] I accepted reluctantly with the understanding that I would have to employ one of my graduate students, Phyllis Pleasants, to keep the books and place the money in the hands of Southern Seminary's Treasurer.[26]

To my greater surprise, Bob Daggy wrote on 3 August 1990 to ask me to succeed Bonnie as Vice-President and later President of the International Thomas Merton Society from 1993 to 1995.[27] I wrote, "I am honored, of course, to serve as an officer in the Thomas Merton Society."[28] I attended the second biennial meeting at Nazareth College in Rochester, New York, in June 1991, and presided over a plenary session during which A.M. Allchin gave a paper on "The Worship of the Whole Creation: Merton and the Eastern Fathers." The meeting in Bill

Perspectives in Religious Studies, 1 (Spring 1974): 66–84; *Cistercian Studies* 10 (1975): 173–89.

[22] "Expansive Catholicism: Ecumenical Perceptions of Thomas Merton," *Religion in Life* 48 (Spring 1979): 63–76; *The Message of Thomas Merton*, ed. Brother Patrick Hart (Kalamazoo MI: Cistercian Publications, 1981) 55–71.

[23] William H. Shannon, President, ITMS, to E. Glenn Hinson, 15 August 1987.

[24] Mary Luke Tobin, Thomas Merton Center for Creative Change, to E. Glenn Hinson, 18 November 1988.

[25] Bonnie Thurston to E. Glenn Hinson, 10 December 1988, responding to my letter to Mary Luke, 2 December 1988.

[26] E. Glenn Hinson to Sister Mary Luke Tobin, 15 December 1988.

[27] Bill Shannon had named a Nominating Committee to choose officers. Bob seems to have departed from that and named people directly. This may be the major reason why some reacted negatively to what happened in the Colorado crisis.

[28] E. Glenn Hinson to Robert E. Daggy, President, ITMS, 14 August 1990.

Shannon's bailiwick turned out well. The next biennial in Colorado Springs, however, encountered serious complications and a puzzling decision by Bob Daggy and Bonnie Thurston to name Father James Conner, a monk at the Abbey of Gethsemani, as president for 1993–1995.

In a letter dated 26 March 1991, well in advance of the Rochester meeting, the Denver Chapter of the ITMS extended an invitation to hold the third triennial meeting in Colorado.[29] Responses at Rochester seemed favorable and enthusiastic. The site committee arranged for the meeting to be held at Colorado College in Colorado Springs from 10–13 June 1993. Unfortunately, in 1992, voters of the state of Colorado passed an amendment to the state constitution that denied protection based on sexual lifestyle and prohibited state or local governments, or any of their agencies, from passing laws which would protect gays from discrimination in jobs, housing, and public accommodations. In January 1993 the Denver District Court issued a temporary injunction to prevent this amendment from taking effect until deemed constitutional by a higher Colorado or perhaps national court. Given Thomas Merton's strong feelings about social justice issues, some ITMS members proposed a boycott. Prior to the injunction, Camaldolese monk, Robert Hale, sent a strong and impassioned statement addressed "To Various Members of the ITMS Board and International Advisors," 29 December 1992. As President, Bonnie Thurston decided that the meeting should be held as planned and notified the Site Committee. She, however, left for Jerusalem on January 4 to teach at St George's College and did not anticipate the volume of pro-boycott mail she would receive. Some correspondents suggested that she should have put the reins in my hands during her absence. On February 8, she circulated a letter to ITMS Officers, Board of Directors, and International Advisors in which she reviewed the strong negative sentiment and then added: "Therefore as of today, 8 February 1993, I resign as President of the International Thomas Merton Society and suggest that my resignation be considered retroactive to November, 1992." The same day, she wrote to me and offered some suggestions as to how I should proceed.

I have never been put in such an embarrassing position, and I would be the first to admit that I may not have acted with the greatest wisdom. Before Bonnie sent her letter of resignation, however, I wrote Robert Hale. I agreed with him that a boycott would "probably speak

---

[29] Kelby K. Cotton, Mountair Christian Church (Disciples of Christ), Lakewood, Colorado, to Robert E. Daggy, 26 March 1991.

more powerfully than anything else on this issue." But I could not stop with that. I went on to say that I thought we had to support Bonnie Thurston's decision to hold the meeting lest it introduce a lot of confusion. "Maybe the little group who will gather in June can lift up their voices enough to get people's attention, and while not as effective as the boycott a cry of outrage will be consistent with Thomas Merton's protest of the war in Vietnam and racism and a lot of other injustices.[30] I wrote a similar response to Jacques Goulet, another strong proponent of a boycott.[31]

Bonnie's letter reached me about two weeks later. Somewhere along the way, Bob Daggy called me to plead with me to write Bonnie and persuade her to reconsider. I did. In my letter I pointed out that I would not feel comfortable stepping into her shoes, that she should not take too seriously the insistence of some that she should have turned things over to me, and that she needed to continue as president for the sake of ITMS. "This fledgling institution needs stability, and you are the person who can give it that. So once again, I entreat you to reconsider. Otherwise the ship will be rudderless."

Somewhere out of this confused situation arose another complication. I'm not sure at what point it happened, but Bonnie Thurston nominated Father James Conner, OCSO, as the President of the International Thomas Merton Society. My failure to attend the Colorado meeting was perhaps the ostensible reason, but it did upset some members of the society that I was not named. Jim Conner, very sensitive to my feelings, wrote a nice note. "I hope that you have not been offended or hurt or put off by anything that was done."[32] I was more hurt than I let him know in my response, but I tried not to let him be the brunt of any latent anger. I explained to him that my absence from the meeting in Colorado Springs should not be interpreted as a protest either of the Gay/Lesbian Rights issue or the new slate of officers and that I thought we should back Bonnie's decision to hold the meeting. I enclosed a copy of my letter to Bonnie. I commended his selection as president. He deserved the office. I would probably have had to decline it for a couple of reasons even if nominated. I was serving as president of

---

[30] E. Glenn Hinson, Vice-President, ITMS, to Robert Hale, Camaldolese Monks, Big Sur, California, 14 January 1993.

[31] E. Glenn Hinson to Jacques Goulet, Mount St Vincent Seminary, Halifax, Nova Scotia, 16 January 1993.

[32] Fr. Jim Conner, ITMS, to E. Glenn Hinson, BTSR, Richmond, 24 June 1993.

the National Association of Baptist Professors of Religion, and my teaching and writing schedule would not have permitted me to carry an extra load. I didn't know how much I could take part in ITMS in the future, but I intended to attend the meeting at St Bonaventure's in Olean, New York in 1995. [33]

In 1994 the Nominating Committee of ITMS requested that I allow my name to be placed on the ballot along with that of Patrick O'Connell. I felt some ambivalence about this but finally decided that it might ease some tensions over the previous election. An election would look better than the appointment of Father Conner had. In a 6 December 1994 letter, Father Conner informed me that O'Connell was elected. He was a worthy candidate in a position to arrange the biennial meeting at St Bonaventure in Olean, New York, in June 1995. I attended and gave my paper on Douglas Steere and Thomas Merton: "Surprising Yokefellows: The Contribution of Douglas V. Steere to Thomas Merton." I thought that would end my participation in ITMS. Patrick O'Connell and friends at Spring Hill College in Mobile, Alabama, however, persuaded me to present a paper in a plenary at the biennial held there in June 1997. I had experienced so many kindnesses from Spring Hill College that I could hardly refuse. For this I revised an address I had given to an ITMS Chapter at St Anselm's in Washington, DC, on 4 May 1996, entitled "Thomas Merton, my Brother: The Impact of Thomas Merton on my Life and Thought."[34]

Although I did not attend ITMS meetings after that, more because of growing deafness rather than any residual resentment, I sustained my membership in the society, continued to read writings by or about Merton, published other articles on his life and thought, and, subsequent to my retirement from BTSR, taught a class on Merton, first at Bellarmine University and then elsewhere. I also took many groups of students to the Abbey of Gethsemani and promoted as effectively as I could what I have thought was Merton's chief message to our day—the urgent need of contemplation in a world of action.

---

[33] E. Glenn Hinson to Fr. James Conner, Abbey of Gethsemani, Trappist, Kentucky, 29 June 1993.
[34] Published in *The Merton Annual: Studies in Culture, Spirituality and Social Concerns*, 11:88–96.

25

SUNSET AND EVENING STAR

My retirement from the Baptist Theological Seminary at Richmond plunged me into a mild bout with depression. Because I'm basically an "up" type, I didn't expect it to happen, but the first semester after leaving Richmond for Louisville I experienced moments of sudden and unaccountable grief. Tears welled up in my eyes at odd times for no obvious reason. A kind of gloom hung over my activities. Where earlier, even after my Oxford *viva*, I climbed out of the doldrums quickly, this one held on most of the fall.

It was not that I didn't have anything to do or was now reduced to meaningless activity. Actually I kept a fairly crowded calendar of activities, as a glance at Appendix D will confirm. With so much going on, you may wonder how I found time to feel down. My own suspicion is that grief inheres in radical changes in one's life work in much the same way it does in death of a loved one, dissolution of a marriage, or loss of a job. Although I had chosen to retire, I felt a terrible emptiness when it came time to start school in the fall, something I had done year after year since September 1937, sixty-two years—sabbaticals excepted. One additional factor may have entered into the equation—departure from a very friendly environment in Virginia to a less hospitable one in Kentucky. A résumé of my invitations to speak in churches, associations, conventions, schools, or other institutions reveals a tremendous disparity between my welcome on the Atlantic seaboard and in Kentucky, as if I had contracted spiritual halitosis when I returned to the latter environment, dominated now by fundamentalists.

Back to the Classroom

Vacation from the classroom did not last long. Before my absence from the classroom could have sunk me into a deep depression, Tony Dunnavant, Dean and Professor of Church History at Lexington Theological Seminary, invited me to teach two classes for the spring semester, 1999–2000—"Significant Persons in Christian Social Ethics" and "Introduction to Church History."[1] Fearful he may have confused me with my former colleague Glen Stassen, who taught ethics at Southern, I hesitated on the former,[2] but accepted his assurances that the ethics course was essentially a Church history course.[3] In January 2000, Louisville Presbyterian Seminary asked me to teach "History of Baptist Churches in the United States" for Baptist students enrolled in their MDiv program.[4] I taught in Lexington on Tuesdays and Thursdays and in Louisville on Wednesdays and Fridays. My weepy moments disappeared soon after the semester began.

Georgian Interlude

A visiting professorship at Candler School of Theology in Atlanta interrupted my teaching at LTS and LPTS. Even before I retired from BTSR, David Key, Coordinator of the Baptist Studies Program at Candler School of Theology, approached me in June 1999 about serving as Visiting Professor at Candler in 2000–01.[5] When I gave my enthusiastic consent, he proceeded over the next couple of months to work out arrangements with the administration there, notifying me on 15 November 1999, that they were ready to send the official invitation.[6] I can scarcely find words adequate to describe my gracious reception by staff and faculty at Candler. My time there reinforced long time friendships with Don Saliers and Roberta Bondi and opened the way for cultivation of new ones. In the fall I taught "Prayer in Christian History: An Ecumenical Approach" and "Baptist Traditions," in the spring "Classics of Christian Devotion" and "Systematic Theology from a Baptist Perspective."[7] Both "Prayer in Christian History" and "Classics of Christian Devotion" surpassed the limit of 25 students set for them. In line with the implications of the course title "Baptist Traditions," I revised somewhat the course content I had used at Louisville Presbyterian Seminary, giving more explicit attention to African-

---

[1] Tony Dunnavant, email message to Glenn Hinson, 23 August 1999.

[2] Glenn Hinson, email message to Tony Dunnavant, 23 August 1999.

[3] Tony Dunnavant, email message to Glenn Hinson, 26 August 1999; Glenn Hinson to Tony Dunnavant, 26 August 1999.

[4] Dianne Reistroffer, Interim Dean and Vice President for Academic Affairs to E. Glenn Hinson, 10 January 2000.

[5] David Key, email message to Glenn Hinson asking for a résumé, 28 June 1999.

[6] David Key, email message to Glenn Hinson, 15 Novemeber 1999.

[7] E. Glenn Hinson to Steven J. Kraftchick, Associate Dean of Academic Affairs, 16 February 2000.

American Baptist churches. I also conducted a reading seminar on early Christianity for three PhD students—one in New Testament and the other two in Church history. During my two semesters at Candler, I also pinch hit for sabbaticant Loyd Allen at McAfee School of Theology, Mercer University, teaching both an "Introduction to Spirituality" and Church history. I developed deep and abiding friendships with students as well as faculty in both institutions.[8]

Teaching at Candler and McAfee sprang a surprise on me soon after I got to Atlanta. Basil Pennington, a fellow member of the Ecumenical Institute of Spirituality, was elected Abbot of Holy Spirit Monastery at Conyers, Georgia, a suburb of Atlanta, and installed September 8. With his gracious assistance, I arranged retreats at Conyers for students in spirituality classes both at Candler and at McAfee. When some retreatants struggled to come up with the "donation" expected, the new abbot, a master irenicist, quickly approved what we could pay while reassuring his more exacting guestmaster that it sufficed. He also led one of the classes in an exercise of centering prayer, an approach to prayer for which he had gained worldwide attention with his popular book *Centering Prayer*. In the spring Victor Kramer, Director of the Aquinas Center of Theology at Emory University and a long time friend through the International Thomas Merton Society, arranged for Father Pennington, a prolific author, and me to speak about our writings in spirituality to a substantial crowd of Candler students and faculty. I distributed a copy of my own bibliography in spirituality.[9]

The welcome I received in the Atlanta area when I taught at Candler and McAfee in 2000–01 contrasted sharply with my muted Kentucky welcome. As soon as David Key circulated word of my advent, I started receiving calls and letters from friends and former students at Southern to invite me to speak or lead retreats in their churches in the Atlanta region. They left scarcely a bare spot on my weekend calendar. The spring schedule grew embarrassingly crowded. I spoke about contemplative lifestyle or some aspect of the spiritual life and led either

---

[8] I preached the ordination sermon for Robin Anderson at First Baptist Church, Decatur, Georgia, on 24 February 2002, and for Ro Ruffin at First Baptist Church, Morrow, Georgia, on 18 March 2007. Both women had served as my teaching assistants in the "Introduction to Spirituality."

[9] "Bibliography of E. Glenn Hinson on Spirituality," *Perspectives in Religious Studies: Essays in Honor of E. Glenn Hinson* 31 (Spring 2004): 99–113.

one day or weekend retreats for a slew of Baptist churches.[10] February 15 I also conducted a "Day Apart" study of *Spiritual Preparation for Christian Leadership* for Methodist clergy in Atlanta at Embry Hills United Methodist Church. Outside the Atlanta area, I addressed an anniversary celebration at Glendale Baptist, Nashville, Tennessee, on March 11.

More academic occasions included lectures related to *Spiritual Preparation for Christian Leadership*,[11] my most recent book, at Iliff School of Theology in Denver (January 22–25); a formal paper on "Reconciliation and Resistance"[12] at the Wesleyan Theological Society meeting in Marion, Indiana (March 3); and a series of lectures on Douglas Steere at Earlham College, Richmond, Indiana (April 21). At Iliff I had the good fortune to breakfast with Huston Smith, who was lecturing on Christianity and other faiths, and to thank him for his influence on my life at a critical stage. We had met only one other time since I left Washington University, when he gave some lectures at Southern Seminary.

In connection with the annual Cooperative Baptist Fellowship meeting in Atlanta, on 28 June 2001, the William H. Whitsitt Society honored former President Jimmy Carter and me with the "Whitsitt Baptist Courage Award." Whitsitt was a president of Southern Seminary forced to resign in 1898 in the face of opposition to his insistence that Baptist history did not follow a "trail of blood" back to Jesus independently of the Catholic Church, but began with English Separatists around 1640. Carter received his award during the evening worship service of the CBF at which he was scheduled to speak. Mine was presented at a packed afternoon session of the Whitsitt Society at which I spoke about "Hope for the Future of Baptists." In this address I raised serious question as to whether CBF or any other group of Baptists could create Baptist/Christian identity in light of (1) growing pluralism in America, (2) the mottled character of all religious bodies, (3) the virtual disappearance of church training since 1970, (4) fundamentalist dominance of the religious airwaves, (5) practical control over the

---

[10] See Appendix D.

[11] E. Glenn Hinson, *Spiritual Preparation for Christian Leadership* (Nashville: Upper Room Books, 1999).

[12] E. Glenn Hinson, "Reconciliation and Resistance: A Case Study," *Wesleyan Theological Journal* 37 (Spring 2002): 25–34. My invitation to address the issue was triggered by a briefer version of "Reconciliation and Resistance" published in *Weavings* 15 (November/December 2000): 40–46.

religious scene in the South by Southern Baptists, and (6) the impact of the "corporation mentality" on American religious life.[13] The award commended me as "one who demonstrated courage within the tradition and heritage of the Baptist faith and in the face of strong opposition had made a lasting contribution in preserving religious liberty, championing soul freedom, pursuing intellectual integrity, upholding human rights, and advocating social justice." When James Dunn, former director of the Baptist Joint Committee, had received his award the year before, he called it "the Baptist stubborn award." I insisted that I would think of it as "the Bertha Brown award," for it was she who taught me faithfulness.

LTS and Baptist Seminary of Kentucky

Before my return to Louisville in 2001, Philip Dare, the Librarian and Acting Dean of Lexington Theological Seminary, contacted me to see if I would again teach an Introduction to Church History at LTS. To my shock and dismay, Tony Dunnavant had died suddenly on February 8 of a pulmonary embolism,[14] leaving a gaping hole in the middle of the LTS faculty. I, of course, quickly agreed and taught both semesters in 2001–02. In the meantime, in June 2001 the faculty of Louisville Presbyterian Seminary contacted me to teach again "History of Baptist Churches in the United States"[15] during the spring semester.

While I engaged in this swirl of activities, a moderate effort to start an alternative seminary in Kentucky was underway. I must confess that I viewed the endeavor with sincere skepticism. On 19 February 2002, Greg Earwood, newly elected President of the Baptist Seminary of Kentucky-to-be, visited me to see if I would be willing to teach Church History and Spirituality when the seminary opened in the fall of 2002. I explained that I would continue to serve as an adjunct professor at LTS in 2002–03 and warned, "I am a high-profile person in Kentucky. The fundamentalists have done a good job of demonizing me. I may hurt rather than help in getting this new seminary off the ground." Greg, however, up to then pastor of Faith Baptist Church in Georgetown, had been my student at Southern Seminary and insisted that I would help more than I would hurt. I expressed the hope that the new seminary would develop and maintain a close relationship with LTS, something

---

[13] E. Glenn Hinson, "Hope for the Future of Baptists," *The Whitsitt Journal* 8 (Fall 2001): 12–15.

[14] Philip Dare, email message to Glenn Hinson, 20 February 2001.

[15] Milton J. Coalter, Acting Dean, LPTS, to E. Glenn Hinson, 6 June 2001.

which potent Landmarkist influence in Kentucky might make difficult.[16] With some reservations still about the prospects of a moderate seminary in Kentucky I agreed to become a part of the "core faculty" as Senior Professor of Church History and Spirituality as the seminary opened in the fall of 2002.

On March 21 I took part in a rally of supporters and potential students at Calvary Baptist Church in Lexington. In a brief extemporaneous speech I said, "I've been skeptical of efforts to start more seminaries, but it looks like the pattern will be to have a moderate seminary in each state where there are significant numbers of Baptists. Perhaps it is our turn." It took some time for me to work out to my own satisfaction a fuller rationale for an alternative Baptist seminary in Kentucky. What I eventually could see more clearly was the importance of preparing ministers to help their people discern how God fits into their lives in today's world in which science plays such a critical role rather than, as at Southern Seminary, into a world that hasn't existed for a century—if ever—guided by Dort Calvinism and hostile to science. BSK opened in the fall of 2002 with two full-time professors—Greg Earwood as President and Professor of Old Testament and Dalen Jackson as Dean and Professor of New Testament. As Senior Professor of Church History and Spirituality, I taught a full load. Several others taught varying amounts as adjuncts. Initially, classes met in Calvary Baptist Church, but, after two years, the seminary moved to the campus of Lexington Theological Seminary. In 2010 it shifted to the campus of Georgetown College, a major supporter from the start.

It disappointed me, but it did not surprise me that Baptist Seminary of Kentucky did not take off in the way BTSR had. In 1991 BTSR was all by itself; by 2002 there were eleven moderate Baptist schools already in operation. More to the point, BTSR enjoyed enthusiastic support of Baptists in Virginia and along the Atlantic coastline; BSK could count only on a much more restricted constituency in a more conservative and less affluent environment.

Differing Church history requirements in the two seminaries created a small problem when I taught at both BSK and LTS in 2002–03.

---

[16] J.M. Pendleton (1811–91), a pastor in Bowling Green, Kentucky, for a time President of Bethel College in Russellville, Kentucky, and later a professor at Union University in Jackson, Tennessee, established the basic tenets of Landmarkism in his book *An Old Landmark Reset*. The chief target of the Landmarkists was Alexander Campbell, founder of the Disciples.

LTS normally required a one-semester survey of Church history, BSK a two-semester survey. For this year alone LTS students were allowed to take the two-semester survey. Nineteen opted also to enroll in "Introduction to Spirituality." The following year, however, LTS hired its former President and Professor of Church History, William Paulsell, to teach again. Each semester until 2008 I taught one or both segments of Church history and an elective course either in Church history or Spirituality. The list of elective offerings is long: Introduction to Christian Spirituality, Classics of Christian Devotion, Prayer in Christian History, Ministers as Spiritual Guides, Mystics of the Church, Women in Christian History, Early Christian Practices, Theology of Religious Experience, History of Christian Spirituality, and Thomas Merton: His Life, Thought, and Spirituality. Electives usually enrolled numerous auditors. After the employment of a full-time professor of Church history in 2008, I limited my teaching to one elective per semester until 2010, when I did not teach either semester.

Since the Baptist Seminary of Kentucky opened in 2002, Louisville Presbyterian Seminary has not called on me to teach Baptist history. However, I have taught several courses in the MA program in spirituality at Bellarmine University which is jointly offered with Louisville Presbyterian Seminary: Introduction to Thomas Merton (Fall 2004), Prayer in Christian History: An Ecumenical Approach (January 2006), Classics of Christian Spirituality (Fall 2006), and The History of Christian Spirituality (Spring 2009).

The Kentucky Issue

The Baptist situation in Kentucky when I returned in 1999 almost certainly contributed in a major way to the sag in my morale. Moderate or Progressive Baptists held sway in the Baptist General Association of Virginia, so much so that, before I retired, frustrated fundamentalists formed a separate association composed of about a hundred small churches. Churches in Virginia looked to the Baptist Theological Seminary at Richmond or to mainline Protestant seminaries such as Princeton, Duke, or Candler to supply their ministers. The Cooperative Baptist Fellowship drew strong support from the larger churches in Virginia. Baptist colleges and universities hewed the moderate line. Churches and schools in adjoining areas along the Atlantic coast (Maryland, DC, North Carolina, South Carolina, Georgia), even where moderates were not a majority, gave the moderate or progressive cause a strong boost, and I felt at home there as they affirmed me and welcomed me to share their lives and ministries.

Not so Kentucky in 1999. Kentucky is a conservative, economically and educationally challenged state. When a more progressive Southern Seminary channeled young ministers into the state's predominantly small churches, the Kentucky Baptist State Convention showed a progressive face. Since Albert Mohler became president in 1993, however, Southern Seminary has shifted to the extreme theological and political right, and fundamentalists now control the state convention. Kentucky boasts a limited number of churches you might characterize as moderate or progressive by virtue of their relationship to the Cooperative Baptist Fellowship, American Baptist Churches, or other denominations and support of Baptist Seminary of Kentucky or other moderate seminaries. Most "moderate" churches maintain a dual alignment with the SBC and CBF, and only a few have separated completely from the SBC. To avoid radical revamping of its educational mission, Georgetown College, founded in 1829, has had to free itself from convention control by establishing an independent board of trustees. University of the Cumberlands (formerly Cumberland College), once hospitable to moderates, seems now to conform itself as closely as it can to the Southern Baptist Convention's theology and politics. Campbellsville University's situation is less clear, but it did adopt the School of Church Social Work when Albert Mohler severed its connection to Southern Seminary.

As you would expect, my Kentucky Baptist connections and activities fit into this much smaller sphere. On returning to Kentucky in 1999 I had only one Baptist invitation—to teach a class at Crescent Hill Baptist Church in Louisville, where I am a member. In 2000, Crescent Hill groups again called on me several times: to answer the question "Why I Am a Baptist?" (January 6); to lecture to a Sunday school class about Teilhard de Chardin (February 20, 27); and to lead a retreat for an adult class (June 10). First Baptist Church, Frankfort, another moderate congregation and strong supporter of the new seminary, asked me to talk about the role of women as deacons in the early Church (May 10). A retreat center with Baptist connections, Cleft Rock, invited me to lead a retreat (May 19–21).

During that same block of time, I taught "What the Psalms Have to Teach Us about Intimacy with God" in an Academy for Spiritual Formation at Mercy Center in Burlingame, California (January 17–22), led retreats at Immanuel Baptist Church in Greenville, North Carolina (March 16–19), and at Dayspring in Maryland, a retreat center of the Church of the Savior in DC (March 31–April 2). I preached Holy Week services for a Mennonite Association in Mound Ridge, Kansas (April 16–19), gave the Matt Kelty Lecture at Lexington Theological Seminary (April 27), and preached the ordination sermon for Francesca Nuzzolese, a former student at Rüschlikon, at Druid Hills Baptist Church in Atlanta (May 7). I taught in *Sursum Corda*, a spiritual directors program of the Episcopal Diocese of South Carolina (May 21–28) and gave lectures in *Audire*, a Roman Catholic spiritual formation program, at San Pedro Center, Winter Park, Florida (June 1–4). I preached an ordination sermon in Richmond on June 25 and did a workshop at the Cooperative Baptist Fellowship annual meeting in Richmond (June 28–30).

Catho-Baptist or Bapto-Catholic

What happens when you experience rejection and alienation within the church family that gave birth to you, nurtured you, and, for a time, encouraged and took pride in you? Some, I suppose, quietly endure, draw back into themselves, and sometimes even act as if everything was okay, just as you see in natural families. Many go to the opposite extreme by leaving home and never again darkening the door of that family, perhaps even organizing a crusade against it or advocating a radical alternative. You will probably have become aware by this time that I've taken a different approach. The hurt I have suffered in the Baptist family has caused me to keep reaching toward my larger family. I sometimes, only partly in jest, call myself a Bapto-Quakero-Methodo-Presbytero-Lutherano-Episcopo-Catholic. I say "partly in jest," because that designation describes pretty well my actual religious identity, and no phase of my life shows that more clearly than this one where I'm "heading off into the sunset." The Baptist connection has still been there, but my ecumenical family has figured more and more prominently in who I am and how my heart beats. Please keep in mind that you can't fully make sense of what has taken place in my life without recognizing that my larger family kept on embracing me even as deafness diminished my ability to engage them. I have to say, that has just blown me away! They have loved me and used me nevertheless!

I will return to Hinson on his deafness in a final chapter; here, I want to elucidate the ecumenical identity that has imposed itself upon me at this point in my life. I scarcely need to underscore more than I have already the impact the Ecumenical Institute of Spirituality has had on my life and work. I should report here, however, that, after 11 September 2001, the institute changed its focus to a certain extent from inter-*Christian* dialogue to inter*faith* dialogue. Experience with two severe winters in 1998 and 1999 also caused us to shift our meetings to more hospitable months. In 2000 we met at Holy Cross Monastery in Berryville, Virginia, October 12-15 to look in depth at Douglas Steere's summons to "mutual irradiation," letting the light of God in us irradiate others and letting ourselves be irradiated by the light of God in them.[17] Following up on that key concept, in 2001 we dialogued with Muslim and Jewish guests at Holy Spirit Monastery in Conyers, Georgia (October 25–28). In 2002 we explored more deeply the Hasidic tradition of Judaism with the help of Rabbi Arthur Waskow of the Shalom Center at the Cenacle in Highland Park, Maryland (October 17–20). In 2003 EIOS had to cancel a meeting scheduled for Dayspring, the retreat center of the Church of the Savior, at which we planned to explore peace perspectives of Muslims, Jews, and Christians. In 2004, thanks to Father Basil Pennington who had returned from his abbacy at Conyers to his home monastery, EIOS met at St Joseph's Abbey, Spencer, Massachusetts (October 14–17), to discuss its future. Due to increasing diminishment of my hearing, with great sadness, I did not attend this or subsequent meetings. Other members did meet, however, at the Cenacle in Lantana, Florida, in 2006, and at the Cenacle Retreat House in Warrenville, Illinois, in 2007. In the latter, numbers having dwindled to a handful, the members voted to cease face-to-face meetings and to share on-line some of the things usually done in meetings. EIOS had lasted more than forty years, and it had immeasurably graced the lives of many who took part in it.

I'm not sure how to speak about the Quaker gene in my spiritual genome. Although I have not felt a strong pull to become a Quaker, key perceptions of these followers of George Fox have seeped into my soul. Some Friends phrases leap from my lips almost instinctively. Isaac Penington's "There is that near you which will guide you. Oh wait for it,

---

[17] Douglas gave the Richard Cary Lecture at the German Yearly Meeting in Bad Pyrmont, Germany, in 1968. It was published under the title *Mutual Irradiation: A Quaker View of Ecumenism*. Pendle Hill Pamphlet 175 (Wallingford PA: Pendle Hill, 1971).

and be sure ye keep to it."[18] John Woolman's "Love was the first motion."[19] Rufus Jones's "The human heart is sensitive to God as the retina is to light waves." [20] Thomas Kelly's "This amazing simplification comes when we 'center down,' when life is lived with singleness of eye, from a holy Center where the breath and stillness of Eternity are heavy upon us and we are wholly yielded to Him."[21] Above all, the Quaker tradition has become vital to me through living on close terms with Douglas and Dorothy Steere and their daughters, Helen and Anne, spending time at Pendle Hill, centering in Meetings, and sharing peace endeavors.

How Methodism wove its concern to intensify the life of God in the hearts of men and women into my heart and mind stands out more patently in my story. I've jokingly cited two reasons why I have not joined the Methodist Church: (1) I can't sing well enough to be a Methodist. (2) I am a "non-methods" person. I would be remiss, however, if I did not confess that I have identified heart and soul with the Methodist obsession with spiritual growth and development that I see at the heart of the Methodist movement, which puts it also at the center of the whole Christian tradition. To have been invited to play a significant role in endeavors that epitomize Methodism—*Weavings, Companions in Christ*,[22] and the Academy for Spiritual Formation—simply boggles my mind. In the Academy the Quaker and the Methodist traditions "shook hands across the aisle," as it were, for the chief architect of the Academy, Danny Morris, drew on the wisdom of Douglas Steere to design its main features.

Following my retirement, invitations to teach in the Academy or adaptations of it such as the 3-Year Covenant Community ratcheted upward year by year, as a glance at Appendix D will verify. My ministry through the Academy reached its peak in 2002 and 2003, the twentieth anniversary of Academy # 1. In those two years the Academy seems to have become almost a full-time work, as I taught a variety of subjects.

---

[18] Penington, *Works*, III: 520; cited by Douglas V. Steere, *Quaker Spirituality*. Classics of Western Spirituality (New York: Paulist Press, 1984) 29.

[19] *The Journal and Major Essays of John Woolman*, ed. Phillips P. Moulton (New York: Oxford University Press, 1971) 127.

[20] Rufus Jones, *A Call to What Is Vital* (New York: Macmillan, 1948) 140.

[21] Thomas R. Kelly, *A Testament of Devotion* (New York: Harper & Row, 1941) 74.

[22] At Janis Grana's invitation I wrote Part 2: "Feeding on the Word: The Mind of Christ," for *Companions in Christ: A Small-Group Experience in Spiritual Formation* (Nashville: Upper Room Books, 2001) 65–110.

The Nevada/California 5-Day Academy held at Mercy Center in Burlingame, California, concluded on 2 May 2003 with a celebration of the twentieth anniversary of this remarkable enterprise. At the behest of Jerry Haas, the Director[23], I gave a keynote address at a banquet that asked an urgent question I once heard Thomas Merton raise: "What do we have to offer the world the world doesn't already have more of than it needs?" The world has more than it needs of earthly "mannas"—self-indulgence as a right, belief that "a little more" will assure ultimate happiness, and a conviction that violence and terror will solve the world's problems. What it doesn't have more of than it needs is the *living* Bread, the Bread that lasts forever. It is the latter that the Academy seeks to awaken and inspire the faithful and the churches to offer to the world. "The paradox of spiritual formation is: by **nature** *nobody's* able; by **grace** *anybody's* able. It's a matter of the Living Word who tabernacled *among* us coming to tabernacle *in* us and to touch the lives of others *through* us…. Our task is *to be, above all, midwives of grace*."[24]

For the next five years, even as my hearing deteriorated further, Jerry Haas and Academy teams still called on me frequently. A faculty member's experience in two-year academies could never match the life-transforming experience of those who worship together for eight weeks, participate in intimate Covenant Groups, hear carefully prepared lectures on sixteen subjects central to spiritual formation, and nurture deep friendships over two years. Nevertheless, even on those one-week stints as both faculty member and learner, I have found the home and the family I have sought since childhood. Now that the digital age has made communication so easy, I continue significant friendships I first struck up in an academy, some dating back almost to the beginning. I watch with great pride and amazement the way the academy helps some to discover their vocation. Academies come pretty close to achieving what Bernard of Clairvaux wanted Cistercian monasteries to be—*scholae caritatis*, "Schools of Love."

Although Baptists have significant historical linkage to John Calvin and Presbyterians, I owe my much more intimate personal Presbyterian bonds to my daughter Elizabeth and to my wife Martha. Elizabeth

---

[23] Jerry Haas, email message to Glenn Hinson, 26 August 2002.

[24] The address, "Offering the World What It Doesn't Already Have More of Than It Needs," was published online and then under the title "More Than Fast Food" in *Rhythm and Fire: Experiencing God in Solitude and Community,* ed. Cynthia Langston Kirk and Jerry Haas (Nashville: Upper Room Books, 2008) 117–19.

received her theological training at Louisville Presbyterian Seminary (MDiv, 1995) and Union Theological Seminary in Richmond (PhD, 2002). She married a Presbyterian minister, Lee Hasty. Both of them are ordained to Presbyterian ministry. On 13 January 2002, I preached the ordination sermon for both of them at St Andrews Presbyterian College in Laurinburg, North Carolina, where Elizabeth taught and Lee worked in administration. When Martha returned to Louisville in 1995, she did not feel comfortable in a Baptist church and joined Highland Presbyterian Church. Highland's pastor, Jim Chatham, was one of Louisville's most outstanding preachers. Quite often, when I did not have a responsibility elsewhere, I attended Highland with her, and we formed close friendships there. In 2009 Martha joined me at Crescent Hill Baptist Church.

A Lutheran link may be the weakest in the chain that binds me closely to other Christians. You may recall that I attended a Lutheran Sunday School as a four or five year old—hardly enough to leave a deep mark. No modern Christian, even a Roman Catholic, however, can overlook the tremendous debt we owe Martin Luther, all of his faults notwithstanding, for his courageous and faithful testimony which set the reformation of the sixteenth century in motion. For me personally that indebtedness has multiplied many times through the witness of Martin Niemöller, the first pastor dispatched to prison for his criticism of Hitler, and Dietrich Bonhoeffer, martyred because of his role in an effort to assassinate *der Führer*.

My Episcopal identity is much firmer and clearer. A lot of Baptists may fail to recognize it, but the Church of England is our mother church by way of the Puritans. A Baptist joining an Anglican or Episcopal Church is going home. Over many years of ecumenical engagement, I have developed close friendships with Anglicans and Episcopalians that made me feel a part of the same family—Stephen Neill, Bishop of the Church of South India; Robert J. Wright, Professor at General Seminary in New York; David Reed, Episcopal Bishop of Kentucky; Georgine Buckwalter, Chaplain at the Episcopal Church Home of Kentucky and one of the brightest students I ever taught, among many others. By request of Bishop Reed, I preached Georgine's ordination sermon for the Episcopal diaconate. Early in July 2003, Elizabeth Conrad, Minister to Children at Christ Church Cathedral in Lexington, Kentucky, initiated what has evolved into an annual rite. We became acquainted through *Sursum Corda*, the spiritual directors program of the Episcopal Diocese of

South Carolina, in which I began to teach in May 2000. Each year since January 2004, I have delivered a series of four or five lectures to the Adult Forum of Christ Church Cathedral. Each time I lectured, I tried to remain for the morning Eucharist, and I must confess that returning to a Baptist congregation left me feeling unfulfilled spiritually. Baptists speak about the Bible a great deal, but they do not saturate their worship with it in the way the Anglican liturgy does! I understand well why some of my most discerning friends have become Episcopalians. Quite comfortably and proudly in 2003 I preached sermons at the ordination of two former students to the Episcopal priesthood, one a Methodist and the other a Baptist—Ellen White at St Andrews Episcopal Church, Arlington, Virginia (January 25), and Daniel Avery at Bruton Parish Church, Williamsburg, Virginia (January 30). Prior to the latter, I led a retreat for Episcopal ministers in the diocese at Bruton Parish.

Although I am using the word "catholic" in a broader sense, as early Christians used it, to mean "universal," it certainly encompasses the Roman Catholic Church as the chief exemplar. You cannot read my story without recognizing what great riches the Roman Catholic Church has poured into my life through self-consciously reaching out toward me in the grand ecumenical era opened for us by Pope John XXIII (1958–63). I think in some ways the Roman Catholic Church has engaged during this era in a search for the true meaning of the word "catholic," and I have found myself pulled into that quest. I know that Thomas Merton was on such a search. As he evolved from what he called a "ghetto Catholic" mentality to an "expansive Catholicism" that looked beyond Christianity toward unity with persons of other faiths and with humankind,[25] so too have I evolved from a "ghetto Baptist" mentality of Cave Spring Landmark Missionary Baptist Church toward the same kind of "expansive Catholicism." Echoing the Apostle Paul, Merton said, "To be truly Catholic is not merely to be correct according to an abstractly universal standard of truth, but also and above all to be able to enter into the problems and joys of all, to understand all, to be all things to all men."[26] He could go further. "If I affirm myself as a Catholic merely by denying all that is Muslim, Jewish, Protestant, Hindu, Buddhist, etc., in the end I will find that there is not much left for me to affirm as a

---

[25] See E. Glenn Hinson, "Expansive Catholicism: Merton's Ecumenical Perceptions," *Religion in Life*, 48 (Spring 1979) 63–76.

[26] Thomas Merton, *Conjectures of a Guilty Bystander* (New York: Doubleday Image Books, 1966) 185.

Catholic: and certainly no breath of the Spirit with which to affirm it."[27]
He would exclude those who narrowly defined the word.

> The 'Catholic' who is the aggressive specimen of a ghetto Catholic
> culture, limited, rigid, prejudiced, negative, is precisely a non-Catholic, at
> least in the cultural sense. Worse still, he may be anti-Catholic in the
> cultural sense and perhaps even, in some ways, religiously, without
> realizing it.[28]

You can see here why I embraced Thomas Merton as "my brother,"
and perhaps also why some "ghetto Baptists" could not abide me. My
ties with Roman Catholics have strengthened through my relationship
with Bellarmine University, where my daughter Elizabeth is Associate
Professor of Theology. Besides teaching there, each semester for a
number of years I have been invited to speak about Merton in
Bellarmine's Elderhostel program. I'm bound to the Roman Catholic
Church through my "brother" Thomas Merton.

Baptist Still But

Alienation from some Baptists and focus on my ecumenical family
should not lead to the assumption that all Baptists turned away from me.
Baptists have honored me far more than I deserve during my sunset
years. In 2002, with the help of the Academy for Spiritual Formation, the
Advent Spirituality Center established the E. Glenn Hinson Institute for
Spiritual Formation. My former colleagues at Southern Seminary, Loyd
Allen and Karen Smith, gave the first set of lectures at Furman
University 10–15 June 2002. Professor Smith subsequently published an
evolved form of her lectures and dedicated the fine book to me.[29]
Stephanie Ford and I delivered the second set at Mars Hill College 7–12
June 2004. She spoke about spiritual disciplines. I used a part of my life
story to illustrate the working of grace in my own life. The National
Association of Professors of Religion celebrated my contribution to
spirituality in a *Festschrift* edited by Loyd Allen.[30] *Review and Expositor*
took note of my contribution to Patristic studies in another *Festschrift*

---

[27] Ibid., 144.

[28] Thomas Merton, *Seeds of Destruction* (New York: Macmillan, 1967) 187–88.

[29] Karen E. Smith, *Christian Spirituality* (London: SCM Press, 2007).

[30] *Perspectives in Christian Spirituality: Essays in Honor of E. Glenn Hinson*, ed. Wm.
Loyd Allen *Perspectives in Religious Studies* 31 (Spring 2004).

edited by Steven R. Harmon,[31] and named me Editor Emeritus. On 27 June 2007, the Cooperative Baptist Fellowship honored me with a banquet called "Bountiful Feast" at the annual meeting in Washington, DC, announcing the establishment of an E. Glenn Hinson Scholarship to encourage Baptists to attend the Academy for Spiritual Formation. Nothing could have gratified or honored me more than to see evidence of a growing relationship between the CBF and United Methodists. On 6 and 7 March 2009, Baptist Seminary of Kentucky honored my fifty years of teaching with an "E. Glenn Hinson Day" and the establishment of an E. Glenn Hinson Lectureship. At the request of Greg Earwood I gave the first two lectures. A group of forty also went with me to the Abbey of Gethsemani, where the monks had prepared a special luncheon in my honor.

Baptists also honored me by continuing to call on me to teach. Although I had to decline an invitation from Hong Kong Baptist Theological Seminary to spend the academic year 2002–03 in Hong Kong, I delivered the Belote Lectures there on 28 January–1 February 2002. Under sponsorship of the Alliance of Baptists, on 10–14 March 2003, I gave a series of lectures on Thomas Merton at the Protestant Seminary in Matanzas, Cuba, spoke about contemplation to a group of students from the University of Havana, and met with a group of ministers in Havana. Perhaps it is symbolic of how my life has turned out that a mission group from Candler School of Theology visited the seminary at Matanzas the same week! In the Oxford Young Scholars Program at Regent's Park College, Oxford, in July 2006, I gave a keynote lecture urging these aspiring Baptist scholars to view their tradition in line with the mainstream of Christianity rather than fundamentalism.

Baptist churches called on me extensively to lecture, preach, and lead retreats. In Kentucky invitations originated from churches supportive of the Baptist Seminary of Kentucky. Outside of Kentucky they came from churches affiliated with the Alliance of Baptists or the Cooperative Baptist Fellowship or Baptists outside the Southern Baptist sphere. I was called on to address a variety of subjects relative to church history or to spirituality.

When I have related my exilic story, I've often had people ask, "Why do you remain a Baptist? Why don't you join us?" My facetious reply has usually been, "Because I would feel guilty to desert so many I

---

[31] *Patristic Retrieval and Baptist Renewal: In Honor of E. Glenn Hinson*, ed. Steven R. Harmon (*Review & Expositor* 101 (Fall 2004).

have infected with my 'heresies.'" A more carefully considered response would be this: I have thought about it often, and many facets of faith I see represented by other traditions attract me. Yet from my broken childhood family days and from my broken church family days on, I have had a "pleasing dream," like William Carey's, that some day humankind would live at one with one another, and that Baptists, even Southern Baptists, would recognize that they too are a part of the world Christian family and also the world human family. Does that sound quixotic, like tilting at windmills? Perhaps so, but Thomas Merton has given me some grounds for thinking it is not. "If I can unite *in myself* the thought and the devotion of Eastern and Western Christendom, the Greek and the Latin Fathers, the Russians with the Spanish mystics," he wrote, "I can prepare in myself the reunion of divided Christians."[32] I could move to another denomination, but I would still be a Baptist and take the Baptist tradition with me. By remaining, I perhaps encourage others to see themselves in union with the whole Body of Christ. I pray that is true.

---

[32] Thomas Merton, *Conjectures of a Guilty Bystander* (Garden City NY: Doubleday Image Books, 1968) 21.

26

NO MOANING AT THE BAR

I've spoken often about my deafness because, since age 27, it has been a major part of my story. Please do not think I have given it so much attention in order to attract sympathy. Depending on its severity, it's an awful handicap. It sets limits to what you can do or how well you can do it. But I don't want any moaning at the bar because I have suffered deafness. Truth to tell, I have learned some critical lessons about living because I have had to cope with deafness. The author of Hebrews is right, we learn obedience through what we suffer, just as the Pioneer and Perfecter of our faith did (Heb 5:8). Actually, in my view, we do more than learn obedience. We take our relationship with God to a deeper level as we learn to live with our vulnerabilities, whatever they may be. How should we think about such diminishments as deafness?

There are some who would say, "It's the will of God." "I believe God causes everything," Neo-Calvinist Albert Mohler, my former student and President of Southern Seminary, declared when he was on the verge of dying from blood clots in his lungs a couple of years ago. I would have to admit that one might find some biblical support for that kind of determinism in, for example, Old Testament texts about God's hardening of Pharaoh's heart (Ex 7:3, 13). It's simple logic, but it leads to devastating conclusions about God as the cause of the deaths of 68 million people in World War II, tsunamis, earthquakes, floods wiping out hundreds of thousands of lives, etc. How could anyone with a modicum of human sensitivity believe in such a god? I could not.

I can understand that deeply devout persons might want to know where God fits into the picture when the intolerable and unthinkable happen. The psalmists certainly did that aplenty. Their wrestling with such questions arose out of the covenant idea. God entered into this covenant with his people, and they had a right to expect something from God just as God had a right to expect something of them. That is the perspective behind John Milton's "Sonnet on His Blindness." One can hear in the background Calvin's concept of the sovereignty of God, but

Milton's experience of vulnerability tempers the harshness of it. Milton argued with God like the psalmists did.

> When I consider how my light is spent
> Ere half my days, in this dark world and wide,
> And that one talent, which is death to hide,
> Lodged with me useless, though my soul more bent
> To serve therewith my Maker, and present
> My true account, lest He, returning, chide:
> "Doth God exact day labor, light denied?"
> I fondly ask; but Patience, to prevent
> That murmur, soon replies, "God doth not need
> Either man's work, or His own gifts; who best
> Bear His mild yoke, they serve Him best.
> His state
> Is kingly. Thousands at His bidding sped,
> And post o'er land and ocean without rest;
> They also serve who only stand and wait."[1]

Milton does not blame God for his blindness. He wants, instead, to know what God expects of him. The answer comes back that they "who best bear [God's] mild yoke, they serve [God] best." No whining; quiet acceptance of one's circumstance is the right attitude. "They also serve who only stand and wait."

I don't think I agree with Milton's assertion, "God doth not need either man's work, or [God's] own gifts." That is a typical scholastic assumption, but it does not recognize fully the two-sidedness of this covenant. Truer to the biblical idea is a declaration by the great fourteenth-century "social mystic" Catherine of Siena: "God needs me as much as I need God." Her assertion shocked me the first time I read it, but on much longer reflection I could see how compelling her logic is. Why does God need us frail and fragile mortals? "Because you have fallen in love with what you have made!"[2] God, too, possessed of infinite compassion, chose vulnerability. And in that vulnerability God can enter fully into our human lot—the very truth Paul learned which has come

---

[1] John Milton, "Sonnet on His Blindness," *1000 Quotable Poems: An Anthology of Modern Verse*, comp. Thomas Curtis Clark, and Esther A. Gillespie (New York: Harper & Brothers, 1937) 1:6.

[2] Catherine of Siena, *The Dialogue*, trans. Suzanne Noffke, Classics of Western Spirituality (New York: Paulist Press, 1980) 325.

home to me. What should have comforted Milton is that God was with him in his blindness. What comforts me is that God is with me in my deafness or whatever else I confront in life. "My grace is sufficient, for my power is perfected in your vulnerability" (2 Cor 12:9).

Let me assert quite bluntly that I do not believe God caused either my loss of hearing or my loss of speech. An explanation of my speech problems is quite simple: I wore myself down physically as I undertook to teach a full load in church history while completing my dissertation in New Testament. Not *God* but *I* must take responsibility for irresponsibility, at least for failure to weigh my limitations.

Explaining deafness is more challenging and complicated. A lot of things contributed to it, none of which points the finger at God. (1) Since my maternal grandmother and my mother suffered hearing loss, genetic factors undoubtedly set some odds against normal hearing. The odds may not have been very high, for my grandmother was the only one of nine children in her family to experience deafness and my mother the only one of four children to do so. I guess the odds may have increased, but I am thankful that neither of my own children has encountered hearing problems. (2) Perhaps connected to some genetic deficiency, I experienced terrible earaches as a child due to infections and had no medical care except Oil of Cloves heated and poured into the ear. For that you can blame rural poverty, living miles from medical help with no convenient transportation except human or animal legs. (3) During the summer between my junior and senior years at Washington U, I did the mandatory six-weeks of anti-aircraft training for the Reserve Officers Training Corp at Fort Bliss, Texas. Before going, I passed a physical that included a hearing test. Today, the army takes care to provide earphones for people exposed to the firing of anti-aircraft batteries. In 1953 the cadre of officers simply cautioned us to put our fingers in our ears when the guns fired, hardly an adequate safeguard. When you were the gunner, moreover, you could not put your fingers in your ears! From this distance it is difficult to recall possible evidence of diminished hearing when I returned from Fort Bliss, but I can remember one incident. One of our professors in political science required our class to attend a lecture by a noted jurist, take notes, and write a summary of his argument. I found that a challenging assignment because I sat a number of rows from the speaker and had to strain to hear what he said. (4) At Southern Seminary, long before I began to teach in 1959, I can think of a few telltale signs that my hearing was fading. When I talked to Martha by phone during our long year of courtship (1955–56), I frequently had to shift the phone from my left ear to my right ear so as to hear more clearly. Typically, I did not let this alarm me but found some rationale such as the noisy phone booth we all had to use in Mullins Hall. When I took my preliminary exams in 1959, diminishment of my hearing was probably helping me to shut the world out as I concentrated on writing my essays. In the middle of the last exam, one of my fellow students almost shouted to get my attention, "Glenn, let's take a break! Haven't you heard us speaking to you the last five minutes?" (5) Soon after I started teaching New Testament, I could no longer ignore the signs of hearing loss, for I knew I could not hear student questions or comments clearly.

Where was God in all of that? Hear me clearly: *God was not causing my hearing loss.* The closest God would come to the cause would be in creating (and the world is still in process) a world in which deafness happens. God surely does not go around bestowing normal hearing on one person and denying it to another. Having said that, however, let me go on to assert this sincere conviction: *God has been with me all the way, even though I have often been incognizant of God's presence and inattentive to God.* May I footnote that with a more documentable assertion: *I'm a fortunate person indeed to have lived through an era when science and technology have taken giant steps to help people with deafness, as well as many other life-limiting debilities.*

Permit me, therefore, to speak of grace abounding in my four-score years so that I was not rendered useless or could only stand and wait! Looking at life from the bright side, I do not feel compelled to whine about what has happened, for I'm the beneficiary of grace greater than all the things that would deny my realization of God's intention for my life. If we are to justify God's involvement in the surd and the absurd of human life, we have to allow for some ironic twists and turns. How you handle your vulnerabilities in life depends to a great extent on the attitude you bring to them. You can throw up your hands in despair from the word go and be overwhelmed. "What can I do?" Or you can recognize that, no matter how difficult your challenge, help will come from somewhere and do your darndest.

The story of Joseph conveys powerfully the truth Paul summed up in Romans 8:28. As I would prefer to translate, "We know that in everything God is working together for good with those who love God, who are called according to [God's] purpose." You know the story.

Jealous brothers connived to get rid of Jacob's pet. Initially they plotted to kill him. As they waited to carry out their vile deed, a slavers caravan happened along, so, opting for money over murder, they sold him to the slavers, who hauled him to Egypt and sold him. They covered their tracks with Jacob by bringing him Joseph's multicolor coat soaked in lamb's blood. In the service of Pharaoh, Joseph rose to power. In the meantime, famine forced the clan to go to Egypt to survive. Irony of ironies, whom should they have to deal with in their plight but the brother they thought they had rid themselves of once and for all? First making them pay a little sweat equity by ordering them to bring Benjamin to Egypt, Joseph forgave them with this paradoxical observation: "Even though you intended to do harm to me, God intended it for good" (Gen 50:20). With malice aforethought they, not God, perpetrated an evil, or perhaps two or three evils. Who can say how God did it, but God turned a rank, rotten shenanigan into something good—saving not only Joseph's life but also the lives of the very kin who tried to do him in.

I think it is appropriate to speak in a similar way in regard to my lifelong battle with deafness. Some might call it coincidence, but I prefer to think that God worked together with me to make something good out of what is in itself bad. Although I had nothing to do with choosing when I would live, my span of life has put at my disposal wonderful advantages for coping with deafness. Consider the more limiting circumstances of Walter Rauschenbusch (1862–1918). Diminishment of hearing forced this powerful voice for social justice to give up his much loved pastoral ministry in "Hell's Kitchen" in New York City. He and his people did not want that, but he knew deafness would limit his ministry to them. Teaching at Colgate-Rochester Seminary, he could have a student stand by his desk and relay the questions to him. The only technology available to aid him was an ear trumpet. By my maternal grandmother's day (18811970) hearing aids had advanced to small radio speakers with wires that plugged into one ear to amplify sound. Grandma Crow carried the radio suspended in front of her by a ribbon around her neck. My mother (1902–1965) refused to use (or perhaps could not afford to buy) one of those until very late in her life, and then only to care for a grandson for a short time.

Incredible advances in my life span have changed the situation of muted persons from night to day. Although well aware of their shortcomings, I sing praises of science and technology as instruments of grace. By the time my deafness required assistance in 1959, science and technology had designed behind-the-ear aids that forced air into the ear to amplify sound. My first hearing aid was embarrassingly large, bigger than my ears. Year by year, however, hearing aids got smaller and more powerful, some small enough to fit within the ear canal. My deafness soon became too severe for me ever to use an in-the-ear aid, but behind-the-ear aids got small enough that they became almost invisible when I let my hair grow over the ear.

As my deafness progressed, the grace of human sensitivity augmented the grace of science and technology. Martha, Chris, Elizabeth, friends, students, colleagues, and acquaintances made allowances. Often they went the second mile to keep from embarrassing me. In 1995, Morton Kelsey, Episcopal priest and Jungian analyst, noticed at a meeting of the Ecumenical Institute of Spirituality that I was having increasing trouble hearing because I had to cross the room to hear what someone with a soft voice said. A hearing-impaired person himself, he took me aside to say, "Glenn, I have a 'friend' who makes money available for ministers to buy the new *Resound* hearing aids (the first digital aids). Would you write to me about it?" The "friend," Morton himself, sent me $3,000 to buy my first digital hearing aids.

I soon discovered that *Resound* had a major limitation; it did not permit one to hear in a noisy crowd. A lot of noise just shut it down. Further medical advances soon came to my aid, however. I went to an otolaryngologist in Richmond to see if a stapedectomy might alleviate some bone deafness; after testing then available, he said no. As I have related earlier, deafness was threatening to put me out of commission entirely. I scarcely heard any of the kind words spoken about me at my retirement fest. When I returned to Louisville in 1999, I went to another otolaryngologist, Mark Severtson, to get a second opinion. He tested me in the same way and reached the same conclusion as the Richmond ENT. Fortunately, a Louisville audiologist fitted me with new digital hearing aids, Widex *Senso*, which increased my hearing markedly even in a crowd. By 2008, however, what little remained of my hearing had dwindled again nearly to the vanishing point. In some frustration, I went to the Heuser Institute in Louisville, where I learned about a still more recent marvel of science and technology—cochlear implants. By happy chance, they sent me to Mark Severtson for testing. This time, when Severtson examined my hearing, he had a new technology for measuring the amount a stapedectomy would improve my hearing by 35 to 50 percent! In April 2009 I had microsurgery on my left ear, in September on my right ear. If my hearing deteriorates further, I may still need to have the cochlear implant, but hope beams at me out there on the horizon. We humans can survive without many things, but we cannot survive without hope.

You can see here that I'm asking you to wrestle with one of the most critical questions a believer has to ask: *Where is God when we have to pass through the dark valleys of life? When we become a Job?* I reject emphatically the deterministic and fatalistic idea that God causes everything, whether good or bad, for some mysterious reasons we may never understand. That image of God is surely not the one we gain from the *Abba/Eema* Jesus spoke about in his parable of the Loving Father (Luke 15:11-32). That father permitted the prodigal to leave home and to waste everything he possessed in profligate living. As a parent, I can readily imagine the pain he suffered when he watched his immature child depart. Yet I know, too, as a parent that he never gave up. Day or night, his thoughts kept beaming down the road on which his son had gone away, and when at last that misguided young man "came to himself" and headed home, this loving father saw him "from afar" and went out to meet him. He raced down the road to throw his arms around him and take him back not as a *servant*, all the prodigal could expect, but as a *son*! Note that the son could not get out the whole spiel he had resolved to speak, "Make me one of your hired hands," before the father directed the servants to clad him in the finest robe, put a ring on his finger, shoes on his feet, and prepare a feast, for "this, my son, has come home."

The story of the prodigal son's return is so captivating that we often gloss over the one about the father's treatment of the pouty elder brother who refused to come in the house to join the celebration for the return of the prodigal. He had good reason to feel resentful. He had stayed home and faithfully discharged the duties of a son. Evidently no one thought to call him from the field, for when he neared the house and heard music and dancing, he had to ask a serving woman, "What's going on here?" She told him, and that just burned him up. He wouldn't go in. He sulked outside. He seethed. Once again, this loving father went out to meet him. When he did, the exemplary brother poured out his sizzling resentment and anger. Can't you visualize it? "All these years I have worked my fanny off, and never once have you so much as killed a baby goat so I could celebrate with my friends." An ordinary father would have turned around and slammed the door in his face. But this was not your typical father. He spoke gently, as to a child. He changed the word, "Child, everything I have is yours. But I had to do this, because this your *brother* has come home." God is a God of infinite compassion!

My encounter with God forces me to wrestle here with a much wider issue than my own deafness as I look back on my life. It compels me to ask: *How* was this God of infinite love Jesus embodied present in the midst of the sad lives of my parents, their lives so scarred by alcoholism and so crushed by poverty? How was this God of infinite love present in the midst of my brother Gene's life, thrust into the world so young, ensnared by alcoholism, and then so early snuffed out? To come closer to home, how has this God of infinite love been present in the life of my son, his promise curtailed by a bi-polar disorder, as he watches everything turn golden for his younger sister?

Chris is very gifted. He did all of the course work for a PhD in Syro-Palestinian archaeology at the University of Chicago. When his major professor succumbed to cancer, he opted out with an MA and, after a couple of years in a quandary, he entered a PhD program at Baylor University in biblical studies. Delayed along the way by his battle with depression, he received his degree in 2002, the same year Elizabeth completed her PhD at Union Theological Seminary in Richmond. He taught as an adjunct professor at the University of Louisville for several years, but his health problems kept him from gaining a permanent position. Two years in a research position for a Louisville company proved too stressful. Elizabeth, meanwhile, taught at St. Andrews Presbyterian College in Laurinburg, North Carolina, for several years and in 2004 became the first woman and first Protestant to teach theology at Bellarmine University in Louisville. She has published several books. In 2009 she was granted tenure and promoted to associate professor. She has received awards for her teaching and plays a significant role in the Presbyterian Church. As I write these words, she is teaching in Hungary on a Fulbright grant. She and Lee have two lovely children—Garrison Douglass and Emme, ages ten and four.

I hope I'm not being brash in thinking that Martha and I have experienced in microcosm what our compassionate heavenly Parent must confront in macrocosm. In 2010 Chris had to give up his research job after suffering a heart attack at age 46. He is not married and has lived with us since he completed his work at Baylor. Since his heart attack, we have had to pay for his health insurance ($460 a month) and his medications, which are exceptionally costly for mental illnesses

($600–750 a month). Add that to the fact that Martha and I now pay Mutual of Omaha nearly $800 a month for supplemental insurance for Medicare, and you can see that medical costs alone consume a huge part of any income we may have. On top of that, however, we have to repay two loans, much of which resulted from Chris's reckless buying, a typical "sin" of severely depressed persons. Buying makes bi-polar persons feel better momentarily; in the long run, it will heap depression on top of depression.

Martha and I love both of our children. We love them with all of the love we are capable of generating. But you can see here that Chris's neediness forces us to act preferentially toward him. Elizabeth and her family fare well on the salaries she and Lee earn, but they have times when they could use some help. We do not have enough additional income, however, to balance what we must, of necessity, expend for Chris or else see him end up as a homeless person. We aren't being fair. We can't be fair without abandoning the person who has the most urgent need. And I'm sure Elizabeth must have moments when she would like to rage at her parents like the elder brother did. We feel a lot of pain.

My own deep pain as a parent burst like a dam about five years ago when I met with a group of American Baptist ministers in Indianapolis to direct them for a year in a spiritual formation program. Just before I left for the first meeting, Chris told me, "Dad, I think I am going to have to take disability." I responded, "Well, if you need to, you should." Throughout the hundred-mile drive to meet with this group, the inequity of my and his career stories kept whirling around in my head and heart. So much in my life had turned up roses. It seemed as if I just stumbled along and, for no explainable reason, wonderful things happened. Here, my son, like my brother, with so much ability, strove to do something he loved, but this terrible mental and emotional disorder rumbled like a rockslide down a mountainside to block his path. When I gathered with this small group of ministers, I wanted to let them know about my emotional fragility. As I told them of my conversation with Chris, I broke down and sobbed. Some must have wondered, "What have we gotten ourselves into?" They had to minister to me before I could provide spiritual direction to them.

Underneath all of this is that urgent question of theodicy. What is God doing in a world so full of disorder, inequity, catastrophe, and, yes, downright evil? What is God doing in a world where tsunamis, earthquakes, and floods snuff out hundreds of thousands of lives?

Richard Dawkins and other atheists would respond, "See. That proves God doesn't exist, that God is a delusion."[3] Even if I concede that they have a point, what I learn from revelation and from my own experience in life cause me to put my money on the reality of the Mysterious Other in the midst of life. What I have had to give up is the idea that God directs everything down to the way my fingers hit these keys on my iMac. God's Almightiness, in my view, has to do with God as the Alpha and the Omega, directing all things toward some meaningful end. What that end will be, none of us can say. Maybe even God can't say, for it's all unfolding step by step under the eye of the Almighty. In the meantime, God works through weakness and suffers as the whole created order groans in birth pangs, awaiting its consummation (Rom 8:22). In place of God as impervious to what we humans experience, I have to make room in my thinking for a vulnerable God of infinite compassion who has chosen to share fully our human lot, yes, the pain of becoming human. What else does the Jesus story tell us?

That God is the compassionate parent of Jesus' parable is what I choose on the basis of revelation to *believe*, not something I can *prove*. It's a conviction I share with the psalmist. "Even though I walk through the darkest valley, I fear no evil, for you are with me; your rod and your staff—they comfort me" (Psalm 23:4–5). I've cited in an earlier chapter a deep insight in Paul's letter to the Philippians that seems so close to what I have learned about the working of grace in our lives. "Work out your own salvation with fear and trembling," he said, "for it is God who is at work in you to give both the motive and the ability to do what pleases God" (Phil 2:12–13; my translation). In the first part Paul seems to aver that we are on our own. God does not hold us on a short leash. Like a wise parent, God does not stand just behind us, looking over our shoulder, ready to yank us back from mistaken desires and actions. We are free, and freedom mandates a responsible approach to life. Taking responsibility is scary, approached "with fear and trembling." A lot of times it overwhelms fragile human beings.

But notice the paradoxical addition, "For God is at work in you to give both the motive and the ability to do what pleases God." "For" (Greek *gar*) connected this inseparably with the first statement—about acceptance of responsibility. It is so important to see that we are not alone. How well we make it in living this responsible life depends, too,

---

[3] Richard Dawkins, *The God Delusion* (Boston and New York: Houghton Mifflin, 2006).

on the fact that God is at work in us. Note, please, what that does *not* say. It does *not* say that God will make your decisions for you. God has given you a mind and a heart to do that. God will not take control of your every thought and deed. God is not a heavenly Zapper! What does God being at work in us do? It gives us (1) motive and (2) ability to do what pleases God. That is grace, Augustine's *donum superadditum*! This does not support determinism or fatalism. Early Christians fought that debilitating outlook among both Greeks and Romans, their fear of *heimarmene* or *fortuna*, "fate." Early Christian apologists especially differentiated Christian "philosophy" from competing philosophies on that critical point. Augustine produced the ultimate response in his classic *City of God*, which he took thirteen years to write. In the modern day, Teilhard de Chardin has expressed the Pauline and Augustinian outlook in relation to an evolutionary model.

As I reflect on my handling of family-related issues and the diminishment of deafness, you may wonder how I face life's ultimate diminishment—death. The prospect of dying confronted me dramatically in late 2010. On September 20, a Monday, I was walking my son's dog, holding the leash in my left hand. My hand suddenly went limp. It wouldn't respond to my brain's signals. When I got home, I told my son, "Chris, I think I may be having a stroke." I had to drive to a drugstore to get it, but I took a 325 mg aspirin, sat down at this keyboard and typed. The hand recovered in about two hours, but my son immediately made an appointment with our internist. The earliest he could see me was Friday morning. When I related my curious experience, he put his stethoscope on my carotid arteries and scheduled immediately a visit to the hospital's lab to have a sonogram of the arteries. During the exam, the technician asked, "Do you ever get dizzy?" I replied, "No. Not in my entire life." But I worried. The result: 90 percent blockage. When the technician relayed that information to my physician, he immediately sent me to a vascular surgeon. The surgeon operated on the right carotid artery on October 12, on the left November 8. He told Martha after the second surgery that the arteries were almost completely blocked. I think that I narrowly missed a massive stroke like the one that claimed my father's life at age 65. I've hallelujahed non-stop from the time I awakened from surgery.

I wrote a blog for *Weavings* on the eve of the first surgery that reflects my faith perspective on this life and death moment. I quote it here:

How Much Faith Life Demands

I can't eat supper or even drink any liquids this evening because I will undergo surgery for removal of plaque from my right carotid artery at 9:00 a.m. tomorrow, October 12, 2010. That is serious surgery. My vascular surgeon says that there is only 2% risk of failure, but I know that the delicacy of an operation on a vessel that supplies blood to my brain doesn't leave much room for even a small miscalculation or error. What it has caused me to think about fourteen hours from the surgery is how much faith, pure naked trust, human life demands.

I don't know Dr. Klamer, the surgeon. Oh, I've met him and liked the straightforward way he spoke. He and his associate gave me clear information about what is going to happen. But I'm trusting my personal physician's recommendation of a colleague in the same hospital, and I'm trusting the hospital and the whole medical community in the city of Louisville, which has an excellent reputation. Is that enough given the desperate need I have for the surgery?

I don't think so, at least not for me. Something as serious as this, however needful, forces me to find within myself a deeper level of faith than I find in medical savvy and institutional reputation. I need God, beyond in our midst. I'm at peace about this because I've learned how to let myself down like a swimmer letting down to trust the buoyancy of the water. The saints through the ages remind me that we live in a sea of love and if I will let myself down into its waters, the waters of grace will hold me up. I've lived a long and grace-filled life. Should I end up among the 2%, I can only say thanks for this inexpressible gift of life that has been mine.

Teilhard de Chardin has helped me to come to this perspective on dying. In *The Divine Milieu* he said, "We must overcome death by finding God in it. And by the same token, we shall find the divine established in our innermost hearts, in the last stronghold which might have seemed able to escape [God's] reach."[4] I have come to think about dying as stepping off into the sea of love and light that God is. God is Love. God is Light. God is Spirit. We need not fear, for God is there just as God is in our midst now.

About a year ago I was asked to do a series of articles on Art of the Resurrection. Artists did not try to depict the resurrection of Jesus until the Renaissance, and they preferred the story of Doubting Thomas in John 20. Caravaggio, one of the key shapers of Renaissance realism,

---

[4] Teilhard de Chardin, *The Divine Milieu* (New York: Harper & Row, 1960) 82.

depicted Thomas thrusting his finger into Jesus' wounded side. Rembrandt van Rijn, however, boldly attempted to depict resurrection from Paul's account in 1 Corinthians 15, where Paul explicitly repudiated those who interpreted resurrection as resuscitation of a corpse. A tragedy, the death of his beloved son Kashia in 1662, inspired Rembrandt to depart from the realism of his mentor Caravaggio toward impressionism. In his *Resurrection*, the Risen Christ has a recognizably human body with angels' wings. However, it is more like the majestic Christ, the Pantocrator, of Byzantine mosaics than the muscular, body-perfect specimens you see in Renaissance paintings. Nevertheless, it is not the human form with angels' wings that catches your eye so much as the eye-blinding light that explodes and bursts behind and all around the Risen One. The Resurrection is an explosion, "a big bang," that gives us a glimpse in time of the power of God to salvation. "God Almighty! God Almighty!" So powerful is the explosion, that it turns the whole surrounding order upside down. The Risen One seems to be ripping away a part of the tomb that had held him. Vague figures, some looking like Roman soldiers, hurtle heels over hind end into the darkness, into a jumble of disarray and disorder. Resurrection is about God's re-creation. So Paul in 2 Corinthians 5:17: "And so if anyone is in Christ, there is a new creation. Old things have passed away. Behold! All things have become new!" That's resurrection.

I will doubtless confirm the suspicions of those inerrantists who did their best to get me out of Southern Seminary, but I don't spend a lot of time thinking about the afterlife in images taken from the book of Revelation. The universe we visualize today does not permit us to think, as ancient people did, of a flat earth with heaven "up there" and hell "down there," and the sun, moon, and stars dangling from the firmament. Physicists report that our sun is one of millions of suns in our galaxy and our galaxy (the Milky Way) is one of more than 150 billion galaxies. Given such a cosmic picture, it makes more sense to me to say that when we die, we participate more fully in God's life than we could while "in the flesh." I realize that I say this in faith because many biologists would insist that souls cannot exist apart from bodies. Could we say in faith anyway that our souls are love energies that animate our bodies while we live? When we die, we add our love energies to those love energies by which God directs the universe toward some ultimately meaningful end? Thence, we would not cease our work on earth but continue our partnership with God to see that God's kingdom might come and God's will be done on earth as in heaven. With this cosmic perspective I confess further that I worry more about the world I'm leaving behind for my children and grandchildren than I do about heaven or hell.

CONCLUSION

THE TOP TEN THINGS
MY LIFE HAS TAUGHT ME

In the Preface to this book I said that I dared to undertake this audacious task with the conviction that others might learn something from hearing my story. In this Conclusion I will try to offer you some help in the learning process by enumerating, as I view it, the top ten things my long life has taught me.

1. At the head of the list of things my life has taught me is that *life is grace, given to me more than planned, earned, or achieved by me*. My parents gave me the gift of life, brought me into the world, nurtured me as well as they could, and equipped me with some of the gifts and skills I needed to benefit from and contribute to this world. When my birth family floundered, ordinary saints in my extended human family noticed my need, scratched around in the soil of my soul, and kept me alive and growing in grace. As hard as I tried to live by my mother's dictum "never owe anyone anything, and you'll have your pride," I would badly distort my story to claim that I made it on my own by sheer grit. The longer and more carefully I look back on my four-score years, the more my heart aches to express my most sincere thanks to every person, every church, every institution, every community, and, yes, every thing that opened floodgates of grace to enable a little red-headed, freckle-faced boy reared in the Missouri Ozarks to live a life that mattered. You will readily recognize that I cannot say "Thank you!" to all humankind for those touches of grace, but I can express unbounded thanks to God for all of them in the confidence and hope that God may convey retroactively and prospectively the desire of my heart to thank them one and all.

If you have read my story, I may amuse you when I insist that showers of grace have fallen on me in profusion even from Baptists in the American South. A Southern Baptist Church in Cuba, Missouri, first awakened me to the claim of God on my life. Another in the St. Louis suburb of Affton drew me deeper into the search for God and God's more urgent expectations. The Southern Baptist Theological Seminary equipped me with some skills to think about God's mysterious presence in our world and some tools for ministry and challenged me to expect great things from God and to attempt great things for God. Then, by God's grace, my limitations notwithstanding, it hired me and opened the way for me to play a modest role in the Church Universal. Even the "Baptist Holy War" in which I suffered some wounds cannot erase the incredible grace Southern Baptists mediated to me.

2. Living my life with a hearing deficiency has taught me that *you have to play the hand you are dealt, making allowances for your limitations.* I won't encumber the point by repeating what I have said in previous chapters about loss of hearing and of voice. It suffices to reiterate that, more than anything else, I had to learn how to let down like a swimmer letting down into the water to discover the buoyancy that is there. As the saints remind us through the ages, we live in a sea of love. We are surrounded by love. If we will let go, we will discover something or someone who holds us up. God's grace, God's gift of Godself, is sufficient, for God has chosen to share our vulnerability.

Coping with deafness and voice trouble helped me to see not only the tolerance but also the genuine care people exercise toward someone who is vulnerable. I can cite some instances where some were not tolerant and understanding, to be sure, but my students displayed wonderful sensitivity from the beginning down to a year or so ago when I endured ten months with maladjusted hearing aids that virtually precluded my hearing anything at all. Let me confess that pride, ego, or whatever you want to call it has exacerbated the problem of deafness throughout my career. I simply do not want to admit that I don't hear something after someone repeats it once or twice. My first impulse is to nod my head up and down as if I did hear and then watch closely to see if the speaker acts surprised by the answer. Little by little, I started to be up front with classes about my inability to hear, as I experienced acceptance not conditional on my hearing. In recent years I have reminded groups who expected to ask questions or make comments that "I'm as deaf as a doorknob."

3. My life has taught me that God will not slap you in the face with a *calling, one of life's cruxes, and give you absolute clarity as to what you should do with your life.* At Washington University I learned after a year or two of floundering, and hearing professors ask what I intended to do with my life and education besides serve myself, that money and prestige do not supply adequate motives for one's life's calling. Before

thinking about a specific vocation, I discovered, I needed to respond to a general calling that comes to all humankind: "Will you live your life from the vantage point of some higher purpose than self-interest?" I have found true what Augustine prayed at the beginning of his *Confessions*, "You have made us for yourself, to praise you, and our heart is restless until it finds rest in you." Witnessing a video about the impoverished children of India whispered to me: "There *is* something you can do besides serve yourself. You can serve God and others." Getting to this point, however, forced me to face the more complex and urgent question: *How* will you serve God and others? Our current cultural milieu seems to make such a query more of a lifelong and unending conundrum than our forbears found. Whereas many of them expected to spend their entire lives committed to a single vocation, we are likely to shift from one job or role to another any number of times in our active careers. The zigs and zags in my own career trajectory, therefore, should not have caught me by surprise. Whereas I trained myself to teach New Testament, Southern Seminary's circumstances and my gift for languages soon pushed me into Patristics and the specialized training that required. Along the way, my focus on persons brought to the surface another calling within this calling, namely, to do something about spiritual formation of ministers. As it turned out, that grew in urgency as an ecumenical revolution and the world's needs generated vastly different attitudes and perceptions about what ministry required. I look back on all of that with exuberant gratitude.

4. My life has confirmed an insight aptly phrased by Douglas Steere: *"Life's interruptions often turn out to be God's opportunities."* I've experienced a lot of "interruptions" in life. Poverty and lack of understanding and guidance with reference to college kept me from moving from high school directly to college, forfeiting scholarship offers. At the time I may have felt some frustration, but at longer range I think it may have done much to clarify my calling. I grew physically, emotionally, and culturally during that year. When I entered Washington University in the fall of 1950, I was far more ready to undertake the rigors of work and study and developed habits that would serve me well for more advanced study.

The most far-reaching, and potentially the most devastating, "interruption" I've experienced grew out of fundamentalist efforts to remove me from the faculty of Southern Seminary, where I had taught for more than thirty years. In the midst of their attacks, the defunding of the International Baptist Theological Seminary at Rüschlikon, Switzerland, seemed for a time to signal the end of my career. As that door slammed shut, however, another opened wide to permit me to make a more significant contribution to the forming of women and men for ministry than I could ever have done had I remained in a long-established institution. Joining a new endeavor permitted me to help shape a curriculum with a focus on spiritual formation for ministry as the integrative factor in ministers' training. Where previously ministers got grounding in the body of divinity and in skills for ministry, now they would have personal formation older institutions struggled to let creep into their curricula.

5. My life has taught me that *persons matter more than projects*. Many deny this point of view. As a matter of fact, one theory of history says that we are like chips in a stream, carried wherever the current leads. The lives of many saints and the bold actions of Pope John XXIII forcefully challenge such a view. Throughout my long teaching career I did my best to *use subjects to teach persons*. That may seem like a contrived distinction to make, but I learned early on to make students rather than academic peers or ecclesiastical superiors the focus of my attention and found very soon that they were *my* teachers. I dedicated *A Serious Call to a Contemplative Lifestyle* to my students with their gift to me in mind. They raised questions I needed to help them wrestle with. I hope you will not conclude that such an approach led to superficial treatment of my subject, church history. Far from it, it forced me to offer more substantive and creative fare. I owe to students the topic that I made the subject of my DPhil dissertation at Oxford. In the 1960s, highly negative attitudes toward the institutional church were the order of the day. As I contemplated a study that would make a worthy contribution to early Christian scholarship, I decided to tackle the issue of the contribution that institutions—baptism, Lord's Supper, discipline, ministry, and organization—made to the winning of the Roman Empire.

Focusing on students and their questions affected my teaching career in a still more dramatic way. Taking my first class in Church history to the Abbey of Gethsemani in 1960 to introduce them to the Middle Ages had an unanticipated impact, adding a dimension to my career I did not envision. Thomas Merton was our host. Inspired by this encounter and subsequent trips to the Abbey the next two or three semesters, in 1963 I introduced a course on the Classics of Christian Devotion. Twenty-three students took it. A year later I had to offer two sections limited to thirty students each, the next year three sections. Tom Sherwood, the registrar, told me that 157 students were on a list waiting to take it.

I don't want to wear this point out, but perhaps you will permit me to mention that I have taught forty different courses during my career. Some of them were handed down from generation to generation, especially Church history requirements. Most of them, however, grew out of my attention to student questions and concerns. At the doctoral level I offered seminars that helped to prepare students for the writing of their dissertations. In the professional area I offered courses that responded to the growing cry of churches and ministers for spiritual formation. In the summer of 1980, for instance, I offered Prayer in Christian History for the first time. Eighty-four students came from all over the United States to take it.

One last word on this point that has a connection with my growing deafness—I regret deeply that the latter, along with my advanced age, has made it much harder for me to engage students as my teachers. Often, I fear, I have been answering questions nobody is asking. Again, though, I am grateful to all who have patiently tried to communicate with me.

6. Perhaps as a by-product of this person-centered focus in teaching, life has taught me that *the object of education should not be simply information but **formation**.* I anticipate seeing some eyebrows arch upward as I say that, for the Baptist tradition, at least as I construe it, emphasizes the voluntary principle in religion, and formation may sound a bit authoritarian, coercive even. Please observe that I am not calling for **indoctrination**. Insofar as I understand it, *formation* is a far cry from indoctrination. In religious terms it entails helping persons to attain their potential as persons and to bring forth their true self made in God's image. I'm sure there is value in memorizing books of the Bible and Bible verses and learning names, dates, places, and happenings. The same applies to church history. The question is: How does such information equip people to live meaningful and fruitful lives? Thomas Merton framed a question we might put forward as a test of the kind of education I have in mind: What do we have to offer the world that the world doesn't already have more of than it needs?

What the "world," specifically American culture, is glutted with and sated on is evident. It has more than it needs of the conviction that self-indulgence is a right. It has more than it needs of belief that naked power and violence are the solution to political problems. It has more than it needs of the assumption that acquiring a little more will bring the ultimate happiness. Is *in*formation the answer? Will *in*formation enable students, ministers, and churches to offer the world what it doesn't already have more of than it needs? I would have to say, "Heck, no!" Perhaps only partly by design, I have invested a good part of my fifty years of teaching to say that. Actually, I am indebted in great part to the fundamentalists who now run the Southern Baptist Convention for this insight. Had they not run me away from my position as David T. Porter Professor of Church History at Southern Seminary, the conviction would never have matured in my mind!

Lest I give my critics too much credit, I hasten to say that it is Thomas Merton who has helped me to frame an answer to this question. I must be honest to confess that I didn't begin to grasp the significance of what Merton was trying to teach until after his untimely death on 10 December 1968. Feeding the wisdom of the contemplative tradition enriched by engagement with oriental wisdom through his own fertile and creative mind, he put forth a powerful case for contemplation in a world of action. We are still trying to grasp the full significance of what he urged.

7. Life has taught me that *you often have to make decisions on faith without certainty.* Life is not a trip down a superhighway. Along the road of life you will enter into tunnels. Sometimes those tunnels are so long you can't see even a pinprick of light at the other end, and you have to proceed with at least one ear attuned to the voice of the Shepherd, "Lo, I am with you always. Do not be afraid."

Many early life experiences had conditioned me to avoid confrontation, to hold back, and to wait until I was sure. When others declined to respond to the comment by Bailey Smith, President of the Southern Baptist Convention, at the National Affairs Briefing in support of the Reagan candidacy that "God Almighty does not hear the prayer of a Jew," I found myself hemmed in and unable to dodge the issue. More than a little alarmed by the radical shift of American politics to the extreme right, I feared that, unchallenged, such thinking could lead to what happened in Germany during the 1930s when no one spoke out. Already a target of fundamentalist attacks, I could make a long list of reasons not to speak, and I had to agonize for hours over the decision to publish my "Open Letter to Dr. Bailey Smith." Not impulse but long and careful reflection caused me to make a leap of faith very similar to the one I had taken when I decided to live my life from the perspective of a wager that God is. It had some of the same yeses and nos as my decision to ask Martha to marry me, that to join the faculty of Wake Forest University, or that to return to Southern Seminary. Somewhere in the decision-making you have to stop chewing on every corner of the dilemma and act in faith with humble recognition that you may be wrong.

8. My life has taught me *that faith can co-exist with what we learn empirically about the world in which we live*. Faith does not depend on "proof" of God, for God is not an object, a thing, whose existence we can "prove." God is the "I AM." As in the scriptures, we "believe" God is. We take a leap of faith, but once we do, we will engage in an earnest search for understanding (*fides quaerens intellectum*). We will look at the world with new eyes in the confidence that we work together with God to see that God's eternal reign may come and God's will be done on earth as in heaven.

My life has taught me, too, that co-existence does not mean uncritical acceptance of everything science and technology do. Humans have used their knowledge for evil as well as for good, so that science must not be allowed to act autonomously. There is a difference between Wisdom and Knowledge. In the sight of Wisdom everything must serve a higher purpose. One of the most perilous things happening today, as science makes incredible advances, however, is to see people of faith repudiating science or people of science negating faith. Fundamentalist Christians negate a modern scientific worldview and insist on acceptance of a biblical one. Official dogma at Southern Seminary today is that the earth is no more than 7,000 years old, give or take a few years, and it was created in seven days in some sort of cataclysmic process. The result is compartmentalization—religion confined to one sphere and science to another. Jesus and the prophets inveighed against such separation in which religion becomes irrelevant to life.

9. My life has taught me *the importance of openness*. We all require some fundamentals, but we will not benefit from fundamentalism. Fundamentalism is a mentality, "I am right. Only if you agree with me can you be right, Christian, saved, or whatever." Life has convinced me that God, the "I AM," Creator of this universe of 150-plus million galaxies, does not have such limited candlepower that God can only illuminate Southern Baptists, "evangelicals," or even Christians. We can be forgiven perhaps for thinking that others would come closer to the

light if they took our way to God, but we need urgently in this day of tense relations between Christians and Muslims to look with new eyes and listen with new ears to scriptures such as the Gospel of John, which is often cited as an "I gotcha!" "I am the way, the truth, and the life; no one comes to the Father except by me!" (John 14:6). That same Gospel also says, "He was that light coming into the world that enlightens *every person*" (John 1:9). Maybe in John 14:6 it is the Universal Christ who speaks, the Christ who is everywhere—in every culture and in every religion. We should at least be open to read other scriptures that confirm the wideness of God's mercy, such as the Apostle Peter's remarkable discovery, "For I perceive truly that God does not discriminate against persons, for in every nation the person who fears God and acts righteously is acceptable to God" (Acts 10:34–35). Jesus himself seems to have backed up the same perspective when he insisted that the tax collector Zacchaeus was *also* "a child of Abraham, for the Son of Man came to seek and to save what has been lost" (Luke 19:10).

10. Finally, my life has taught me that *wholeness and holiness require transparency and honesty*. In this memoir I've done my level best to be transparent. I spent the early years of my life trying to wear an image I thought people wanted to see. I kept others at arms length lest they see my faults or become aware of my vulnerabilities. I never let any of my fellow students at Washington U know where I came from. When I spoke to others, especially significant others such as professors, I spent much of my time wondering what kind of impression I was making on them.

I've always thought of myself as a fast learner, but on this, one of the most central truths in human life, I caught on slowly. Sometimes you can't catch onto lessons like this until you are looking up to see bottom. Loss of hearing and voice in quick succession brought my vulnerability to my attention. The slow struggle to recover my voice said, "You are who you are. Accept it!" Intensive study of Augustine's *Confessions* and Søren Kierkegaard's *Purity of Heart* among Classics of Christian Devotion confronted me with my double-mindedness and play-acting. Kierkegaard especially put me through a wringer about my false self that stood in the way of "willing one thing," viz. what God expects. At this early stage I didn't have access to Thomas Merton's *Journals*, for they were not published until 25 years after he died, but he often underscored for my students the critical importance of transparency, and you can see in his journals how he practiced that. Honesty must begin with ourselves, with a recognition and confession of our own woundedness. The word "humility" isn't in vogue today in our culture, but it is still at the heart of the spiritual life. The unknown fourteenth-century author of *The Cloud of Unknowing* gave a definition I find helpful—to have a proper self-estimate, aware both of one's neediness and of God's infinite compassion. Nothing, surely, confirms this insight more profoundly than Jesus' Parable of the Loving Father. The prodigal son had first to "come to himself" (Luke 15:17).

I could add a hundred other things my life has taught me. I pray that you will have seen some of them in reading *A Miracle of Grace*. Meantime, think about what your years on earth have taught you.

APPENDIX A

RESPONSES OF DR. E. GLENN HINSON
FOR
Academic Personnel Committee
Board of Trustees
The Southern Baptist Theological Seminary
February 3, 1992

Concern #1: Regarding Scripture

I believe the New Testament is a totally trustworthy guide in all matters of faith and practice. The text of it which we now possess through textual criticism is entirely reliable, though scholars may differ on particular readings. Early manuscript transmission by hand copying allowed many variant readings, but modern methods of study have allowed scholars to recover essentially what the original authors wrote.

Mr. Michael quotes from page 110 of *Jesus Christ* to conclude I have used a negative connotation by using the word "embellishment" in describing the New Testament text. I use the word "embellishment" in the sense of "additions" as its etymology from the Greek *emballein* would imply. An embellishment could range from the addition of a single word to theological interpretations or expansions on earlier accounts. The word does not carry either a negative or a positive connotation. When one compares Matthew and Luke with Mark, which both used, one can readily see some of these additions or expansions, for example, in the temptation accounts. Mark gives a very terse statement, kind of a summary, in Mark 1:12–13. Matthew and Luke give expanded accounts which interpret the temptation experience (Matt 4:1–11, Luke 4:1–13). Similarly, Matthew's and Luke's account of healing miracles (Matt 9:1–8; Luke 5:17–26) give somewhat different versions than Mark (2:1–12). Scholars talk about these variations as "embellishments." On pages 66–67 of *Jesus Christ* I have done my best to establish the authenticity of Jesus' healing ministry without trying to deny totally what is fairly obvious to readers of these passages. I have admitted that "Some embellishment undoubtedly occurred," but then I went on to say, "Discounting somewhat for embellishment, therefore, impressive evidence of Jesus' healing ministry remains. Likewise, I have had to admit "embellishment" in accounts of Jesus' appearances in response to persons in early Christian times who did not believe in the reality of the resurrection or even of Jesus during his earthly life (p. 110) based on comparison of the different accounts. But I have gone on to add: "Although embellishments like these deserve to be treated with caution, clashing as they do with other evidences, the very existence of the Christian movement depended upon an authentic and profound experience which lay behind even the embellishments." In saying that, I do not question the authenticity of the accounts. I am simply making clear that they differ as all reputable New Testament scholars point out and can be seen in reading the texts. Yet I go on to affirm the crucial point, that is, the "authentic and profound experience which lay behind even the embellishments."

Concern #2: Regarding the Resurrection

The quotation, "The risen Christ had not a physical but a spiritual body," (p. 11) is a virtual quotation from 1 Corinthians 15. The dispute of those who have trouble with it is with Paul and not with me, but I cite the paragraph in which it appears.

Paul sustained neither of those views, and it is perhaps safest to reconstruct the experience of the first believers from him since the matter was of crucial significance for him and his apostolate. Paul was convinced that the Christ who appeared to him belonged to another order of existence than the Christ the disciples had known in the flesh. The risen Christ had not a physical but a spiritual body. Flesh and blood, Paul contended, cannot inherit the kingdom of God. The perishable physical nature has to give way to the imperishable spiritual nature.

Concern #3: Regarding the Divinity of Jesus

I accept the formula of Nicaea-Constantinople in 381:

… one Lord Jesus Christ, the Son of God, begotten from the Father, only-begotten, this, from the substance of the Father, God from God, light from light, true God from true God, begotten not made, of one substance with the Father, through Whom all things came into being, things in heaven and things on earth, Who because of us men and because of our salvation came down and became incarnate, becoming man, suffered and rose again on the third day, ascended to the heavens, and will come to judge the living and the dead;

This is my personal faith, and I have taken part in an international study of the Nicene Creed for many years now. I do not hesitate to affirm it as my faith. It properly preserves both the divinity and the humanity of Jesus.

In *Jesus Christ* I have done everything I can *as a historian* to establish a foundation for this in Jesus' self-understanding. I have pointed out that he had "a unique sense of authority," which he reflected in his calling of disciples and in his teaching (p. 68). "Jesus was not an ordained rabbi, … but he spoke and acted with authority which rabbis did not claim (Mark 1:22, 27)." (p. 69) I have argued, further, that Jesus' claims to authority greater than that of scribes and Pharisees were rooted in his "unique filial consciousness" (p. 84). Not only in *Jesus Christ* but in many writings I have pointed out the intimacy of Jesus' relationship with God reflected in his use of the term "abba," which was not merely a way Jesus prayed but the way. "The teaching of Jesus about God's fatherhood reflected deep personal experience, an experience of intimate communion in prayer." (p. 85f.) Repeatedly I have noted that Jesus believed the Kingdom of God was present and coming to realization in himself. I have observed the implications of the charge of blasphemy made against Jesus by the Jewish Sanhedrin vis-à-vis his consciousness of divinity. More or less summarizing all that I said previously on this in *Jesus Christ*, I said: "His citation of the Son of Man saying from Daniel 7:11 came dangerously close to a direct claim of divinity, and, as the writer contended earlier, Jesus' assertions of authority in both deed and word did so even more." (p. 103)

The passage selected from *Jesus Christ* to illustrate that I question the divinity of Jesus is one in which I was presenting views of others and the quotation stopped just as it got to my personal view. (From pages 83–84).

All that I have said in these paragraphs are others' views. I believe that a careful, objective reading of the next five paragraphs beyond the material quoted will show that I have done my best in the passage to establish the basis for the early Church's claims of Jesus' divinity in his own self-understanding. What does "unique sense of sonship" mean except that his sense of sonship is not that of other persons, and that is why he had such a powerful sense of authority. The way Jesus addressed God as "Abba" is, in my mind, the strongest ground we have for affirming what we do about him in the creeds.

In writing an account of the origins of Christianity, however, I cannot go on, *as a historian*, to theologize about these evidences. I have to stay with the evidence given in the Gospels. I am bound to let the scripture determine my faith rather than making my faith determine the scriptures. *As a Christian*, I affirm the Creed. It states my personal faith.

Concern #4: Regarding the "Error" of Jesus

The quotation from page 76: "Indeed, it is difficult to avoid the conclusion that Jesus expected the return of the Son of Man and the consummation to occur within his own lifetime (Mark 13:30). His 'error' was due to prophetic fore-shortening." Sounds more alarming out of context than in it. The use of quotation marks quite clearly means "so-called error" as I have seen some of my critics admit that they recognized. The larger quotation, however, also proves that I had in mind a defense of the biblical evidence. The next paragraph after the one quoted by Mr. Michael reads:

Was this a change in Jesus' thinking? Some scholars have suggested that it was. In the earlier phase of his ministry he may have taught what C. H. Dodd has called "realized eschatology," that is, he stressed the Kingdom of God in its present aspects. By the time he reached Jerusalem, however, he may have shifted to the future tense. He majored on the fate of Jerusalem, the eschatological aspect of the kingdom, and his return. That he taught his own return seems to be implied in the parables of the thief at midnight, the waiting servants, the talents, and the ten virgins.

Looking back over these quotations, I believe one can see the pattern of deliberate effort to cast what I have said in the worst light. To sum up the main features of this: (1) Statements I wrote twenty years ago are being circulated as if I had just published them and thus was threatening to infect the whole world with them when, in fact, the book *Jesus Christ* has been out of print more than ten years and I have made no effort to have it reprinted. (2) By taking quotations out of context, those who are circulating this list of quotations prevent readers from seeing that I was making a strenuous effort to sustain the content of scriptures against radical New Testament criticism in every instance. (3) By inserting editorial comments in several of the quotes published in the *Indiana Baptist*, my general comments about historical methodology have been completely distorted, drawing a conclusion which subsequent material in the book disproves. (4) Perniciously, views of my summaries of the views of other persons (quotes from pp. 64, 76) have been quoted as mine when I have gone on to refute them in subsequent paragraphs. (5) In the instance of the concern on the resurrection, Mr. Michael is deliberately contradicting the Apostle Paul and not me and proposing a radical problem for the Christian concept of resurrection. I would suggest that he open to I Corinthians 15:44 and read what it says. The Risen Christ participates in God's life so that the physical body had to be transformed into a spiritual body.

E. Glenn Hinson
Approved for release to Trustees
From Oxford University
January 26, 1992

Concern #5: Regarding Other Religions

In the statement quoted I am addressing one of the most serious problems in the history of Christianity, that of Christian responsibility for the persecution of people of other religious persuasions. This problem is particularly acute with reference to Jewish people. Anyone who knows the history of Christianity will be aware of centuries of the grossest forms of persecution of the Jews by Christians which culminated during the period of the Third Reich in Germany in a deliberate effort to extirpate all Jews. It is essential that we get at the root of the problem of intolerance as it developed in early Christian history.

Can one believe that God disclosed himself in other religions? We must believe that he did in Judaism, for Jesus was a Jew. Christians ought to have the highest respect for the Jewish people because Judaism is our parent religion. Did God reveal himself in other cultures and religions than Judaism? That, too, we must acknowledge. As the Apostle Paul reminds in Romans 1:18ff., accountability to God depends on the recognition that God made himself known to other peoples with sufficient clarity that they are without excuse. Observe in Romans 1:19 that Paul uses the present tense: "Wherefore the knowledge of God is manifest among them, for God manifested it to them"

If Mr. Michael will look closely at what I have said, he will see that I was not presenting a dogmatic position. Rather, I presented what others have seen as viable options. Roman Catholics, who are the most successful of any religious group in mission work, have developed a policy of cooperation. In many parts of the world missionaries have had to learn how to cooperate with people of other faiths. In Israel, for Instance, they work under restrictions which prohibit efforts to win Jews, but some of them have gained the respect of the Jewish people by cooperation which bodes well for Christian influence and witness.

I do not understand the objection Mr. Michael has to defining the task of the churches as "helping modern persons to recover the ground of being and to cope with dehumanization and depersonalization." Does he question whether people today experience loss of hope, dehumanization, and depersonalization? This is only another way of saying what the churches have always tried to do. In early Christianity they spoke about that as delivering people from the control of demons and fear of fate.

In the United States, where more than ninety percent of the people claim some kind of church affiliation, my comment about the mission not necessarily implying conversion or incorporation into the church may not seem defensible. It has to do, however, with the world situation in which Christianity finds itself today in countries where Christians are a minuscule portion of the population. Conversion in Muslim countries will lead to execution of the converts. Should missionaries seek to put people at such risk? In India the government forbids evangelism by missionary organizations, but the hospital and nutrition program at Bangalore have led to the forming of a dozen or more churches without deliberate conversion and incorporation.

The suggestion that I may be teaching "contrary to the whole Abstract when he advocates the legitimacy of other world religions and suggests that we cooperate with non-Christian religions rather than convert their adherents" sounds like a desperate way to find some basis for Mr. Michael's accusations. I am not questioning any of the "unique doctrines of Christianity" in what I am brainstorming about. I am trying, rather, to prevent the distortion of those doctrines by bigoted application which has brought disrepute on Christianity in the past and will continue to hurt Christian witness if we do not repent of past bigotries and modify our behavior. Whether we want to admit it or not, Christians have no witness to Jewish people because of the holocausts of the past. Contrary to what Mr. Michael thinks, other religions do not "stand in opposition to Christianity" "by their very nature." Our most basic Christian doctrines, belief in one God and messiah, come from Judaism. To recognize truth in other religions does not negate the unique teachings of Christianity.

APPENDIX B

Major Engagements by Type Listed Chronologically
Last Years at Southern Seminary, 1985–92 (Chapters 19–22)

Academy for Spiritual Formation

2–17 February 1985: Academy # 1 Scarritt-Bennett Center, Nashville,
Tennessee: Contemporary Spiritualities

24–29 August 1987: Academy # 2 Camp Sumatanga, Alabama:
Contemporary Spiritualities

4–9 April 1988: -Day Academy Cedar Rapids, Iowa: History of Christian
Spirituality

1–6 November 1988: Academy # 3 St. Benedict's Center, Madison,
Wisconsin: History of Christian Spirituality

30 October–4 November 1989: Academy # 4 Camp Sumatanga, Alabama:
New Testament Spirituality

18–23 February 1990: Alabama 5-Day Academy, Blue Lake, Andalusia,
Alabama: History of Christian Spirituality

4–9 May 1992: Academy # 6 Camp Sumatanga, Alabama: Christian
Spirituality and Cultural Spiritualities

Endowed Lectureships

5–10 August 1984: Douglas Steere Lectures, Bayview, Michigan: "Significant
Religious Voices of the 20th Century"

11–13 October 1985: Harwell Lectures, University of Alabama: "Getting in
Touch with the Working of Grace"

13–15 February 1987: Brooks Hays Lectures, Pulaski Heights BC, Little Rock,
Arkansas: "Spiritual Formation in Social Transformation"

19–20 February 1987J. Hybert Pollard Lectures, Linfield College,
McMinnville, Oregon: "Ways to Pray"

31 March 1987: Paul Wattson Memorial Lecture, Catholic U of America:
"The Influence of Fundamentalism on Ecumenical Dialogue"

1 February 1989: Dahlberg Lectures on Peacemaking, FBC, Phoenix, Arizona

28–28 February 1989: Staley Lectures, William Carey College, Hattiesburg,
Mississippi: "Early Christian Outreach into the Roman Empire"

14–15 November 1989: Carver-Barnes Lectures, Southeastern Baptist
Seminary: "Baptist Heroes and Heroines"
6–7 March 1991: Hughey Lectures, International Baptist Seminary,
Rüschlikon, Switzerland: "Baptists and Religious Liberty"
26 May 1991: Cuthbert Allen Memorial Lecture Ecumenical Institute, WFU
and Belmont Abbey: "Ecumenical Spirituality"
26–27 February 1992: Edwin Stephens Griffiths Lectures, S. Wales Baptist
College, Cardiff, Wales: "Ecumenical Spirituality"

Lectures at Colleges, Universities, and Seminaries

22–24 October 1984: Alice Lloyd College, Pippa Passes, Kentucky: Prayer in
Christian History
16–17 January 1985: Asbury Seminary, Wilmore, Kentucky
30 March 1985: Kentucky Baptist Student Union, Berea College, Kentucky:
"The Church and World Issues"
4 October 1985: University of Kentucky: "The Integrative Power of the
Judaeo-Christian Tradition"
7–8 October 1986: Union Theological Seminary, New York, 150th
Anniversary: "Spiritual Preparation for Apocalypse: Dietrich
Bonhoeffer"
26 October 1986: Berea College: "Contemplative Lifestyle"
30 October–1 November 1986Mercer University Medical School, Macon,
Georgia: "Prayer in Relation to Healing"
5 November 1987: University of South Carolina BSU
16–18 January 1987General Theological Seminary, New York
4–8 July 1988: Furman University Pastors School
21–23 October 1988Spring Hill College, Mobile, Alabama: "Thomas Merton
on Ecumenism"
27–29 January 1989: Baylor University Faculty Retreat
26–27 April 1990: Spring Hill College, Mobile, Alabama Christus Institute:
"Models of the Church in History" (with Avery Dulles)
27 November 1990: General Theological Seminary, New York

Lectures in Church History or Baptist History at Churches

7 July 1985: Ridgewood Baptist Church, Louisville, Kentucky
21 June 1987: Buechel Park Baptist Church, Louisville, Kentucky
16 February 1989: Calvary Episcopal Church: Lectures on John Bunyan
8–9 April 1989: FBC, Hyattsville, Maryland: "The Priesthood of Believers"
20 January 1991: St. Matthews Baptist Church, Louisville, Kentucky

24 March 1991: Highland Baptist Church, Louisville, Kentucky
1–7 April 1991: FBC, West Lafayette, Indiana

Lectures on Spirituality at Churches

9–12 September 1984: FBC, Kannapolis, North Carolina
28 October 1984: University Baptist Chapel, Cincinnati, Ohio
25–27 January 1985: Parkway Village BC, Memphis, Tennessee
22–24 March 1985: FBC, Silver Spring, Maryland: *A Serious Call to a Contemplative Lifestyle*
20–21 September 1985: Hartford Baptist Church, Ohio County, Kentucky
13–15 October 1985: First Friends Meeting, Richmond, Indiana
3, 10, 17, 24 November 1985Calvin Presbyterian Church, Louisville, Kentucky
7–9 February 1986: Greenwood Forest Baptist Church, Cary, North Carolina
14–16 March 1986: FBC, Ashland, Kentucky: "Growth in Discipleship"
6–9 April 1986: Broadway Baptist Church, Fort Worth, Texas
20–23 April 1986: Orange Baptist Church, Orange, Virginia
17–20 July 1986: Glendale Baptist Church, Nashville, Tennessee
27 July 1986: Highland Baptist Church, Louisville, Kentucky
12 October 1986: FBC, Prescott, Arkansas
14–16 November 1986: Temple Baptist Church, Champaign-Urbana, Illinois
13–15 March 1987: Kensington Baptist Church, Washington, DC
22, 29 March; 5, 12 April 1987: FBC Hyattsville, Maryland
17–19 April 1987: Chevy Chase Baptist Church, Washington, DC
1–3 May 1987: Temple Hills Baptist Church, Temple Hills, Maryland
15–17 May 1987: Temple Baptist Church, Memphis, Tennessee
1–4 October 1987: College Parkway Baptist Church, Arnold, Maryland
12–14 February 1988: Covenant Church, Reston, Virginia
14, 21, 28 August; 1 Sept. 1988: St. Andrews United Church of Christ, Louisville, Kentucky
16, 23 October 1988: Jeff Street Baptist Church, Louisville, Kentucky
24–26 September 1989: FBC, Chattanooga, Tennessee
6–8 October 1989: St. Charles Avenue Baptist Church, New Orleans, Louisiana
1, 15 March 1990: Broadway Baptist Church, Louisville, Kentucky
18–21 March 1990: FBC, Wilson, North Carolina
1–4 April 1990: Bethlehem Baptist Church, Texas, Kentucky
2–4 November 1990: Huguenot Road Baptist Church, Richmond, Virginia: "Sermon on the Mount"

11 November 1990: University Baptist Church, Austin, Texas
10 February 1991: Highland Baptist Church, Louisville, Kentucky
15–17 February 1991: FBC, Auburn, Alabama
10 March 1991: Shalom Baptist Church, Louisville, Kentucky
12–14 April 1991: Rutledge Baptist Church, Rutledge, Tennessee

Retreats Led for Churches or Other Organizations

10 November 1984: St. Matthews Baptist Church, Louisville, Kentucky
6–8 December 1984: Providence Baptist Church, Charlotte, North Carolina
24–26 May 1985: FBC, Lenoir, North Carolina
2–26 February 1985: Virginia Ministers Conference, Roslyn, Richmond, Virginia: "Interior Life of the Minister"
28 February–2 March 1986: Tennessee Ministers Conference, Gatlinburg, Tennessee
18–20 September 1987: Second Baptist Church, Lubbock, Texas
23–26 September 1987: Baptist Student Union, University of Richmond, Richmond, Virginia
10 October 1988: Buechel Presbyterian Church, Louisville, Kentucky

Lectures in Denominational Gatherings

13–19 August 1984: Baptist Student Conference, Ridgecrest, North Carolina: "Contemplative Lifestyle"
1–2 November 1984: South Carolina Ministers Conference, Columbia, South Carolina
8–9 November 1984: Washington, DC, Baptist Convention
26–27 November 1984: Ohio Baptist Convention Pastors Conference
9–10 July 1986: BSU Directors, Tennessee, TSU, Cookeville, Tennessee
14 June 1987: Baptist Campus Ministers' Pre-SBC Meeting, St. Louis
21 September 1987: SBC Church Leadership Conference, Southern Seminary: "Developing Spiritual Leadership"
20–21 February 1988: Student Missions Conference, Southern Seminary: "Spirituality and Missions"
8–12 August 1988: Virginia Baptist General Association, Eagle Eyrie
20 February 1989: Texas Baptist Christian Life Commission Convocation: "A Spirituality for the 1990's"
24–25 February 1989: Student Missions Conference, Southern Seminary
18–19 May 1990: Virginia Alliance of Baptists: "The Barbarian Invasions of the SBC"
1–5 October 1990: Ecclesiology Conference, Southern Seminary

1–2 February 1991: North Carolina Baptist Student Union, Raleigh, North Carolina

21–23 March 1991: Student Missions Conference, Southern Seminary

Lectures to American Baptist Churches or Other Groups

20 March 1985: American Baptist Churches General Board, Valley Forge, Pennsylvania

21 April 1985: FBC, Summitsville, Indiana

4–6 August 1985: Judson Memorial Baptist Church, Washington, DC

2–3 October 1985: FBC, Champaign, Illinois

21–24 February 1986: Regional Prayer Conference, ABC, Manhattan, Kansas: Series of Four Lectures on Prayer

7–9 March 1986: Toledo Conference of the American Baptist Churches

2 March 1987: West Virginia Baptist Convention, ABC, Charleston

16–17 March 1987: Ohio Young Pastors Conference, ABC

11–13 March 1988: Bellewood Baptist Church, Syracuse, New York

6–8 May 1988: FBC, Cannelton, Indiana

7 August 1988: Peakland Baptist Church, Lynchburg, Virginia

16–21 July 1989: ABC Prayer Conference, Green Lake, Wisconsin

5 May 1990: FBC, Camp Spring, Maryland

5–10 August 1990: FBC, West Lafayette, Indiana

4–5 February 1991: American Baptist Churches in Philadelphia

Lectures on Peacemaking

13–16 November 1984: Sojourners Retreat on Peacemaking, Kirkridge

15–17 April 1985: Peacemaking Forum, Dayton Oaks Camp, Berne, Iowa

25–26 July 1985: Peace Convocation, SBC Christian Life Commission, Nashville

31 July 1985: Downtown Kiwanis, Louisville, Kentucky: "The Spirituality of Peacemaking"

7 September 1985: Peacemaking Conference, Washington, DC: Keynote: "Biblical Perspectives on Peacemaking"

20–21 January 1986: Peace Convo, SBC Christian Life Commission, Charlotte, North Carolina

2 July 1987: *Baptistische Seminar*, Buckow, East Germany: "Baptist Attitudes toward War and Peace since 1914"

1 February 1989: Dahlberg Lectures on Peacemaking, FBC, Phoenix, Arizona

E. Glenn Hinson

Lectures to Special Groups

25–26 March 1985: Troops, Fort Polk, Alexandria, Louisiana: Lectures on
"Grace" and "Ecumenism"
31 July 1985: Downtown Kiwanis, Louisville, Kentucky: "The Spirituality of
Peacemaking"
7–8 June 1991: Servant Leadership School, Church of the Savior,
Washington, DC

Lectures to Ministers Groups

10 April 1985: Ecumenical Ministers Conference, Jeffersonville, Indiana:
"Christian Humanism"
29 April 1985: Highland (Louisville) Shepherds
31 March–2 April 1986Buffalo, New York, area churches, ABC: "Devotional
Life of the Christian Minister"
10 June 1989: Women in Ministry, SBC Pre-Convention Meeting: Workshop
on Listening
5–7 July 1991: Middletown Baptist Church, Middletown, Kentucky

Presentations to Professional Societies

1–3 August 1985: *Societas Liturgica*, Boston University, Boston: "BEM from a
Baptist Perspective"
18–24 August 1991: International Patristics Conference, Oxford, England:
"Women among the Martyrs"

Ordinations and Installations

23 August 1987: Ernie Elder's ordination, FBC, Memphis, Tennessee
22 May 1988: James R. White's ordination, FBC, Charlestown, Indiana
8 May 1989: Georgine Buckwalter's ordination to Episcopal Diaconate,
Christ Church Cathedral, Louisville, Kentucky
29 July 1990: Sandra Hack (Polaski), ordination, Glendale BC, Nashville,
Tennessee
14 October 1990: Gene Corbin, ordination, Northside BC, Jackson,
Mississippi
24 February 1990: David S. Hunsicker, installation, First Christian, New
Albany, Indiana
2 June 1991: Tom Son Ordination, FBC, Bloomington, Indiana

Lectures on Thomas Merton

30 October 1988: St. James Catholic Church, Louisville, Kentucky: "The Merton I Knew"

10–13 October 1988: Oakhurst Baptist Church, Atlanta: "Merton's Social Criticism and Humanism"

25–27 May 1989: Merton Conference, Bellarmine University: "Merton on Ecumenism"

17 December 1990: St. Frances of Rome Catholic Church, Louisville, Kentucky: "Merton's Many Faces"

13–16 June 1991: International Thomas Merton Society, Rochester, New York: "Surprising Yokefellows: Thomas Merton and Douglas V. Steere"

Ecumenical Lectures

28–30 September 1984: American Academy of Ecumenists, Cincinnati, Ohio: "Confessing Apostolic Faith"

25 October 1984: TEAM-A Meeting, Southern Seminary: "Spiritual Preparation of Ministers"

18–20 April 1989: National Workshop on Christian Unity, Indianapolis, Indiana: " Building Community: One Body of Christ"

23 May 1989: Our Lady of Sorrows Catholic Church, St. Louis, Missouri: "Scriptural Perspectives on Baptism"

28–30 August 1989: Atlantic Ecumenical Conference, Ontario, Canada

29–30 September 1989: North American Academy of Ecumenists, Louisville, Kentucky

9 November 1989: Week of Prayer for Christian Unity, Nashville, Tennessee

24 January 1990: Week of Prayer for Christian Unity, Louisville, Kentucky

14 January 1991: Week of Prayer for Christian Unity, Louisville Presbyterian Seminary

14 March 1991: Jewish/Christian Dialogue, Mobile, Alabama

Lectures to Groups Other than Baptist

4 November 1984: Central Presbyterian Church, Louisville, Kentucky: World Hunger

5 May 1985: Mareno Christian Church, Mareno, Indiana

16 February 1986: Central Presbyterian Church, Louisville, Kentucky

5 October 1986: Calvary Episcopal Church, Louisville, Kentucky

8 February 1987: First Presbyterian Church, Columbus, Indiana: "Spiritual Preparation for Apocalypse: Dietrich Bonhoeffer"

25 April 1987: Jennings, Florida, Small Churches Regional Conference

10 December 1988: St. Francis in the Fields Episcopal Church, Louisville, Kentucky

3 March 1989: Hillview Cumberland Presbyterian Church, Louisville, Kentucky

20–21 October 1989: UMC Annual Conference, Longview, Texas

7–8 June 1989: Denominational Executives Retreat, Roslyn, Richmond, Virginia: History of Christian Spirituality

13 February 1990: Episcopal Clergy Conference, Louisville, Kentucky: "The Contribution of the Churches to the E. European Revolution"

18 April 1990: Bartholomew County Ministerial Association, Columbus, Indiana

APPENDIX C

Major Engagements by Types Listed Chronologically
Baptist Seminary at Richmond, 1992–99 (Chapters 23–24)

Academy for Spiritual Formation

18–23 October 1993 Academy # 7 Mercy Center, Burlingame, California:
New Testament Communities and Our Communities

19–24 February 1995 Michigan 5-Day Academy DeWitt, Michigan: A
Serious Call to a Contemplative Lifestyle

23–29 April 1996 Academy # 10 Mercy Center, Burlingame, California:
Protestant Spirituality

11–16 May 1997 Colorado 5-Day Academy Sedalia, Colorado: Using the
Bible in Spiritual Formation

8–13 June 1997 5-Day Academy Camp Caraway, North Carolina: History
of Christian Spirituality

27 October–1 November 1997 Academy # 13 Camp Sumatanga,
Alabama: Protestant Spirituality?

18–23 May 1999 Academy # 14 Sinsinnawa, Wisconsin: Using the Bible
in Spiritual Formation

14–19 June 1999 Youth 5-Day Academy, Indianapolis, Indiana: Using the
Bible in Spiritual Formation

23–25 July 1999 3-Year Covenant Community, Waycross Center, Indiana:
"Sacraments and Faith Tradition"

7–12 November 1999 New York 5-Day Academy Silver Bay, New York:
New Testament Spirituality

Endowed Lectureships

3 November 1993 Roland Bainton Lecture, Yale University:
"Inclusiveness in Teaching and Writing Church History: The Case of
Marcella"

28 February–25 April 1995 Westminster Canterbury Lectures, Richmond,
Virginia: Prayer in Christian History

23–24 October 1995 Horton Lectures, Brewton Parker College, Mount
Vernon, Georgia

5–6 March 1996 Staley Lectures, Cumberland College, Williamsburg,
Kentucky

22–23 April 1997 Hoover Lectures, FBC, Ashland, Virginia

24 February 1998 Vivian B. Harrison Lectures, Mount Olive College, Mount Olive, North Carolina

1–2 February 1999 Staley Lectures, Averitt College, Danville, Virginia

Lectures at Colleges, Universities, and Seminaries

6–10 July 1992 University of Richmond Pastors School, Richmond, Virginia: "Mature Faith"

8–9 October 1992 Mercer University, Macon, Georgia: "The Background of the Moderate Movement"

11 January 1993 Georgetown College Pastors School, Georgetown, Kentucky: Keynote address: "Spiritual Preparation for Christian Ministry"

28 January 1993 Brewton-Parker College, Mount Vernon, Georgia: "Contemplative Lifestyle"

22 February 1993 Duke Divinity School Baptist House of Studies, Durham, North Carolina

8 March 1993 Presbyterian School of Christian Education, Richmond, Virginia: "Development of the Minister's Devotional Life"

10 May 1993 Houston Baptist University, Houston, Texas

4–5 June 1993 Wilmington College, Wilmington, Ohio: "The Impact of Thomas Kelly on American Religious Life"

23 January 1995 Cumberland College, Williamsburg, Virginia: "Mature Faith"

10–11 April 1995 Bluefield College, Bluefield, Virginia

5 July 1995 Presbyterian School of Christian Education, Richmond, Virginia

21 September 1995 Wingate College, Monroe, North Carolina

1 October 1995 College of William and Mary, Williamsburg, Virginia: "Spiritual Disciplines"

1 February 1996 Union Theological Seminary, Richmond, Virginia: "Spirituality in the Baptist Tradition"

9–10 April 1996 Randolph Macon College, Lynchburg, Virginia

20 October 1996 Hollins College, Roanoke, Virginia

23 January 1997 James Madison University, Harrisonburg, Virginia

23–24 May 1997 Staley Lectures, Lees McClain College, Banner Elk, North Carolina

14 September 1997 Hollins College, Roanoke, Virginia

6 December 1997 Virginia Tech Baptist Student Union Banquet, Blacksburg, Virginia

2 February 1998 Furman University Lectures in Religion, Greenville, South Carolina

24 March 1998 Guilford College, Guilford, North Carolina (Ministers Meeting)

7 April 1998 Averitt College, Danville, Virginia (Chapel)

21 September 1998 Wake Forest University, Winston-Salem, North Carolina

10–11 September 1999 John Leland Center, Washington, DC

Lectures in Church History or Baptist History at Churches

18–20 September 1992 University Baptist Church, Baltimore, Maryland

18 October 1992 Salem Baptist Church, Salem, North Carolina

27 June 1993 Williamsburg Baptist Church, Williamsburg, Virginia

21–16 January 1996 FBC, West Lafayette, Indiana: "Christianity and the Arts"

6, 13, 20, 27 April 1997 Williamsburg Baptist Church, Williamsburg, Virginia: "Early Christianity from Book of Acts"

Lectures on Spirituality at Churches

2 August 1992 Melbourne Heights Baptist Church, Louisville, Kentucky

11–14 October 1992 FBC, Winston-Salem, North Carolina

19 October 1992 FBC, Greenwood, South Carolina

4, 11, 18 November 1992 River Road Baptist Church, Richmond, Virginia

17 January 1993 Moratico BC, Kilmarnock, Virginia: "Introduction to the Sermon on the Mount"

22–24 January 1993 Second Baptist, Lubbock, Texas

24–26 January 1993 Huguenot Road Baptist Church, Richmond, Virginia: "The Sermon on the Mount"

27–28 February 1993 Central Baptist Church, Daytona Beach, Florida

17 March 1993 Grace Baptist Church, Richmond, Virginia

24, 31 March 1993 River Road Baptist Church, Richmond, Virginia

28 March 1993 Luther Rice Baptist Church, Washington, DC

2 April 1993 Churchland Baptist Church, Chesapeake, Virginia

18 April 1993 Triangle Baptist Church, Triangle, Virginia

21, 28 April 1993 River Road Baptist Church, Richmond, Virginia

18, 25 April 1993 FBC, Silver Spring, Maryland [p.m.]

25 April 1993 FBC, Winchester, Virginia [8:30 a.m.]

25 April 1993 Calvary Baptist Church, Washington, DC [11:00 a.m.]
9 May 1993 FBC, Richmond, Texas
16 May 1993 Bedford Baptist Church, Bedford, Virginia
25 May 1993 Richmond Hill, Richmond, Virginia
2 June 1993 Lakeside Baptist Church, Richmond, Virginia
19 June 1992 Midlothian Baptist Church, Richmond, Virginia
26–27 September 1993 First Baptist Church, Rochester, New York
16–17 October 1993 Marion Baptist Church, Marion, Virginia
20–21 November 1993 Bon Air Baptist Church, Richmond, Virginia
15, 22, 29 November 1993 Churchland Baptist Church, Chesapeake,
    Virginia
6 December 1993 Churchland Baptist Church, Chesapeake, Virginia
8 December 1993 Ginter Park Baptist Church, Richmond, Virginia
8–11 January 1995 Hilton Baptist Church, Newport News, Virginia
22 January 1995 Thalia Lynn Baptist Church, Virginia Beach, Virginia
5 February 1995 Speedway Baptist Church, Indianapolis, Indiana
25–26 February 1995 Myers Park Church, Charlotte, North Carolina
10–12 March 1995 FBC, West Lafayette, Indiana
3, 15, 22 March 1995 FBC, Ashland, Virginia
21 March–2 April 1995 Providence Baptist Church, Charlotte
7–9 April 1995 Glade Baptist Church, Blacksburg, Virginia
30 April 1995 Westhampton Baptist Church, Richmond, Virginia
29 July–2 August 1995 Eufala Baptist Church, Eufala, Oklahoma
27 September 1995 Farmville Baptist Church, Farmville, Virginia
30 September–1 October 1995University Baptist Church, Baltimore,
    Maryland
28–29 October 1995 Central Baptist Church, Richmond, Virginia
3, 10, 17 March 1995 Community of Grace Church, Richmond, Virginia
10–11 February 1996 Fredericksburg Baptist Church, Fredericksburg,
    Virginia
14, 21, 28 February 1996 Derbyshire Baptist Church, Richmond, Virginia
6 March 1996 Derbyshire Baptist Church, Richmond, Virginia
20, 27 March 1996 FBC, Ashland, Virginia
22–24 March 1996 University Baptist Church, Baton Rouge, Louisiana
11–14 April 1996 College Park Baptist Church, Orlando, Florida
19–21 April 1996 FBC, Chattanooga, Tennessee
5 May 1996 Ettrick Baptist Church, Matoaca, Virginia
20–22 September 1996 FBC, Radford, Virginia
20 October 1996 Calvary Baptist Church, Roanoke, Virginia

1–2 February 1997 Talbot Park Baptist Church, Norfolk, Virginia
26 February 1997 Ginter Park Baptist Church, Richmond, Virginia
22–25 June 1997 FBC, Wilson, North Carolina
27–30 September 1997 New Vision Baptist Church, Richmond, Virginia
8 October 1997 River Road Baptist Church, Richmond, Virginia
12 October 1997 FBC, Murfreesboro, North Carolina
24–26 October 1997 Crestwood Baptist Church, Louisville, Kentucky
4 November 1997 River Road Baptist Church, Richmond, Virginia
16 November 1997 North Riverside Baptist Church, Newport News,
      Virginia
7–8 December 1997 Blacksburg Baptist Church, Blacksburg, Virginia
27 January 1998 FBC, Greenville, South Carolina
4, 11 March 1998 Ravensworth Baptist Church, Springfield, Virginia
15 March 1998 Oak Chapel, Orange, Virginia
22 March 1998 Riverchase Baptist Church, Birmingham, Alabama
25 March 1998 FBC, Ashland, Virginia
12 September 1998 Beth Carr Baptist Church, Halifax, Virginia
18 October 1998 Churchland Baptist Church, Chesapeake, Virginia
7, 14, 21, 28 February 1999Ginter Park Baptist Church, Richmond,
      Virginia: *Love at the Heart of Things*
7–9 March 1999 FBC, Memphis, Tennessee
12–14 March 1999 FBC, Richmond, Virginia
28 March 1999 Bagby Memorial Baptist Church, Burkesville, Virginia
11 April 1999 Westover Hills Baptist Church, Richmond, Virginia
14 April 1999 FBC, Ashland, Virginia
23–24 April 1999 Boulevard Baptist Church, Falls Church, Virginia
9 May 1999 Beale Memorial Baptist Church, Richmond, Virginia
26 May 1999 Ginter Park Baptist Church, Richmond, Virginia
12 September 1999 Knollwood Baptist Church, Winston-Salem, North
      Carolina

Retreats Led for Churches or Other Organizations

18 September 1992 Presbyterian School of Christian Education,
      Richmond, Virginia
27 October 1992 Richmond Hill Spiritual Directors, Richmond, Virginia
28 January 1993 Georgia Baptist Ministers, Callaway Gardens, Georgia
5–7 February 1993 Richmond Hill Association, Richmond, Virginia
1–2 March 1993 Richmond Deacons Retreat, Richmond Hill, Richmond,
      Virginia

30 April–2 May 1993 West End Baptist Church, Petersburg, Virginia

1 May 1993 FBC, Silver Spring, Maryland [p.m.]

6–8 May 1993 Texas Ministers Retreat, DeWitt Ranch, La Grange, Texas

25–26 June 1993 Richmond Hill RUAH Staff Retreat, Richmond, Virginia

19–22 August 1993 Upper Essex Baptist Church, Upper Essex, Virginia

30–31 August 1993 Richmond Hill Staff Retreat, Richmond Hill, Richmond, Virginia

1 September 1993 Richmond Hill Workshop, Richmond, Virginia

10–11 September 1993 Richmond Hill Spiritual Directors Retreat, Richmond, Virginia

24–25 September 1993 Richmond Hill Ministers Retreat, Richmond, Virginia

3–5 March 1995 Watts Street Baptist Church, Durham, North Carolina

24–26 April 1995 Older Adult Retreat at Eagle Eyrie, VBGA Assembly

12–13 April 1995 Avilá Retreat House, Durham, North Carolina

17–19 July 1995 BGAV Retreat, Eagle Eyrie, BGAV Assembly

8–10 September 1995 South Main Baptist Church, Houston, Texas, at Laity Lodge

15–17 September 1995 BGAV Retreat, Eagle Eyrie, BGAV Assembly

16–18 October 1995 CBF Youth Ministers at St. Meinrad Archabbey, Indiana

17–18 November 1995 FBC, Ashland, Virginia, deacon retreat

2–3 December 1995 Community of Grace Baptist Church at Richmond Hill, Richmond

26–28 January 1996 Talbot Park Baptist Church, Norfolk, Virginia at Williamsburg

25–26 March 1996 Staff of the DC Baptist Convention at Williamsburg, Virginia

10–11 May 1996 Christian Psychotherapy Services, Virginia Beach, Virginia

6–7 September 1996 King's Grant Baptist Church deacon's retreat, King's Grant, Virginia

10–11 January 1997 FBC, Greenville, South Carolina, at White Oak Retreat Center

19–20 February 1997 Richmond Hill, Richmond, Virginia

7–9 March 1997 Vienna Baptist Church, Vienna, Virginia at George Washington Park

30–31 May 1997 Franklin Baptist Church, Franklin, Virginia, retreat at Wakefield

28 February–1 March 1998 Winfree Memorial Baptist Church, Richmond, Virginia
3, 10 May 1998 Trinity Baptist Church, Richmond, Virginia
2–3 October 1998 Northeast Baptist Student Retreat, Princeton area, New Jersey
5 October 1998 Middle Penn Baptist Ministers Retreat, Philly area, Pennsylvania
6–8 November 1998 Immanuel Baptist Church, Greenville, North Carolina, at Richmond Hill
15–16 May 1999 Mount Vernon Baptist Association Retreat, Mount Vernon, Virginia
12 June 1999 Crescent Hill Baptist Church, Louisville, Kentucky
15 September 1999 FBC, Lynchburg, Virginia
18–19 September 1999 Broaddus Memorial Baptist Church, Charlottesville, Virginia
1–2 October 1999 FBC, Austin, Texas

Lectures in Denominational Gatherings

3–4 October 1992 Alliance of Baptists FBC, Clinton, Maryland
25–27 February 1993 Texas Alliance of Baptists Beaumont, Texas
27–28 May 1993 Campus Ministers, Virginia Baptist General Association, Roslyn, Richmond, Virginia
24–26 August 1993 Richmond Baptist Association, Richmond, Virginia: "Mission in the Inner City"
3–5 August 1995 Gathering of Baptists Interested in Spirituality, Mars Hill, North Carolina
11 September 1995 Baptist General Association of Virginia, Richmond, Virginia: "Contemporary Retreats"
14–16 March 1996 Alliance of Baptists, Myers Park Church, Charlotte, North Carolina
1 April 1996 Appomattox Baptist Association at New Hope BC, Virginia
22 April 1996 North Carolina/Virginia Religious Educators at Second Baptist, Richmond
17–29 June 1996 Cooperative Baptist Fellowship, Richmond, Virginia, "Break Out"
9 September 1996 BGAV Study, Richmond, Virginia: "Contemplation"
18–19 November 1996 Shenandoah Baptist Association Pastors Conference

26–28 June 1997 Cooperative Baptist Fellowship, Louisville, Kentucky, "Break Out"

8 September 1997 BGAV Study, Richmond, Virginia: "Contemplative Retreats"

17–18 October 1997 American Baptist Churches of Michigan, East Lansing, Michigan

10–11 November 1997 BGAV, Roanoke, Virginia

22 March 1998 Alabama Cooperative Baptist Fellowship

28–30 May 1998 Women's Missionary Union of Virginia, Richmond, Virginia

25–27 June 1998 Cooperative Baptist Fellowship, Birmingham, Alabama, "Break Out"

14 September 1998 BGAV Study, Richmond, Virginia

31 October 1998 Cooperative Baptist Fellowship of Virginia, Richmond, Virginia

24–26 June 1999 Cooperative Baptist Fellowship, Birmingham, Alabama, "Break Out"

Lectures on Peacemaking

14 November 1992 Virginia Baptist General Association Peace Conference, Richmond, Virginia

23–25 August 1996 FBC, Martinsville, Virginia

Lectures to Special Groups

22–25 October 1992 Center for the Study of Ethics and Culture, Gethsemani, Kentucky

14 March 1995 Richmond Area Christian Educators: "Mature Faith"

11 May 1995 Ministry to Ministers Wellness Retreat, Rockville, Virginia

9–10 June 1995 RUAH Spiritual Direction Program, Richmond Hill, Richmond: "Some Great Spiritual Directors"

22 May–5 October Ministry to Ministers Wellness Retreat, Rockville, Virginia

6–7 October 1995 Baptist/Humanist Dialogue, University of Richmond, Richmond: "Must Humanism Be Secular?"

5–11 August 1996 Spirituality Institute, Northern Baptist Seminary, Chicago

25–27 October 1996 Accomack Memorial Hospital, Northampton, Virginia

4 December 1996 Ministry to Ministers Wellness Retreat, Rockville,
Virginia
9–10 May 1997 Christian Psychotherapists, Sandbridge, Virginia
14–15 November 1997RUAH Spiritual Direction Program, Richmond
Hill, Richmond
5 December 1997 Ministry to Ministers Wellness Retreat, Rockville,
Virginia
7 February 1998 Spiritual Directors of South Carolina, FBC, Columbia,
South Carolina
22 May 1998 Ministry to Ministers Wellness Retreat, Rockville, Virginia
18 August 1998 Wayne E. Oates Institute, Louisville, Kentucky:
"Spiritual Preparation for Christian Leadership"
9–10 October 1998 RUAH Spiritual Direction Program, Richmond Hill,
Richmond
11 December 1998 Ministry to Ministers Wellness Retreat, Rockville,
Virginia
30 April 1999 Ministry to Ministers Wellness Retreat, Rockville, Virginia

Lectures to Ministers Groups

20 May 1993 Ministers Support Group, Tabernacle BC, Richmond,
Virginia
8 November 1993 Virginia Baptist Pastors Conference, Richmond,
Virginia
26 February 1996 Virginia Ministers Discussion Group, Richmond,
Virginia
8 January 1997 Ashland Clergy Association, Ashland, Virginia
12–14 January 1997 Ministers Council of Wisconsin retreat
22 March 1997 Ministers of Southside Baptist Association, Farmville,
Virginia
5 May 1997 Roanoke Valley Ministers Association, Roanoke, Virginia
23 March 1998 Richmond Ministers Association, Richmond, Virginia
1 April 1998 Retired Ministers Association, Richmond, Virginia
24 March 1999 Ashland Clergy Association, Ashland, Virginia

Presentations to Professional Societies

9 January 1993 Conference on Post-Modernism, Abbey of Gethsemani,
Kentucky: "Rootedness in Tradition and Global Spirituality"

19 March 1993 National Association of Baptist Professors of Religion, Charleston, South Carolina: Response to review of *The Church Triumphant*

21–26 August 1995 International Patristics Conference, Oxford, England: "Women Biblical Scholars in Early Christianity"

Lectures on Thomas Merton

4 May 1996St. Anselm's Abbey, Washington, DC: "Thomas Merton, My Brother"

12–14 May 1997International Thomas Merton Society, Spring Hill College, Mobile: "Thomas Merton, My Brother"

Ecumenical Lectures

9–10 May 1995 Clergy Study Day, Diocese of Raleigh, Morehead, North Carolina

20 October 1995 Society of the Companions of the Holy Cross, Roslyn, Richmond

20–24 January 1999 Consultation on Christian Churches Uniting, St. Louis, Missouri

16 September 1999 Baptist/Catholic Dialogue, Richmond, Virginia

Lectures at Churches Other than Baptist

6–7 February 1995 Evangelical Covenant Church, Rosemont, Illinois

9–11 August 1996 All Saints Episcopal Church at Shrinemont, Staunton, Virginia

29 September 1996 Christ the King Lutheran Church, Richmond, Virginia

6 October 1996 St. Paul's Episcopal Church, Richmond, Virginia

13 October 1996 Grace and Holy Trinity Church, Richmond, Virginia

10 November 1996 Christ Church Episcopal, Richmond, Virginia

9 February 1997 St. Andrews Episcopal Church, Richmond, Virginia

16, 23 February 1997 St. Stephen's Episcopal Church, Richmond, Virginia

2–4 March 1997 Radford Presbyterian Church, Radford, Virginia

19–24 May 1997 *Sursum Corda*, Episcopal Diocese of South Carolina

21 September 1997 Christ the King Lutheran Church, Richmond, Virginia

17–19 April 1998 Pendle Hill, Wallingford, Pennsylvania (Douglas Steere)

24–26 April 1998 Covenant Community of Michigan, Lansing, Michigan: "Evoking and Confirming Gifts"

11 November 1998 Crestwood Presbyterian Church, Richmond, Virginia

16 November 1998 St. James Episcopal Church, Richmond, Virginia
18 November 1998 Brentwood Presbyterian Church, Richmond, Virginia
19–22 November 1998 Community Covenant Church, Phenix City, Alabama
10 March 1999 River Road Presbyterian Church, Richmond, Virginia
18, 25 April–2 May 1999 Seventh Street Christian Church, Richmond, Virginia
20 September 1999 Benedictine Pastoral Center, Bristow, Virginia

Ordinations and Installations

1 November 1992 Sara Sellers, ordination, Tappahanock BC, Tappahanock, Virginia
19 November 1995 Donna Hopkins, ordination, Calvary Baptist Church, Roanoke, Virginia
23 November 1997 Linnea Petty, ordination, Triangle Baptist Church, Triangle, Virginia
20 September 1998 Chris Chapman, installation, Knollwood BC, Winston-Salem, North Carolina
2 May 1999 Timothy Irving, ordination, FBC, Petersburg, Virginia

APPENDIX D

Major Engagements by Types Listed Chronologically
In a Busy Retirement, 2000–Present (Chapters 25–26)
N.B. Calendars for 2004 and 2005 seem to have been lost.

Academy for Spiritual Formation

17–22 January 2000 California 5–Day Academy Mercy Center, Burlingame, California: Psalms in Spiritual Formation

23–28 April 2000 Academy # 16 Camp Sumatanga, Alabama: New Testament Communities and Our Communities

29 April–4 May 2001 Pennsylvania 5–Day Academy for Spiritual Formation, Pendle Hill, Wallingford, Pennsylvania

26–28 July 2001 Michigan 3–Year Covenant Community Spirituality and Health

9–14 April 2002 Academy # 17 Oblate Renewal Center, San Antonio, Texas: New Testament Spirituality

13–18 May 2002 Academy # 18 Sinsinnawa, Wisconsin: Using the Bible in Spiritual Formation

30 September–5 October 2002 Academy # 19 Mercy Center, Burlingame, California: History of Christian Spirituality

16–21 March 2003 Florida 5–Day Academy Leesburg, Florida: *Spiritual Preparation for Christian Leadership*

3–6 April 2003 Spirit Streams Retreat La Casa de Maria, Santa Barbara, California: *Feeding on the Word*

27 April–3 May 2003 California/Nevada 5–Day Academy Mercy Center, Burlingame, California: New Testament Spirituality

25–29 August 2003 Colleague Covenant Forum Memphis, Tennessee: Using the Bible in Spiritual Formation

16–21 November 2003 Oklahoma 5–Day Academy Canyon Camp, Oklahoma: Using the Bible in Spiritual Formation

2–7 November 2003 Minnesota 5–Day Academy Christ the King, Buffalo, Minnesota: Foundations of Hope

26–31 January 2004 Academy # 21 Bon Secours, Marriottsville, Maryland: New Testament Spirituality

26 September–1 October 2004 Nashville 5-Day Academy Camp Garner Creek, Tennessee: Foundations of Hope

17–22 January 2005 Academy # 20 Camp Sumatanga: New Testament Communities and Our Communities

3–8 April 2005 Nebraska 5-Day Academy St. Benedict's Retreat House, Schuyler, Nebraska: New Testament Communities and Our Communities

23–29 April 2006 Texas 5-Day Academy Lakeview Conference Center, Palestine, Texas: History of Christian Spirituality

11–16 February 2007 Academy # 24 Mercy Center, Burlingame, California: Protestant Spirituality

30 September–5 October 2007 Kansas 5-Day Academy Spiritual Life Center, Wichita, Kansas: Praying the Psalms

14–18 October 2007 North Carolina 5-Day Academy Salter Path, North Carolina: Praying the Psalms and Contemplative Lifestyle

4–10 May 2008 Academy # 26 Oblate Renewal Center, San Antonio, Texas: Protestant Spirituality

27 January–1 February 2009 Academy # 27 Bon Secours, Marriottsville, Maryland: Protestant Spirituality

Academy # 29 Mercy Center, Burlingame, California: New Testament Spirituality

Endowed Lectureships

27 April 2000 Matt Kelty Lecture, Lexington Theological Seminary, Kentucky

20–21 January 2002 Hamrick Lectures, FBC, Charleston, South Carolina

28 January–1 February Belote Lectures, Hong Kong Baptist Seminary, Hong Kong

7–8 October 2006 Leuschner Lectures, Seventh & James Baptist Church, Waco, Texas

6–7 March 2009 E. Glenn Hinson Lectures, BSK, Lexington, Kentucky

Lectures at Colleges, Universities, and Seminaries

22–25 January 2001 Iliff School of Theology, Denver, Colorado: *Spiritual Preparation for Christian Leadership*

21 April 2001 Earlham College, Richmond, Indiana

9–10 July 2001 Gardner-Webb College, Boiling Springs, North Carolina

10–15 June 2002 Hinson Institute, Furman University, Greenville, South Carolina

19 August 2002 Earlham College and Bethany Theological Seminary, Dayton, Ohio

10–14 March 2003 Matanzas Seminary, University of Havana, Cuba
6 January 2006 Lipscomb University Faculty Retreat, Nashville,
Tennessee
21–29 July 2006 Regent's Park College, Oxford University, Oxford,
England: Keynote for Oxford Young Scholars Program
12 May 2007 Baptist Seminary of Kentucky, Lexington, Kentucky
(commencement)
24 January 2008 Bellarmine University, Louisville, Kentucky:
"Perspectives on Ecumenism Today"

Lectures in Church History or Baptist History at Churches

6 January 2000 Crescent Hill Baptist Church "Barnette's Buddies": "Why
I Am a Baptist"
10 May 2000 FBC, Frankfort, Kentucky: Deacons in Early Christianity
23 June 2002 Broadway Baptist Church, Louisville, Kentucky
4, 11 June 2006 Highland Presbyterian Church, Louisville, Kentucky:
"Separation of Church and State" "Christians and Politics"

Lectures on Spirituality at Churches

20, 27 February 2000 Crescent Hill Baptist Church: "Teilhard de
Chardin's Spirituality"
16–19 March 2000 Immanuel Baptist Church, Greenville, North Carolina
8 October 2000 FBC, Auburn, Alabama
25 October, 1 November 2000 Oakhurst Baptist Church, Atlanta
10, 17, January 2001 FBC, Greenville, South Carolina
9–11 February 2001 FBC, Morrow, Georgia
23–25 February 2001 FBC, Savannah, Georgia
11 March 2001 Glendale Baptist Church, Nashville
4 April 2001 Northside Drive Baptist Church, Atlanta
6–8 April 2001 National Heights Baptist Church, Atlanta
8 May 2001 Verdery Springs Baptist Church, Atlanta
10–13 June 2001 Kirkwood Baptist Church, Kirkwood, Missouri
22 July 2001 Crescent Hill Baptist Church, Louisville, Kentucky
21–24 October 2001 Ball Camp Church, Knoxville, Tennessee
6–10 January 2002 Calder Baptist Church, Beaumont, Texas
18–19 January 2002 St. Andrews Baptist Church, Columbia, South
Carolina
15–16 March 2001 Calvary Baptist Church, Lexington, Kentucky
5 May 2002 Elizabeth Baptist Church, Shelby, North Carolina

22 September 2002 Lexington Ave Baptist Church, Danville, Kentucky
7–10 March 2003 Weatherly Heights Baptist Church, Huntsville,
Alabama
10–12 February 2006 Grace Baptist Church, Tullahoma, Tennessee
12 March 2006 Deer Park Baptist Church 100th anniversary, Louisville,
Kentucky
29 April 2007 FBC, London, Kentucky

Retreats Led for Churches or Other Organizations

31 March–2 April 2000 Servant Leadership Retreat, Dayspring, Church of
the Savior, DC
19–21 May 2000 Cleft Rock Retreat Center, Corbin, Kentucky
10–11 June 2000 Crescent Hill Baptist Church, Louisville, Kentucky
11–12 December 2000 Candler Student Retreat, Holy Spirit Monastery,
Conyers, Georgia
3 February 2001 FBC, Greenville, South Carolina
16–18 March 2001 Church of the Servant Jesus, Atlanta
23–25 March 2001 Oakmont Baptist Church, Greenville, North Carolina,
at Camp Caraway
31 March 2001 Oakhurst Baptist Church, Atlanta
30 November–2 December 2001 Church of the Servant Jesus, Atlanta
22, 24 February 2002 Oakmont Baptist Church, Greenville, North
Carolina, at Camp Caraway
20 May 2006 Crescent Hill Baptist Church, Louisville, Kentucky
27–29 March 2009 University Baptist Church, Starkville, Mississippi

Lectures in Denominational Gatherings

13 November 2000 Georgia Cooperative Baptist Fellowship, Atlanta
28 June 2001Whitsitt Society, Atlanta (Baptist Courage Award): "The
Future of Baptists"
5–7 April 2002 Alliance of Baptists Convocation, WFU, Winston–Salem,
North Carolina
28 March 2006 BGAV Study, Richmond, Virginia
27–30 June 2007 Cooperative Baptist Fellowship, Washington, DC

Lectures to Special Groups

23–28 May 2000 *Sursum Corda*, Episc Diocese of South Carolina Spiritual
Direction Program
1–4 June 2000 *Audire*, San Pedro Center, Winter Park, Florida

22–23 March 2002 Baptist Hospital Chaplains retreat, New Harmony, Indiana

25–31 May 2003 *Sursum Corda*, Episc Diocese of South Carolina Spiritual Direction Program

27–31 October 2003 *Sursum Corda* Refresher, St. Christopher, South Carolina

20–22 August 2003 Palmetto Health, Columbia, South Carolina retreat

24–26 April 2008 College of Prayer, Washington, DC

24–25 July 2009 Seminary Friends, U of the Cumberlands, Williamsburg, Kentucky: "Four Centuries of Baptist Spirituality"

Lectures to Ministers Groups

14–16 December 2007United Methodist Clergy of Indiana, Knobs Haven, Loretto, Kentucky

29 July 2008United Methodist Clergy, Mt. St. Francis, New Albany, Indiana

Presentations to Professional Societies

3 March 2001Wesleyan Theological Society, Marion, Indiana

Lectures on Thomas Merton

15–17 September 2006 St. Mary's Retreat Center, Sewanee, Tennessee

11 October 2006 Elderhostel, Merton Studies Center, Bellarmine U, Louisville, Kentucky

1–2 December 2006 Stillpoint Spirituality Program, Nashville, Tennessee

7, 14, 21, 28 March 2007 Crescent Hill Baptist Church, Louisville, Kentucky

28 March 2007 Elderhostel, Merton Studies Center, Bellarmine U, Louisville, Kentucky

10 October 2007 Elderhostel, Merton Studies Center, Bellarmine U, Louisville, Kentucky

5 March 2008 Elderhostel, Merton Studies Center, Bellarmine U, Louisville, Kentucky

8 October 2008 Elderhostel, Merton Studies Center, Bellarmine U, Louisville, Kentucky

31 October–2 November 2008 Richmond Hill, Richmond, Virginia: "Thomas Merton: His Life, Thought and Spirituality"

21–23 November 2008 The Anchorage, retreat at Kanuga Retreat Center, North Carolina: "Thomas Merton: His Life, Thought and Spirituality"

14 October 2009 Elderhostel, Merton Studies Center, Bellarmine U, Louisville, Kentucky

15 October 2010 Elderhostel, Merton Studies Center, Bellarmine U, Louisville, Kentucky

Ecumenical Lectures

2 November 1996 Federation of Churches and Synagogues, Baton Rouge, Louisiana

Lectures at Churches Other than Baptist

16–19 April 2000 Mennonite Association, Moundridge, Kansas: Holy Week Services

15 February 2001 Embry Hills United Methodist Church, Atlanta

5, 12, 19 February 2003First Christian Church, Mount Sterling, Kentucky

5–6 June 2003 Indiana Methodist Conference, Indiana University, Bloomington

10–13 October 2003 Trinity Episcopal Church, Midland, Texas

18, 25 October 2006 James Lees Presbyterian Church, Louisville, Kentucky

2–4 March 2007 Trinity Episcopal Church, Clemson, South Carolina at Kanuga

28 September 2007 Thomas Jefferson Unitarian Universalist Church, Louisville, Kentucky

Lectures at Christ Church Cathedral, Lexington, Kentucky

(5 Sundays in January and February)
2004 Using the Bible in Spiritual Formation
2005 Ways of Praying
2006 Thomas Merton: His Life, Thought and Spirituality
2007 *A Serious Call to a Contemplative Lifestyle*
2008 Great Texts for a Healthy Spirituality
2009 The Fourteenth-Century English Mystics
2010 Shapers of Anglican Spirituality
2011 Early Christian Foundations of Spirituality
2012 Major Creative Women Contributors to Christian Spirituality

Ordinations and Installations

7 March 2000 Francesca Nuzzolese, ordination, Druid Hills BC, Atlanta

25 June 2000 Christiane Radano, ordination, Leigh Street BC, Richmond, Virginia

1 October 2000 Theresie Houghton, ordination, Fredericksburg Baptist Church, Virginia

4 November 2001 Nicki Royal Peet, ordination, Williamsburg Baptist Church, Virginia

13 January 2002 Elizabeth Hinson–Hasty, ordination, St. Andrew Presbyterian College, Laurinburg, North Carolina

24 February 2002 Robin Anderson, ordination, FBC, Decatur, Atlanta

5 May 2002 Lisa Allison, ordination, Trinity Church, Richmond, Virginia

25 January 2003 Ellen White, ordination to Episcopal Priesthood, St. Andrews Episcopal Church, Arlington, Virginia

30 January 2003 Daniel Avery, ordination to Episcopal Priesthood, Bruton Parish Church, Williamsburg, Virginia

9 November 2003 Laura Mannes, ordination, Webster Groves BC, St. Louis, Missiour

18 March 2007 Ro Ruffin, ordination, FBC, Morrow, Georgia

19 August 2007 Jim Hunter, installation, FBC, Corbin, Kentucky

15 November 2009 Katie Anderson, ordination, Lexington Ave BC, Danville, Kentucky

PERSONAL WRITINGS ARRANGED CHRONOLOGICALLY WITHIN TYPES OF PUBLICATIONS

Books

The Church: Design for Survival. Nashville: Broadman Press, 1967. 128 pp.

Glossolalia. Tongue Speaking in Biblical, Historical, and Theological Perspectives. Nashville & New York: Abingdon Press, 1967. With Frank Stagg, and Wayne E. Oates. 110 pp.

Zweitausend Jahren der Zungenreden (*Glossolalia* in German translation). Kassel: Oncken Verlag, 1968.

Seekers after Mature Faith: A Historical Introduction to the Classics of Christian Devotion. Waco TX: Word Books, 1968. 250 pp.

First and Second Timothy and Titus, Broadman Bible Commentary, Volume XI. Nashville: Broadman Press, 1971.

A Serious Call to a Contemplative Life-style. Philadelphia: Westminster, 1974. 125 pp.

Soul Liberty. Nashville: Convention Press, 1975. 138 pp.

Jesus Christ, The Church of Our Fathers. Vol 1. Gaithersburg MD: Consortium Press, 1977. 187 pp.

The Integrity of the Church. Nashville: Broadman Press, 1978. 198 pp.

Editor, *Doubleday Devotional Classics.* New York: Doubleday, 1978. 3 vols. 1,361 pp.

The Reaffirmation of Prayer. Nashville: Broadman Press, 1979. 144 pp.

A History of Baptists in Arkansas. Little Rock: Arkansas Baptist State Convention, 1979. xv + 487 pp.

Editor, *The Early Church Fathers* in Broadman Christian Classics. Vol. 1. Nashville: Broadman Press, 1980. 536 pp.

The Evangelization of the Roman Empire. Macon GA: Mercer University Press, 1981. 332 pp.

The Priesthood of All Believers. Nashville: Church Training Department, Sunday School Board, SBC, 1981.

Are Southern Baptists Evangelicals? With James Leo Garrett, Jr. Macon GA: Mercer University Press, 1983.

Adult Bible Study Quarterly, July–September 1982. Sunday School Board, Southern Baptist Convention. 80 pp.

Editor and Translator, *Understandings of the Church.* Sources of Early Christian Thought. Philadelphia: Fortress Press, 1986.

The Community of Faith: God's Workshop for Peace. Baptist Peacemaker
International Spirituality Series. No. 3. Louisville KY: International Division
of Baptist Peacemaker, 1986.
Coauthor. *Grounds for a Common Witness: Confessing One Faith.* Cincinnati OH:
Forward Movement Publications, 1988. 68 pp.
Religious Liberty. Louisville: Glad River Publications, 1991. Revised version of
Soul Liberty.
A Serious Call to a Contemplative Lifestyle. Rev. ed. Macon GA: Smyth & Helwys,
1993.
Spirituality in Ecumenical Perspective. Louisville: Westminster/John Knox, 1993.
200 pp.
Vozes do Cristianismo Primitivo, translated and with articles added by Paulo
Siepierski. San Paulo, Brazil: Tematica Publicacoes, 1993. 146 pp.
The Church Triumphant: A History of Christianity up to 1300. Macon GA: Mercer
University Press, 1995. xxi + 492 pp.
The Early Church: Origins to the Dawn of the Middle Ages. Nashville: Abingdon
Press, 1996. 384 pp.
Love at the Heart of Things: A Biography of Douglas V. Steere. Wallingford PA and
Nashville: Pendle Hill Publications and the Upper Room, 1998. xvi + 391 pp.
Spiritual Preparation for Christian Leadership. Nashville: The Upper Room, 2000.
218 pp.

Pamphlets

Transcending Rage: A Spiritual Approach to Anger. Cincinnati OH: Forward
Movement Publications, c. 1994. Originally published in *Weavings* 9
(March/April 1994).
Editor, *Traveling In,* by Douglas V. Steere, edited by E. Glenn Hinson. Pendle Hill
Pamphlets, 324. Wallingford PA: Pendle Hill Publications, 1995.
On Coping with Your Anger. Cincinnati OH: Forward Movement Publications,
1996.
Doing Faith Baptist Style: Voluntarism in *The Baptist Style for a New Century.*
Nashville: Baptist History and Heritage Society and the William H. Whitsitt
Baptist Heritage Society, 2001.
Who Interprets the Bible for Baptists? Baptist Heritage Library Nashville: Baptist
History and Heritage Society, 2003. 46 pp.

Articles in Dictionaries and Encyclopedias

"Southern Baptist Theological Seminary." In *Encyclopedia of Southern Baptists.* Vol.
3, edited by Davis C. Woolley. Nashville: Broadman Press, 1971. 178–83.
"Ecumenism and Southern Baptists." Ibid. Vol 4. 2190–91.
"Constantinianism." In *The Encyclopedia of Religion,* edited by Mircea Eliade. New
York: Macmillan; London: Collier Macmillan, 1987. 4:71–72.

"Irenaeus." Ibid. 7:280–83.

"Justin Martyr." Ibid. 8:220–23.

"Tertullian." Ibid. 14:406–8.

"The Instructor and *Miscellanies* of Clement of Alexandria." In *Christian Spirituality*, edited by Frank N. Magill and Ian P. McGreal. San Francisco: Harper & Row, 1988. 1–6.

"The Life of St. Anthony by Athanasius." In *Christian Spirituality*. 19–23.

"The Saints' Everlasting Rest by Richard Baxter." Ibid. 303–8.

"Pilgrim's Progress and *Grace Abounding* by John Bunyan." Ibid. 320–25.

"The Journal of George Fox." Ibid. 340–45.

"A Serious Call to a Devout and Holy Life by William Law." Ibid. 353–58.

"The Diary of David Brainerd by Jonathan Edwards." Ibid. 372–77.

"A Testament of Devotion by Thomas Kelly." Ibid. 530–35.

"On Listening to Another by Douglas Steere." Ibid. 576–81.

"Infant Baptism." In *Encyclopedia of Early Christianity*, edited by Everett Ferguson. New York: Garland Publishing, 1990. 461–62.

"Fasting." Ibid. 344–45.

"Missions." Ibid. 605–09.

"Meditation, Forms of." In *Harper's Dictionary of Religious Education*, edited by Iris V. Cully and Kendig Brubaker Cully. San Francisco: Harper & Row, 1990. 403–05.

"Prayer." In *Harper's Dictionary of Religious Education*. 494–97.

"Baptist and Quaker Spirituality." In *Christian Spirituality: Post-Reformation and Modern*, edited by Louis Dupré and Don E. Saliers. New York: Crossroad, 1989. 324–38.

"Canon." In *Mercer Dictionary of the Bible*, edited by Watson E. Mills. Macon GA: Mercer University Press, 1990. 130–35.

"Clement, First." Ibid. 159–60.

"Diognetus, Epistle to." Ibid. 214–15.

"Egerton 2 Papyrus." Ibid. 235.

"Eusebius." Ibid. 273.

"Ignatius." Ibid. 401–2.

"Interpretation, History of." Ibid. 408–10.

"Irenaeus." Ibid. 410–11.

"Justin Martyr." Ibid. 484.

"Mandeans, Mandaeism." Ibid. 544–45.

"Mani, Manichaeism." Ibid. 545–46.

"Patristic Literature." Ibid. 654–57.

"Roman Empire." Ibid. 769–72.

"Literature, Devotional." In *Dictionary of Pastoral Care and Counseling*, edited by Rodney L. Hunter. Nashville: Abingdon Press, 1990. 654–56.

"Ministry (Protestant Tradition)." In *Dictionary of Pastoral Care and Counseling*. 734–37.

"Spirituality (Protestant Tradition)." Ibid. 1222–23.

"Church Order." In *Dictionary of the Ecumenical Movement*, edited by Nicholas Lossky, Jose Miguez Bonino, John Pobee, Thomas Stransky, Geoffrey Wainwright, and Pauline Webb. Geneva: WCC Publications; Grand Rapids MI: Eerdmans, 1991. 184–86.

"Apostolic Fathers." In *Layman's Bible Dictionary*. Nashville: Holman Bible Publishers, 1991. 96–97.

"Tradition." In *New Handbook of Christian Theology*, edited by Donald W. Musser and Joseph Price. Nashville: Abingdon Press, 1992. 489–91.

"Callistus." In *Dictionary of Judaism in the Biblical Period*, edited by Jacob Neusner and William Scott Green. New York: Macmillan, 1996. 1:112.

"Justin." In *Dictionary of Judaism in the Biblical Period*. 2:360.

"Tertullian." Ibid. 2:628.

"Ecumenism, Baptist Attitudes." In *Dictionary of Baptists in America*, edited by Bill J. Leonard. Downers Grove IL: InterVaristy Press, 1994. 110–11.

"Evangelicalism, Baptist." Ibid. 114.

"McGlothlin, William Joseph." Ibid. 177.

"Prayer, Baptist Views." Ibid. 223–24.

"Prayer Meeting." Ibid. 224.

"The Southern Baptist Theological Seminary." Ibid. 225.

"Spirituality, Baptist Approaches." Ibid. 255.

"Williams, William." Ibid. 290.

"Yates, Kyle Monroe." Ibid. 298.

"Marcella." In *Encyclopedia of Early Christianity*, edited by Everett Ferguson et al. Rev. ed. New York and London: Garland Publishing, 1997. 2:713.

"Thomas Merton." In *A New Handbook of Christian Theologians*, edited by Donald W. Musser and Joseph L. Price. Nashville: Abingdon Press, 1995.

"Edgar Young Mullins." In *Makers of Christian Theology in America*, edited by Mark G. Toulouse and James O. Duke. Nashville: Abingdon Press, 1997. 348–53.

"Admonition to Parliament, The (1572)." *Die Religion in Geschichte und Gegenwart*, 4 Aufl. Tübingen: J.C.B. Mohr [Paul Siebeck] 1998. 1:121.

"Alford, Henry [1810–71]." Ibid. 1:295–96.

"Arnold, Matthew [1822–88]." Ibid. 1:295–96.

"Arnold, Thomas [1795–1842]." Ibid. 1:295–96.

"Barlow, William [ca. 1565–1613]." Ibid. 1:1111.

"Barnett, Samuel Augustus [1844–1913]." Ibid. 1:1122.

"Bennett, William James Early [1804–1886]." Ibid. 1:1303.

"Benson, Richard Meux [1824–1915]." Ibid. 1:1304.

"Bigg, Charles [1840–1908]." Ibid. 1:1559.

"Bloxam, John Rouse [1807–91]." Ibid. 1:1645.

"Borrow, George [1803–1881]." Ibid. 1:1701.

"Bowden, John William [1798–1844]." Ibid. 1:1701.

"Breda, Declaration of." Ibid. 1:1743.

"Brooke, Stopford Augustus [1832–1916]." Ibid. 1:1771.

"Christentum III, 4. Vorreformatorische und nachreformatorische Kirchen." In *Die Religion in Geschichte und Gegenwart*, 4. Aufl. Tubingen: J.C.B. Mohr (Paul Siebeck) 1999. 2:218–19.

"Ambrose of Milan." In *Upper Room Dictionary of Spiritual Formation*. Nashville: Upper Room Books, 2003. 18–19.

"Anthony of Egypt." Ibid. 22.

"Athanasius of Alexandria." Ibid. 26–27.

"Augustine of Hippo." Ibid. 27–28.

"Basil of Caesarea." Ibid. 32.

"Baxter, Richard." Ibid. 32–33.

"Bunyan, John." Ibid. 46–47.

"Cassian, John." Ibid. 51–52.

"Chrysostom, John." Ibid. 57–58.

"Clement of Alexandria." Ibid. 60–61.

"Cyprian of Carthage." Ibid. 72–73.

"Cyril of Jerusalem." Ibid. 73.

"Ephrem Syrus." Ibid. 96.

"Fox, George." Ibid. 111–12.

"Glossolalia." Ibid. 117.

"Gregory I." Ibid. 120–21.

"Gregory of Nazianzus." Ibid. 121.

"Gregory of Nyssa." Ibid. 121.

"Ignatius of Antioch." Ibid. 140–41.

"Impassibility." Ibid. 144.

"Irenaeus of Lyons." Ibid. 146–47.

"Jerome." Ibid. 150.

"Jones, Rufus." Ibid. 154.

"Kelly, Thomas R." Ibid. 159–60.

"King, Jr., Martin Luther." Ibid. 162–63.

"Law, William." Ibid. 166–67.

"Neoplatonism." Ibid. 199.

"Origen." Ibid. 204–5.

"Pelagianism." Ibid. 212–13.

"Pietism." Ibid. 218–19.

"Plotinus." Ibid. 220.

"Quakers." Ibid. 231.

"Scripture." Ibid. 247.

"Steere, Douglas V." Ibid. 261.

"Tertullian." Ibid. 270–71.

"Unceasing Prayer." Ibid. 279–80.

"Woolman, John." Ibid. 293–94.

E. Glenn Hinson

"Ministers as Midwives and Mothers of Grace." In *Handbook of Spirituality for Ministers: Perspectives for the 21st Century*, edited by Robert J. Wicks. New York and Mahwah NJ: Paulist Press, 2000. 642–55.
"Baptism." In *A New Handbook of Christian Theology*, edited by Donald W. Musser and Joseph L. Price. Nashville: Abingdon Press, 2003. 59–60.
"Charismatic Movement." In *Upper Room Dictionary of Christian Spiritual Formation*. Nashville: Upper Room Books, 2003. 56.
"Humanism." Ibid. 136.
"Jansenism." Ibid. 149–50.
"Tradition." In *Handbook of Christian Theology,* edited by Donald W. Musser and Joseph L. Price. Nashville: Abingdon Press, 2003. 516–18.
"William Taylor." In *Die Religion in Geschichte und Gegenwart*, 4. Aufl. Tubingen: J.C.B. Mohr (Paul Siebeck) 1999. 8, 102.
"Baptists." In *The Encyclopedia of Arkansas History & Culture*. Little Rock AK: Butler Center for Arkansas Studies, 2005.
"Baptist Spirituality." In *Dictionary of Christian Spirituality*, edited by Glen Scogie. Grand Rapids MI: Zondervan, 2011. 291–83.
"Freedom of Choice." Ibid. 461.
"*Fuga Mundi.*" Ibid. 465.
"Hermits and Anchorites." Ibid. 498–99.
"Love." Ibid. 587–89.
"Peace." Ibid. 658–59.
"Sacred and Secular." Ibid. 729–31.
"Syrian Spirituality." Ibid. 783.
"Teilhard de Chardin, Pierre." Ibid. 787–88.
"American Spirituality." In *Westminster Dictionary of Spirituality*. Philadelphia: Westminster Press, 1983. 8-11.
"Ecumenism and Southern Baptists." In *Encyclopedia of Southern Baptists*. 4:2190–91.
"Review and Expositor." In *Encyclopedia of Southern Baptists*. 4:2440.
"Augustine." In *Great Thinkers of the Western World*, edited by Ian P. MacGreal. San Francisco: HarperCollins, 199. 213–16.
"Origen." In *Great Thinkers of the Western World*. 64–67.
"George Fox." In *Great Thinkers of the Western World*. 72–75.

Essays in Festschriften

"Eric Charles Rust: Apostle to an Age of Science and Technology." In *Science, Faith and Revelation: An Approach to Christian Philosophy*, edited by Robert E. Patterson. Nashville: Broadman Press, 1979. 13–25.
"Dale Moody: Bible Teacher Extraordinaire." *Perspectives in Religious Studies* 14. Macon GA: Mercer University Press, 1987. 3–18.

"Penrose St. Amant: Dean at Southern, 1959–1969." *Perspectives in Religious Studies* 16. Essays in Honor of Penrose St Amant (Winter 1989): 41–51.

"Essene Influence in Roman Christianity: A Look at the Second-Century Evidence." In *Perspectives in Contemporary New Testament Questions.* Festschrift for T.C. Smith, edited by Edgar V. McKnight. Lewiston/Queenston/Lampeter: Edwin Mellen Press, l992. 63–74.

"Ecumenical Spirituality." In *Spirituality in Ecumenical Perspective,* edited by E. Glenn Hinson. Essays in Honor of Douglas and Dorothy Steere. Louisville: Westminster/John Knox Press, 1993. 1–14.

"The Quest for Integrity in Early Christianity: Third and Fourth Century Baptismal and Catechetical Procedures in the Shaping of Human Motives and Goals." *Perspectives in Religious Studies* 24. *Festschrift* for Theron Price (Spring 1997): 49–64.

"Modern Pluralism and John 14:6." In *Gemeinschaft der Kirchen und gesellschaftliche Verantwortung: Die Würde des Anderen und das Recht anders zu denken: Festschrift für Professor Dr. Eric Geldbach,* edited by Lena Lybaek, Konrad Raiser, Stefanie Schardien. *Ökumenische Studien,* Band 30. Münster: LIT Verlag, 2004. 401–10.

"Oh, Baptists, How Your Corporation Has Grown!" In *Distinctively Baptist: Essays on Baptist History: A Festschrift* in Honor of Walter B. Shurden. Macon GA: Mercer University Press, 2005. 17–34.

"Baptists and the Social Gospel and the Turn toward Social Justice: 1898–1917)." In *Turning Points in Baptist History: Essays in Honor of Harry Leon McBeth,* edited by Michael E. Williams and Walter B. Shurden. Macon GA: Mercer University Press, 2008. 235–48.

"Human Rights in Early Christian Perspective." In *Resurrection and Responsibility: Essays on Theology, Scripture, and Ethics in Honor of Thorwald Lorenzen.* Eugene, Oregon: Pickwick Publications, 2009. 165–84.

Essays in Symposia

"A Theology of the Urban Mission." In *Toward Creative Urban Strategy,* edited by George A. Torney. Waco TX: Word Books, 1970. 24–42.

"The Significance of Glossalalia in the History of Christianity." In *Speaking in Tongues: Let's Talk About It,* edited by Watson E. Mills. Waco TX: Word Books, 1973. 61–80.

"My Faith Is Paradoxical." In *What Faith Has Meant to Me,* edited by Claude A. Frazier. Philadelphia: Westminster Press, 1975. 85–94.

"William Carey and Ecumenical Pragmatism." *Journal of Ecumenical Studies* 17 (Spring, 1980): 73–83; and in *Baptists and Ecumenism,* edited by Glenn Igleheart and William Jerry Boney. Philadelphia: Judson Press, 1980.

"Expansive Catholicism: Ecumenical Perceptions of Thomas Merton." In *The Message of Thomas Merton*, edited by Patrick Hart. Cistercian Studies Series, No. 42. Kalamazoo MI: Cistercian Publications, 1981. 55–71.

"Who Shall Suffer Injury at Our Hands?" *Waging Peace: A Handbook for the Struggle to Abolish Nuclear Weapons*, edited by Jim Wallis. San Francisco: Harper & Row, 1982. 146–52.

"Voluntarism and Holy Obedience." In *Prayer and Holy Obedience in a War-Wracked World: Papers from a Quaker-Southern Baptist Colloquy*, edited by Glenn Igleheart. Atlanta: Home Mission Board, SBC, 1982. 5–25.

"Seeking a Suitable Spirituality in a Sect Becoming Catholic." In *Living with Apocalypse*, edited by Tilden H. Edwards. San Francisco: Harper & Row, 1984. 148–68.

"Recovering the Pastor's Role as Spiritual Guide." In *Spiritual Dimensions of Pastoral Care*, edited by Gerald L. Borchert and Andrew D. Lester. Philadelphia: Westminster Press, 1984–5. 27–41.

"The Apostolic Faith as Expressed in the Writings of the Apostolic and Church Fathers." In *The Roots of Our Common Faith*, edited by Hans Georg Link. Faith and Order Paper, No. 119. Geneva: World Council of Churches, 1984. 115–25.

"Christianity a No Parking Religion." In *The Way of Faith*, edited by James M. Pitts. Wake Forest NC: Chanticleer Publications, 1985. 67–73.

"Puritan Spirituality." In *Protestant Spiritual Traditions*, edited by Frank C. Senn. New York/Mahwah NJ: Paulist Press, 1986. 165–82.

"The Significance of Glossolalia in the History of Christianity." In *Speaking in Tongues: A Guide to Research on Glossolalia*, edited by Watson E. Mills. Grand Rapids MI: Eerdmans, 1986. 181–204.

"Oriental Orthodox Christology: A Southern Baptist Perspective." In *Christ in East and West*, edited by Paul R. Fries and Tiran Nersoyan. Macon GA: Mercer University Press, 1987.147–54.

"The Contemplative View." In *Christian Spirituality: Five Views of Sanctification*, edited by Donald L. Alexander. Downers Grove IL: InterVarsity Press, 1988. 171–89.

"The Church and Its Ministry." In *The Minister and the Ministry*, edited by Daniel O. Aleshire and George W. Knight. Nashville: Seminary Extension Department, 1989. 1–7.

"How Do We Worship?" With Gerald Austin. In *To Understand Each Other*, edited by Fisher Humphreys and Aquin O'Neil. *The Theological Educator* 39 (Spring 1989): 75–87.

"The Nicene Creed Viewed from the Standpoint of the Evangelization of the Roman Empire." In *Faith to Creed*, edited by S. Mark Heim. Grand Rapids MI: Eerdmans, 1991. 117–28.

"Patristic Views of the Church: Unity and Diversity in the Second Century." In *The People of God: Essays on the Believers' Church*, edited by Paul Basden and David S. Dockery. Nashville: Broadman Press, 1991. 181–92.

"The Contribution of Women to Spirituality." With Molly Marshall-Green. In
Becoming Christian, edited by Bill J. Leonard. Louisville: Westminster/John
Knox Press, 1990. 116–30, 205–6.

"The Aha! Sign." *Rivers in the Desert*, edited by Rowland Croucher. Sutherland,
Australia: Albatross Books, 1991. 326–32.

"The Background to the Moderate Movement." In *The Struggle for the Soul of the
SBC*, edited by Walter B. Shurden. Macon GA: Mercer University Press, l993.
l–l6.

"One Baptist's Dream: A Denomination Truly Evangelical, Truly Catholic, Truly
Baptist." In *Southern Baptists and American Evangelicals: The Conversation
Continues*, edited by David S. Dockery. Nashville: Broadman & Holman
Publishers, 1993. 201–17.

"Fundamentalism and World Consciousness." In *The Struggle Over the Past:
Fundamentalism and the Modern World*, edited by William M. Shea. Lanham,
New York & London: The College Theological Society, l993. 223–28.

"The Contemplative Roots of Baptist Spirituality." In *Ties that Bind: Life Together
in the Baptist Vision*, edited by Gary Furr and Curtis Freeman. Macon GA:
Smyth & Helwys, l994. 69–82.

"The Compelling Power of the Word of God." In *Proclaiming the Baptist Vision:
The Bible*, edited by Walter B. Shurden. Macon GA: Smyth & Helwys, 1994.
35–42.

"l and 2 Timothy and Titus." In *Mercer One-Volume Commentary*. Macon GA:
Mercer University Press, l993. 1253–62.

"An Unexpected Ecumenical Surprise." In *Encounters for Unity*, edited by G.R.
Evans, Lorelei F. Fuchs, and Diane C. Kessler. Norwich: Canterbury Press,
1995. 94–99.

"Prayers and Litanies." In *Worship Resources for Christian Congregations: A
Symphony for the Senses*, edited by Donald Nixon and C. Welton Gaddy.
Macon GA: Smyth & Helwys, 1995. 85, 109–10, 250–51, 262.

"Litany for a Holocaust Remembrance." In *For the Living of These Days*, edited by
Peggy Haymes and Michael Hawn et al. Macon GA: Smyth & Helwys, 1995.

"Horizonal Persons." In *Communion, Community, Commonweal: Readings for
Spiritual Leadership,* edited by John S. Mogabgab. Nashville: Upper Room
Books, 1995, 181–87.

"Edgar Young Mullins." In *Makers of Christian Theology in America*, edited by
Mark G. Toulouse and James O. Duke. Nashville: Abingdon Press, 1997. 348–
53.

"Living Christ, you who were not minded to cling to eternal glory." In *Simple
Blessings for Sacred Moments*, edited by Isabel Anders. Liguori MO:
Liguori/Triumph, 1998. 109.

"Must Humanism Be Secular?" In *Freedom of Conscience: A Baptist/Humanist
Dialogue*, edited by Paul D. Simmons. Amherst NY: Prometheus Press, 2000.
182–93.

"Feeding on the Word: The Mind of Christ." In *Companions in Christ Participant's Book* Nashville: Upper Room Books, 2001. 67–109.

"Ministers as Midwives and Mothers of Grace." In *Handbook of Spirituality for Ministers: Perspectives for the 21st Century*, edited by Robert J. Wicks. New York and Mahwah NJ: Paulist Press, 2000. 642–55.

"The Authority of Tradition: A Baptist View." In *The Free Church and the Early Church*, edited by D.H. Williams. Grand Rapids MI: Eerdmans, 2002. 141–61.

"Great Tests for a Healthy Spirituality." In *The Pastor's Study Bible*. Nashville: Abingdon Press, 2007. 4:115–58.

"For a Nation's Change of Heart." In *Prayers for the New Social Awakening: Inspired by the New Social Creed*, edited by Christian T. Iosso and Elizabeth Hinson-Hasty. Louisville: Westminster/John Knox Press, 2008. 150–53.

"More than Fast Food." In *Rhythm & Fire*, edited by Jerry P. Haas and Cynthia Langston Kirk. Nashville: Upper Room Books, 2008. 117–19.

"The Influence of Friedrich Schleiermacher on E.Y. Mullins." In *Schleiermacher in America*, edited by Jeffrey Wilcox and Terrence Tice.

"Harbingers to Humankind." In *Hope: Its More than Wishful Thinking*, compiled by Amy Lyles Wilson. Nashville: Fresher Air Books (The Upper Room), 2010. 29–30.

Major Articles

Biblical Studies

"Hodayoth III, 6–18: In What Sense Messianic?" *Revue de Qumran* 2 (Feb 1960): 183–204.

"The Christian Household in Colossians, 3:18-4:1." *Review and Expositor* 70 (Fall 1973): 495–506.

"Reconciliation and Resistance." *SBC Today* (January 1988): 14–15.

"Persistence in Prayer in Luke/Acts." *Review and Expositor* 104 (Fall 2007): 721–36.

Patristics

"Christian Teaching in the Early Church." *Review and Expositor* 59 (Summer 1962): 258–73.

"Baptism in Early Church History." *Review and Expositor* 65 (Winter 1968): 23–31.

"The Lord's Supper in Early Church History." *Review and Expositor* 66 (Winter 1969): 15–24.

"The Nature and Origin of Catholicism." *Review and Expositor* 72 (Winter 1975): 71–89.

"Confessions or Creeds in Early Christian Tradition." *Review and Expositor* 76 (Winter 1979): 5–16.

"Evidence of Essene Influence in Roman Christianity: An Inquiry." *Studia Patristica*. Oxford and New York: Pergamon Press, 1982. 18:697–701.

"Did Hippolytus Know Essenes Firsthand?" *Studia Patristica* 18.3:283–9.
"Women among the Martyrs." *Studia Patristica*, edited by Elizabeth A.
    Livingstone. Leuven: Peeters Press, 1993. 25:423–28.
"When the World Collapsed: The Spirituality of Women during the Barbarian
    Invasion of Rome." *Perspectives in Religious Studies* 20 (Summer l993): 113–130.
"Women Biblical Scholars in the Late Fourth Century: The Aventine Circle."
    Studia Patristica. Leuven: Peeters, 1997. 33:319–24.
"Some Things I've Learned from the Study of Early Christian History." *Review
    and Expositor* 101 (Fall 2004): 729–44.

Ecumenism
"The Ecumenical Movement: Threat or Hope? A reply to Henry A. Buchanan
    and Bob W. Brown." *Christian Century* 81 (23 December 1964): 1592–95.
"Southern Baptists and Ecumenism: Some Contemporary Patterns." *Review and
    Expositor* 66 (Summer 1969): 287–98.
"Ecumenism." *The Theological Educator* 8 (Spring 1978): 50–57.
"William Carey and Ecumenical Pragmatism." *Journal of Ecumenical Studies* 17
    (Spring 1980): 73–83.
"Baptism and Christian Unity: A Baptist Perspective." In *Baptism: An Ecumenical
    Starting Point*, edited by George Kilcourse. Lexington: Kentucky Council of
    Churches, 1982. 20–31.
"Towards a Common Confession of Apostolic Faith Today." *Ecumenical Trends* 21
    (July–August 1983): 108–11.
"The Life of Grace within Us: Defining the Issues." *Southwestern Journal of
    Theology* 28 (Spring 1986): 6–10.
"Creeds and Christian Unity: A Southern Baptist Perspective." *Journal of
    Ecumenical Studies* 23 (Winter 1986): 25–36.
"Defining Diversity and Unity: The Churches' Quest for Catholicity." *Sojourners*
    (November 1986): 41–42.
"Church as Koinonia—Starting Point and Destination of Ecumenical Endeavor."
    Verbum 28 (1987): 351–360.
"The Lima Text as a Pointer to the Future: A Baptist Perspective." *Studia Liturgica*
    16 (1986): 92–99.
"L'influence du fondamentalisme sur le dialogue oecumenique." *Oecumenisme*
    (September 1988): 16–18.
"Southern Baptists, Christology, and Ecumenical Relationships." *Ecumenical
    Trends* 19 (February 1990): 22–24.
"The Influence of Fundamentalism on Ecumenical Dialogue." *The Journal of
    Ecumenical Studies* 26 (Summer 1989): 468–82.
"An Unexpected Ecumenical Surprise." *Encounters for Unity*, edited by G.R.
    Evans, Lorelei F. Fuchs, and Diane C. Kessler. Norwich: Canterbury Press,
    1995. 94–99.

Church History
"The Church: Liberator or Oppressor of Women?" *Review and Expositor* 72 (Winter 1975): 19–30.
"Ordination in Christian History." *Review and Expositor* 79 (Fall 1981): 485–96.
"The Historical Involvement of the Church in Social Ministries and Action." *Review and Expositor* 85 (Spring 1988): 233–42.
"Pastoral Authority and the Priesthood of Believers from Cyprian to Calvin." *Faith and Mission* 7 (Fall 1989): 6–23.

Baptist History
"Baptist Education and American Culture." *Review and Expositor* 60 (Winter 1964): 541–54.
"The Authority of the Christian Heritage for Baptist Faith and Practice." Published by Commission on Baptist Doctrine of the BWA, from the annual meeting at Einsiedeln, Switzerland, 14–16 July 1973. 1–17.
"Historical Patterns of Lay Leadership in Ministry in Local Baptist Churches." *Baptist History and Heritage* 13 (January 1978): 26–34.
"The Authority of the Christian Heritage for Baptist Faith and Practice." *Search* (Spring 1978): 6–24.
"The Southern Baptists: A Concern for Experiential Conversion." *Christian Century* 95 (7–14 June 1978): 610–15.
"The Baptist Experience in the United States." *Review and Expositor* 79 (Spring 1982): 217–30.
"Southern Baptists and the Liberal Tradition in Biblical Interpretation." *Baptist History and Heritage* 19 (July 1984): 16–20.
"Between Two Worlds: Southern Seminary, Southern Baptists, and American Theological Education." *Baptist History and Heritage* 20 (April 1985): 28–35.
"Baptistische Grundsaetze und Fundamentalismus." *Una Sancta* 47 (1992): 12–18.
"The Baptist World Alliance: Its Identity and Ecumenical Involvement." *The Ecumenical Review* 46 (October 1994): 406–11.
"E.Y. Mullins as Interpreter of the Baptist Tradition." *Review and Expositor* 96 (Winter 1999): 109–22.
"Baptist Contributions to Liberalism." *Baptist History and Heritage* 35 (Winter 2000) 39–54.
"Trends in Baptist Spirituality." *Christian Spirituality Bulletin* 7 (Fall/Winter 1999): 1, 3–7.
"Baptist Approaches to Spirituality." *Baptist History and Heritage* 37 (Spring 2002): 6–31.
"Lessons from Baptist History." *Hill Road* 6 (June 2003): 75–98. Chinese.
"Mullins on Confessions of Faith." *Baptist History and Heritage* 43 (Winter 2008): 49–60.

Southern Baptist Convention
"The SBC—Houston, 1979." *Christian Century* 96 (18–25 July 1979): 225-277.
"Baptism: A Southern Baptist Dilemma." *Liturgy* 4 (Winter 1983): 39–44.
"SBC at Pittsburgh: Fundamentalism with a Benign Face." *Christian Century* 100 (6–13 July 1983): 639–40.
"Endangered Species: Will the Baptist Tradition Survive?" *Report from the Capitol* (September 1993): 4–6, 14.
"Hope for the Future of Baptists." *Whitsitt Journal* 8 (Fall 2001): 12–15.

Contemporary Issues
"Toward Creative Urban Strategy: A Theology for Urban Mission." *Home Missions* 40 (September 1969): 20–29.
"Ordination: Is a New Concept Needed?" *Search* 2 (July 1972): 40–46.
"Future Shock and the Christian Mission." *The Quarterly Review* 33 (April 1973): 4–16.
"A Rationale for Baptist Higher Education." *Search* 4 (Fall 1973): 11–21.
"Theological Education 1977: A Southern Baptist Context." *Christian Century* 94 (2–9 February 1977): 93–95.
"The Crisis of Teaching Authority in Roman Catholicism." *The Journal of Ecumenical Studies* 14 (Winter 1977): 66–68.
"Baptists and Evangelicals: What Is the Difference?" *Baptist History and Heritage* 16 (April 1981): 20–32.
"Neo-Fundamentalism: An Interpretation and Critique." *Baptist History and Heritage* 16 (April 1981): 33–42, 49.
"Religion's Tryst with Politics." *Review and Expositor* 83 (Spring 1986): 209–220.
"Christlicher Fundamentalismus: Hoffnung oder Katastrophe für das europäische Christentum?" *Okumenische Rundschau* 41 (Oktober 1992): 449–63.
"Historical and Theological Perspectives on Satan." *Review and Expositor* 89 (Fall 1992): 475–87.
"The Educational Task of Baptist Professors of Religion on the Edge of a New Millennium." *Perspectives in Religious Studies* 22 (Fall 1995): 227–37.
"Forming Baptist Identity(ies) in American Higher Education." *Perspectives in Religious Studies* 34 (Winter 2007): 365–75.

Thomas Merton
"Merton's Many Faces." *Religion in Life* 42 (Summer 1973): 153–67.
"The Catholicizing of Contemplation: Thomas Merton's Place in the Church's Prayer Life." *Perspectives in Religious Studies* 1 (Spring 1974): 66–84; *Cistercian Studies* 10 (1975): 173–89.
"Expansive Catholicism: Ecumenical Perceptions of Thomas Merton." *Religion in Life* 48 (Spring 1979): 63–76.

E. Glenn Hinson

"*Contemptus Mundi—Amor Mundi*: Merton's Progression from World Denial to World Affirmation." *Cistercian Studies* 26 (1991): 339–49. Spanish translation in *Cistercium*.

"Thomas Merton My Brother: The Impact of Thomas Merton on My Life and Thought." *The Merton Annual*, vol. 11, edited by George A. Kilcourse, Jr. (Sheffield, England: Sheffield Academic Press, 1999) 89–96.

"Loneliness as a Key to the Merton Story." *Cistercian Studies* 40 (2005): 395–410.

Spirituality, Spiritual Formation

"The Spiritual Formation of the Minister as a Person." *Review and Expositor* 70 (Winter 1973): 73–85.

"The Problems of Devotion in the Space Age." *Review and Expositor* 71 (Summer 1974): 293–301.

"Prayer in an Economy of Abundance." *Religion in Life* 44 (Autumn 1975): 269–80.

"Spiritual Development: A Baptist View." *The NICM Journal* 2 (Spring 1977): 84–94.

"Morton T. Kelsey: Theologian of Experience." *Perspectives in Religious Studies* 9 (Spring 1982): 5–20.

"Prayer in John Bunyan and the Early Monastic Tradition." *Cistercian Studies* 18 (1983): 217–30.

"Douglas V. Steere: Irradiator of the Beams of Love." *Christian Century* 102 (24 April 1985): 416–19.

"Southern Baptist and Medieval Spirituality: Surprising Similarities." *Cistercian Studies* 20 (1985): 224–36.

"The Spiritual Formation of the Minister." *Review and Expositor* 83 (Fall 1986): 587–95.

"Baptists and Spirituality: A Community at Worship." *Review and Expositor* 84 (Fall 1987): 649–58.

"Spiritual Preparation for Apocalypse: Learning from Bonhoeffer." *Cistercian Studies* 23 (1988): 156–68.

"A Social Spirituality for the 1990's." *SBC Today* (September 1989): 18; (October 1989): 18; (November 1989): 19.

"Social Involvement and Spirituality." *The Merton Annual*, vol. 3, edited by Robert E. Daggy, et al. New York: AMS Press, 1990. 217–29.

"Midwives and Mothers of Grace." *Theological Educator* 43 (Spring 1991): 65–79.

"Historical Perspectives on Spirituality." *Review and Expositor* 88 (Fall 1991): 331–42.

"Rootedness in Tradition and Global Spirituality." *The Merton Annual: Studies in Culture, Spirituality, and Social Concerns*, vol. 6. Collegeville MN: The Liturgical Press, 1994. 6–22.

"The Impact of Thomas Kelly on American Religious Life." *Quaker Religious Thought* 27 (July 1995): 11–22.

"Dear St. Benedict: A Letter of Appreciation for What Your Sons and Daughters Have Meant to Me." *Lexington Theological Quarterly* 35 (Spring 2000): 1–13.
"The Progression of Grace: A Re-reading of *The Pilgrim's Progress*." *Spiritus* 3 (Fall 2003): 251–62.
"A Surge of Spirituality." *Christian Century* 122 (20 September 2005): 38–40.
"Improving Our Listening and Seeing." *Christian Reflection: Mysticism*. Waco TX: Baylor University, 2005. 77–84.
"Ignatian and Puritan Prayer: Surprising Similarities." *The Merton Annual 2007*, edited by Victor A. Kramer. Louisville KY: Fons Vitae, 2007. 20:79–92.
"The Abbey of Our Lady of Gethsemani: An Appreciation." *Conversations* 5 (Fall/Winter 2007): 36–37.

Worship
"The Theology and Experience of Worship: A Baptist View." *The Greek Orthodox Theological Review* 22 (Winter 1977): 417–27.
"Reassessing the Puritan Heritage in Worship/Spirituality: A Search for a Method." *Worship* 53 (July 1979): 318–26.
"Private Springs of Public Worship." *Review and Expositor* 80 (Winter 1983): 109–117. 240; *The Navy Chaplain*, 4:22–28.
"The Spirituality of Baptism and the Lord's Supper in the Context of Worship." *Hill Road* 3 (2000): 64–85. Chinese.

Peacemaking
"SBC's Peacemaking Convo: How Significant Was It?" *Christian Century* 96 (14 March 1979): 268–69.
"Disarmament of the Heart." *Faith and Mission* 4 (Fall 1986): 3–12.
"Baptist Attitudes toward War and Peace since 1914." *Baptist History and Heritage* 39 (Winter 2004): 98–116.

Personal
"I Am Not a Heretic." *SBC Today* (July 1986): 14–15.

Articles in Weavings

"An Ordinary Saint." *Weavings* 2 (March/April 1987): 31–33.
"Making the Most of the Time." *Weavings* 6 (January/February, 1991): 38–43.
"On Coping with Your Anger." *Weavings* 9 (March/April 1994): 32–39.
"Horizonal Persons." *Weavings* (March/April 1995): 22–29.
"Kindlers and Purifiers of Dreams." *Weavings* (May/June 1996): 38–45.
"Having the Mind of Christ." *Weavings* March/April 1997): 16–21.
"Praying without Ceasing." *Weavings* May/June 1998): 34–43.
"On Being 'God's Pencil'." *Weavings* 13 (November/December 1998): 31–37.

"Relentless Optimist." *Weavings* 14 (November/December 1999): 34–40.
"Reconciliation and Resistance." *Weavings* 15 (November/December 2000): 40–46.
"The Road to Emmaus." *Weavings* 16 (November/December 2001): 32–38.
"At Eternity's Converging Point." *Weavings*17 (May/June 2002): 20–27.
"Luminous Saints." *Weavings* 18 (May/June 2003): 28–35.
"Suffering and Hope." *Weavings* (July/August 2003): 6–14.
"Editor's Introduction." *Weavings* 19 (May/June 2004): 2–3.
"Loneliness as a Crucible of Grace." *Weavings* 20 (March/April 2005): 17–24.
"*Autarkeia*: Recovering a Philosophy of Enough." *Weavings* 20 (November/December 2005): 37–44.
"The Quantity Quotient Behind Busyness." *Weavings* 14 (January/February 2007): 14–21.
"Not Giving Up." *Weavings* 14 (July/August, 2007): 6–14.
"Impasse and the Sufficiency of Grace." *Weavings* 15 (January/February 2008): 35–43.
"The Absence of God." *Weavings* 25.1 (Winter 2009–2010): 6–12.
"Little Efforts Matter." *Weavings* 25.2 (Spring 2010–2011): 30–36.
"Fortunate Fencing." *Weavings* 26.1 (Fall 2010–2011): 36–41.
"Church as *Schola Caritatis*, *Weavings* 26. 4 (Spring 2011–2012): 40–47.
"Elpisizing." *Weavings* 27.1 (Fall 2011–2012)
"*Epektasis:* Antidote to Fear of Change." *Weavings* 27.3 (Summer 2011–2012)

Reviews of Classics in Weavings

A Serious Call to a Devout and Holy Life. By William Law. *Weavings* (September/October 1986): 41–42.
A Testament of Devotion. By Thomas R. Kelly. *Weavings* (September/October 1986): 43–44.
The Journal of John Woolman, Weavings 1 (November/December 1986): 42–44.
The Confessions of Augustine, Weavings 2 (March/April 1987): 40–42.
Le Milieu Divin. By Teilhard de Chardin. *Weavings* 2 (May/June 1987): 44–45.

INDEX

Index

Activities: Lecturing, Teaching, Consulting

Society for the Study of Christian Spirituality 336, 337
South Wales Baptist College, Cardiff, Wales 310
Southeastern Baptist Theological Seminary, Wake Forest, NC 242, 248, 266
Southern Baptist Convention annual meetings
Houston 1979 229
St Louis 1980 230, 272
Dallas 1985 261
St Louis 1987 265, 268
Southern Seminary faculty morale crisis (1973-74) 154-156
Staley Lectures, Union University, Jackson, TN 249
Sursum Corda 351, 355
Tantur Ecumenical Institute, Jerusalem, Israel 180-185, 285
Theological Education Association of Mid-America (TEAM-A) 158
Themes in sermons, lectures, retreats 325-327
Theology of Religious Experience 349
Thomas Merton: His Life, Thought, and Spirituality 349
Towards the Common Expression of Apostolic Faith Today
Faith and Order, WCC 211
Faith and Order, NCC 211-213, 249
Twelfth International Patristics Conference, Oxford 1995 334
Union Theological Seminary, Richmond, VA 316, 317, 321, 322, 331, 355, 367
University of Notre Dame 278
University of Richmond, Richmond, VA 316
University of the Cumberlands, Williamsburg, KY 350
Virginia Tech University, Blacksburg, VA 248-249
Volunteers of America 76, 112
Wainwright House, Rye, NY 169
Wake Forest Divinity School 253
Wake Forest University 241-242, 243-254, 282, 322, 380
Weavings 274, 337, 353, 370-371
Wilkinson Lectures, Northern Baptist Theological Seminary, Chicago 1980 239
Wingate College, Wingate, NC 248
Women in Christian History 349
Yad Vashem, Jerusalem, Israel 181

Organizations, Institutions, and Places Author Was Involved With

A & P, Affton, MO 63, 68, 69, 70, 71, 72, 73, 74, 75, 77, 98, 104, 105, 201
A & P, St Matthews, KY 75, 108, 111
Alliance of Baptists 296, 299, 313, 316, 327, 328, 358
American Academy of Religion 253, 336
American Baptist Churches 280-281, 350, 368
American Baptist General Board, Valley Forge, PA 281

Publications Discussed in the Text

E. Glenn Hinson

Issues and Writings Alluded to or Discussed

446

Index

Honors and Awards

Miscellaneous